SATURDAY AM

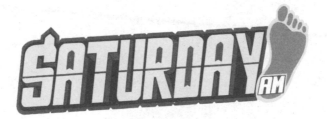

PRESENTS...

HAMMER

VOLUME 1

THE OCEAN KINGDOM

STORY AND ART BY *JEYODIN*

ROCKPORT

CONTENTS

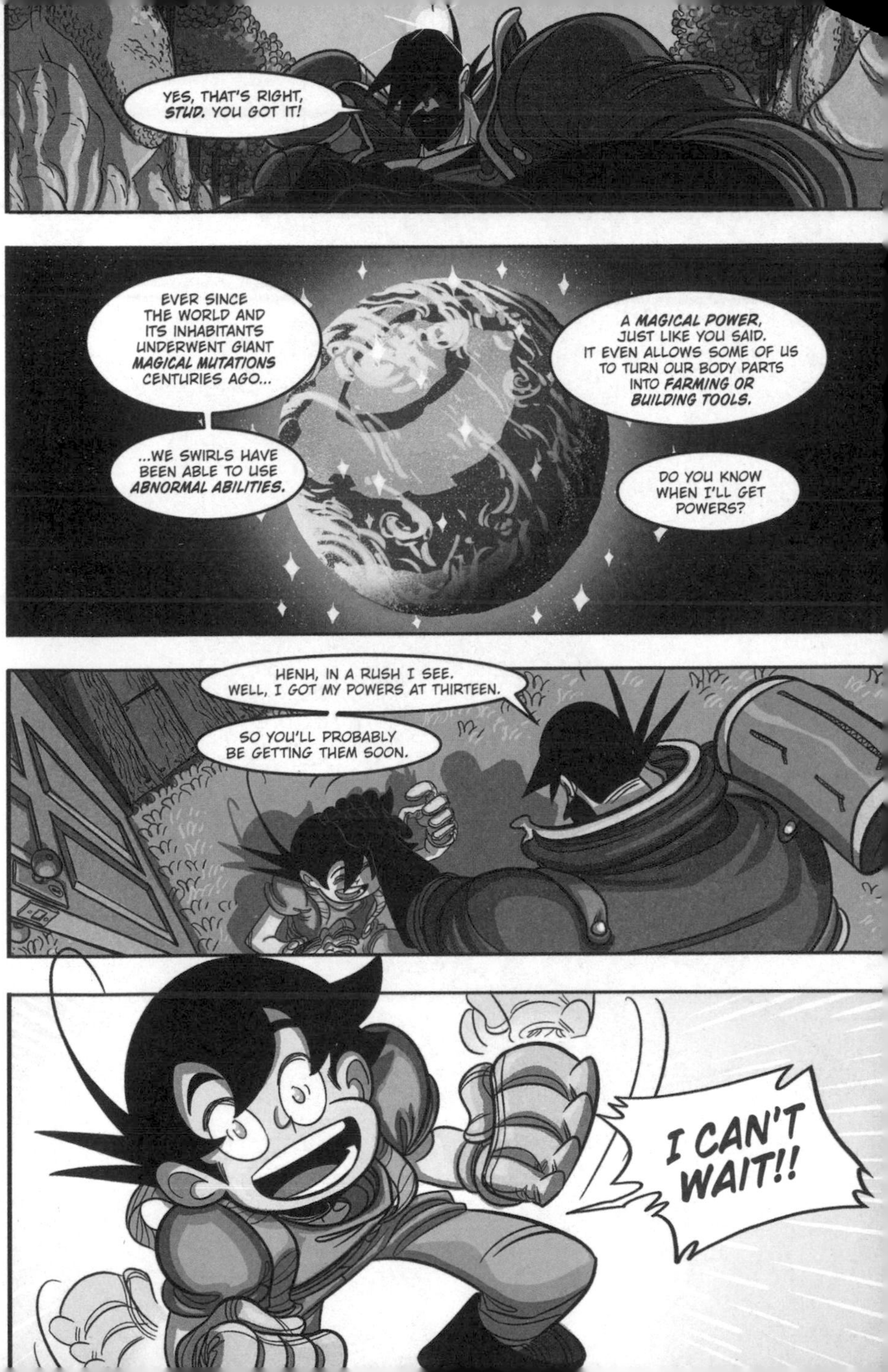
YES, THAT'S RIGHT, STUD. YOU GOT IT!
EVER SINCE THE WORLD AND ITS INHABITANTS UNDERWENT GIANT MAGICAL MUTATIONS CENTURIES AGO...
...WE SWIRLS HAVE BEEN ABLE TO USE ABNORMAL ABILITIES.
A MAGICAL POWER, JUST LIKE YOU SAID. IT EVEN ALLOWS SOME OF US TO TURN OUR BODY PARTS INTO FARMING OR BUILDING TOOLS.
DO YOU KNOW WHEN I'LL GET POWERS?
HENH, IN A RUSH I SEE. WELL, I GOT MY POWERS AT THIRTEEN.
SO YOU'LL PROBABLY BE GETTING THEM SOON.
I CAN'T WAIT!!

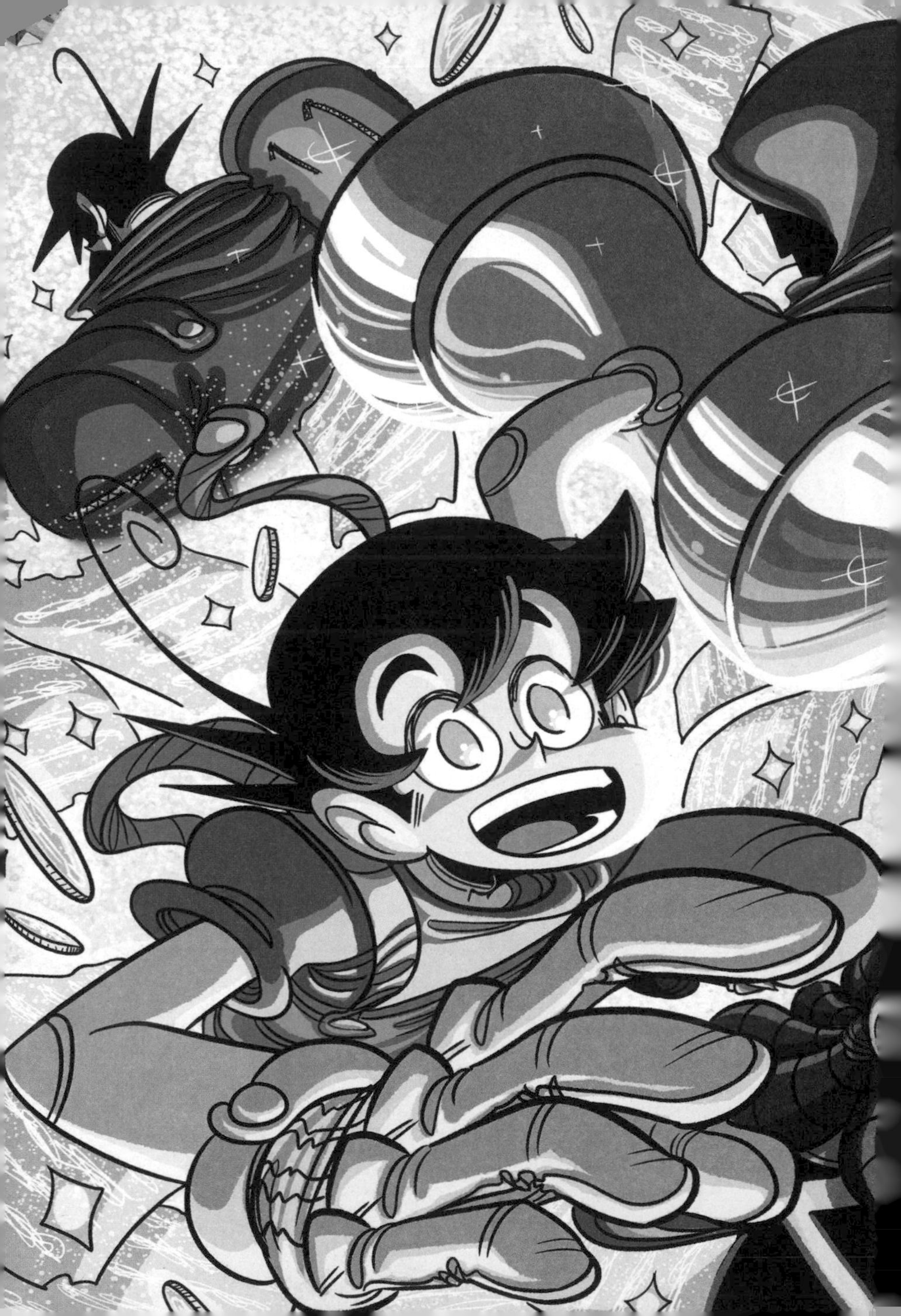

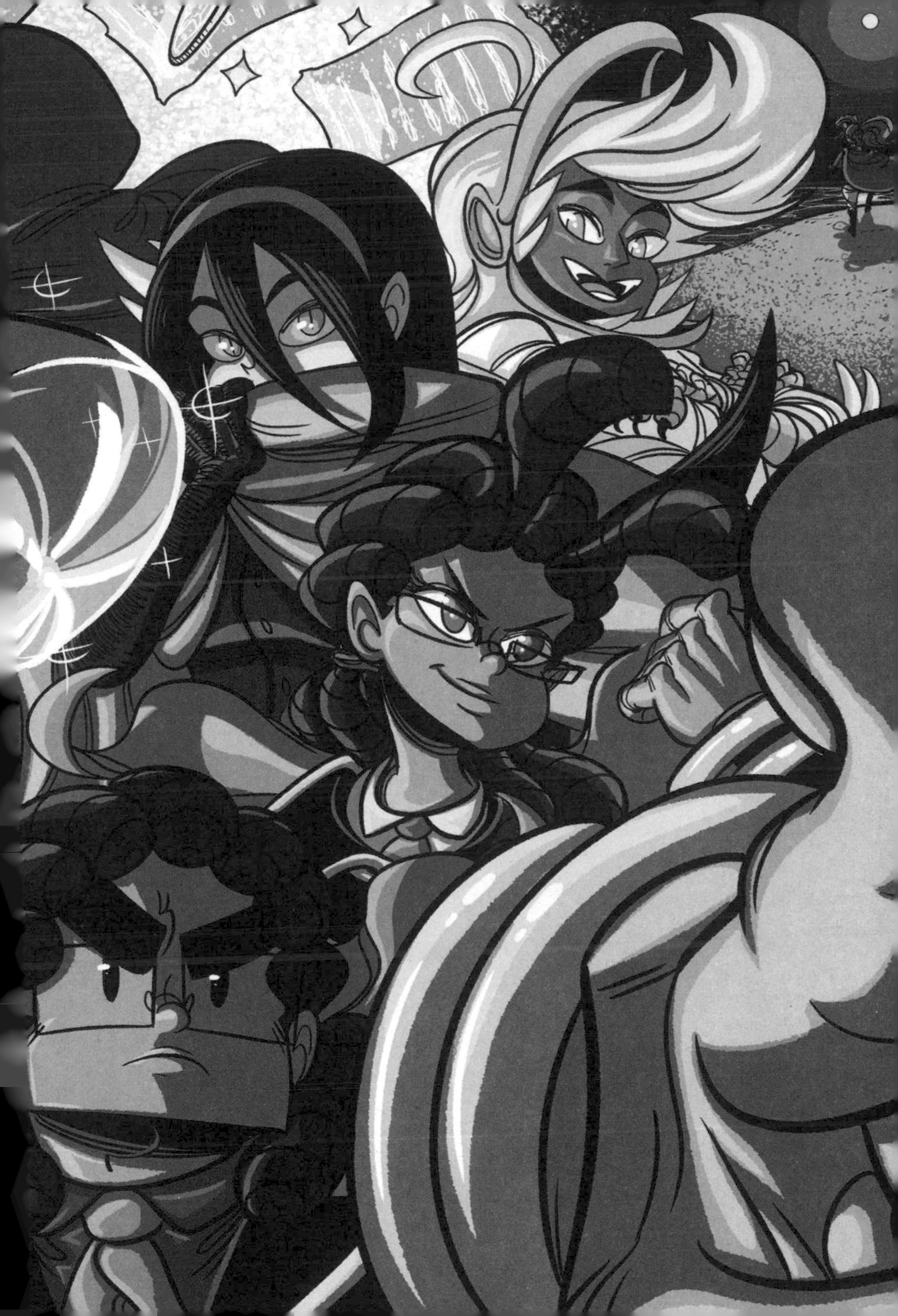

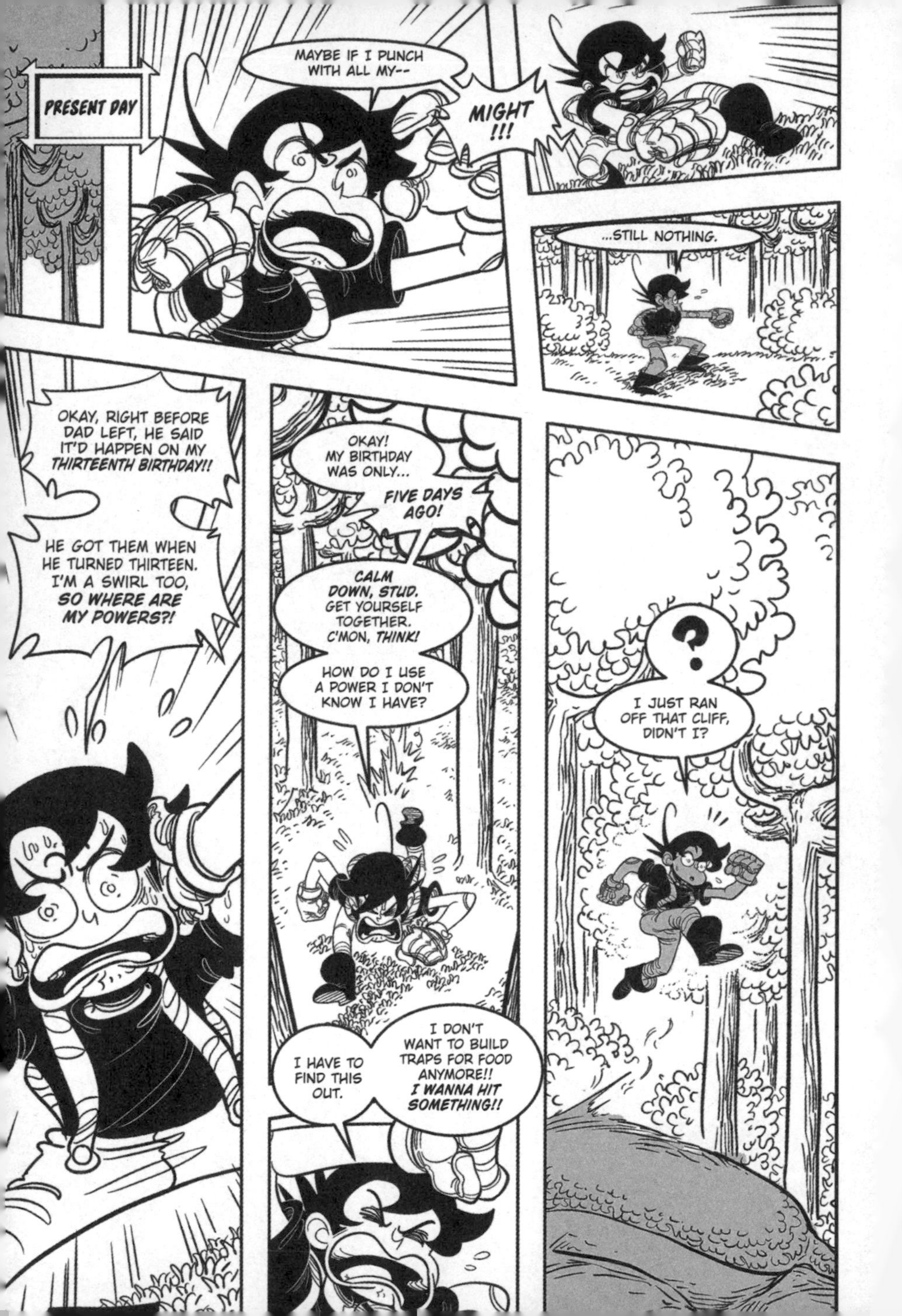
PRESENT DAY
MAYBE IF I PUNCH WITH ALL MY--
MIGHT !!!
...STILL NOTHING.
OKAY, RIGHT BEFORE DAD LEFT, HE SAID IT'D HAPPEN ON MY THIRTEENTH BIRTHDAY!!
HE GOT THEM WHEN HE TURNED THIRTEEN. I'M A SWIRL TOO, SO WHERE ARE MY POWERS?!
OKAY! MY BIRTHDAY WAS ONLY...
FIVE DAYS AGO!
CALM DOWN, STUD. GET YOURSELF TOGETHER. C'MON, THINK!
HOW DO I USE A POWER I DON'T KNOW I HAVE?
I HAVE TO FIND THIS OUT.
I DON'T WANT TO BUILD TRAPS FOR FOOD ANYMORE!! I WANNA HIT SOMETHING!!
?
I JUST RAN OFF THAT CLIFF, DIDN'T I?

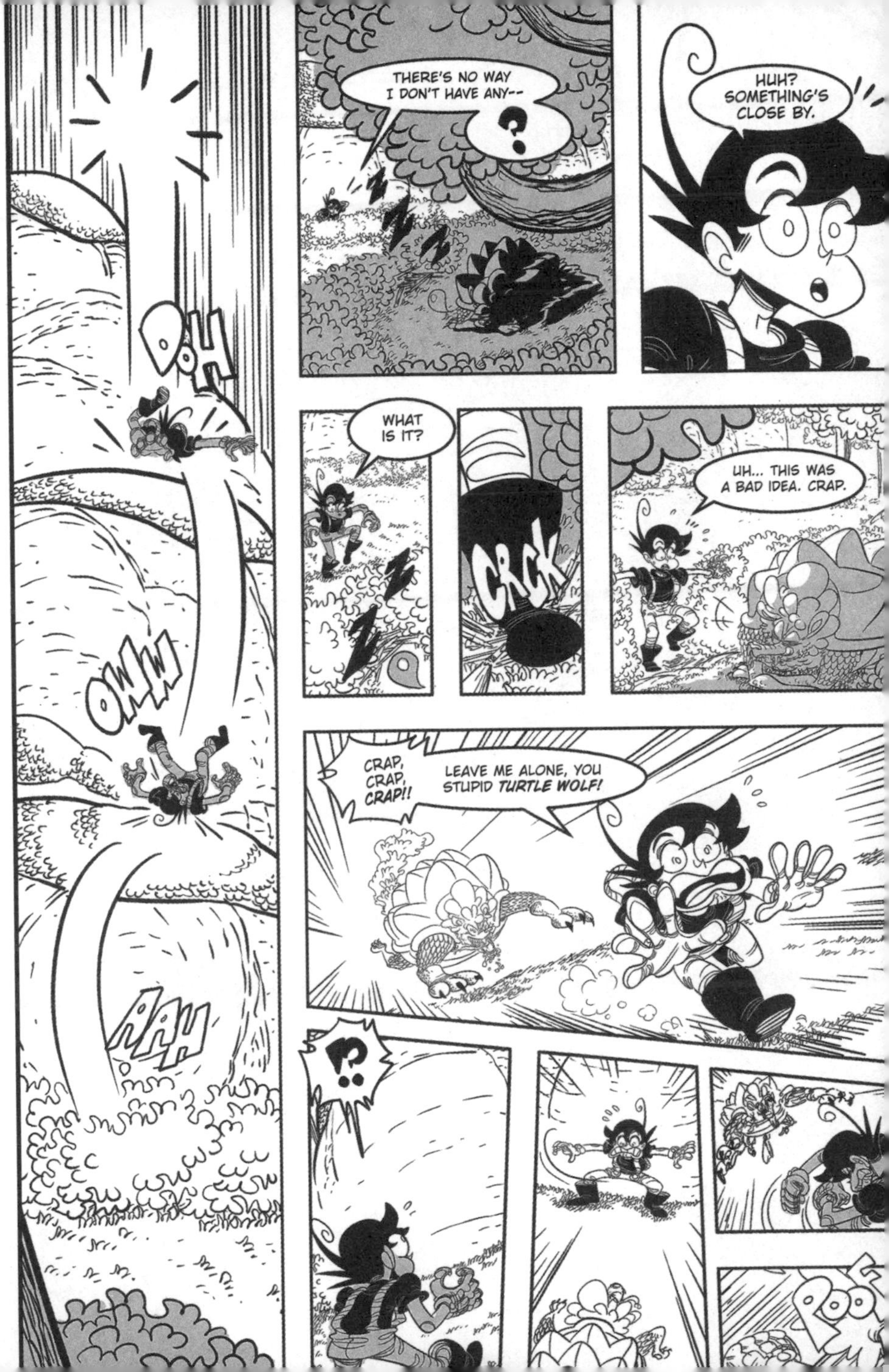
DOOH
OWW
AAH
THERE'S NO WAY I DON'T HAVE ANY--
?
HUH? SOMETHING'S CLOSE BY.
WHAT IS IT?
CRCK
UH... THIS WAS A BAD IDEA. CRAP.
CRAP, CRAP, CRAP!!
LEAVE ME ALONE, YOU STUPID *TURTLE WOLF!*
!?
POO

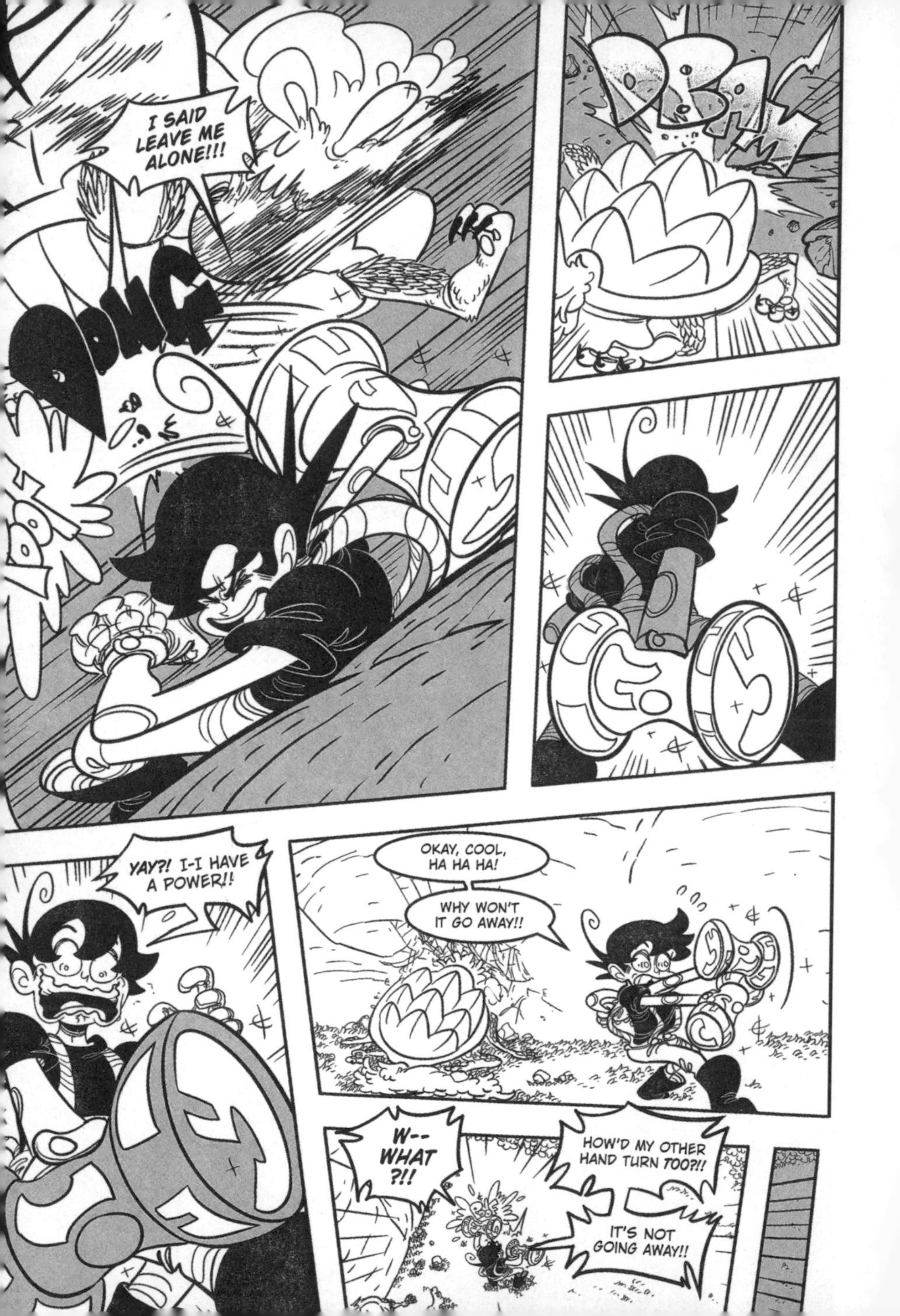
I SAID LEAVE ME ALONE!!!
YAY?! I-I HAVE A POWER!!
OKAY, COOL, HA HA HA!
WHY WON'T IT GO AWAY!!
W-- WHAT ?!!
HOW'D MY OTHER HAND TURN TOO?!!
IT'S NOT GOING AWAY!!

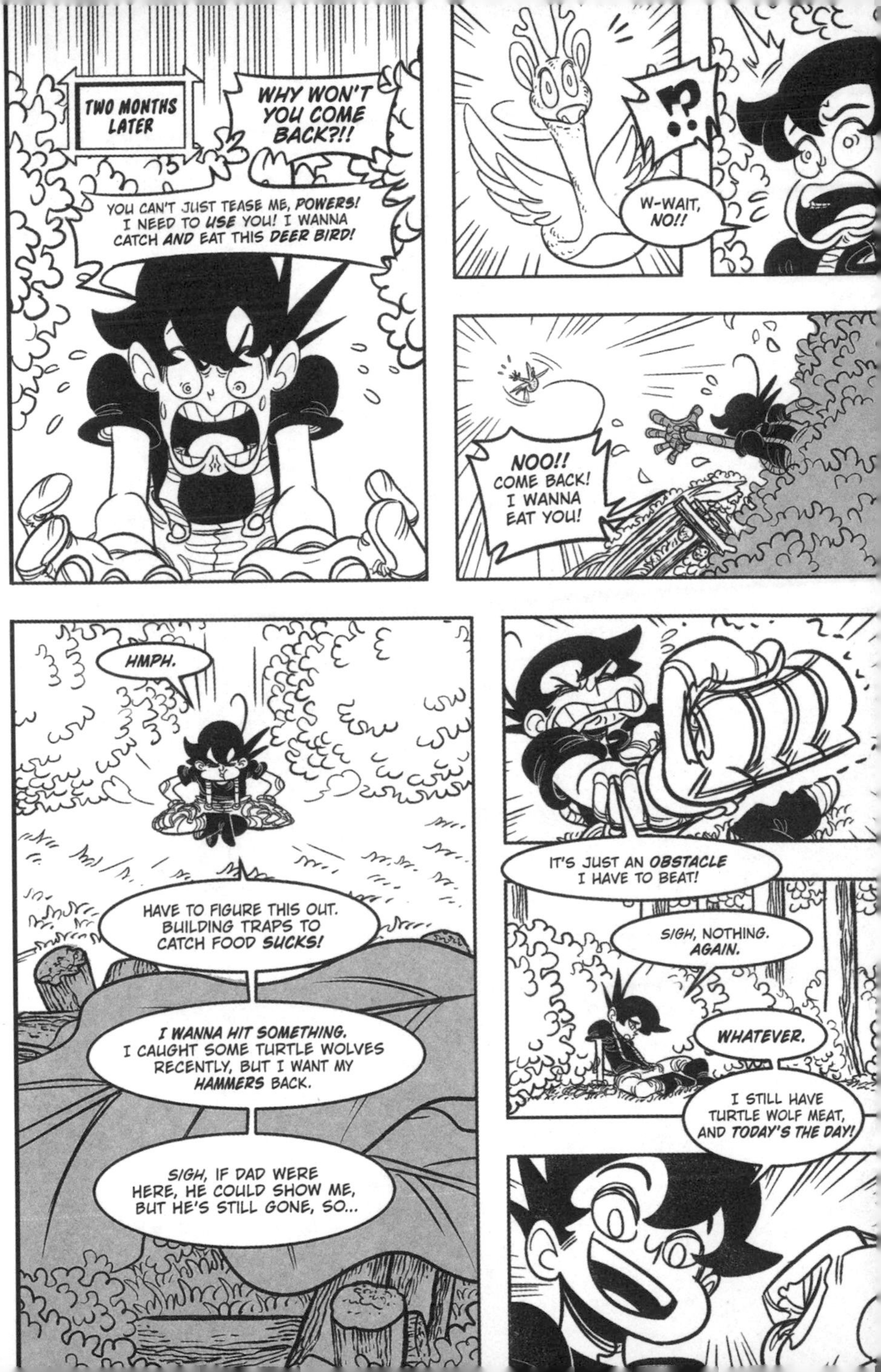
TWO MONTHS LATER
WHY WON'T YOU COME BACK?!!
YOU CAN'T JUST TEASE ME, POWERS! I NEED TO USE YOU! I WANNA CATCH AND EAT THIS DEER BIRD!
!?
W-WAIT, NO!!
NOO!! COME BACK! I WANNA EAT YOU!
HMPH.
HAVE TO FIGURE THIS OUT. BUILDING TRAPS TO CATCH FOOD SUCKS!
I WANNA HIT SOMETHING. I CAUGHT SOME TURTLE WOLVES RECENTLY, BUT I WANT MY HAMMERS BACK.
SIGH, IF DAD WERE HERE, HE COULD SHOW ME, BUT HE'S STILL GONE, SO...
IT'S JUST AN OBSTACLE I HAVE TO BEAT!
SIGH, NOTHING. AGAIN.
WHATEVER.
I STILL HAVE TURTLE WOLF MEAT, AND TODAY'S THE DAY!

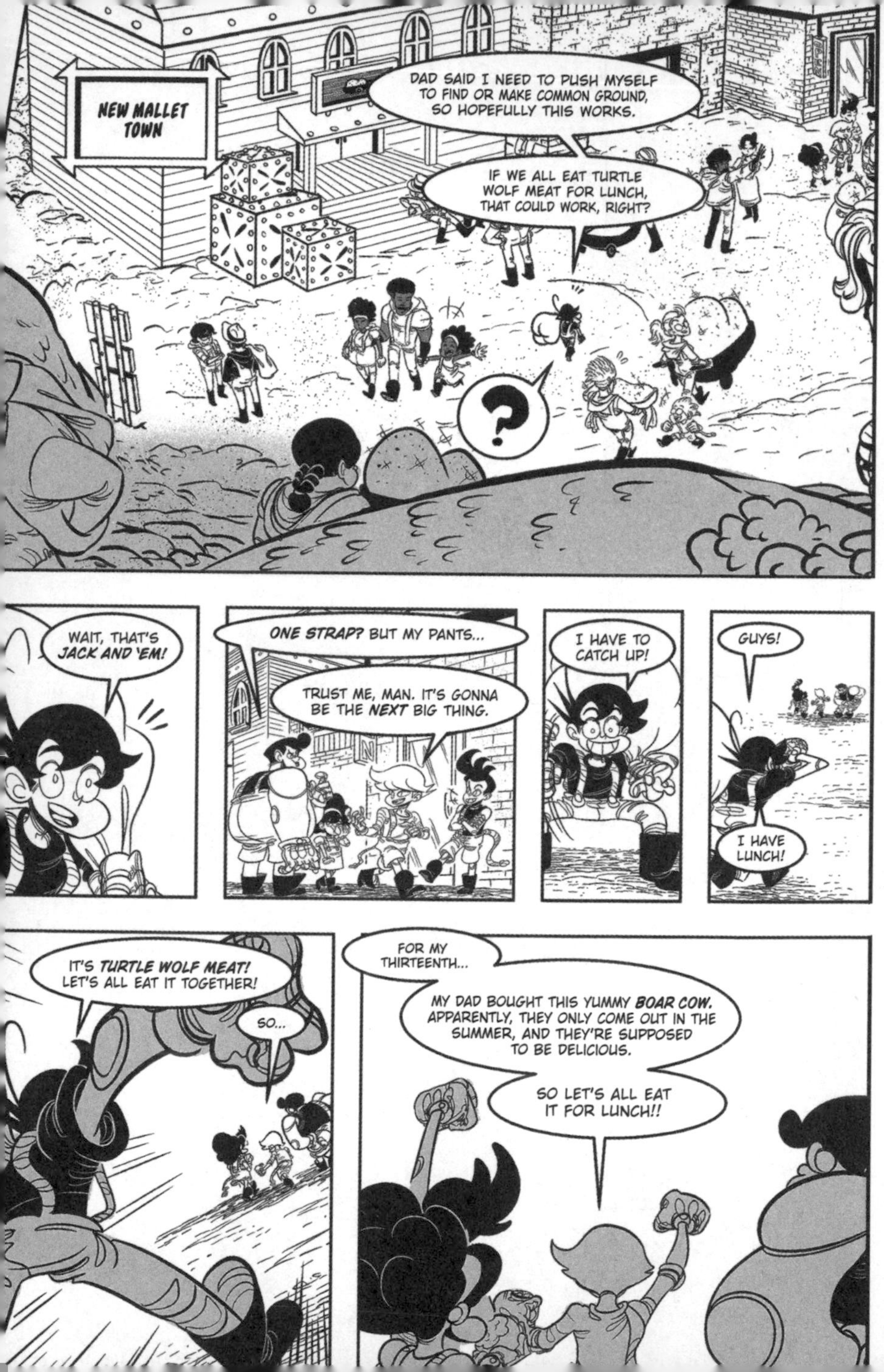
NEW MALLET TOWN
DAD SAID I NEED TO PUSH MYSELF TO FIND OR MAKE COMMON GROUND, SO HOPEFULLY THIS WORKS.
IF WE ALL EAT TURTLE WOLF MEAT FOR LUNCH, THAT COULD WORK, RIGHT?
?
WAIT, THAT'S JACK AND 'EM!
ONE STRAP? BUT MY PANTS...
TRUST ME, MAN. IT'S GONNA BE THE NEXT BIG THING.
I HAVE TO CATCH UP!
GUYS!
I HAVE LUNCH!
IT'S TURTLE WOLF MEAT! LET'S ALL EAT IT TOGETHER!
SO...
FOR MY THIRTEENTH...
MY DAD BOUGHT THIS YUMMY BOAR COW. APPARENTLY, THEY ONLY COME OUT IN THE SUMMER, AND THEY'RE SUPPOSED TO BE DELICIOUS.
SO LET'S ALL EAT IT FOR LUNCH!!

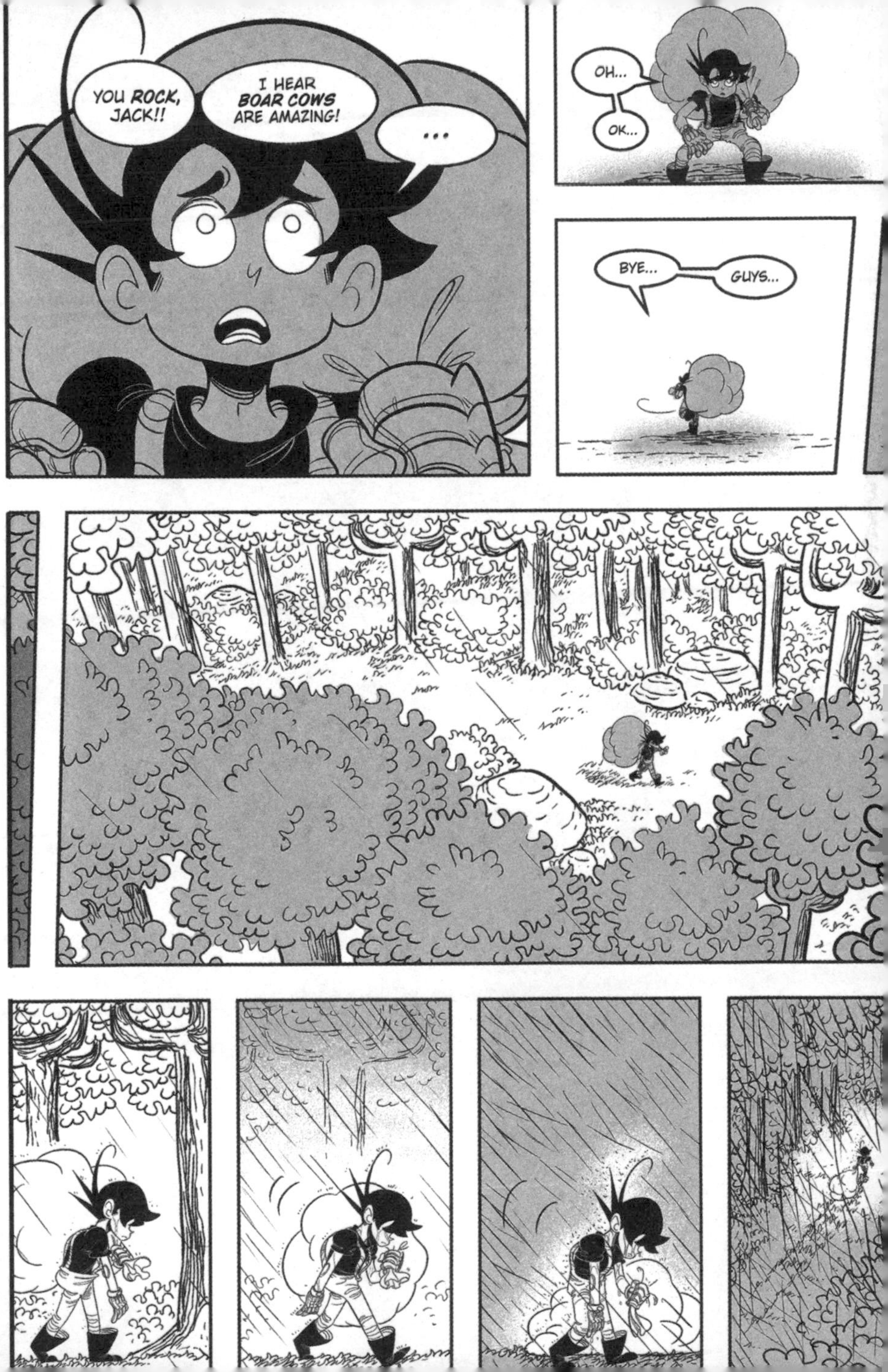
YOU ROCK, JACK!!
I HEAR BOAR COWS ARE AMAZING!
...
OH...
OK...
BYE...
GUYS...

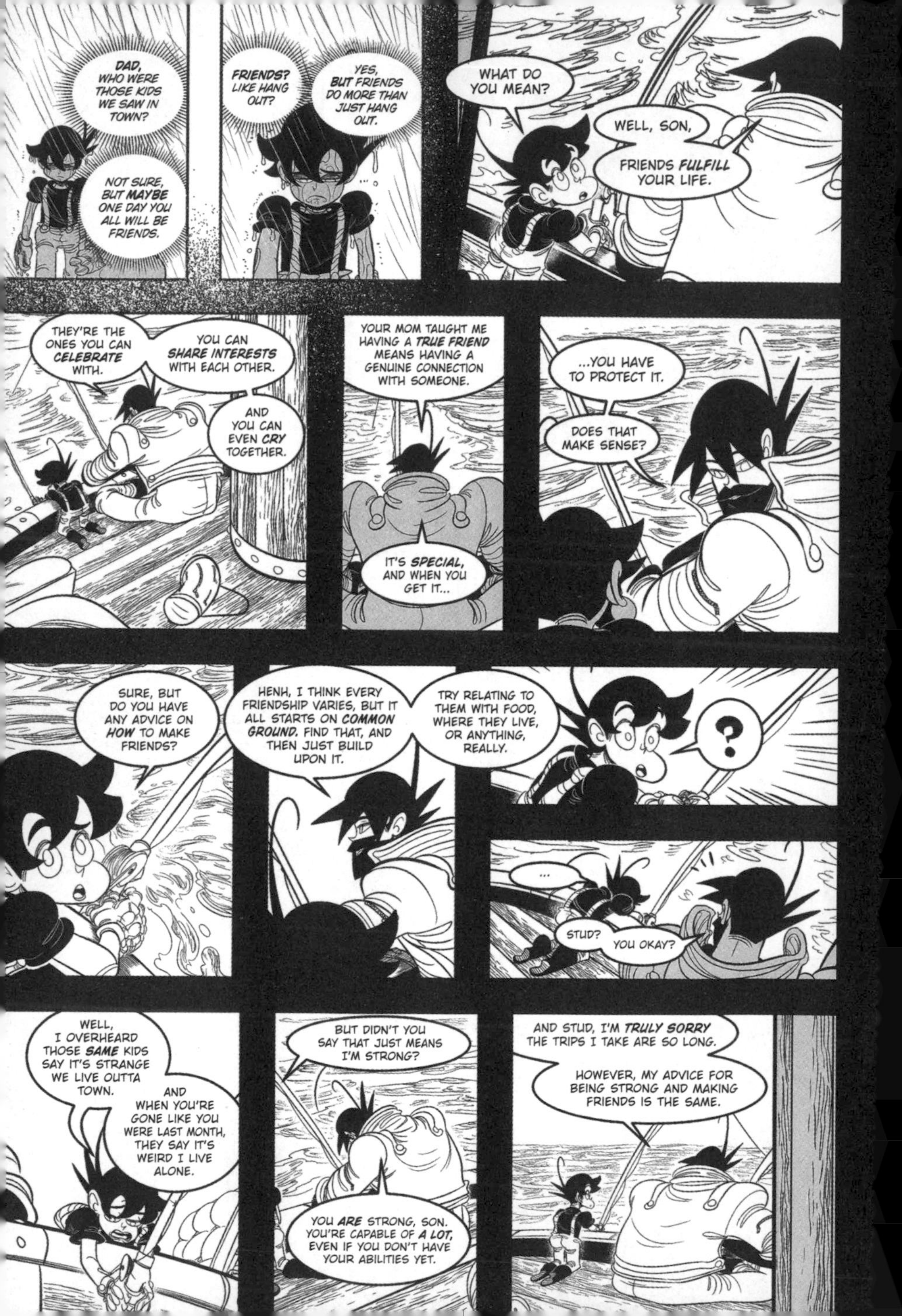
DAD, WHO WERE THOSE KIDS WE SAW IN TOWN?
NOT SURE, BUT MAYBE ONE DAY YOU ALL WILL BE FRIENDS.
FRIENDS? LIKE HANG OUT?
YES, BUT FRIENDS DO MORE THAN JUST HANG OUT.
...
WHAT DO YOU MEAN?
WELL, SON,
FRIENDS FULFILL YOUR LIFE.
THEY'RE THE ONES YOU CAN CELEBRATE WITH.
YOU CAN SHARE INTERESTS WITH EACH OTHER.
AND YOU CAN EVEN CRY TOGETHER.
YOUR MOM TAUGHT ME HAVING A TRUE FRIEND MEANS HAVING A GENUINE CONNECTION WITH SOMEONE.
IT'S SPECIAL, AND WHEN YOU GET IT...
...YOU HAVE TO PROTECT IT.
DOES THAT MAKE SENSE?
SURE, BUT DO YOU HAVE ANY ADVICE ON HOW TO MAKE FRIENDS?
HENH, I THINK EVERY FRIENDSHIP VARIES, BUT IT ALL STARTS ON COMMON GROUND. FIND THAT, AND THEN JUST BUILD UPON IT.
TRY RELATING TO THEM WITH FOOD, WHERE THEY LIVE, OR ANYTHING, REALLY.
?
...
STUD?
YOU OKAY?
WELL, I OVERHEARD THOSE SAME KIDS SAY IT'S STRANGE WE LIVE OUTTA TOWN.
AND WHEN YOU'RE GONE LIKE YOU WERE LAST MONTH, THEY SAY IT'S WEIRD I LIVE ALONE.
BUT DIDN'T YOU SAY THAT JUST MEANS I'M STRONG?
YOU ARE STRONG, SON. YOU'RE CAPABLE OF A LOT, EVEN IF YOU DON'T HAVE YOUR ABILITIES YET.
AND STUD, I'M TRULY SORRY THE TRIPS I TAKE ARE SO LONG.
HOWEVER, MY ADVICE FOR BEING STRONG AND MAKING FRIENDS IS THE SAME.

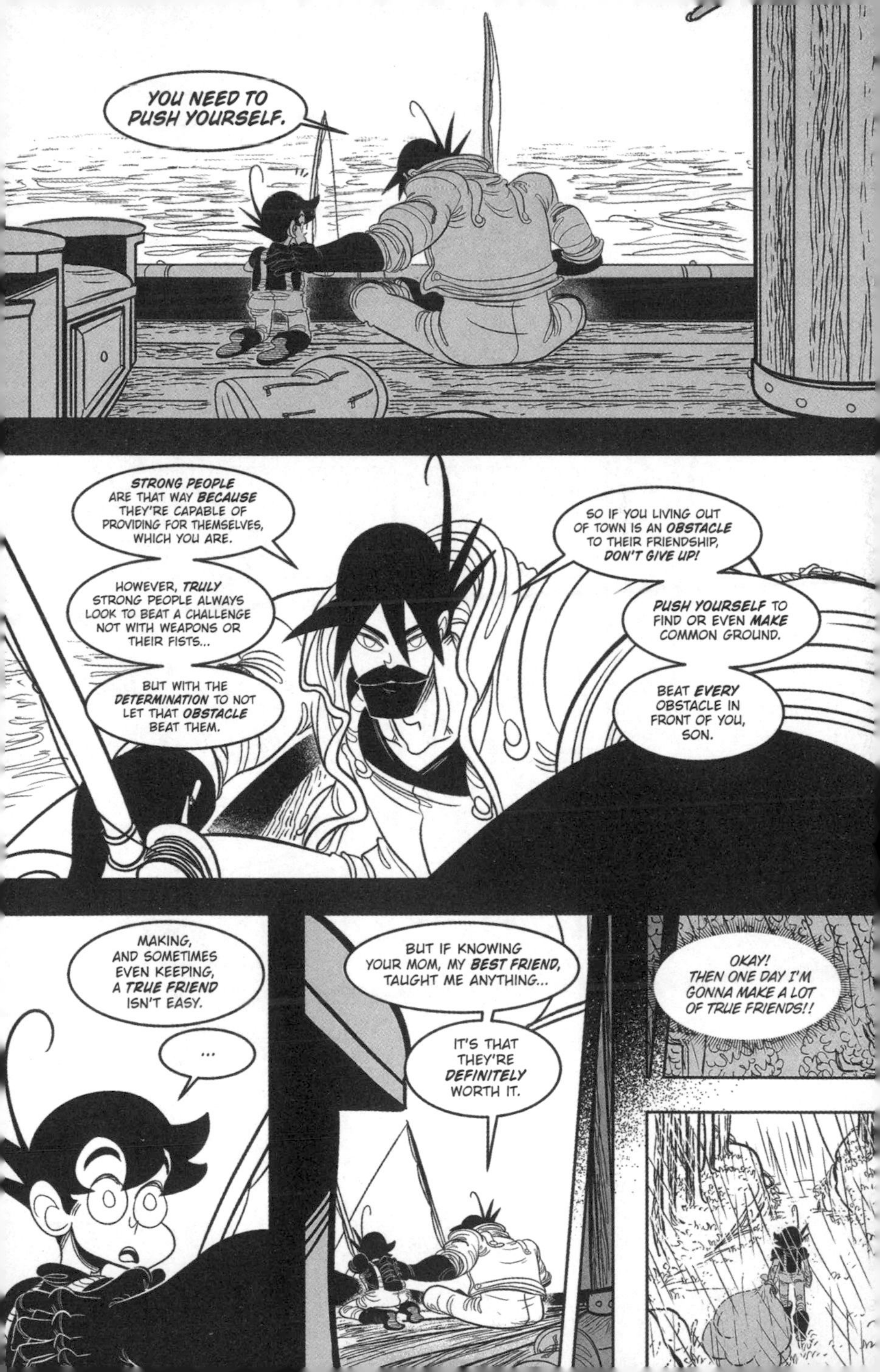
YOU NEED TO PUSH YOURSELF.
STRONG PEOPLE ARE THAT WAY BECAUSE THEY'RE CAPABLE OF PROVIDING FOR THEMSELVES, WHICH YOU ARE.
HOWEVER, TRULY STRONG PEOPLE ALWAYS LOOK TO BEAT A CHALLENGE NOT WITH WEAPONS OR THEIR FISTS...
BUT WITH THE DETERMINATION TO NOT LET THAT OBSTACLE BEAT THEM.
SO IF YOU LIVING OUT OF TOWN IS AN OBSTACLE TO THEIR FRIENDSHIP, DON'T GIVE UP!
PUSH YOURSELF TO FIND OR EVEN MAKE COMMON GROUND.
BEAT EVERY OBSTACLE IN FRONT OF YOU, SON.
MAKING, AND SOMETIMES EVEN KEEPING, A TRUE FRIEND ISN'T EASY.
...
BUT IF KNOWING YOUR MOM, MY BEST FRIEND, TAUGHT ME ANYTHING...
IT'S THAT THEY'RE DEFINITELY WORTH IT.
OKAY! THEN ONE DAY I'M GONNA MAKE A LOT OF TRUE FRIENDS!!

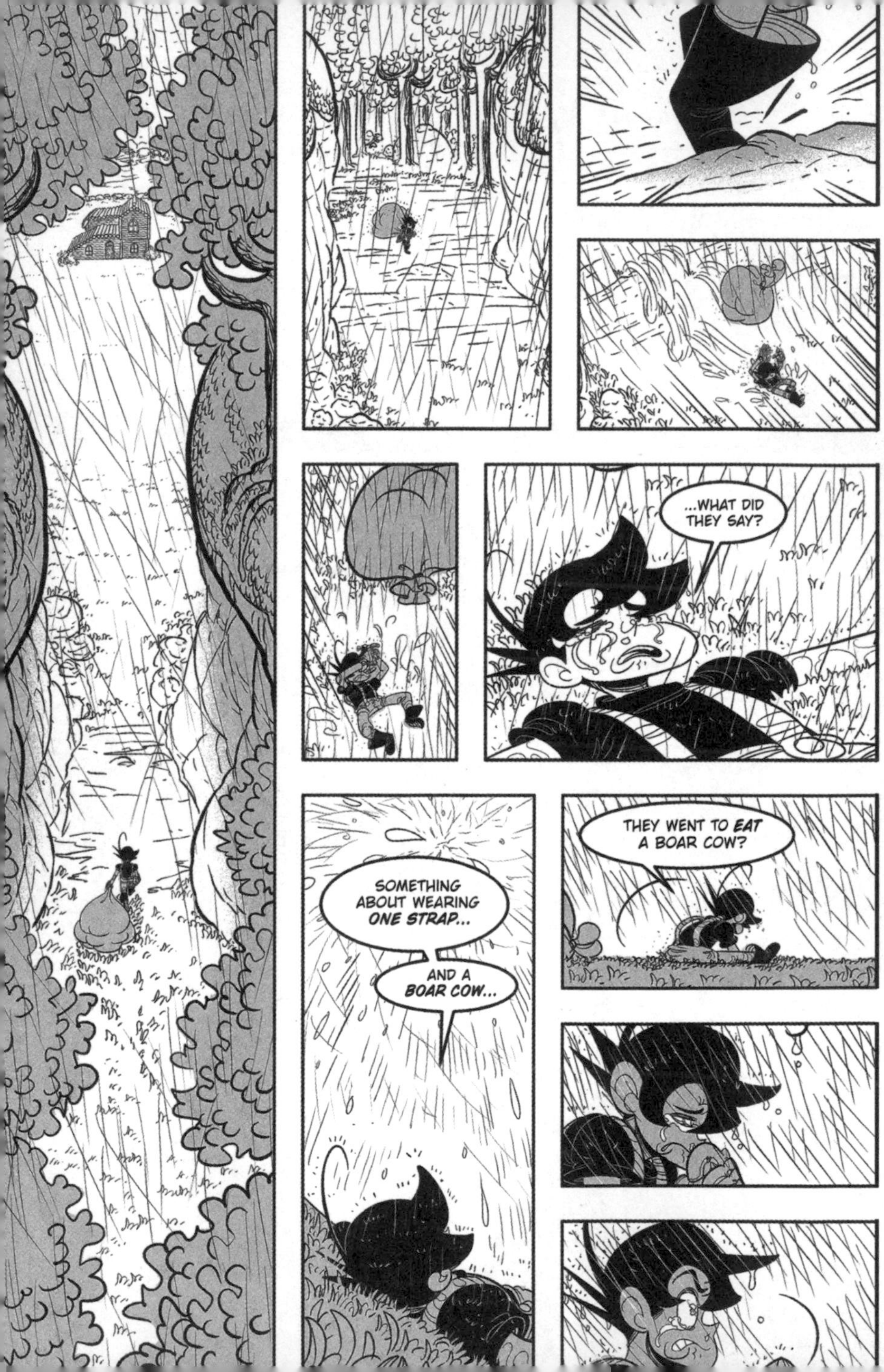
...WHAT DID THEY SAY?
SOMETHING ABOUT WEARING *ONE STRAP...*
AND A *BOAR COW...*
THEY WENT TO *EAT* A BOAR COW?

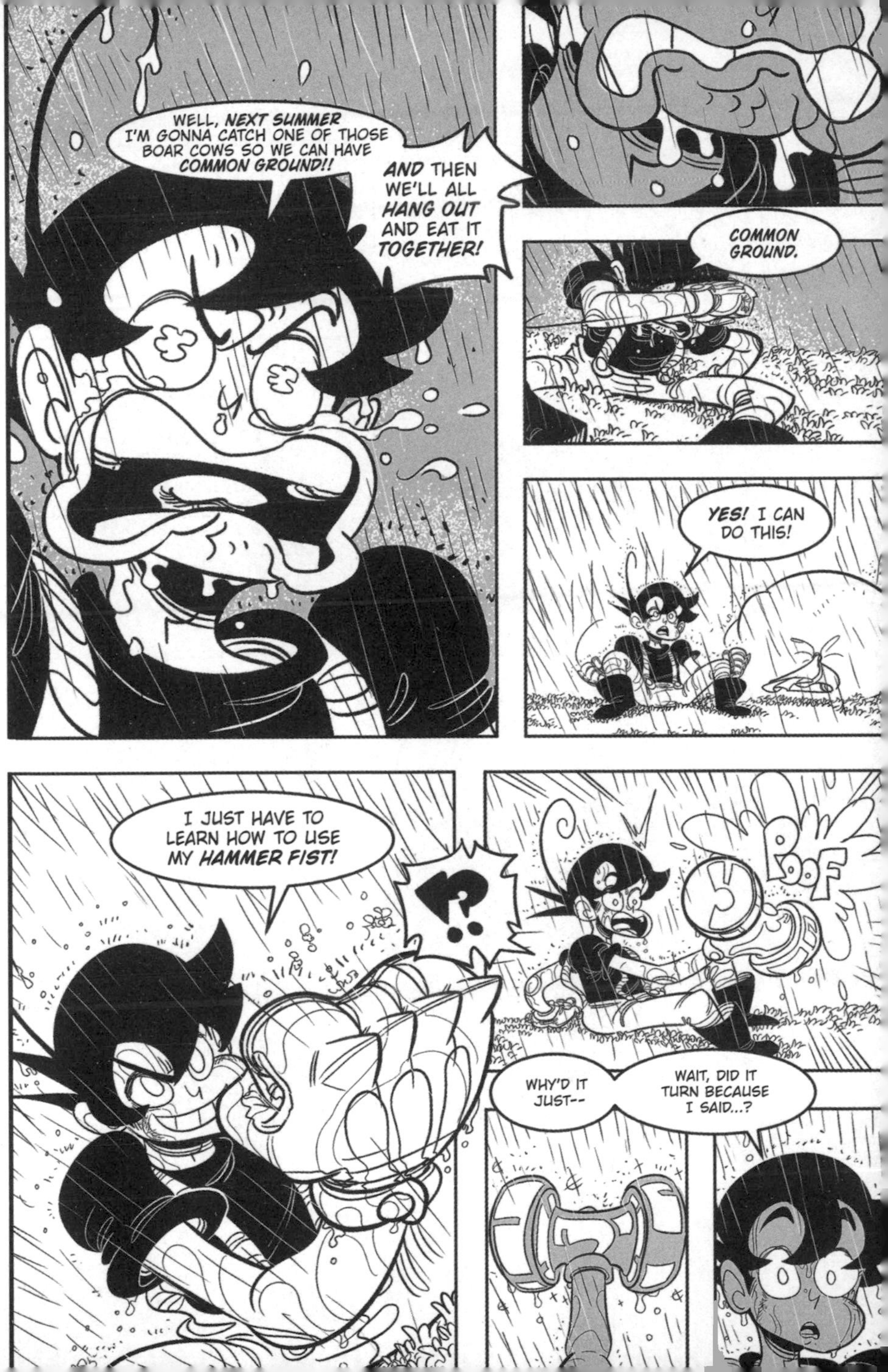
WELL, NEXT SUMMER I'M GONNA CATCH ONE OF THOSE BOAR COWS SO WE CAN HAVE COMMON GROUND!!
AND THEN WE'LL ALL HANG OUT AND EAT IT TOGETHER!
COMMON GROUND.
YES! I CAN DO THIS!
I JUST HAVE TO LEARN HOW TO USE MY HAMMER FIST!
?!
POOF
WHY'D IT JUST--
WAIT, DID IT TURN BECAUSE I SAID...?

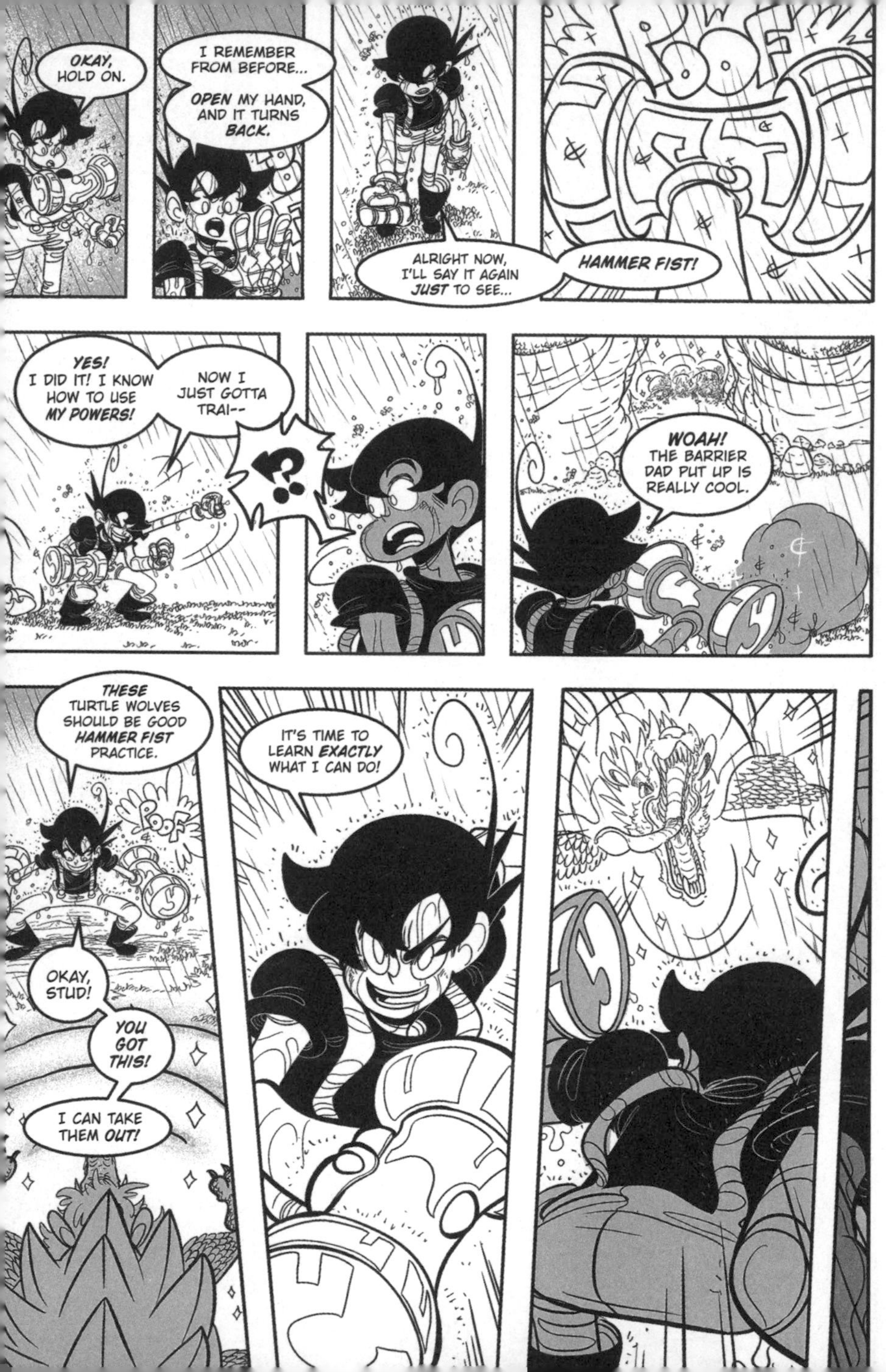
OKAY, HOLD ON.
I REMEMBER FROM BEFORE...
OPEN MY HAND, AND IT TURNS BACK.
ALRIGHT NOW, I'LL SAY IT AGAIN JUST TO SEE...
HAMMER FIST!
POOF
YES! I DID IT! I KNOW HOW TO USE MY POWERS!
NOW I JUST GOTTA TRAI--
?!
WOAH! THE BARRIER DAD PUT UP IS REALLY COOL.
THESE TURTLE WOLVES SHOULD BE GOOD HAMMER FIST PRACTICE.
POOF
OKAY, STUD!
YOU GOT THIS!
I CAN TAKE THEM OUT!
IT'S TIME TO LEARN EXACTLY WHAT I CAN DO!

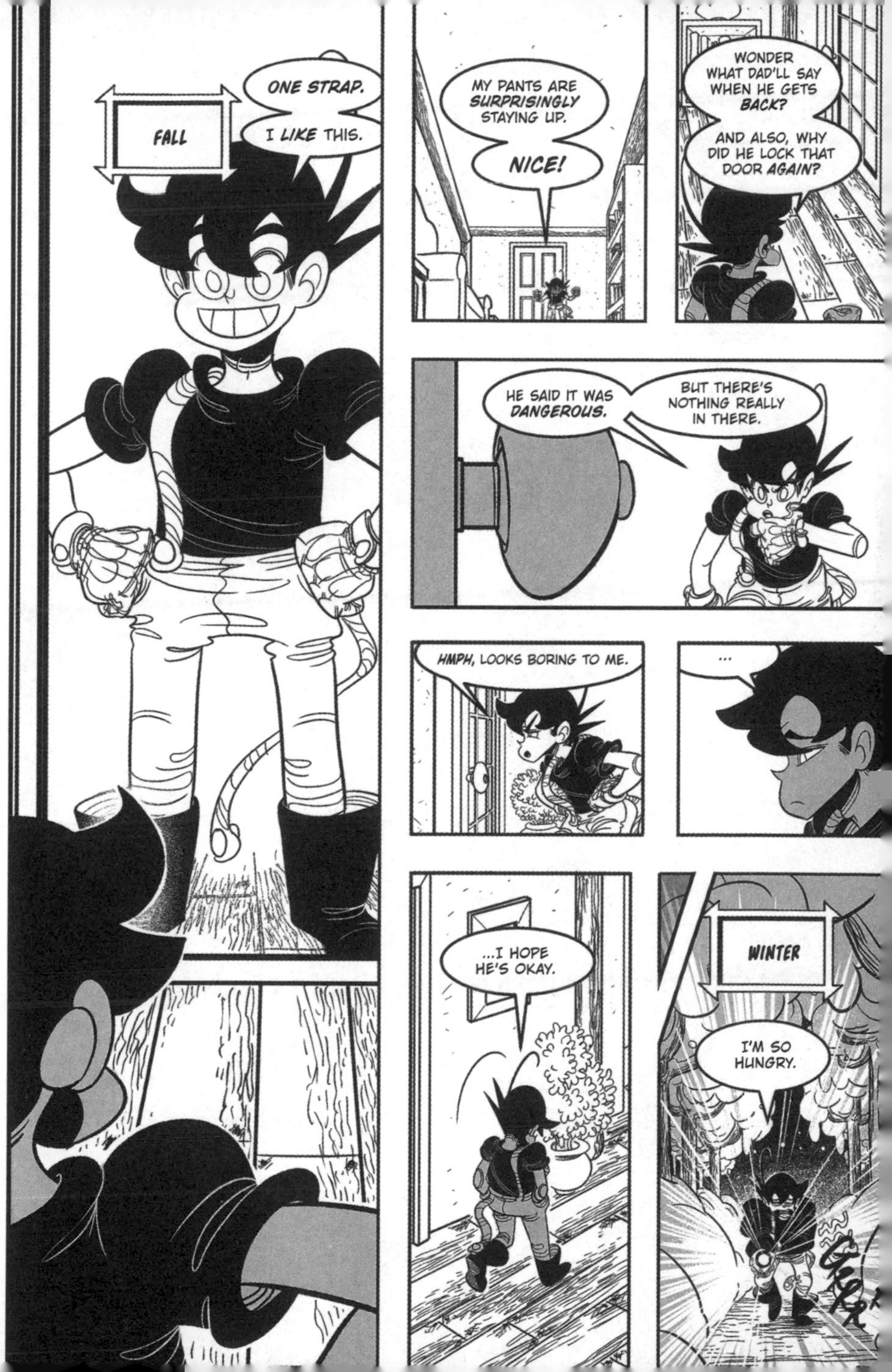
FALL
ONE STRAP.
I LIKE THIS.
MY PANTS ARE SURPRISINGLY STAYING UP.
NICE!
WONDER WHAT DAD'LL SAY WHEN HE GETS BACK?
AND ALSO, WHY DID HE LOCK THAT DOOR AGAIN?
HE SAID IT WAS DANGEROUS.
BUT THERE'S NOTHING REALLY IN THERE.
HMPH, LOOKS BORING TO ME.
...
...I HOPE HE'S OKAY.
WINTER
I'M SO HUNGRY.
GRRR

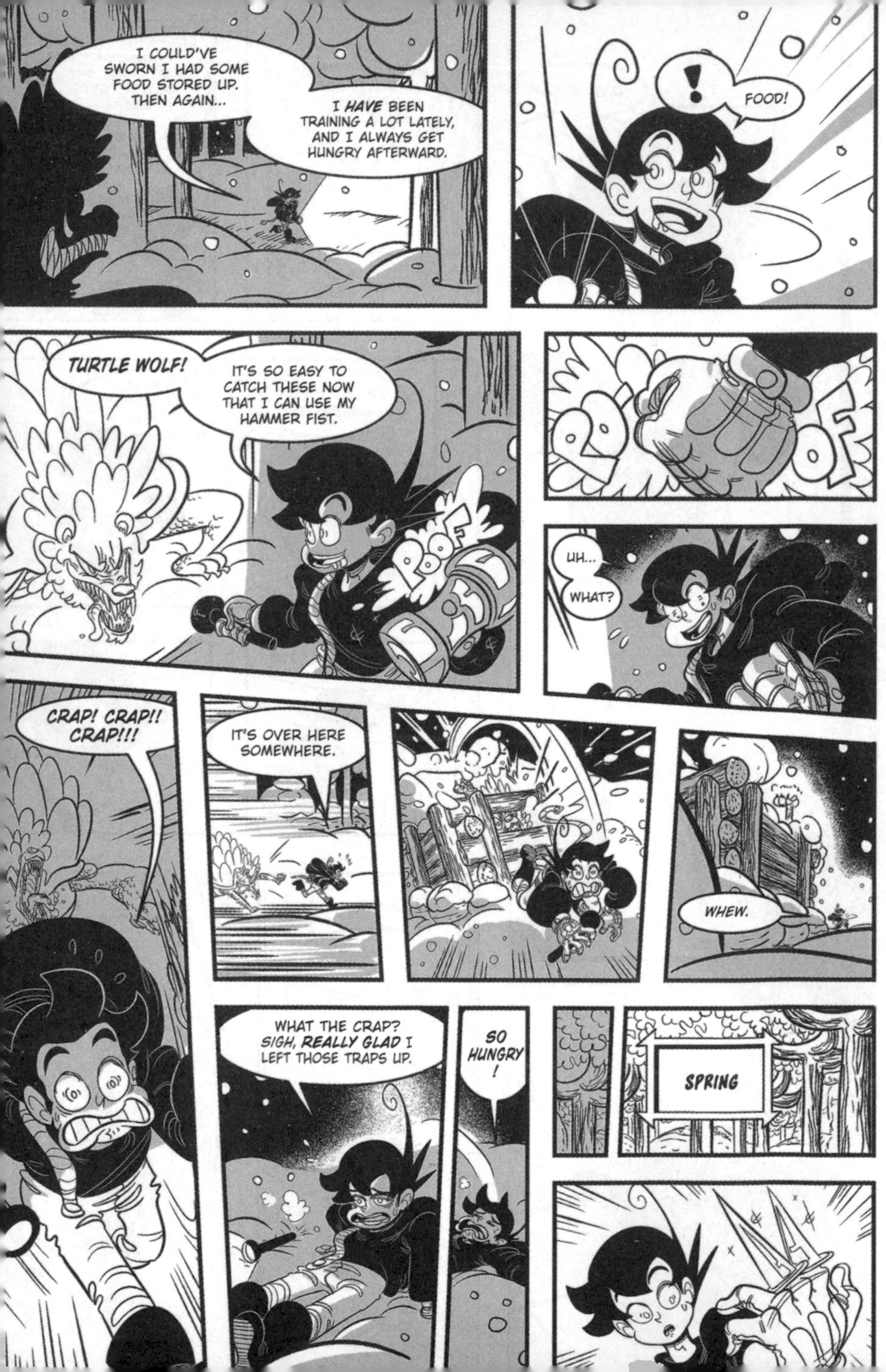
I COULD'VE SWORN I HAD SOME FOOD STORED UP. THEN AGAIN...
I *HAVE* BEEN TRAINING A LOT LATELY, AND I ALWAYS GET HUNGRY AFTERWARD.
!
FOOD!
TURTLE WOLF!
IT'S SO EASY TO CATCH THESE NOW THAT I CAN USE MY HAMMER FIST.
POOF
UH...
WHAT?
CRAP! CRAP!! CRAP!!!
IT'S OVER HERE SOMEWHERE.
WHEW.
WHAT THE CRAP? *SIGH, **REALLY GLAD*** I LEFT THOSE TRAPS UP.
SO HUNGRY!
SPRING

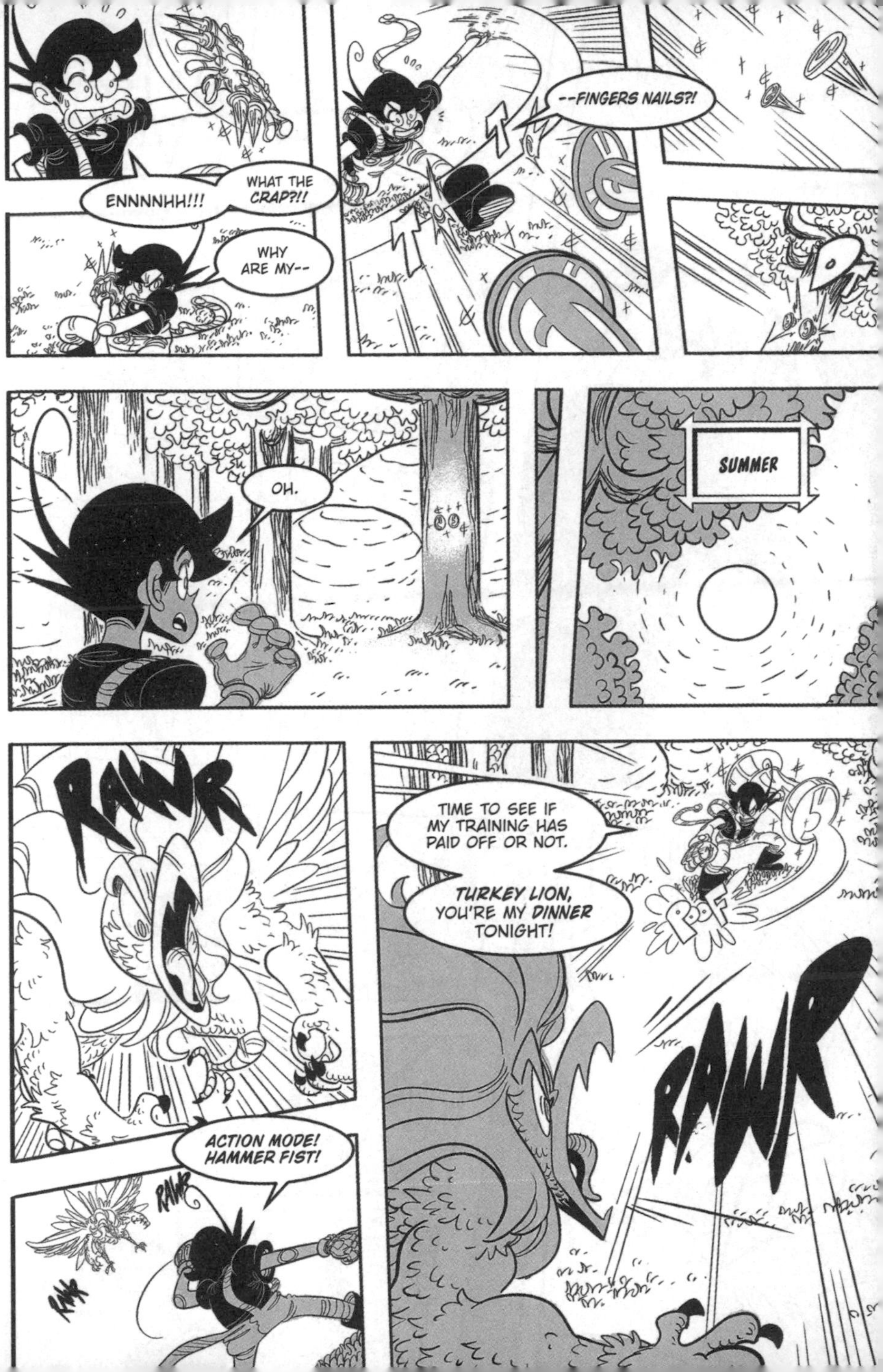
ENNNNHH!!!
WHAT THE CRAP?!!
WHY ARE MY--
--FINGERS NAILS?!
OH.
SUMMER
RAWR
ACTION MODE! HAMMER FIST!
RAWR
RAWR
TIME TO SEE IF MY TRAINING HAS PAID OFF OR NOT.
TURKEY LION, YOU'RE MY DINNER TONIGHT!
POOF
RAWR

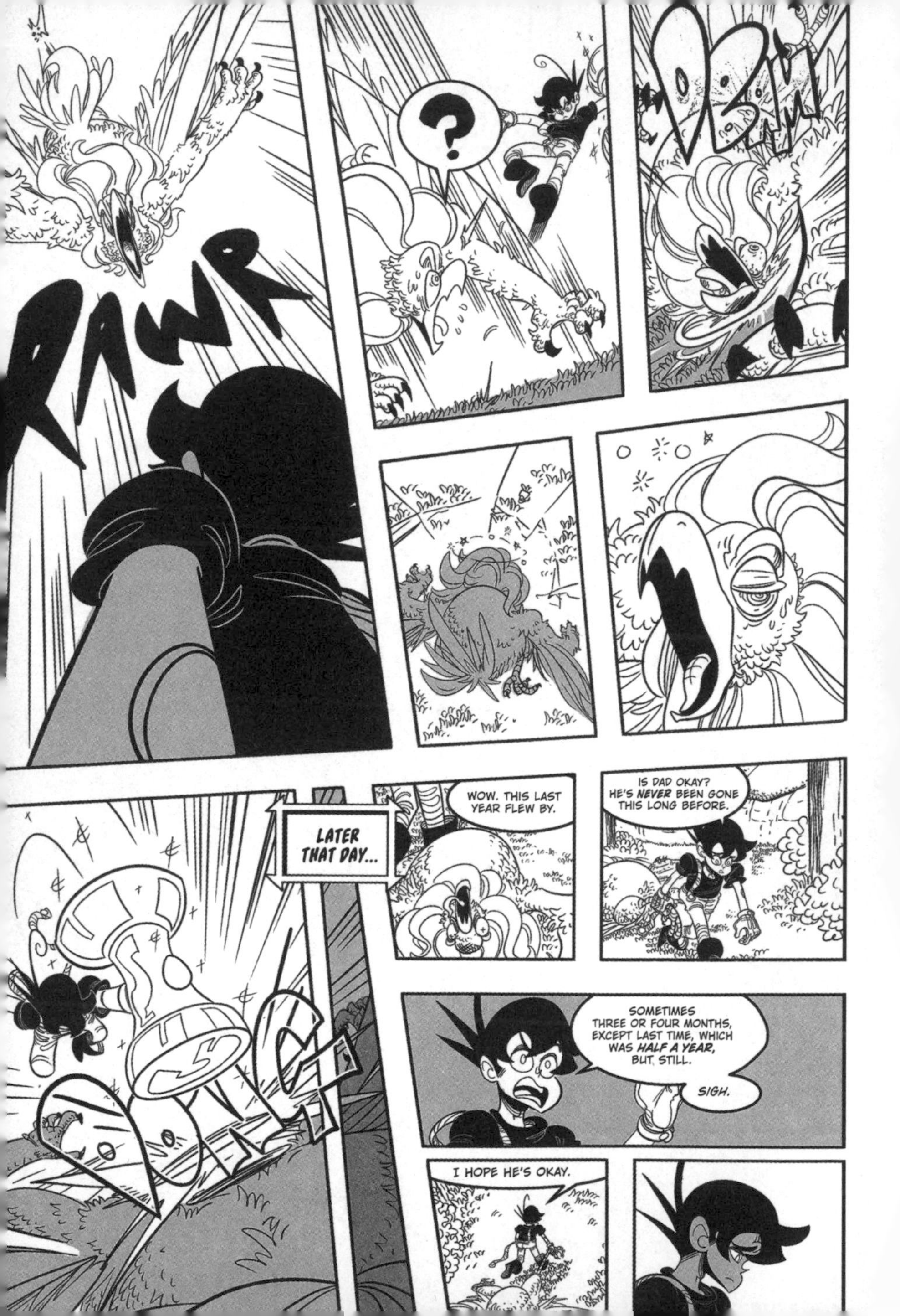
RAWR
?
LATER THAT DAY...
WOW. THIS LAST YEAR FLEW BY.
IS DAD OKAY? HE'S *NEVER* BEEN GONE THIS LONG BEFORE.
SOMETIMES THREE OR FOUR MONTHS, EXCEPT LAST TIME, WHICH WAS *HALF A YEAR,* BUT, STILL.
SIGH.
I HOPE HE'S OKAY.

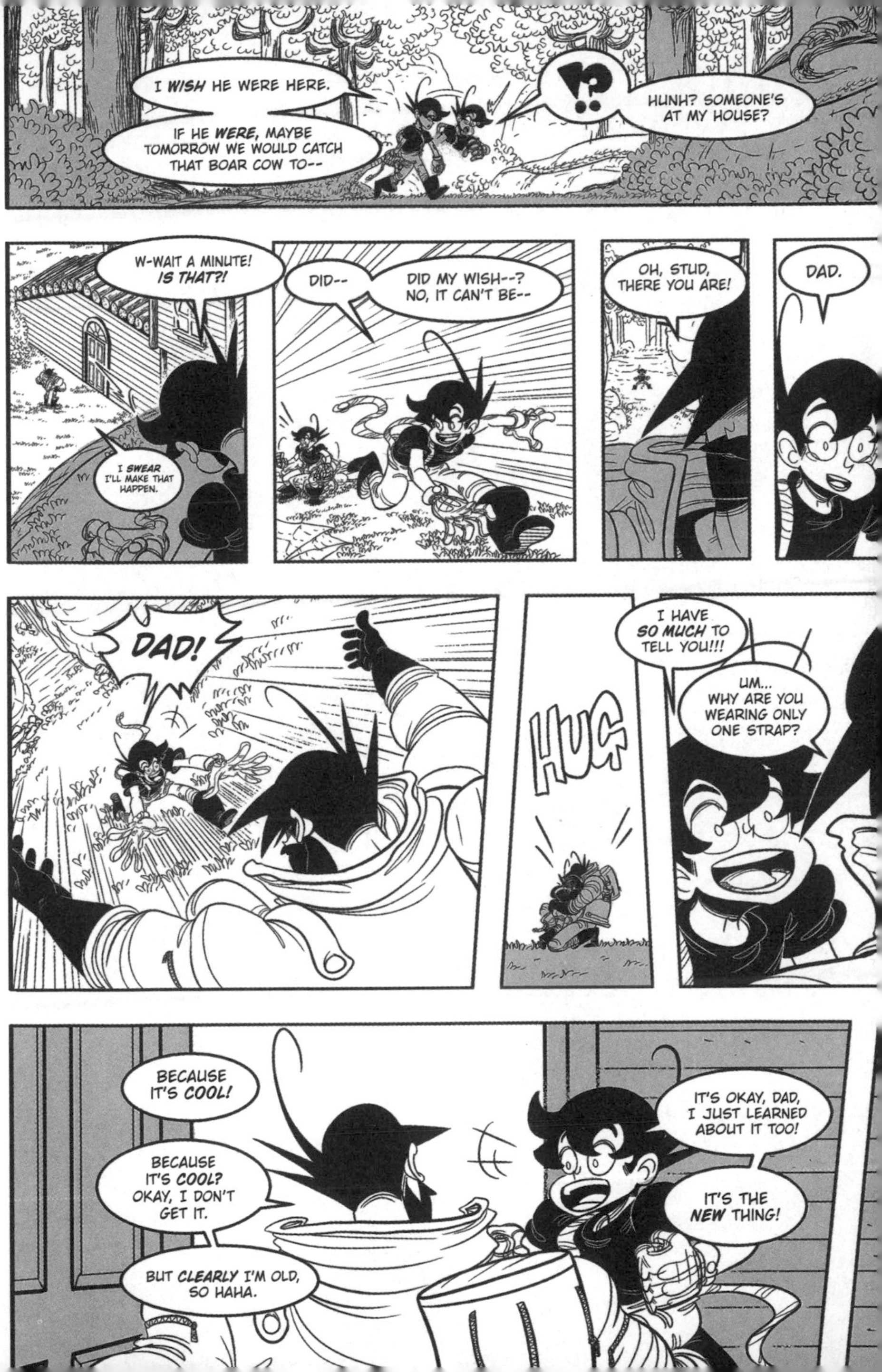
I WISH HE WERE HERE.
IF HE WERE, MAYBE TOMORROW WE WOULD CATCH THAT BOAR COW TO--
!?
HUNH? SOMEONE'S AT MY HOUSE?
W-WAIT A MINUTE! IS THAT?!
I SWEAR I'LL MAKE THAT HAPPEN.
DID--
DID MY WISH--? NO, IT CAN'T BE--
OH, STUD, THERE YOU ARE!
DAD.
DAD!
HUG
I HAVE SO MUCH TO TELL YOU!!!
UM... WHY ARE YOU WEARING ONLY ONE STRAP?
BECAUSE IT'S COOL!
BECAUSE IT'S COOL? OKAY, I DON'T GET IT.
BUT CLEARLY I'M OLD, SO HAHA.
IT'S OKAY, DAD, I JUST LEARNED ABOUT IT TOO!
IT'S THE NEW THING!

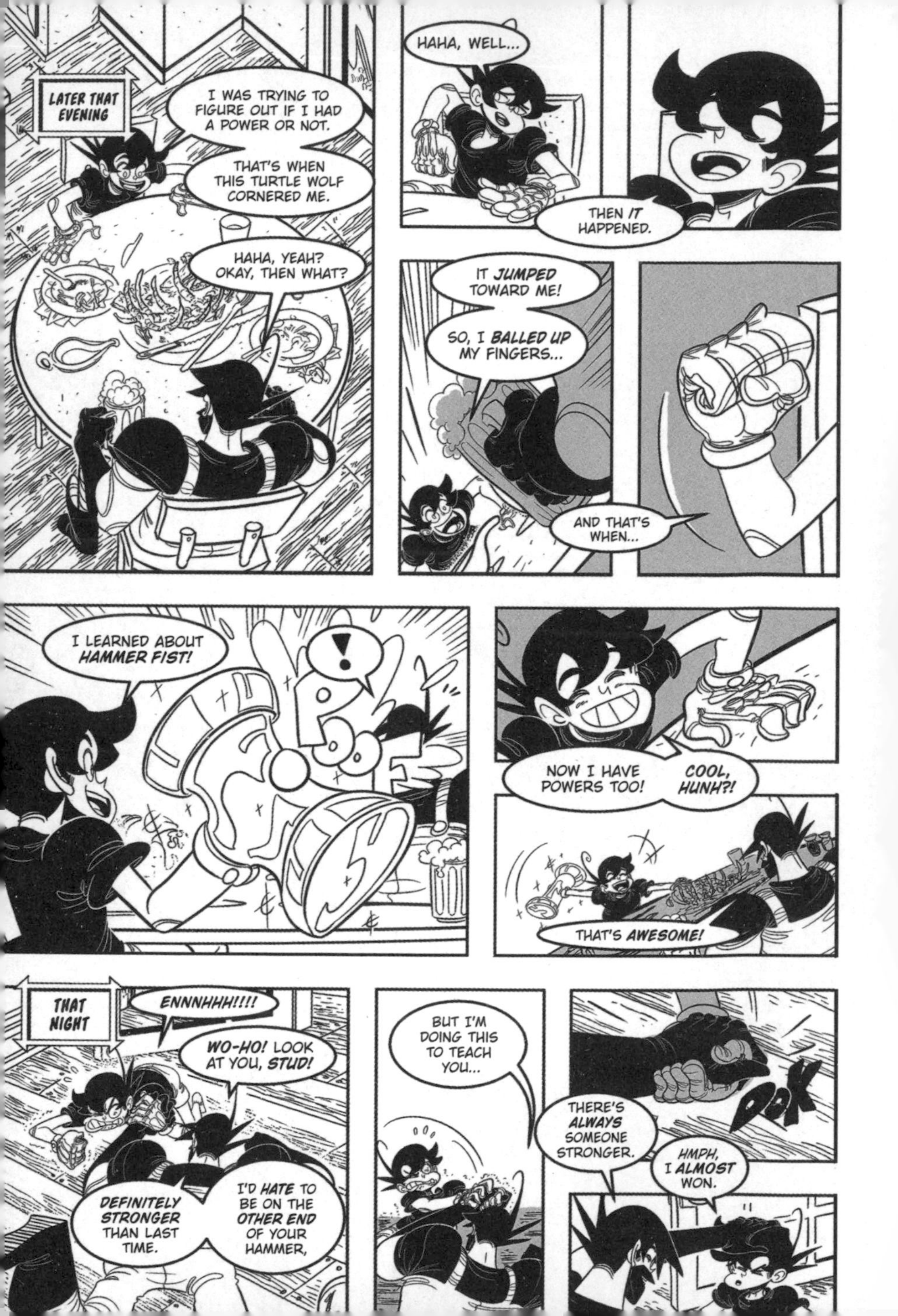
LATER THAT EVENING
I WAS TRYING TO FIGURE OUT IF I HAD A POWER OR NOT.
THAT'S WHEN THIS TURTLE WOLF CORNERED ME.
HAHA, YEAH? OKAY, THEN WHAT?
HAHA, WELL...
THEN *IT* HAPPENED.
IT *JUMPED* TOWARD ME!
SO, I *BALLED UP* MY FINGERS...
AND THAT'S WHEN...
I LEARNED ABOUT *HAMMER FIST!*
!
POOF
NOW I HAVE POWERS TOO!
COOL, HUNH?!
THAT'S *AWESOME!*
THAT NIGHT
ENNNHHH!!!!
WO-HO! LOOK AT YOU, *STUD!*
DEFINITELY STRONGER THAN LAST TIME.
I'D *HATE* TO BE ON THE *OTHER END* OF YOUR *HAMMER*,
BUT I'M DOING THIS TO TEACH YOU...
DOK
THERE'S *ALWAYS* SOMEONE STRONGER.
HMPH, I *ALMOST* WON.

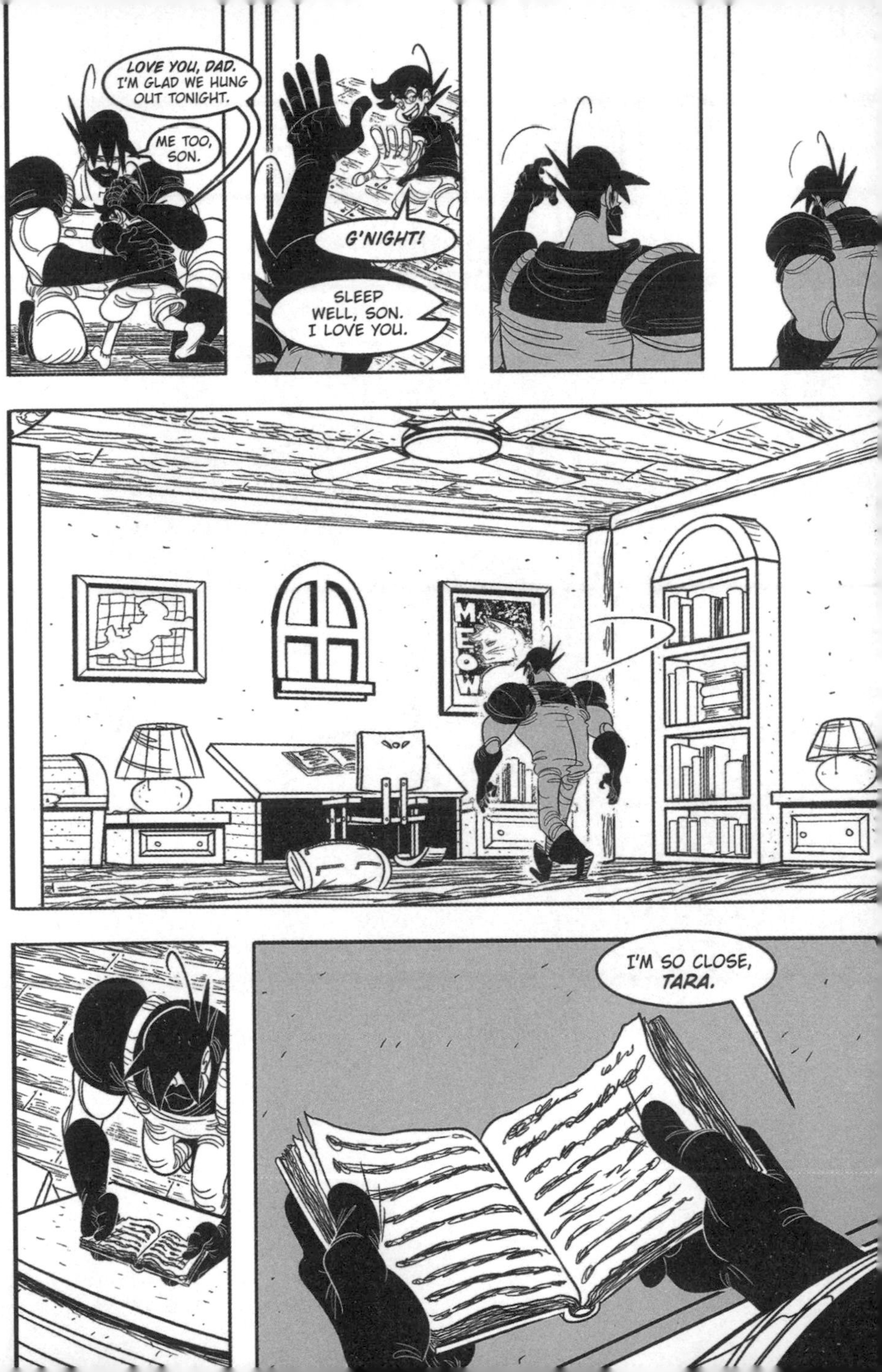
LOVE YOU, DAD. I'M GLAD WE HUNG OUT TONIGHT.
ME TOO, SON.
G'NIGHT!
SLEEP WELL, SON. I LOVE YOU.
MEOW
I'M SO CLOSE, TARA.

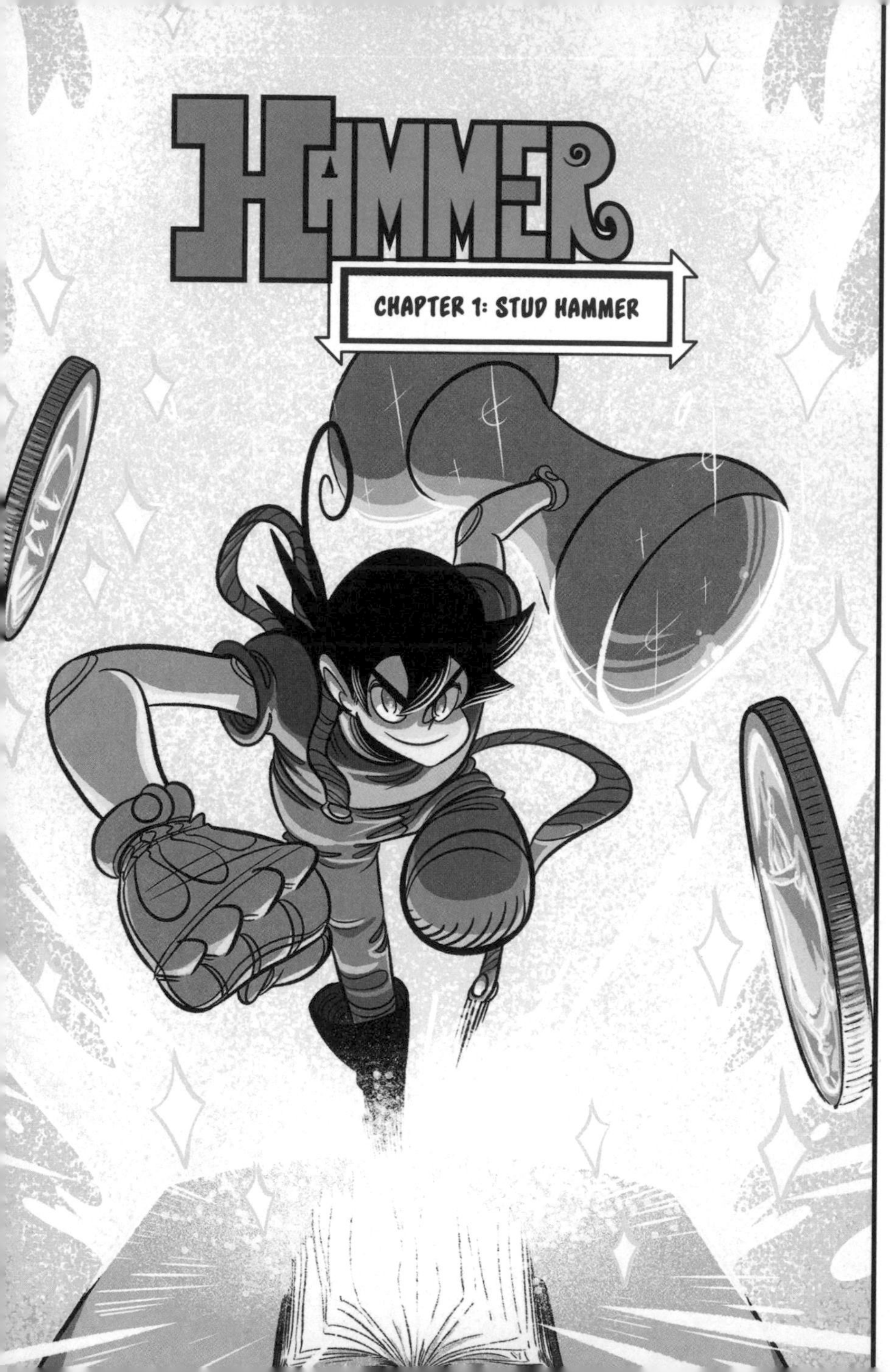
HAMMER
CHAPTER 1: STUD HAMMER

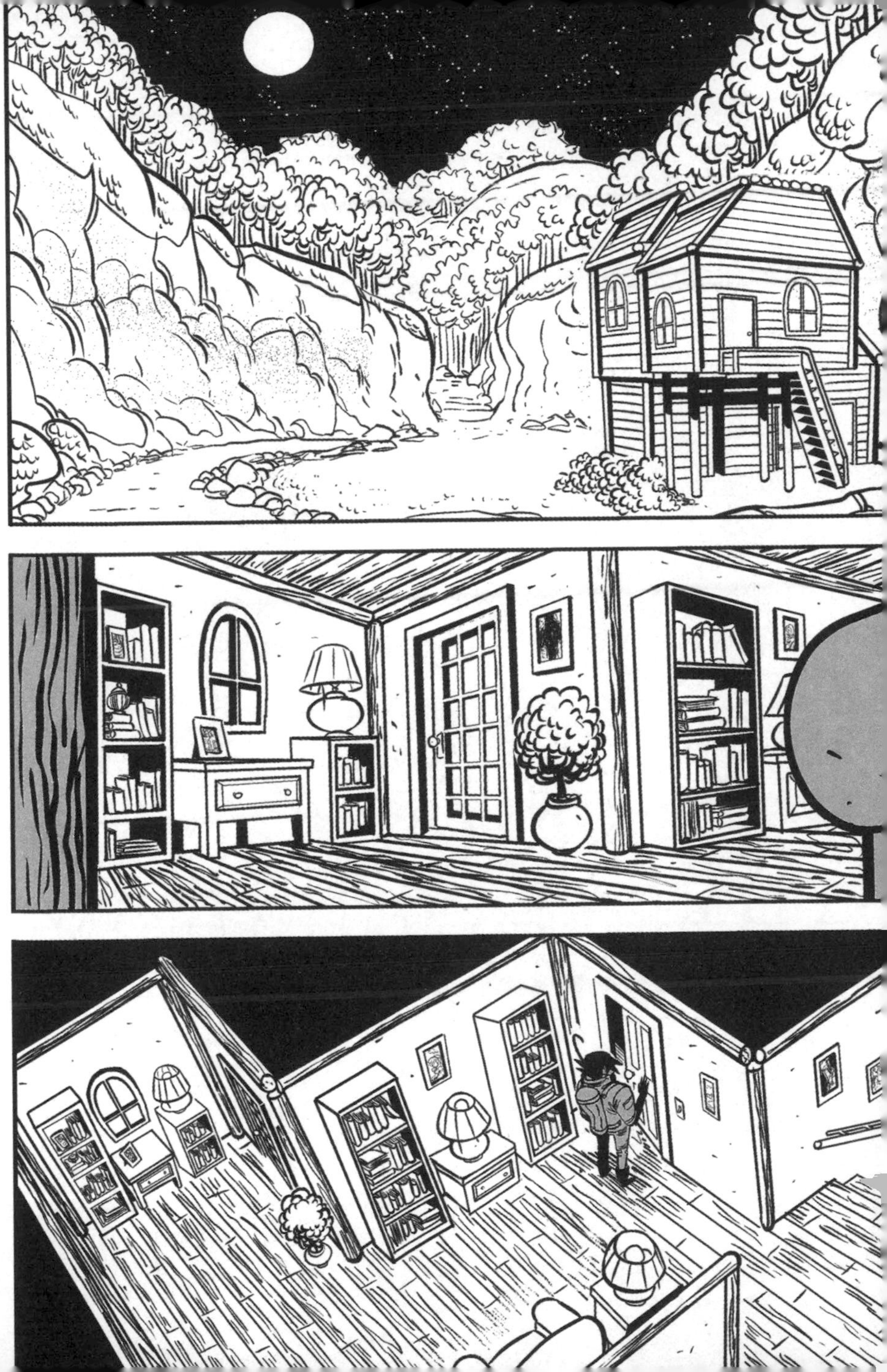

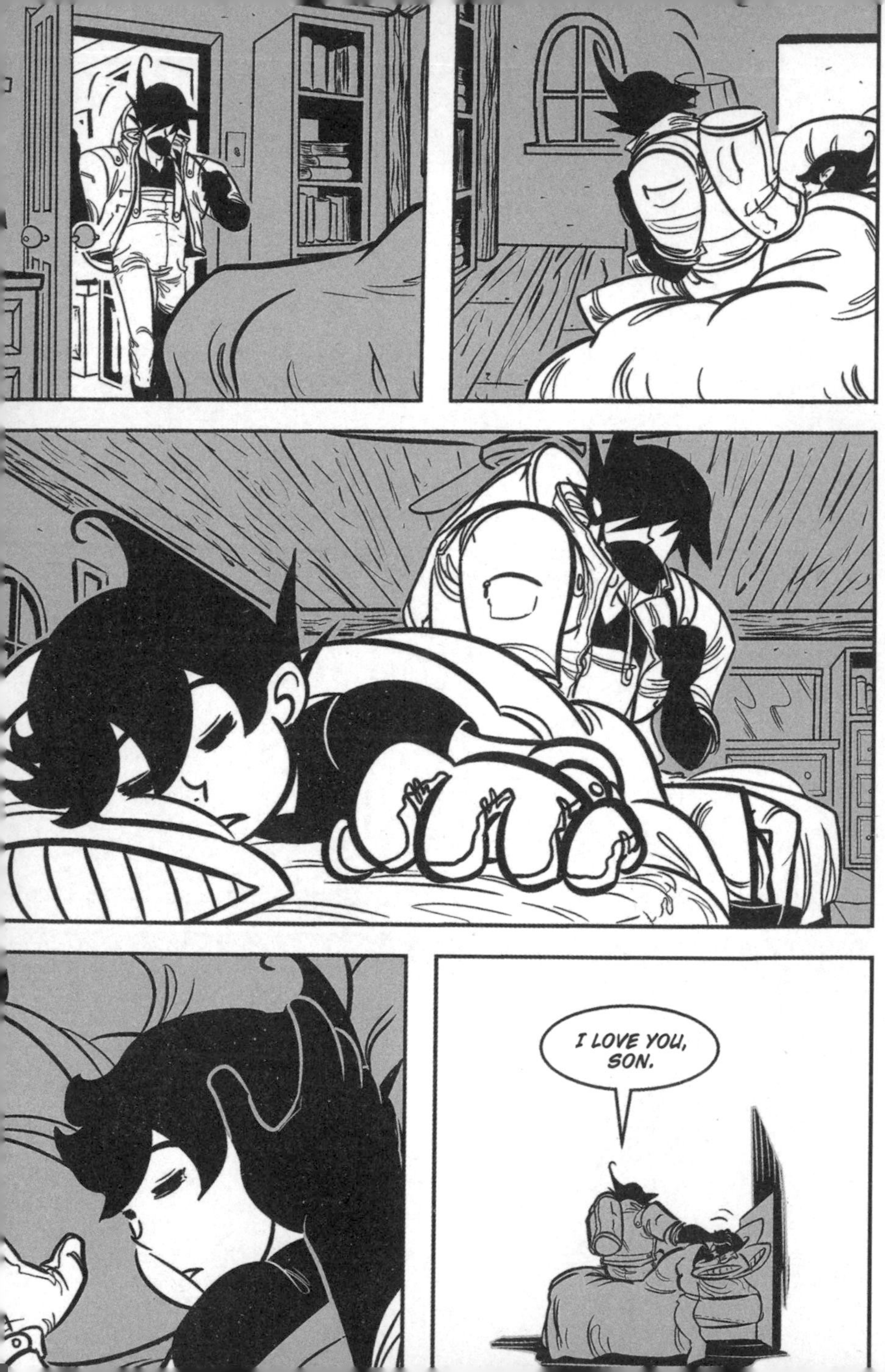
I LOVE YOU, SON.

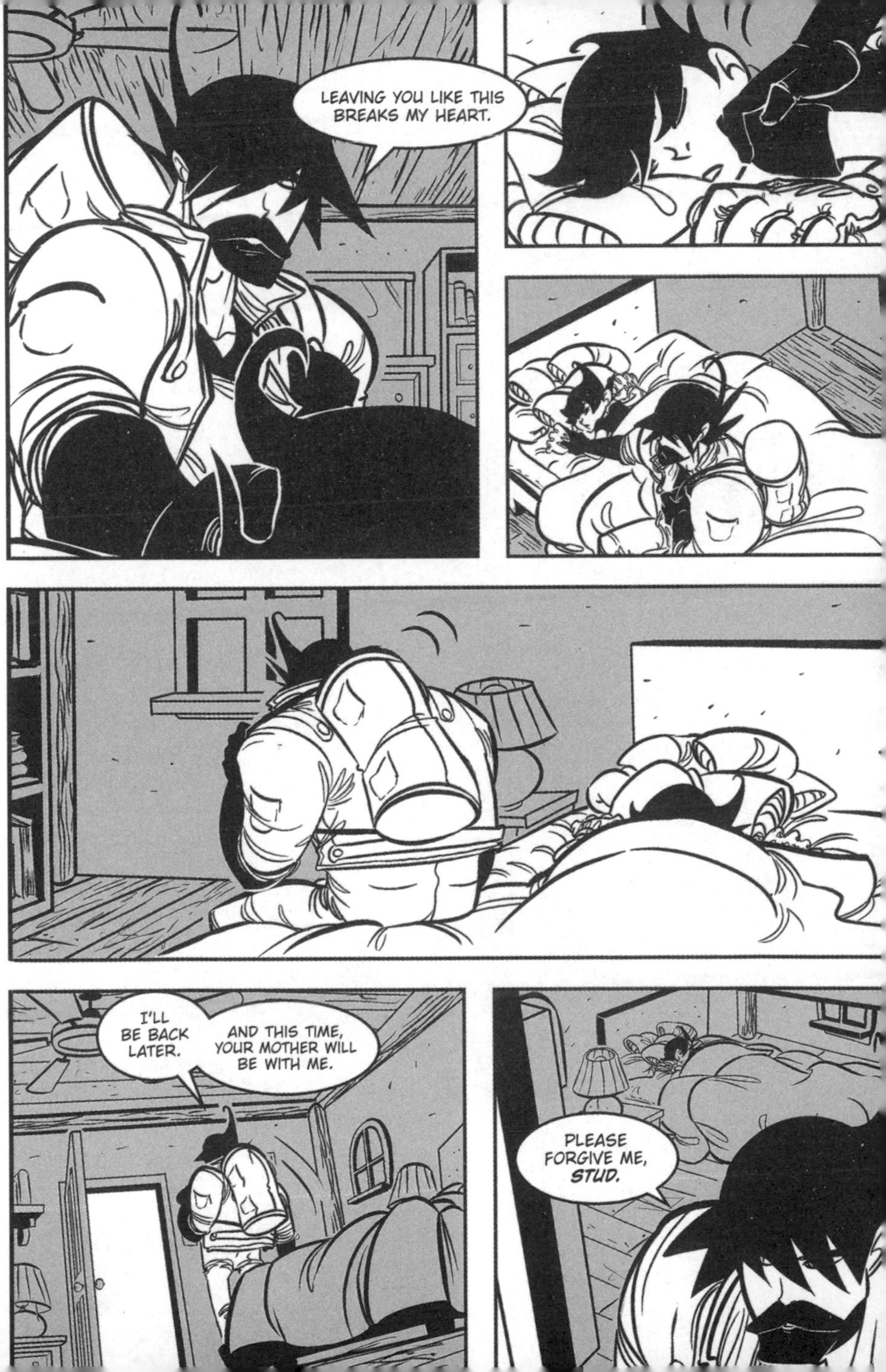
LEAVING YOU LIKE THIS BREAKS MY HEART.
I'LL BE BACK LATER.
AND THIS TIME, YOUR MOTHER WILL BE WITH ME.
PLEASE FORGIVE ME, *STUD*.

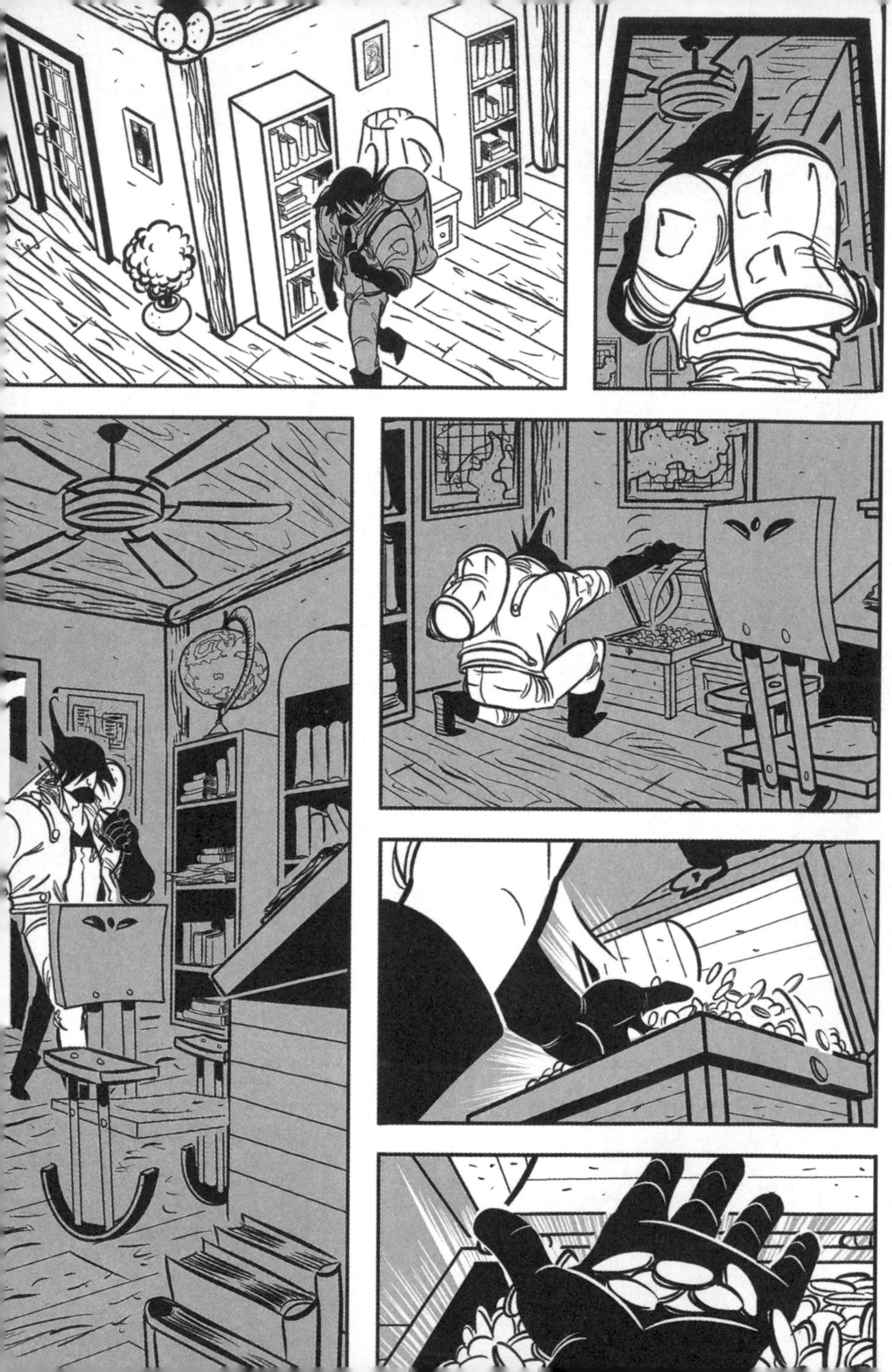

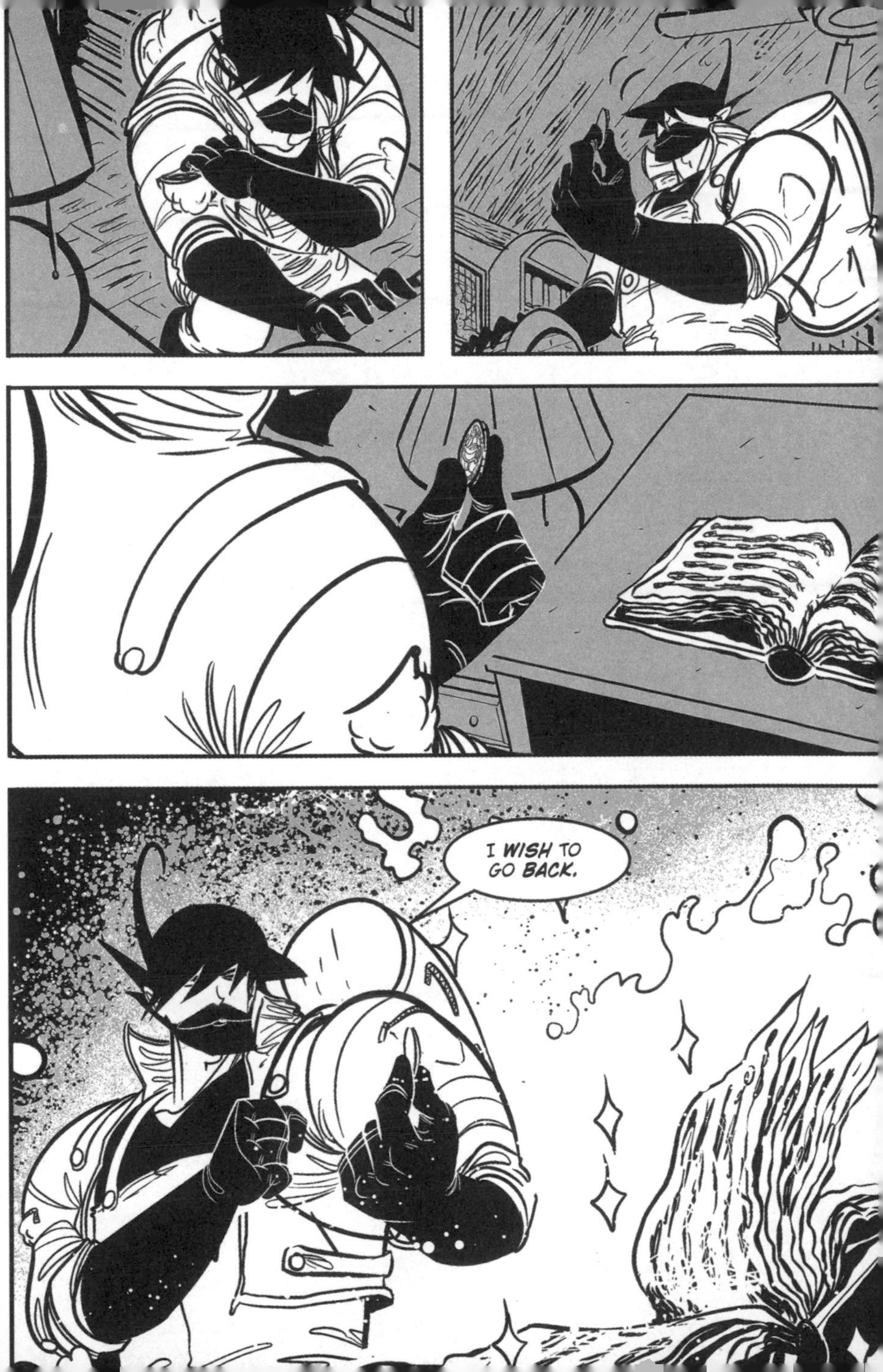
I WISH TO GO BACK.

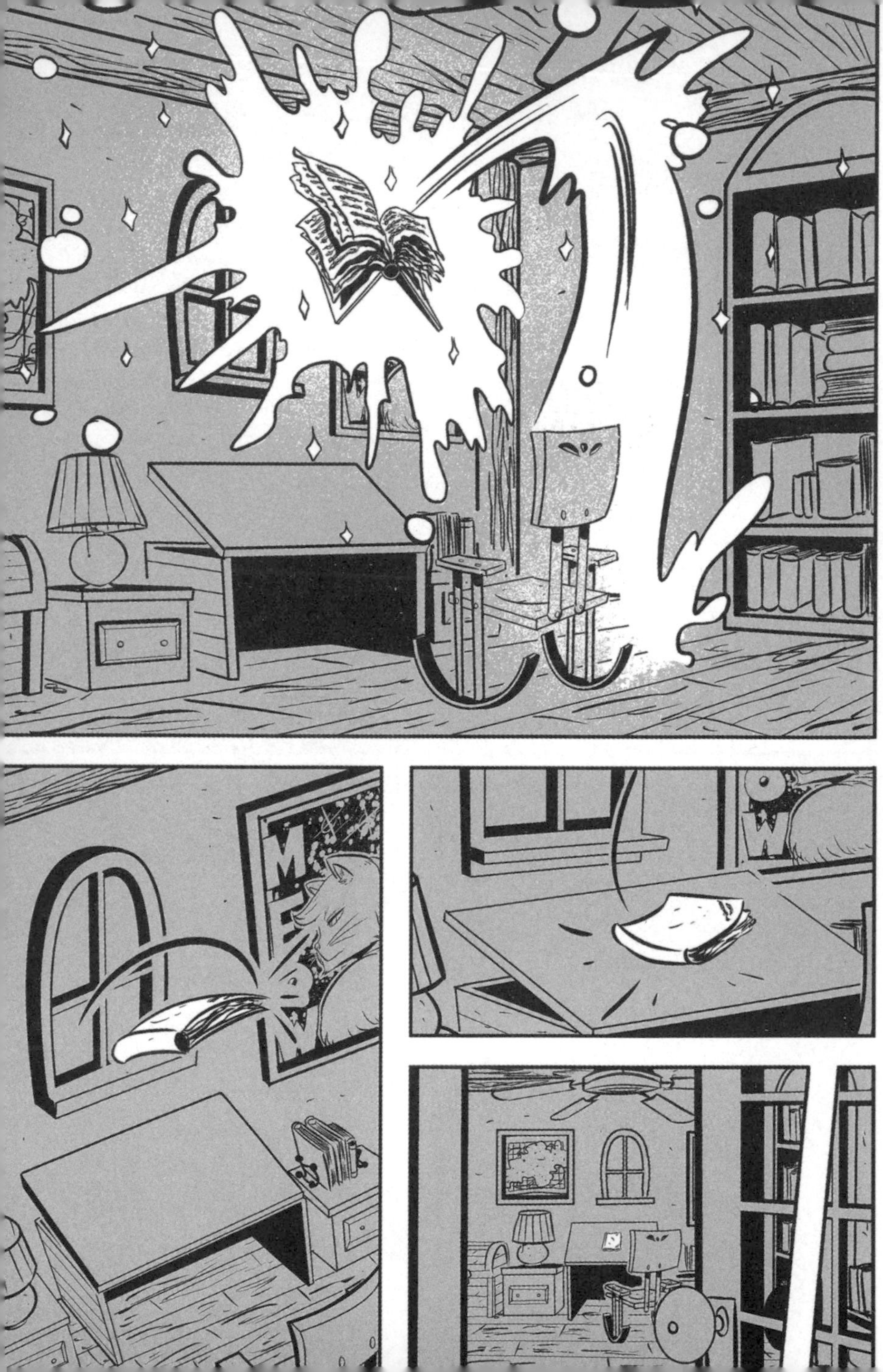
MEW

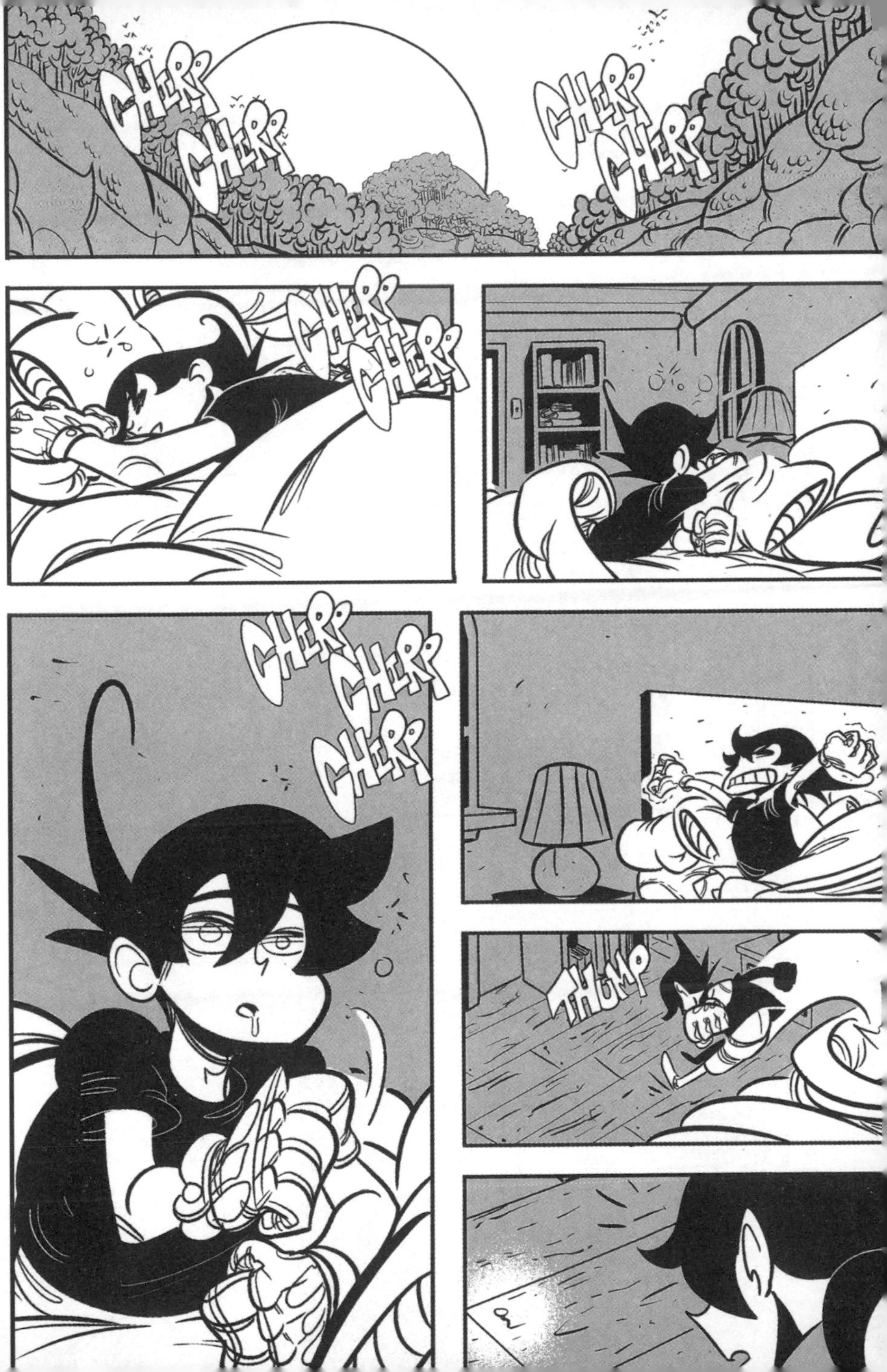
CHIRP CHIRP
CHIRP CHIRP
CHIRP CHIRP
CHIRP CHIRP CHIRP
THUMP

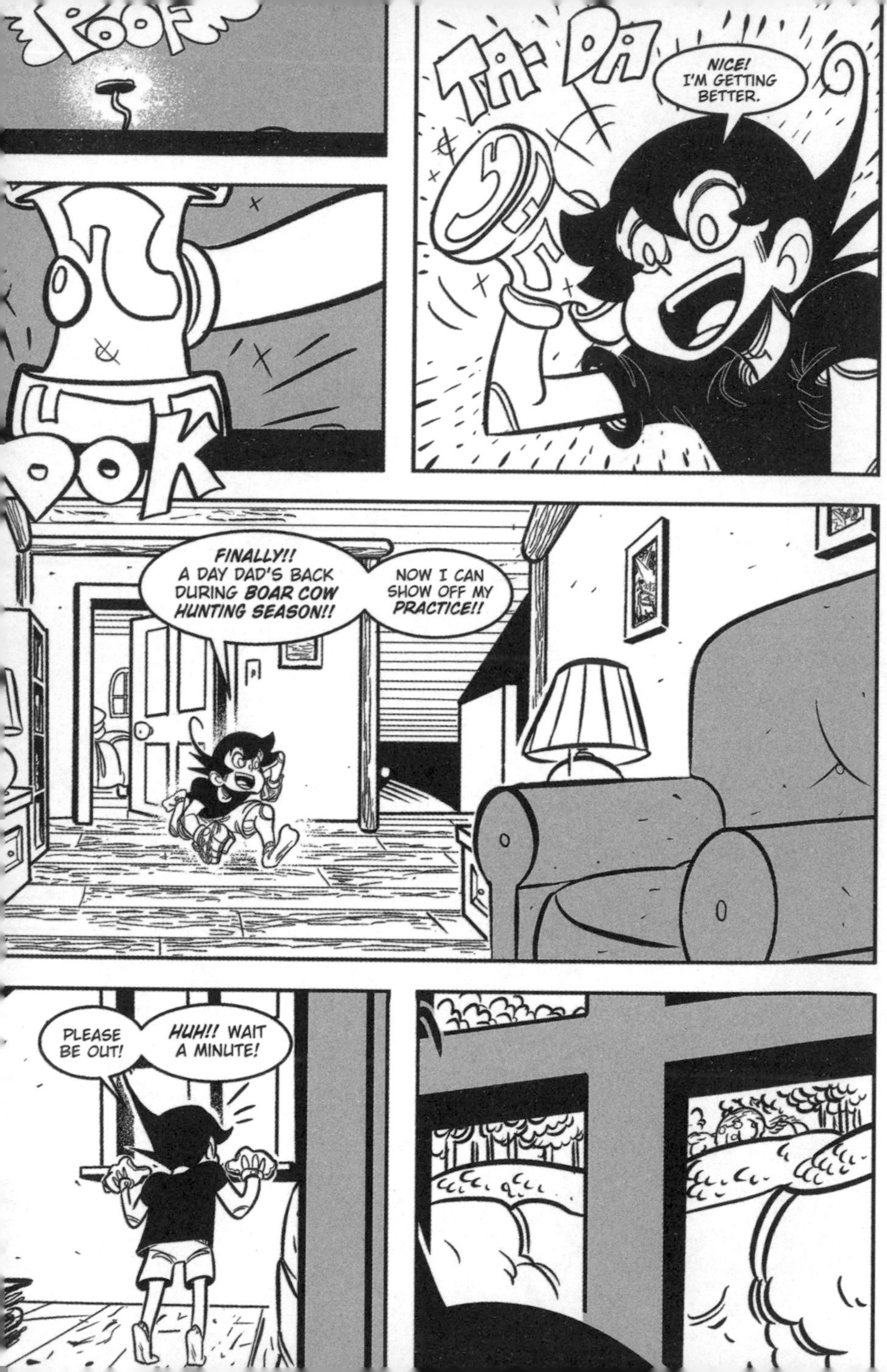
POOF
TA-DA
NICE! I'M GETTING BETTER.
DOK
FINALLY!! A DAY DAD'S BACK DURING BOAR COW HUNTING SEASON!!
NOW I CAN SHOW OFF MY PRACTICE!!
PLEASE BE OUT!
HUH!! WAIT A MINUTE!

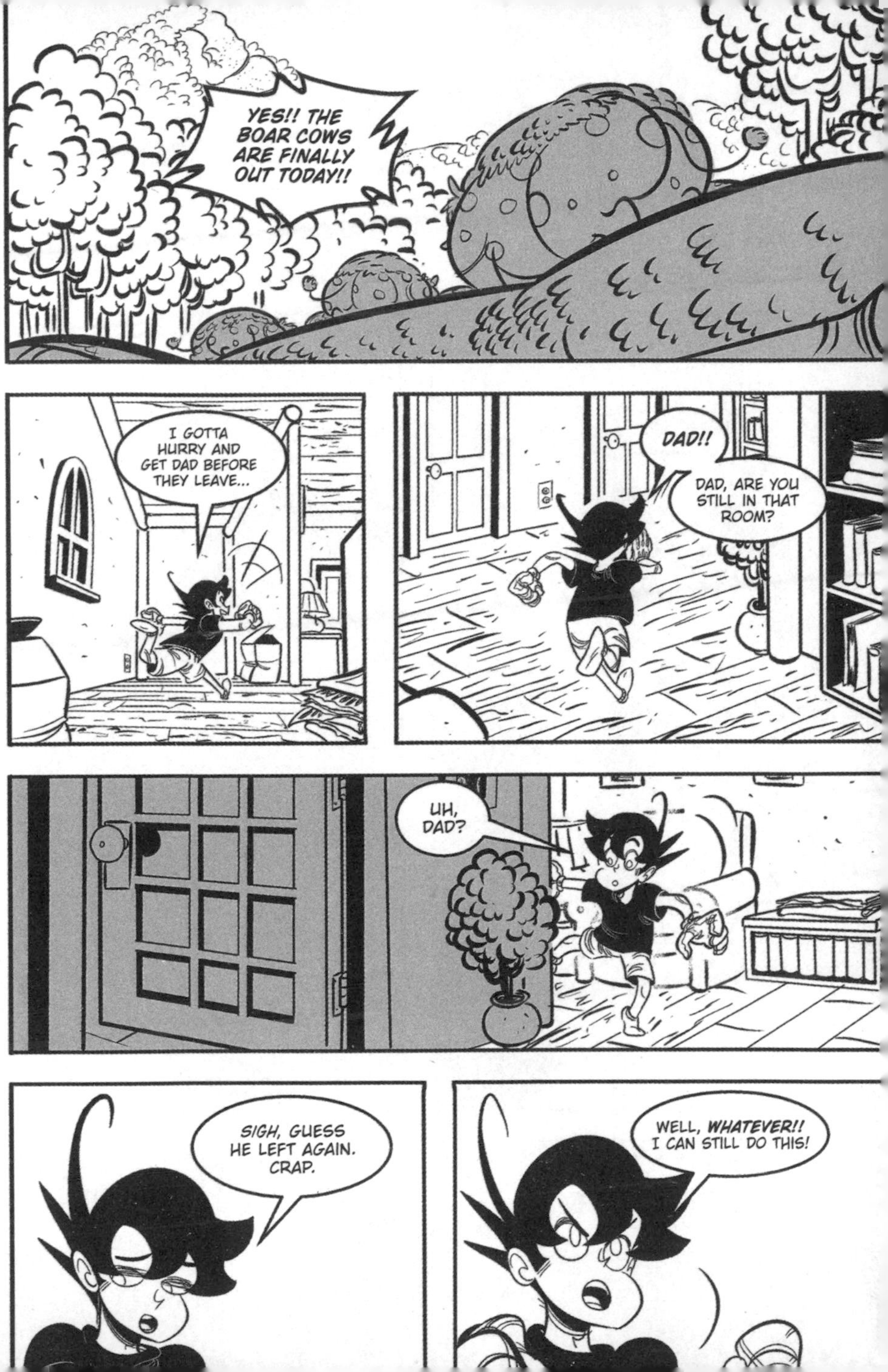
YES!! THE BOAR COWS ARE FINALLY OUT TODAY!!
I GOTTA HURRY AND GET DAD BEFORE THEY LEAVE...
DAD!!
DAD, ARE YOU STILL IN THAT ROOM?
UH, DAD?
SIGH, GUESS HE LEFT AGAIN. CRAP.
WELL, WHATEVER!! I CAN STILL DO THIS!

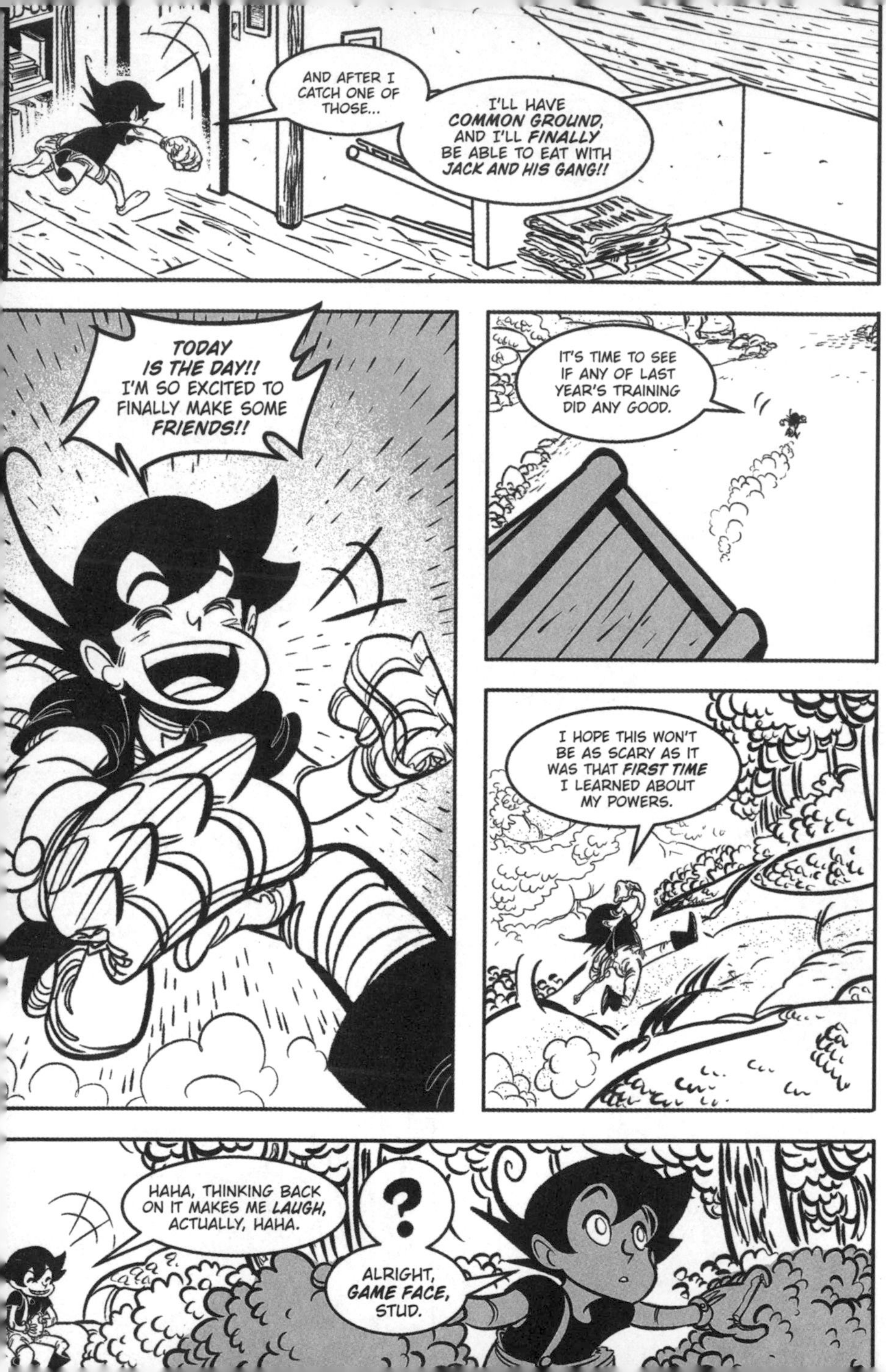
AND AFTER I CATCH ONE OF THOSE...
I'LL HAVE COMMON GROUND, AND I'LL FINALLY BE ABLE TO EAT WITH JACK AND HIS GANG!!
TODAY IS THE DAY!! I'M SO EXCITED TO FINALLY MAKE SOME FRIENDS!!
IT'S TIME TO SEE IF ANY OF LAST YEAR'S TRAINING DID ANY GOOD.
I HOPE THIS WON'T BE AS SCARY AS IT WAS THAT FIRST TIME I LEARNED ABOUT MY POWERS.
HAHA, THINKING BACK ON IT MAKES ME LAUGH, ACTUALLY, HAHA.
?
ALRIGHT, GAME FACE, STUD.

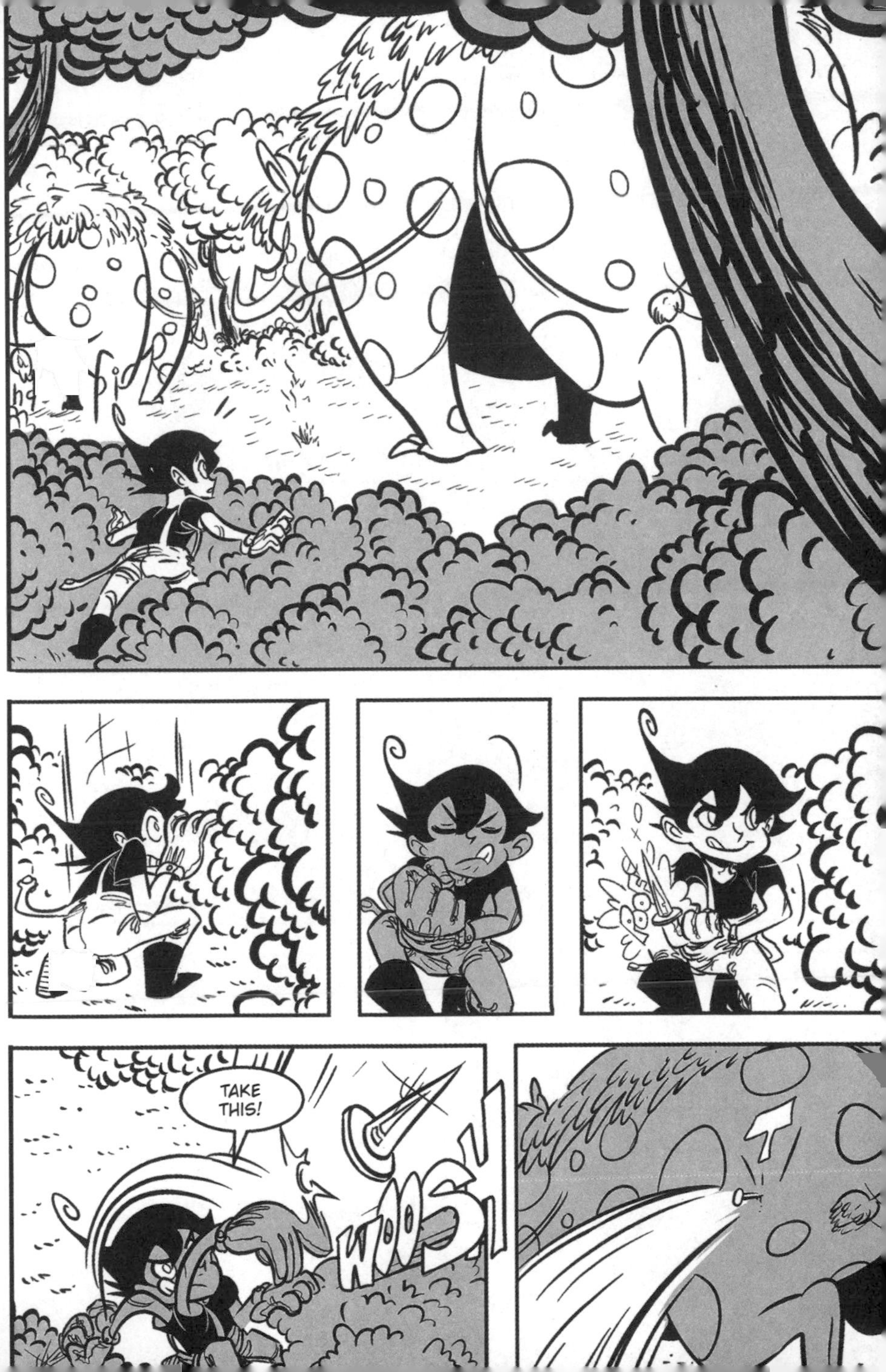
TAKE THIS!
WOOSH!

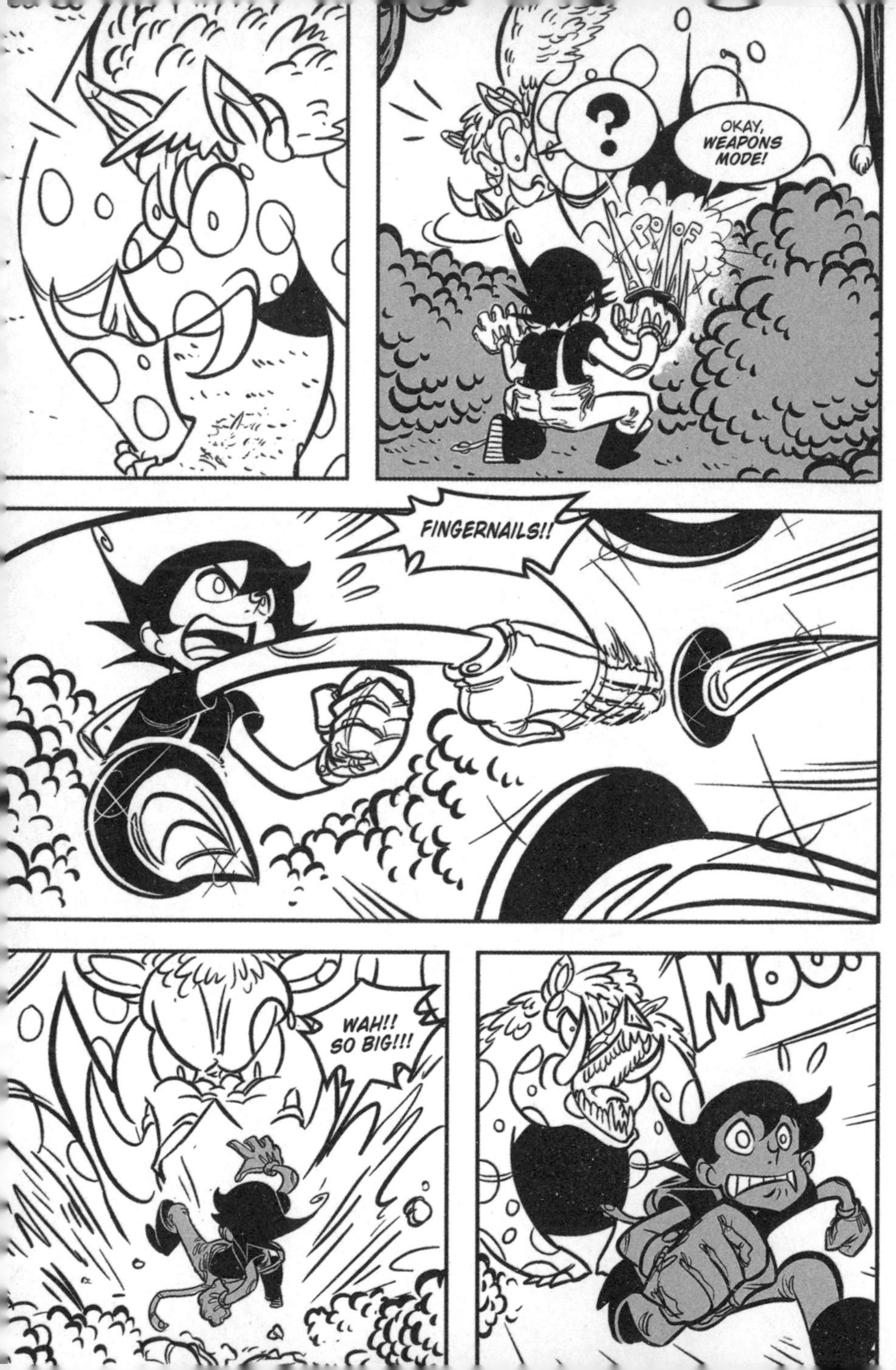
?
OKAY, WEAPONS MODE!
POOF
FINGERNAILS!!
WAH!! SO BIG!!!
MOO

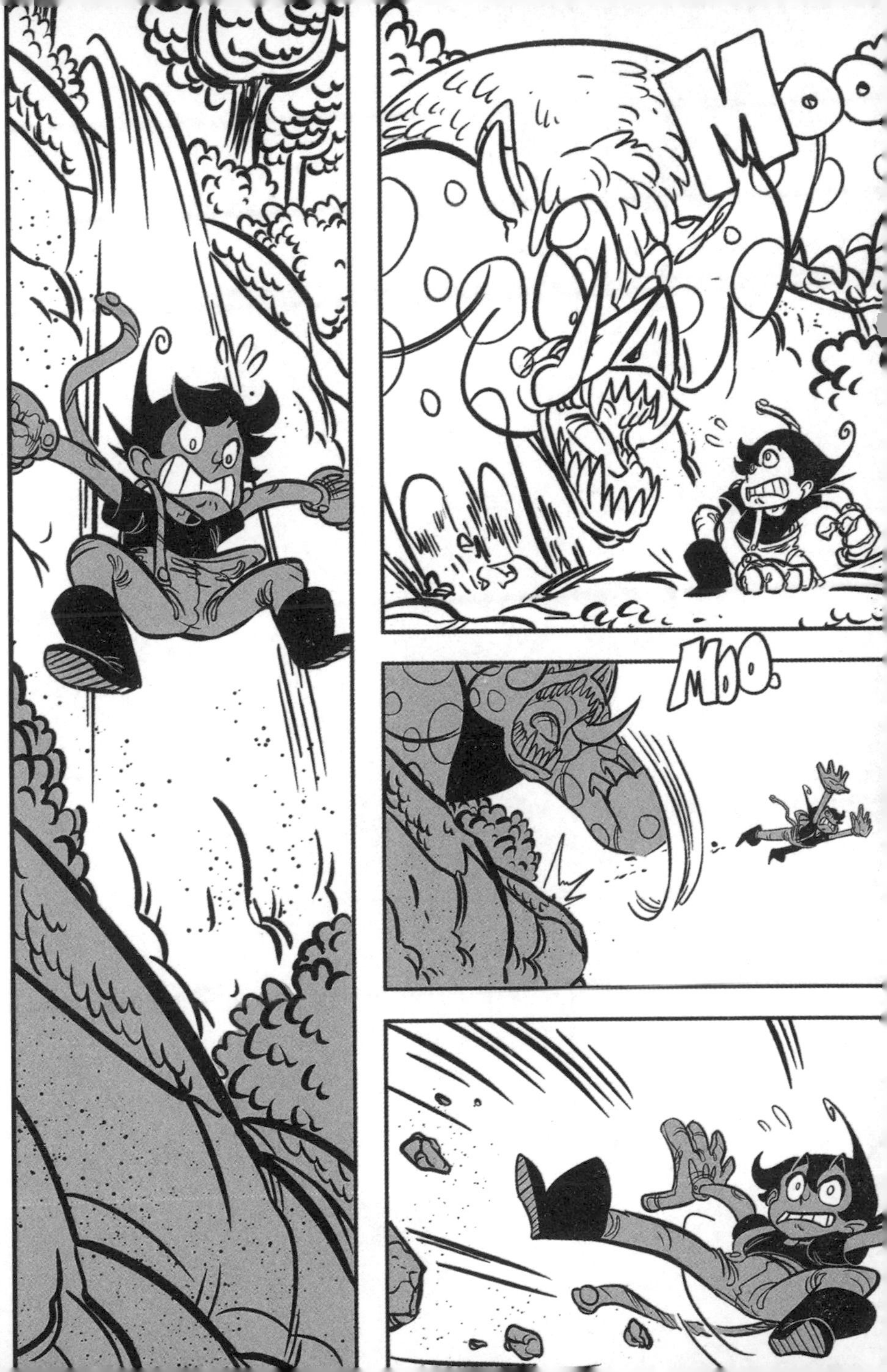
MOO
MOO.

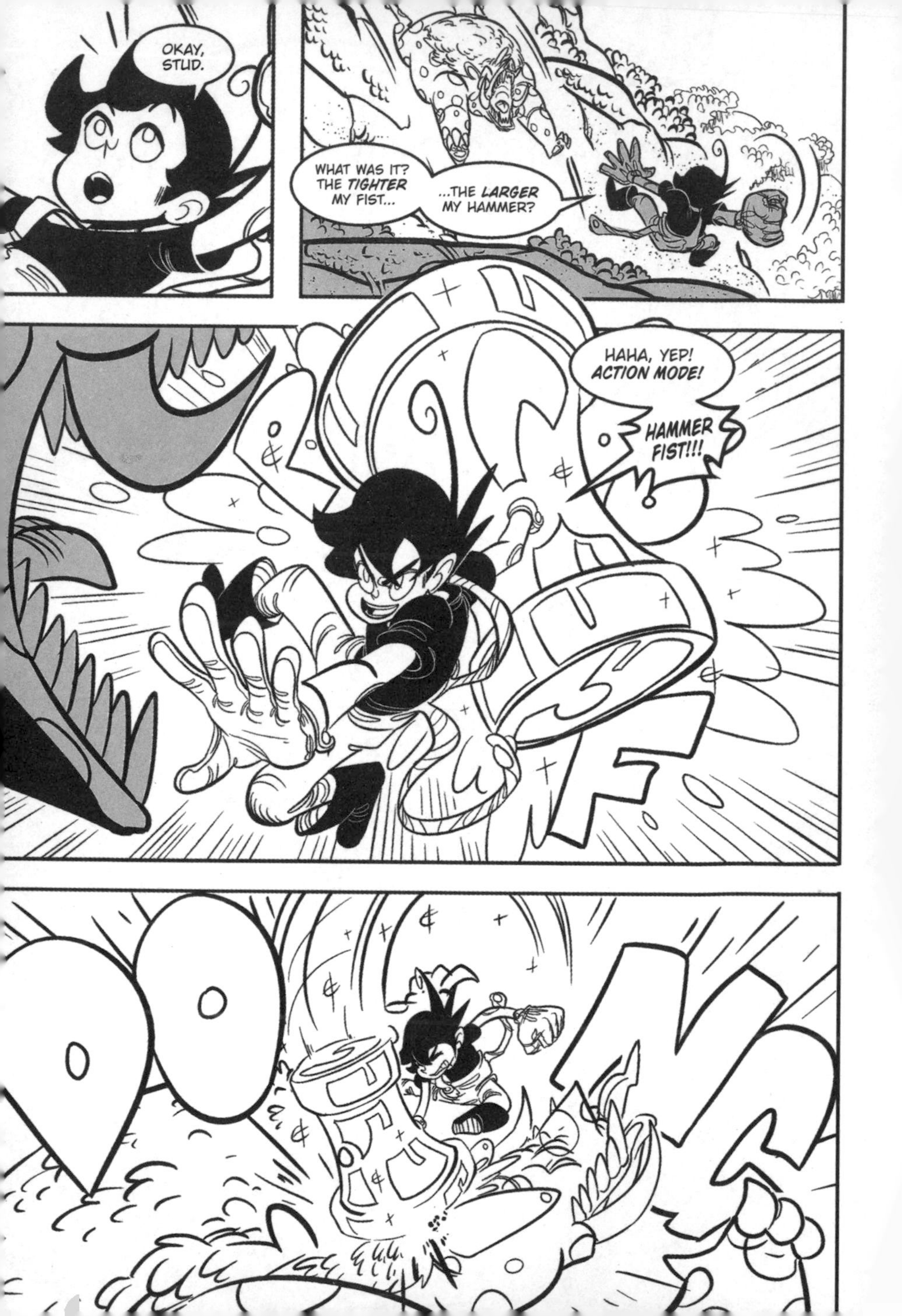
OKAY, STUD.
WHAT WAS IT? THE TIGHTER MY FIST...
...THE LARGER MY HAMMER?
HAHA, YEP! ACTION MODE!
HAMMER FIST!!!

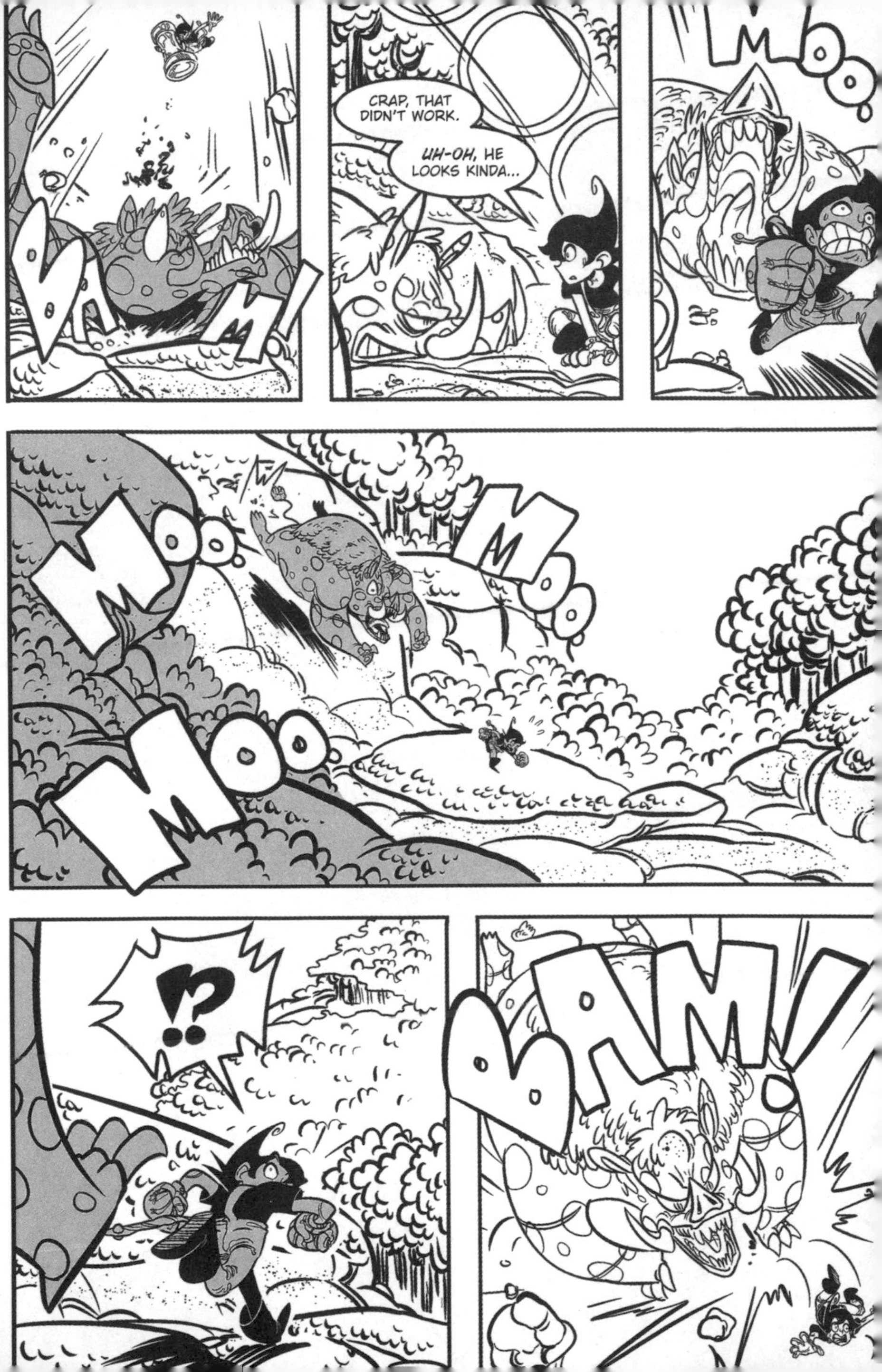
WHAM!
CRAP, THAT DIDN'T WORK.
UH-OH, HE LOOKS KINDA...
MOO
MOO
MOO
MOO
!?
BAM!

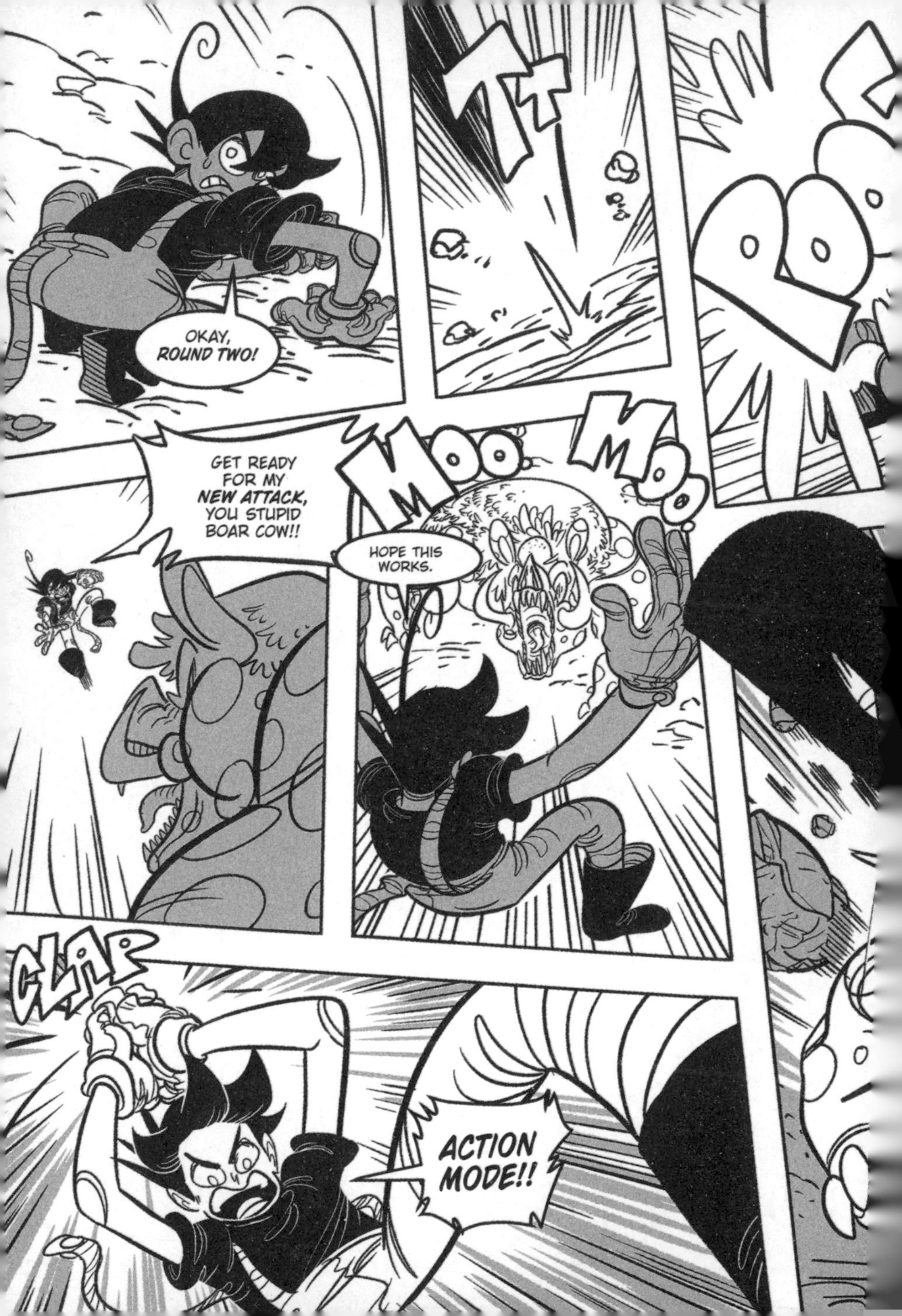
OKAY, ROUND TWO!
GET READY FOR MY NEW ATTACK, YOU STUPID BOAR COW!!
MOO.
MOO
HOPE THIS WORKS.
CLAP
ACTION MODE!!

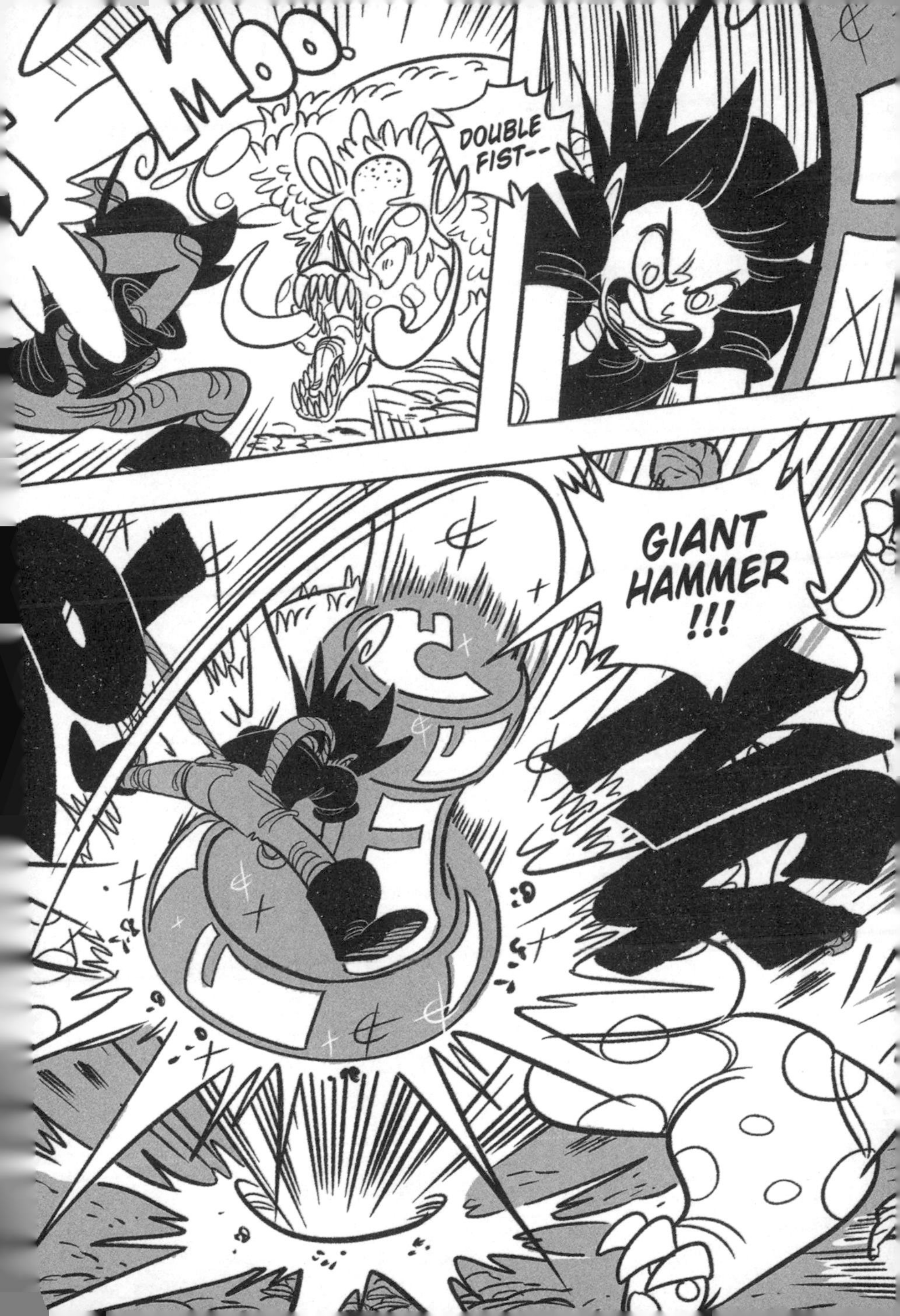
MOO!
DOUBLE FIST--
GIANT HAMMER !!!

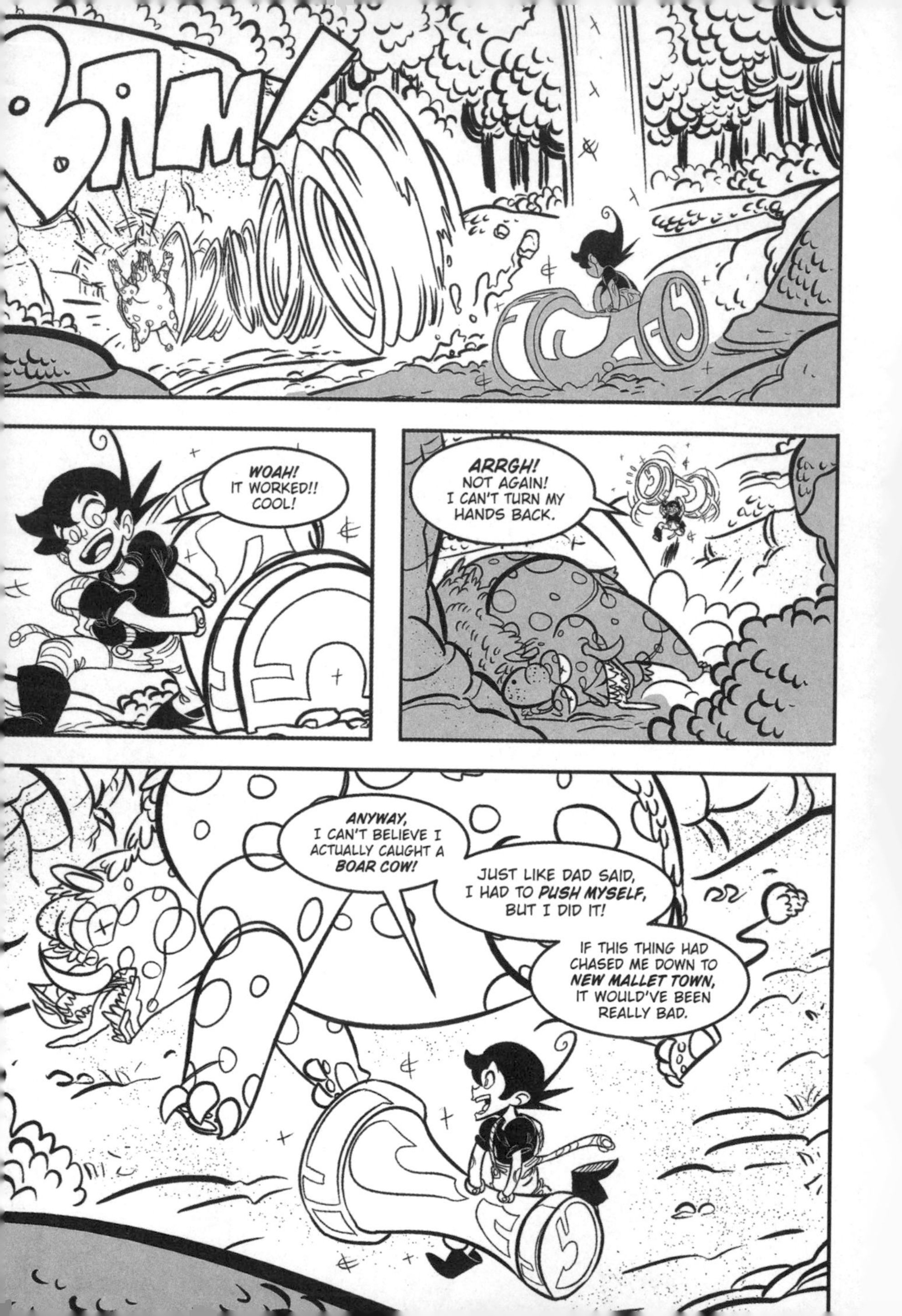
BAM!
WOAH! IT WORKED!! COOL!
ARRGH! NOT AGAIN! I CAN'T TURN MY HANDS BACK.
ANYWAY, I CAN'T BELIEVE I ACTUALLY CAUGHT A BOAR COW!
JUST LIKE DAD SAID, I HAD TO PUSH MYSELF, BUT I DID IT!
IF THIS THING HAD CHASED ME DOWN TO NEW MALLET TOWN, IT WOULD'VE BEEN REALLY BAD.

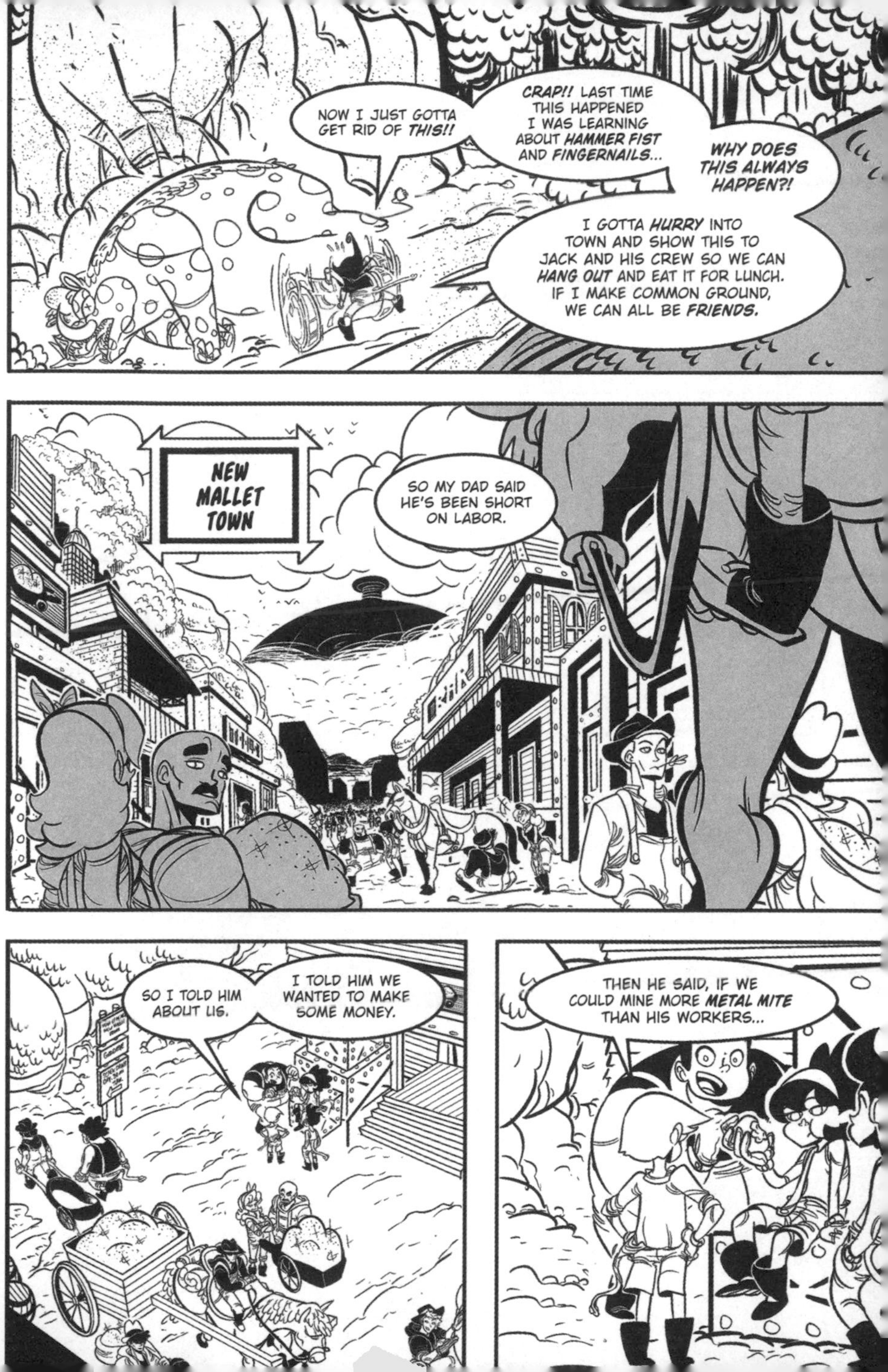
NOW I JUST GOTTA GET RID OF *THIS!!*
CRAP!! LAST TIME THIS HAPPENED I WAS LEARNING ABOUT *HAMMER FIST* AND *FINGERNAILS...*
WHY DOES THIS ALWAYS HAPPEN?!
I GOTTA *HURRY* INTO TOWN AND SHOW THIS TO JACK AND HIS CREW SO WE CAN *HANG OUT* AND EAT IT FOR LUNCH. IF I MAKE COMMON GROUND, WE CAN ALL BE *FRIENDS.*
NEW MALLET TOWN
SO MY DAD SAID HE'S BEEN SHORT ON LABOR.
SO I TOLD HIM ABOUT US.
I TOLD HIM WE WANTED TO MAKE SOME MONEY.
THEN HE SAID, IF WE COULD MINE MORE *METAL MITE* THAN HIS WORKERS...

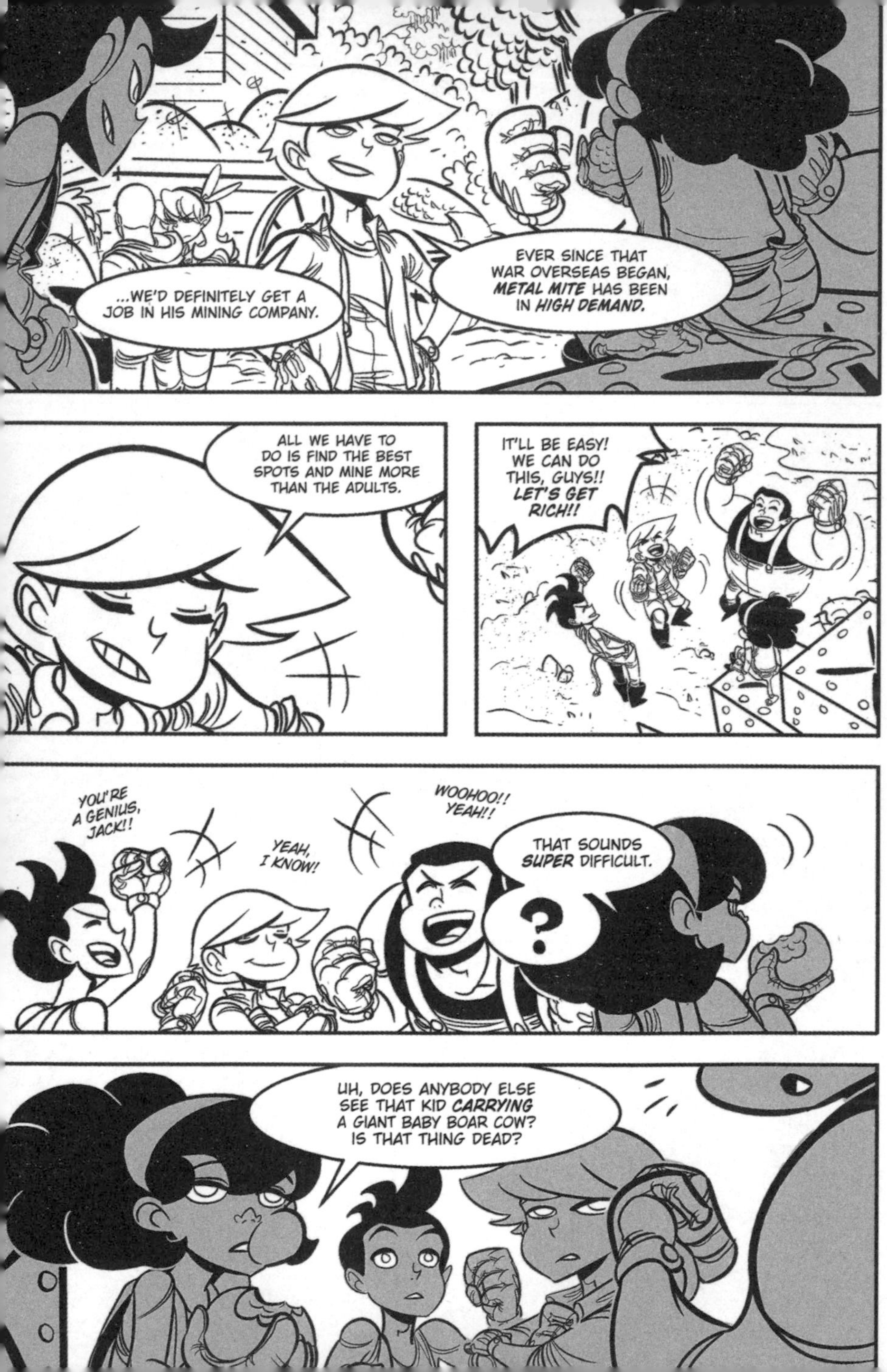
...WE'D DEFINITELY GET A JOB IN HIS MINING COMPANY.
EVER SINCE THAT WAR OVERSEAS BEGAN, ***METAL MITE*** HAS BEEN IN ***HIGH DEMAND.***
ALL WE HAVE TO DO IS FIND THE BEST SPOTS AND MINE MORE THAN THE ADULTS.
IT'LL BE EASY! WE CAN DO THIS, GUYS!! ***LET'S GET RICH!!***
YOU'RE A GENIUS, JACK!!
YEAH, I KNOW!
WOOHOO!! YEAH!!
THAT SOUNDS ***SUPER*** DIFFICULT.
?
UH, DOES ANYBODY ELSE SEE THAT KID ***CARRYING*** A GIANT BABY BOAR COW? IS THAT THING DEAD?

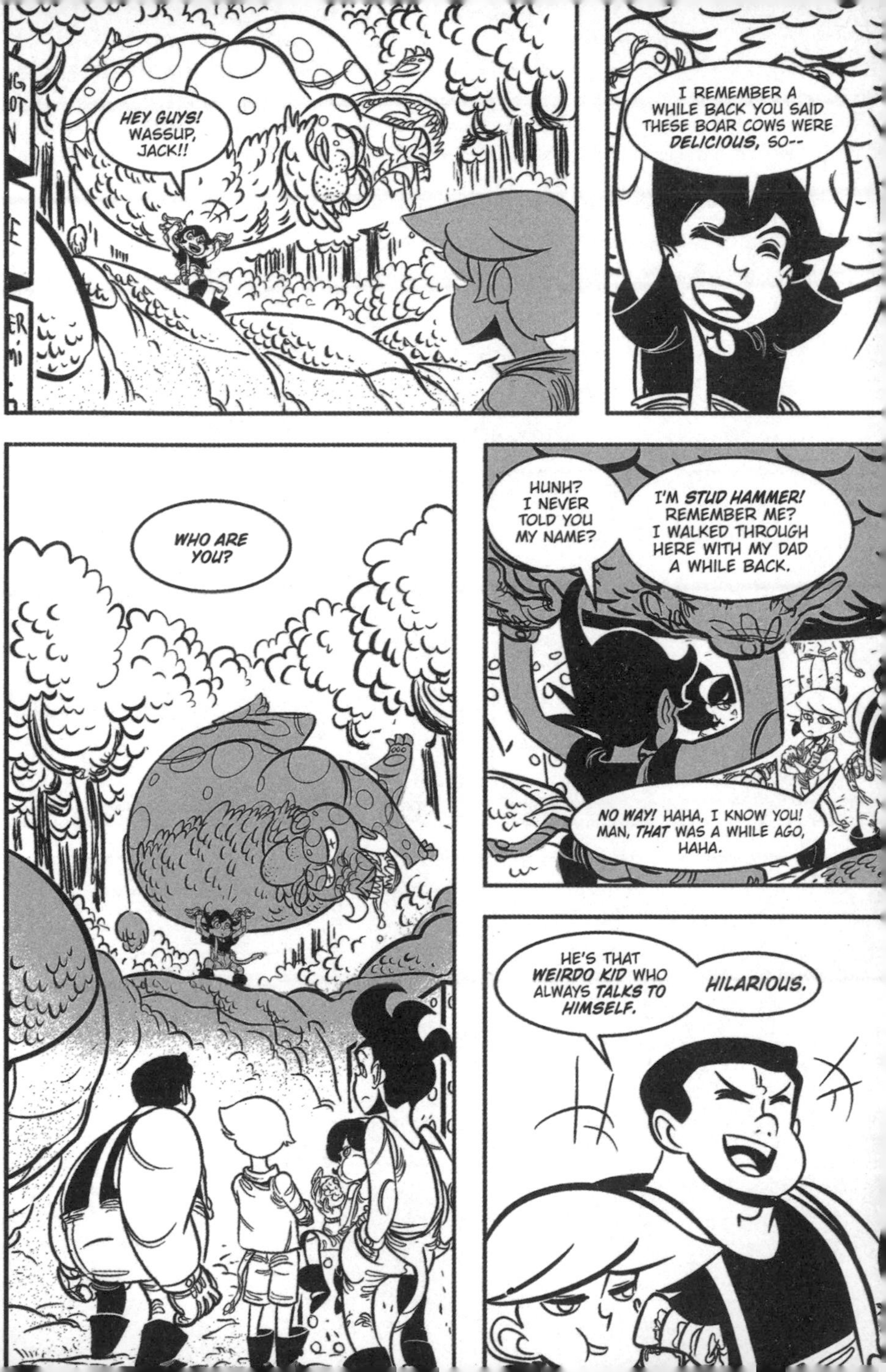
HEY GUYS! WASSUP, JACK!!
I REMEMBER A WHILE BACK YOU SAID THESE BOAR COWS WERE DELICIOUS, SO--
WHO ARE YOU?
HUNH? I NEVER TOLD YOU MY NAME?
I'M STUD HAMMER! REMEMBER ME? I WALKED THROUGH HERE WITH MY DAD A WHILE BACK.
NO WAY! HAHA, I KNOW YOU! MAN, THAT WAS A WHILE AGO, HAHA.
HE'S THAT WEIRDO KID WHO ALWAYS TALKS TO HIMSELF.
HILARIOUS.

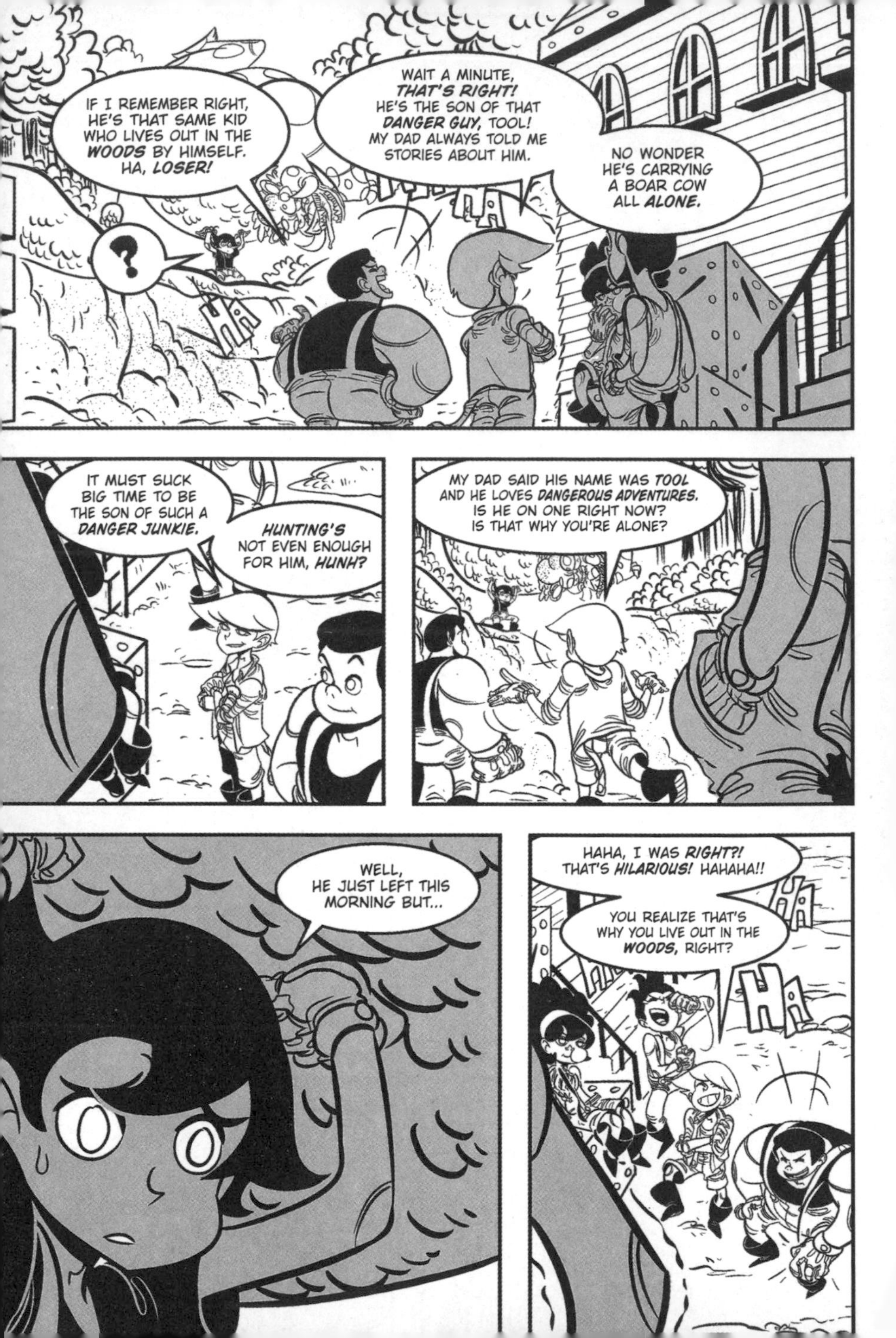
IF I REMEMBER RIGHT, HE'S THAT SAME KID WHO LIVES OUT IN THE **WOODS** BY HIMSELF. HA, **LOSER!**
?
WAIT A MINUTE, **THAT'S RIGHT!** HE'S THE SON OF THAT **DANGER GUY,** TOOL! MY DAD ALWAYS TOLD ME STORIES ABOUT HIM.
NO WONDER HE'S CARRYING A BOAR COW ALL **ALONE.**
IT MUST SUCK BIG TIME TO BE THE SON OF SUCH A **DANGER JUNKIE.**
HUNTING'S NOT EVEN ENOUGH FOR HIM, **HUNH?**
MY DAD SAID HIS NAME WAS **TOOL** AND HE LOVES **DANGEROUS ADVENTURES.** IS HE ON ONE RIGHT NOW? IS THAT WHY YOU'RE ALONE?
WELL, HE JUST LEFT THIS MORNING BUT...
HAHA, I WAS **RIGHT?!** THAT'S **HILARIOUS!** HAHAHA!!
YOU REALIZE THAT'S WHY YOU LIVE OUT IN THE **WOODS,** RIGHT?

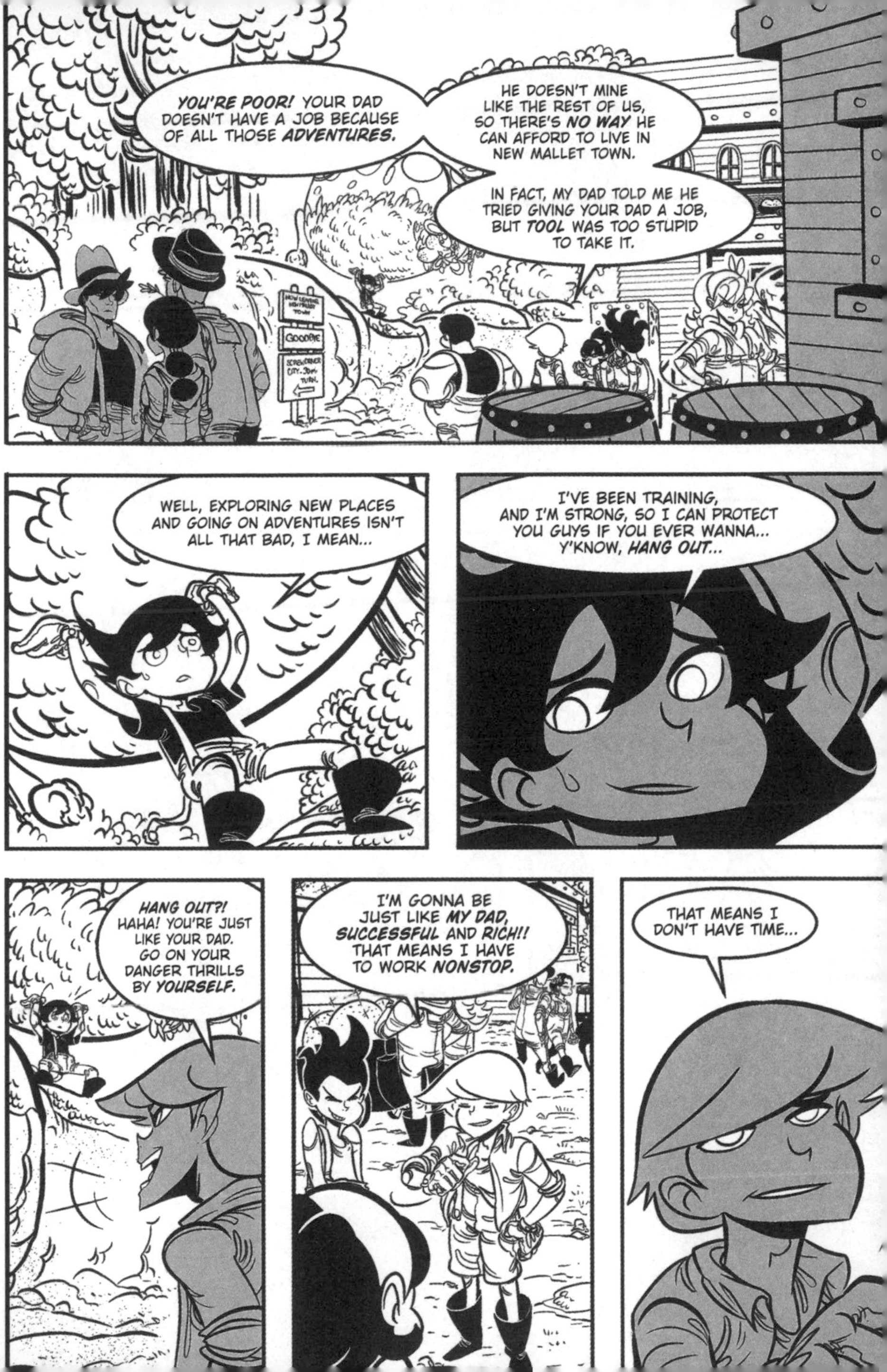
YOU'RE POOR! YOUR DAD DOESN'T HAVE A JOB BECAUSE OF ALL THOSE ADVENTURES.
GOODBYE
HE DOESN'T MINE LIKE THE REST OF US, SO THERE'S NO WAY HE CAN AFFORD TO LIVE IN NEW MALLET TOWN.
IN FACT, MY DAD TOLD ME HE TRIED GIVING YOUR DAD A JOB, BUT TOOL WAS TOO STUPID TO TAKE IT.
WELL, EXPLORING NEW PLACES AND GOING ON ADVENTURES ISN'T ALL THAT BAD, I MEAN...
I'VE BEEN TRAINING, AND I'M STRONG, SO I CAN PROTECT YOU GUYS IF YOU EVER WANNA... Y'KNOW, HANG OUT...
HANG OUT?! HAHA! YOU'RE JUST LIKE YOUR DAD. GO ON YOUR DANGER THRILLS BY YOURSELF.
I'M GONNA BE JUST LIKE MY DAD, SUCCESSFUL AND RICH!! THAT MEANS I HAVE TO WORK NONSTOP.
THAT MEANS I DON'T HAVE TIME...

...TO BE FRIENDS WITH A *WEIRDO*.

W-WEIRDO?

MOO

!?

LEAVING
TALLOT
TOWN

DOBB

WORNER
30mi.
TURN.

MOO

POW

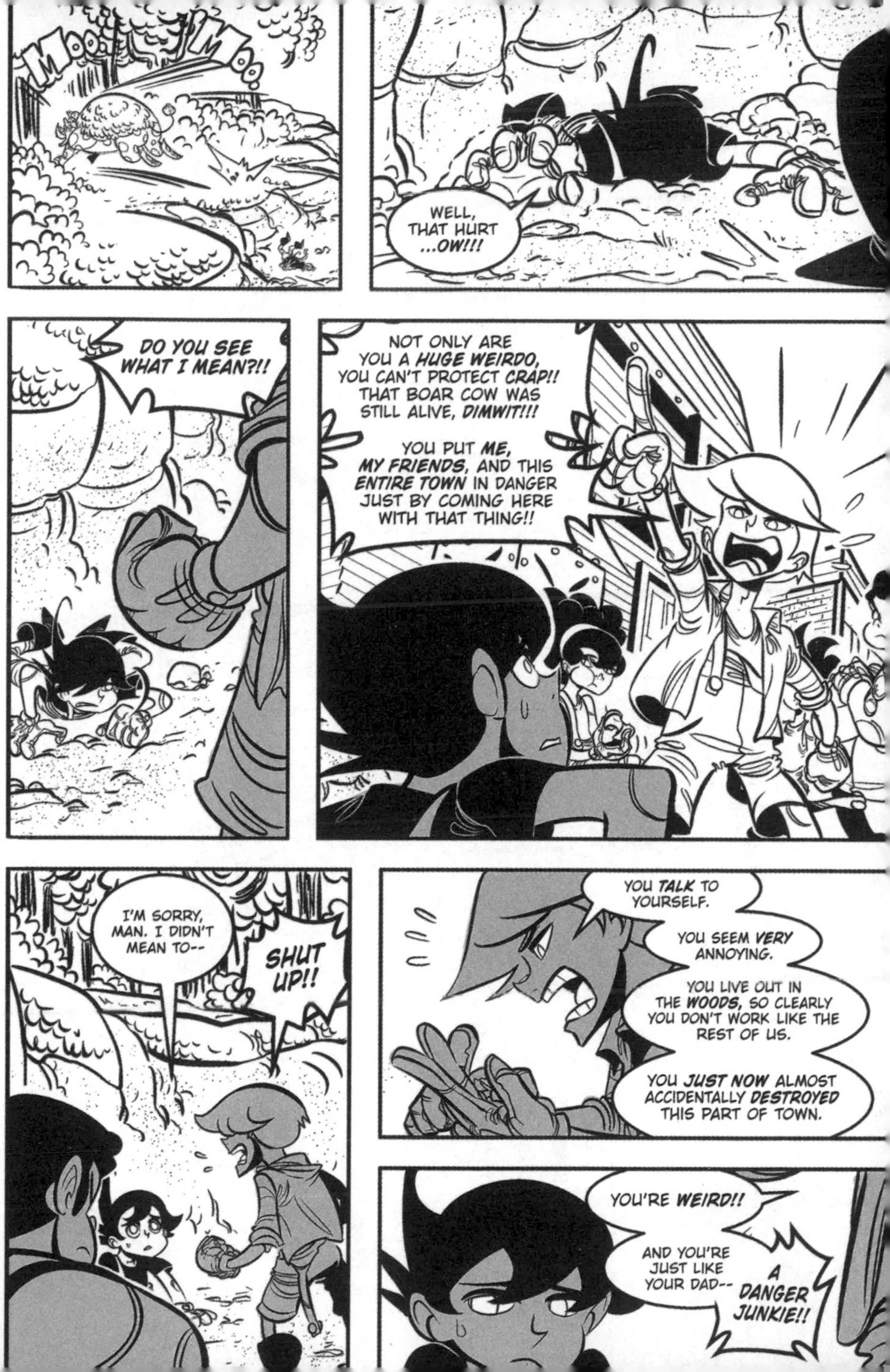
MOO MOO
WELL, THAT HURT ...OW!!!
DO YOU SEE WHAT I MEAN?!!
NOT ONLY ARE YOU A HUGE WEIRDO, YOU CAN'T PROTECT CRAP!! THAT BOAR COW WAS STILL ALIVE, DIMWIT!!!
YOU PUT ME, MY FRIENDS, AND THIS ENTIRE TOWN IN DANGER JUST BY COMING HERE WITH THAT THING!!
I'M SORRY, MAN. I DIDN'T MEAN TO--
SHUT UP!!
YOU TALK TO YOURSELF.
YOU SEEM VERY ANNOYING.
YOU LIVE OUT IN THE WOODS, SO CLEARLY YOU DON'T WORK LIKE THE REST OF US.
YOU JUST NOW ALMOST ACCIDENTALLY DESTROYED THIS PART OF TOWN.
YOU'RE WEIRD!!
AND YOU'RE JUST LIKE YOUR DAD--
A DANGER JUNKIE!!

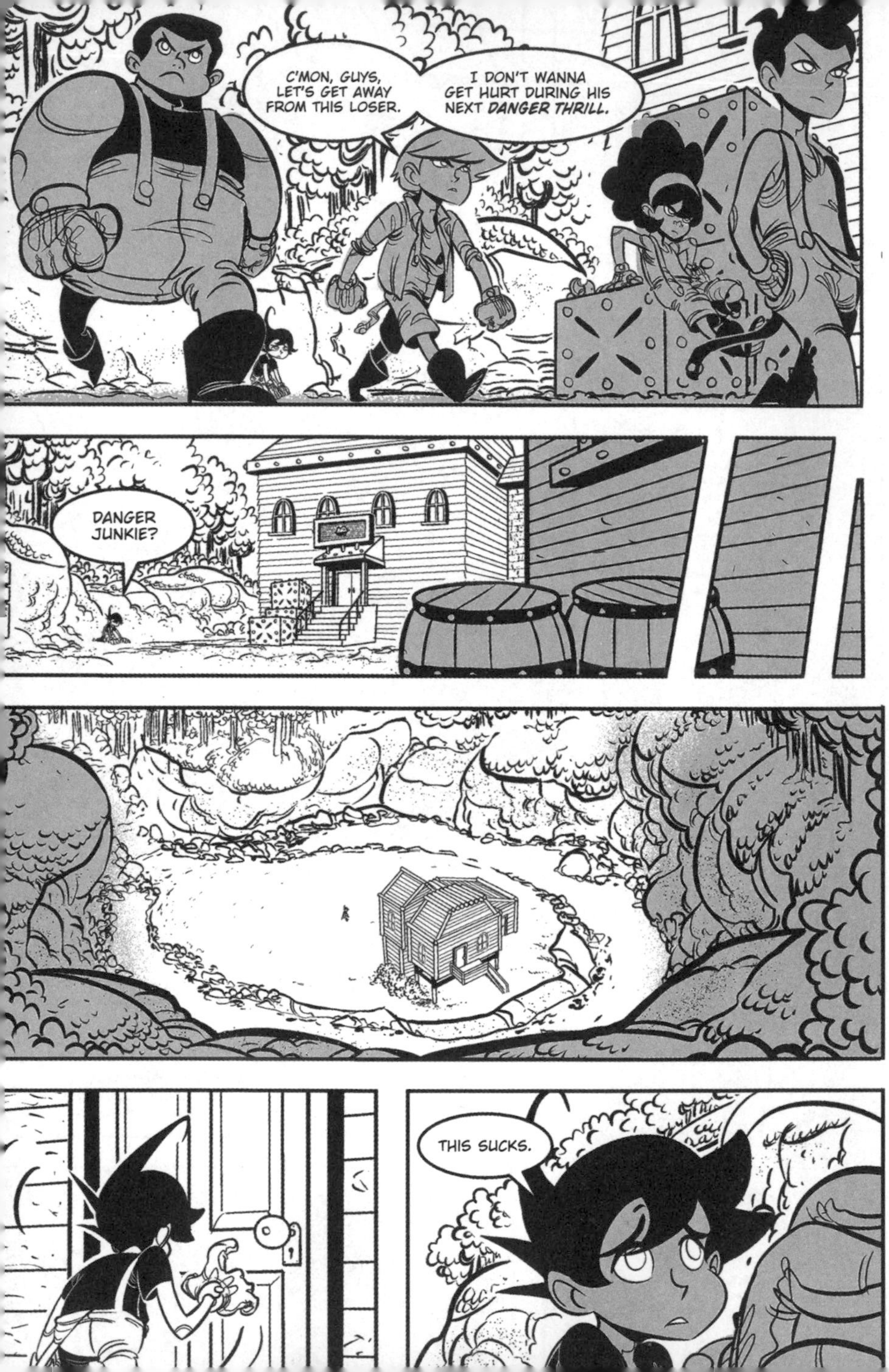
C'MON, GUYS, LET'S GET AWAY FROM THIS LOSER.
I DON'T WANNA GET HURT DURING HIS NEXT *DANGER THRILL.*
DANGER JUNKIE?
THIS SUCKS.

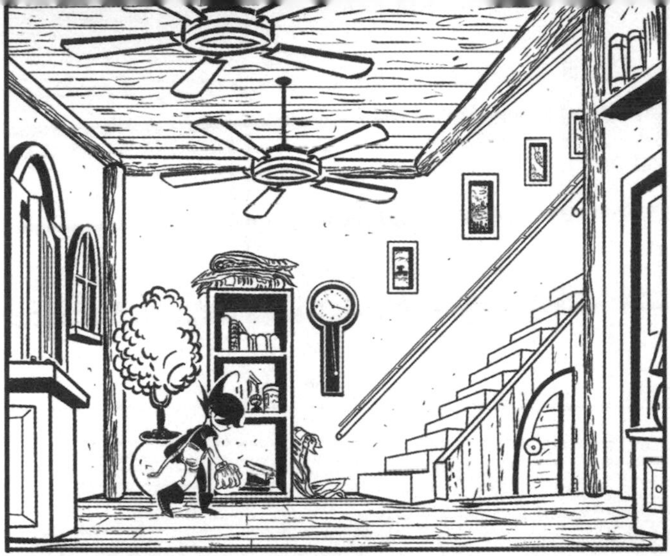
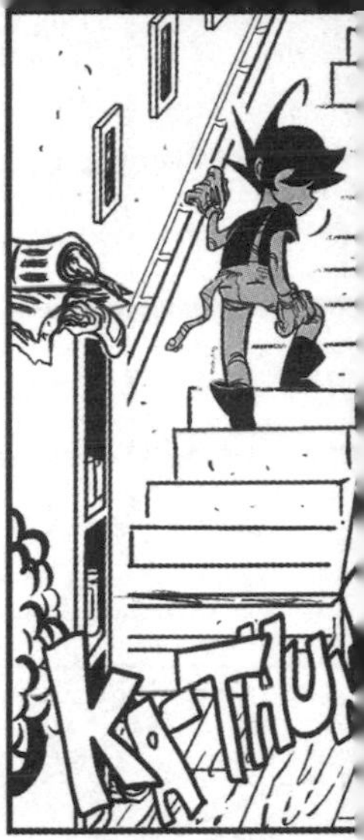
KA-THU
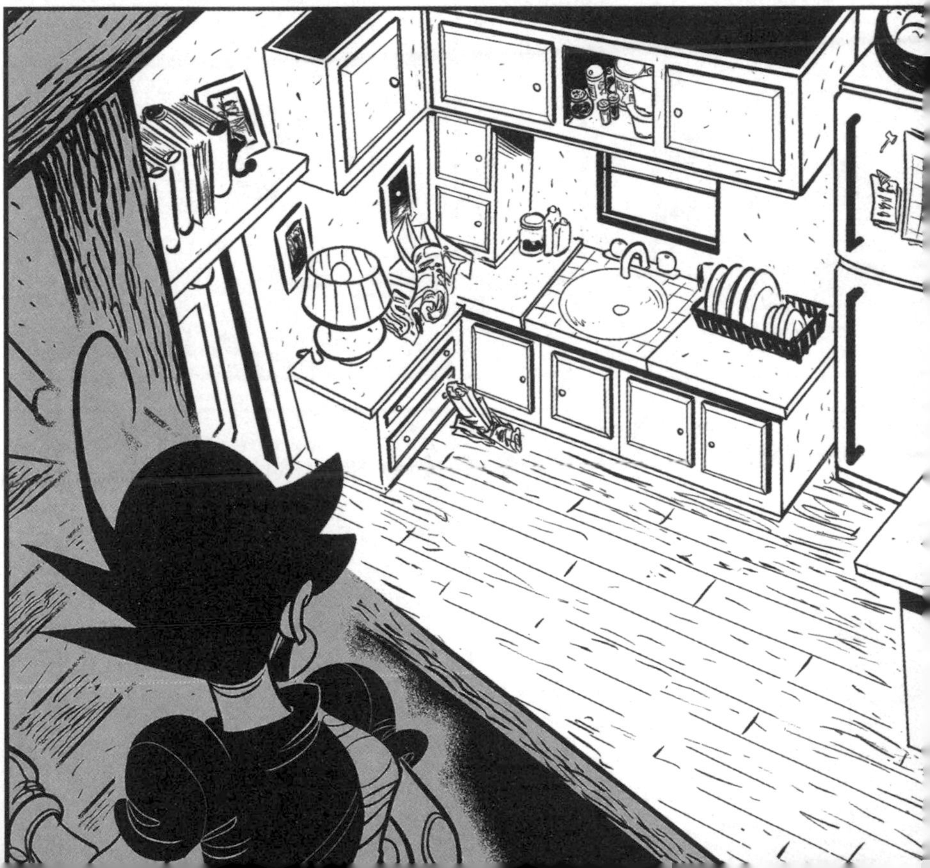

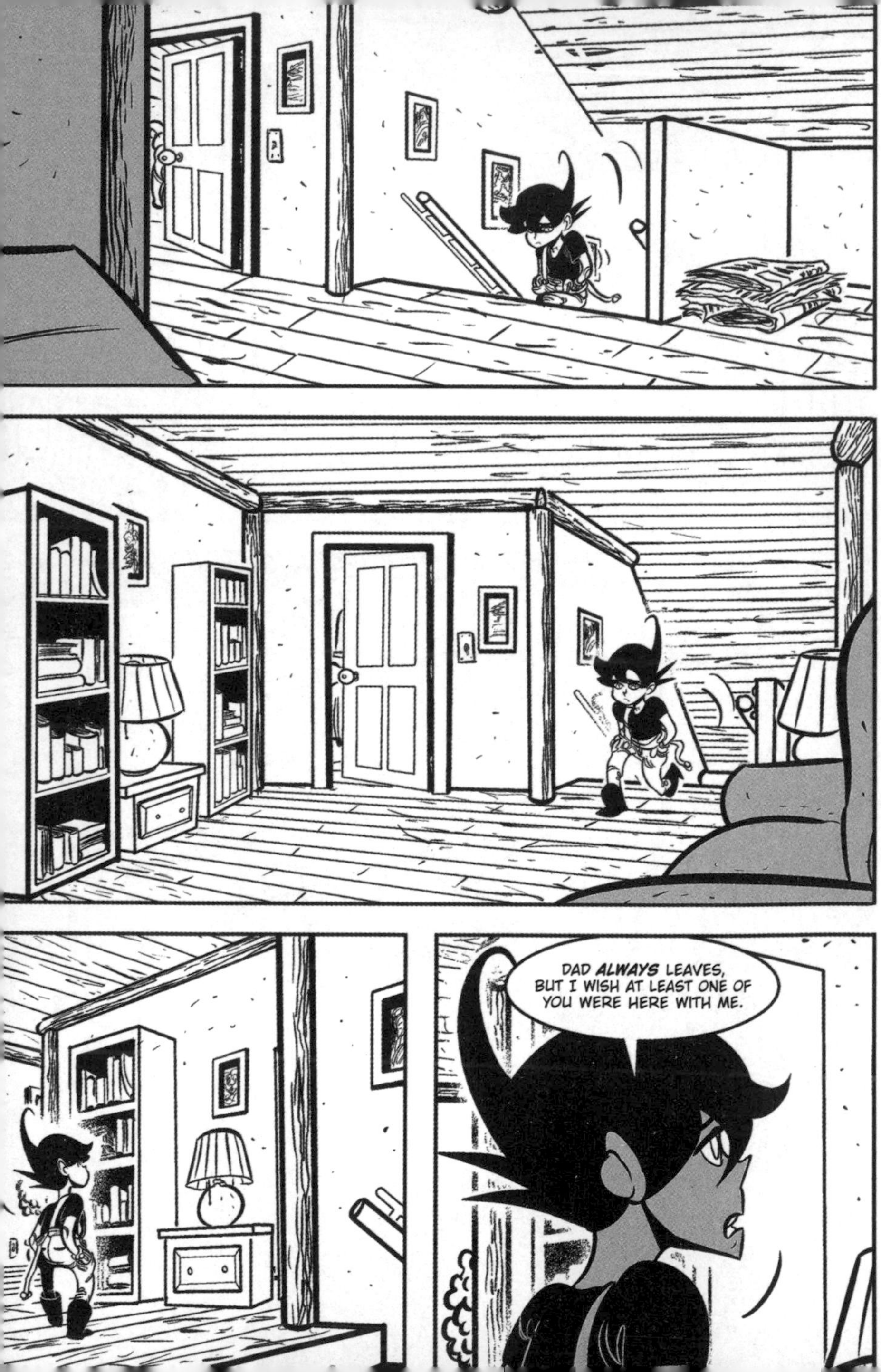
DAD ALWAYS LEAVES, BUT I WISH AT LEAST ONE OF YOU WERE HERE WITH ME.

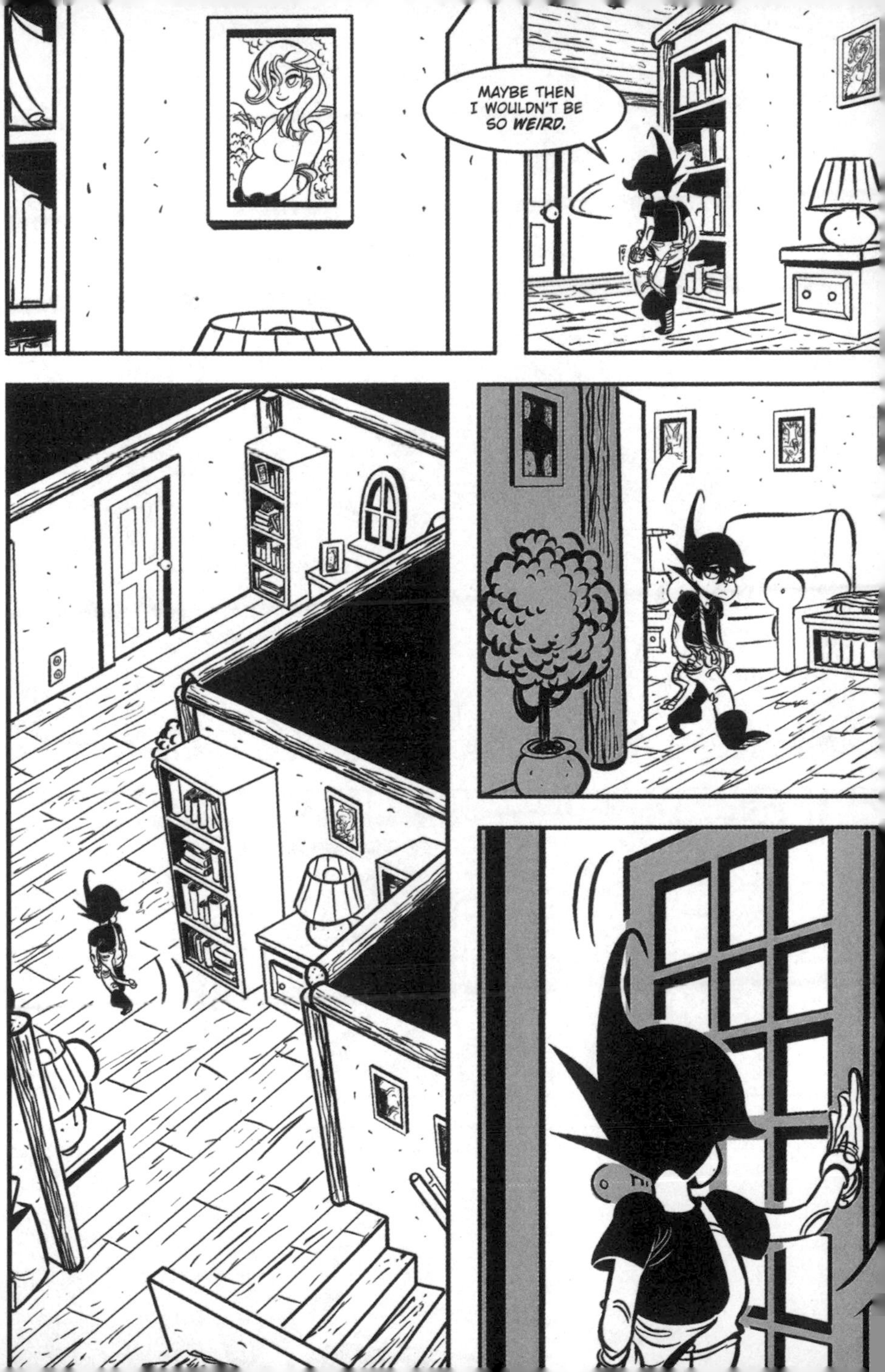
MAYBE THEN I WOULDN'T BE SO WEIRD.

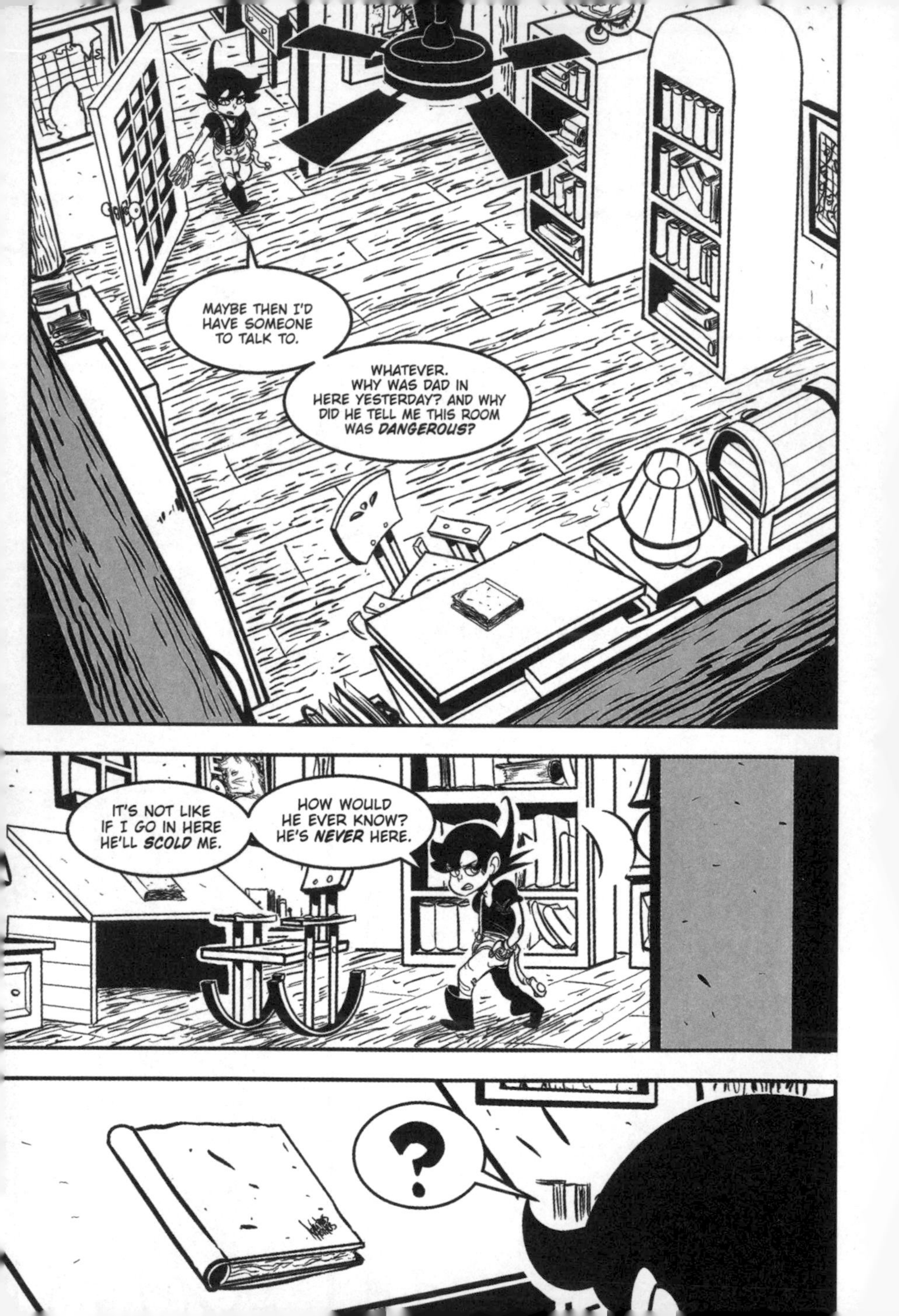
MAYBE THEN I'D HAVE SOMEONE TO TALK TO.
WHATEVER. WHY WAS DAD IN HERE YESTERDAY? AND WHY DID HE TELL ME THIS ROOM WAS *DANGEROUS*?
IT'S NOT LIKE IF I GO IN HERE HE'LL *SCOLD* ME.
HOW WOULD HE EVER KNOW? HE'S *NEVER* HERE.
?

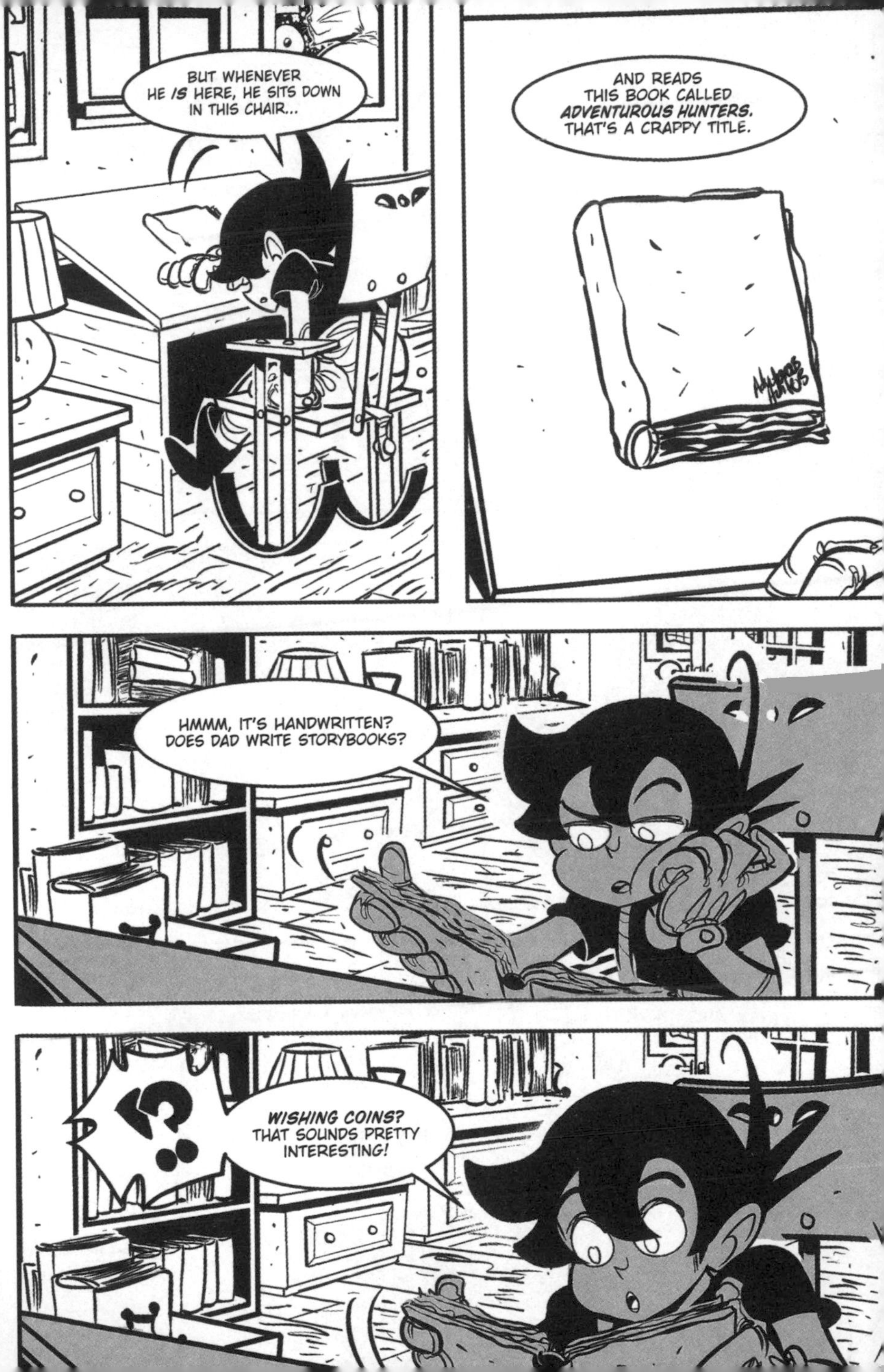
BUT WHENEVER HE *IS* HERE, HE SITS DOWN IN THIS CHAIR...
AND READS THIS BOOK CALLED ***ADVENTUROUS HUNTERS.*** THAT'S A CRAPPY TITLE.
HMMM, IT'S HANDWRITTEN? DOES DAD WRITE STORYBOOKS?
?!
WISHING COINS? THAT SOUNDS PRETTY INTERESTING!

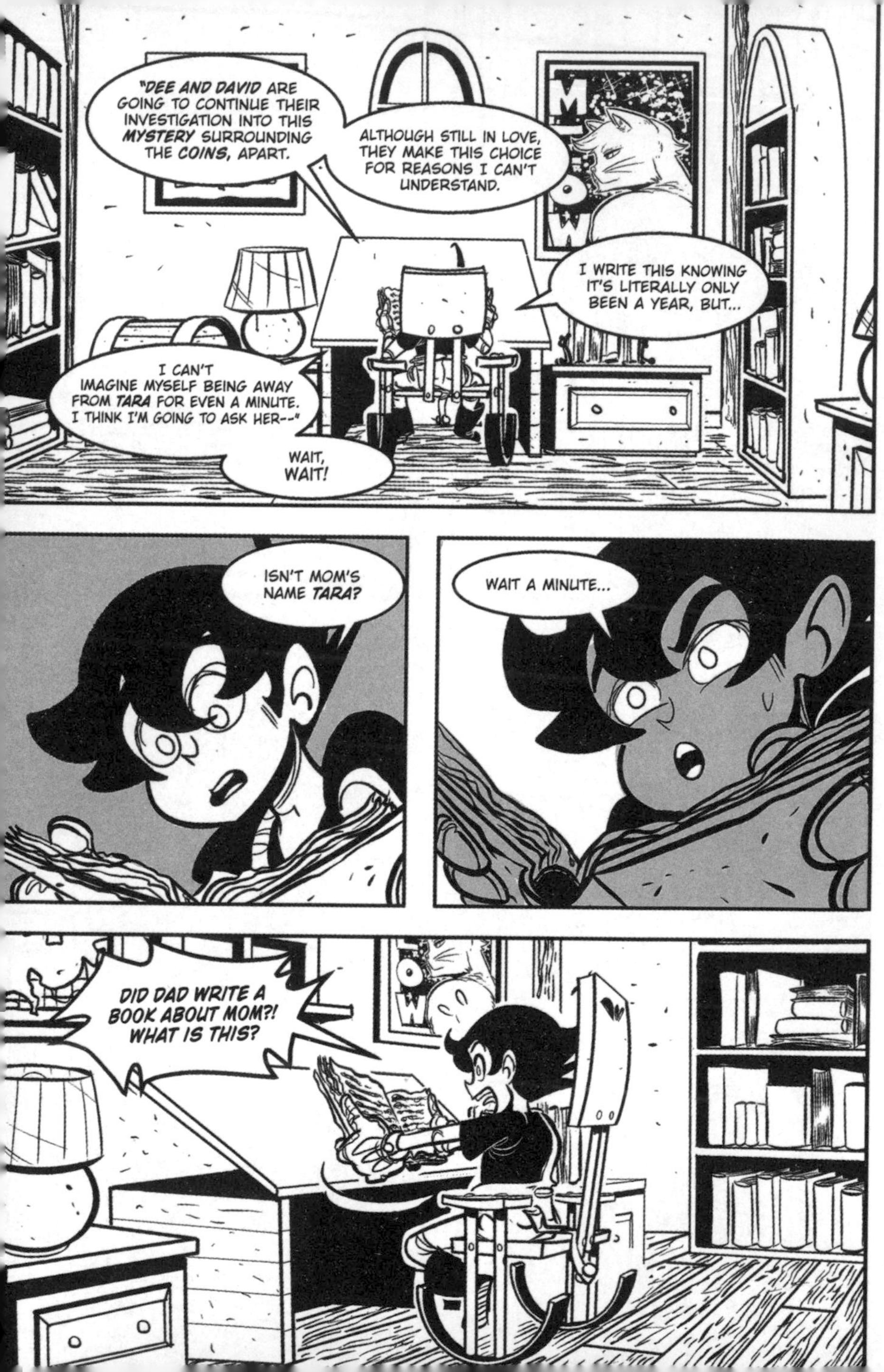
"DEE AND DAVID ARE GOING TO CONTINUE THEIR INVESTIGATION INTO THIS MYSTERY SURROUNDING THE COINS, APART.
ALTHOUGH STILL IN LOVE, THEY MAKE THIS CHOICE FOR REASONS I CAN'T UNDERSTAND.
I WRITE THIS KNOWING IT'S LITERALLY ONLY BEEN A YEAR, BUT...
I CAN'T IMAGINE MYSELF BEING AWAY FROM TARA FOR EVEN A MINUTE. I THINK I'M GOING TO ASK HER--"
WAIT, WAIT!
ISN'T MOM'S NAME TARA?
WAIT A MINUTE...
DID DAD WRITE A BOOK ABOUT MOM?! WHAT IS THIS?

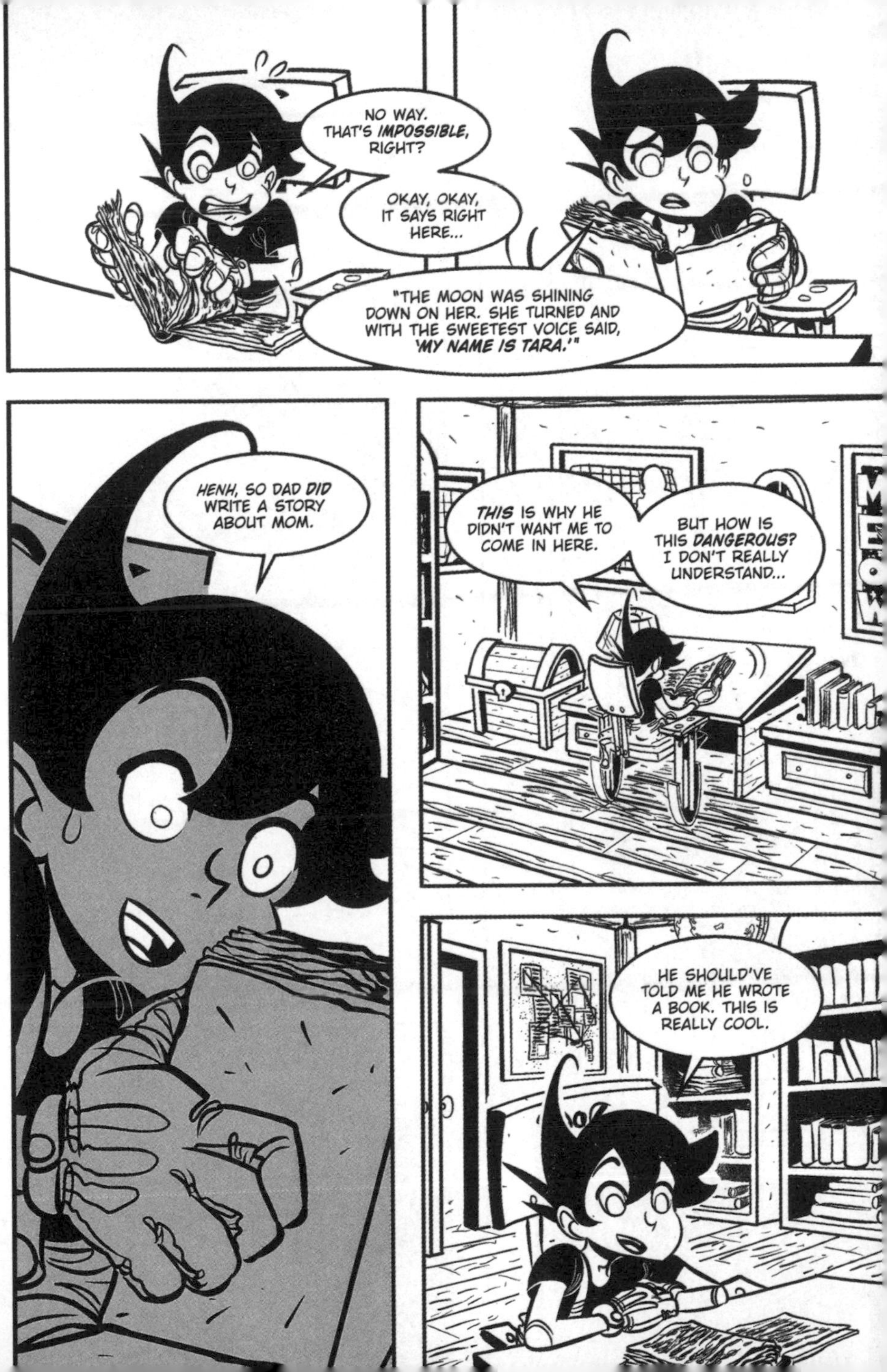
NO WAY. THAT'S *IMPOSSIBLE,* RIGHT?
OKAY, OKAY, IT SAYS RIGHT HERE...
"THE MOON WAS SHINING DOWN ON HER. SHE TURNED AND WITH THE SWEETEST VOICE SAID, ***'MY NAME IS TARA.'***"
HENH, SO DAD *DID* WRITE A STORY ABOUT MOM.
THIS IS WHY HE DIDN'T WANT ME TO COME IN HERE.
BUT HOW IS THIS *DANGEROUS?* I DON'T REALLY UNDERSTAND...
MEOW
HE SHOULD'VE TOLD ME HE WROTE A BOOK. THIS IS REALLY COOL.

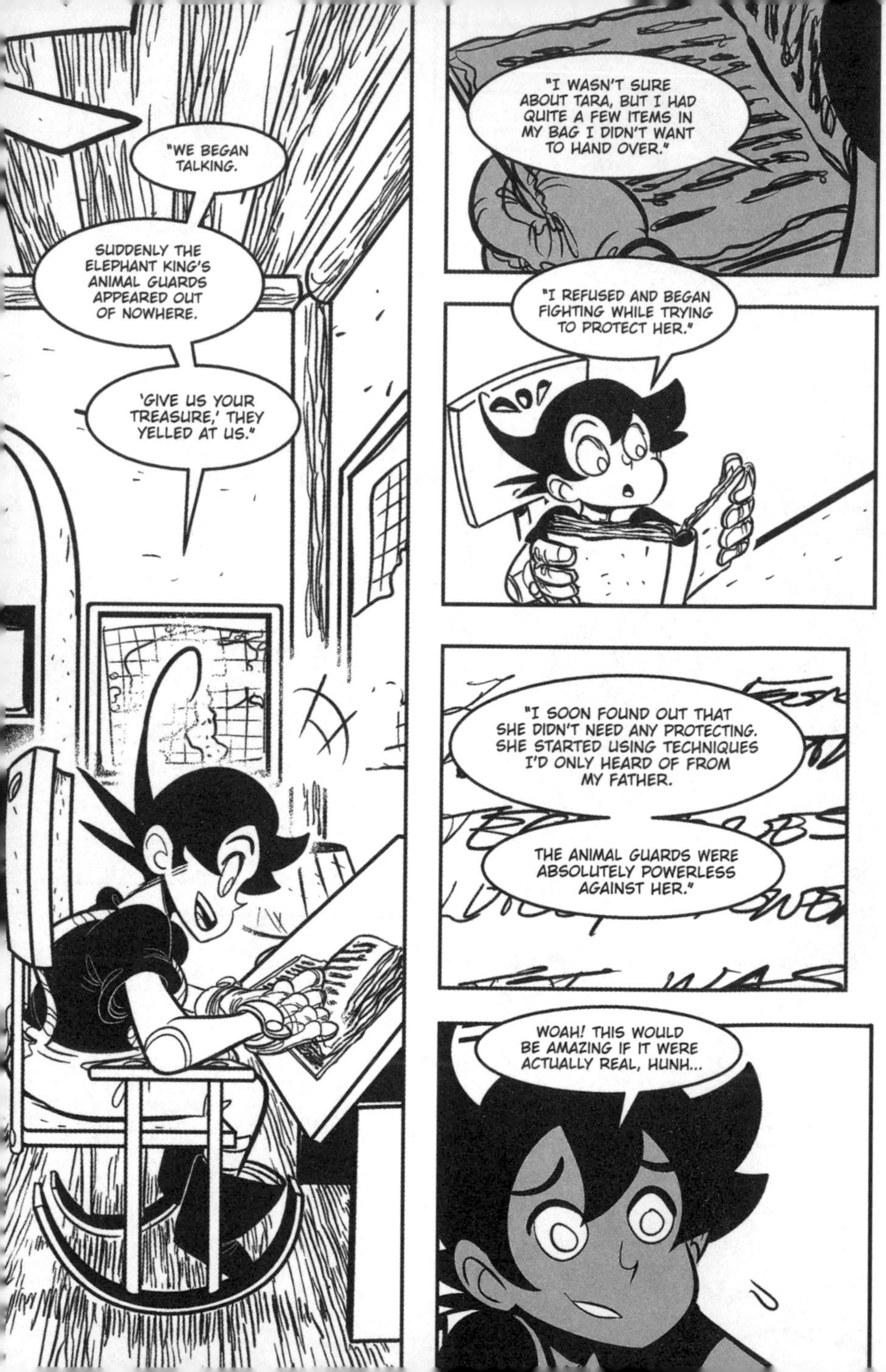
"WE BEGAN TALKING.
SUDDENLY THE ELEPHANT KING'S ANIMAL GUARDS APPEARED OUT OF NOWHERE.
'GIVE US YOUR TREASURE,' THEY YELLED AT US."
"I WASN'T SURE ABOUT TARA, BUT I HAD QUITE A FEW ITEMS IN MY BAG I DIDN'T WANT TO HAND OVER."
"I REFUSED AND BEGAN FIGHTING WHILE TRYING TO PROTECT HER."
"I SOON FOUND OUT THAT SHE DIDN'T NEED ANY PROTECTING. SHE STARTED USING TECHNIQUES I'D ONLY HEARD OF FROM MY FATHER.
THE ANIMAL GUARDS WERE ABSOLUTELY POWERLESS AGAINST HER."
WOAH! THIS WOULD BE AMAZING IF IT WERE ACTUALLY REAL, HUNH...

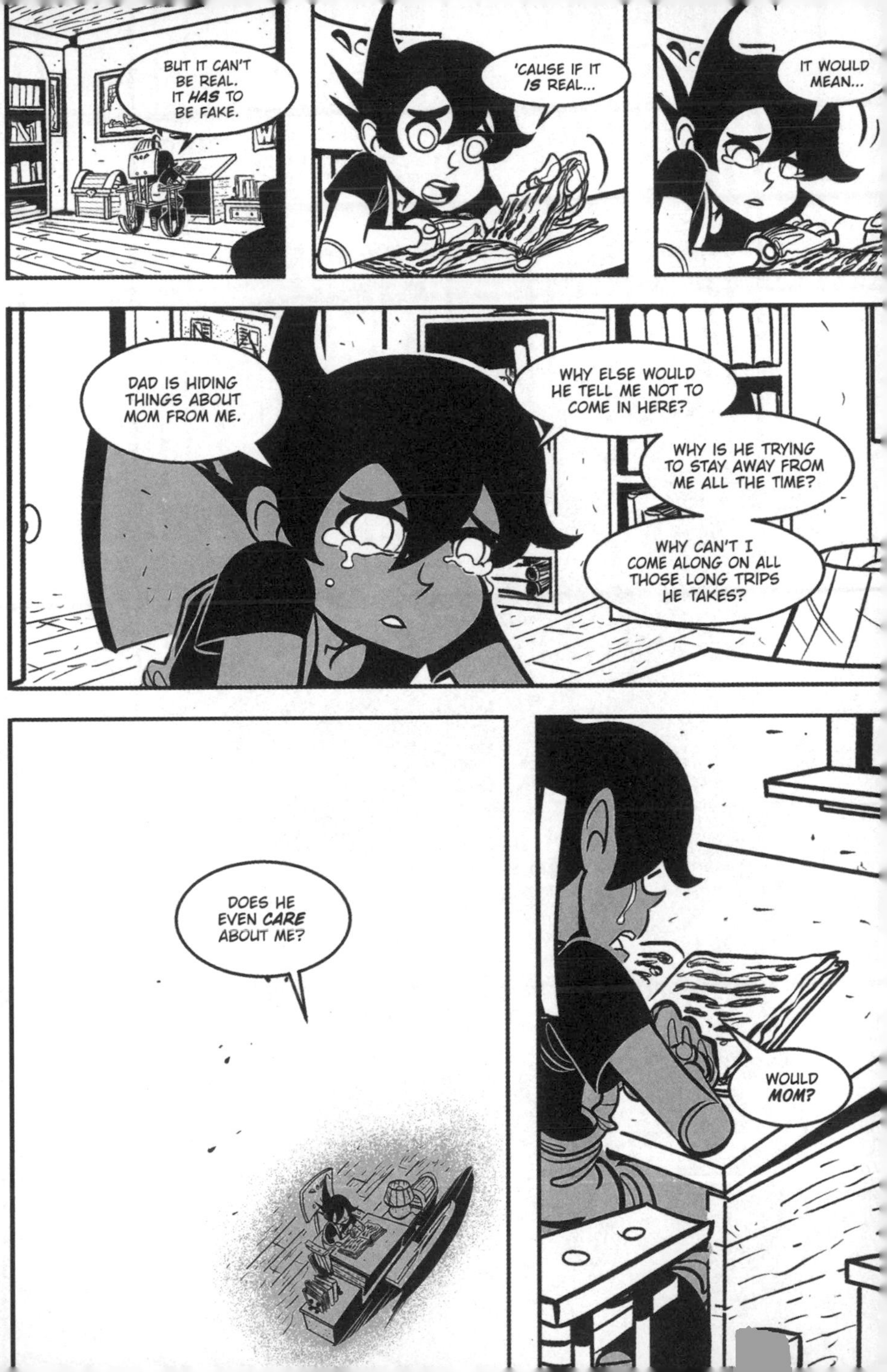
BUT IT CAN'T BE REAL. IT HAS TO BE FAKE.
'CAUSE IF IT IS REAL...
IT WOULD MEAN...
DAD IS HIDING THINGS ABOUT MOM FROM ME.
WHY ELSE WOULD HE TELL ME NOT TO COME IN HERE?
WHY IS HE TRYING TO STAY AWAY FROM ME ALL THE TIME?
WHY CAN'T I COME ALONG ON ALL THOSE LONG TRIPS HE TAKES?
DOES HE EVEN CARE ABOUT ME?
WOULD MOM?

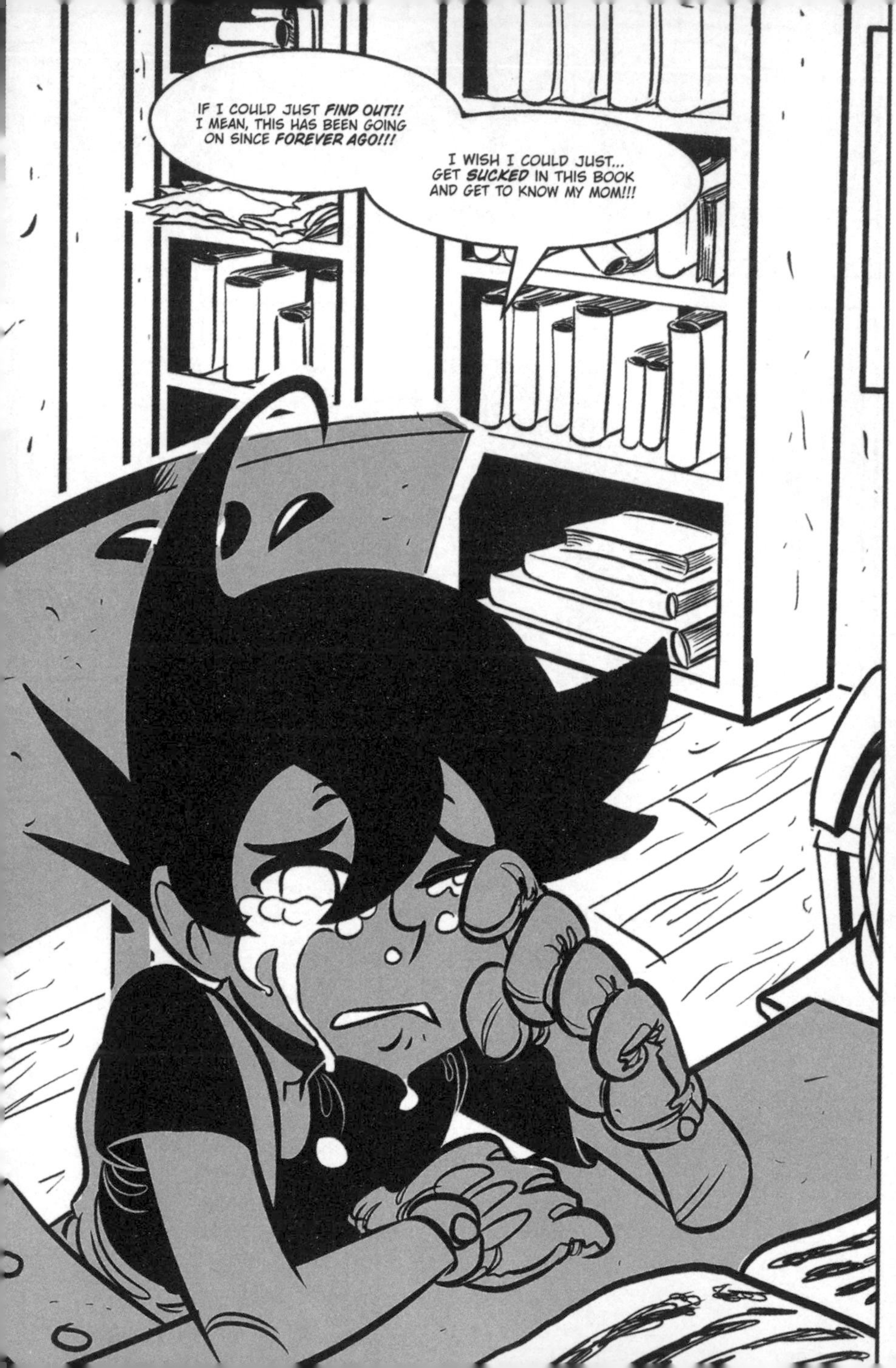
IF I COULD JUST FIND OUT!! I MEAN, THIS HAS BEEN GOING ON SINCE FOREVER AGO!!!
I WISH I COULD JUST... GET SUCKED IN THIS BOOK AND GET TO KNOW MY MOM!!!

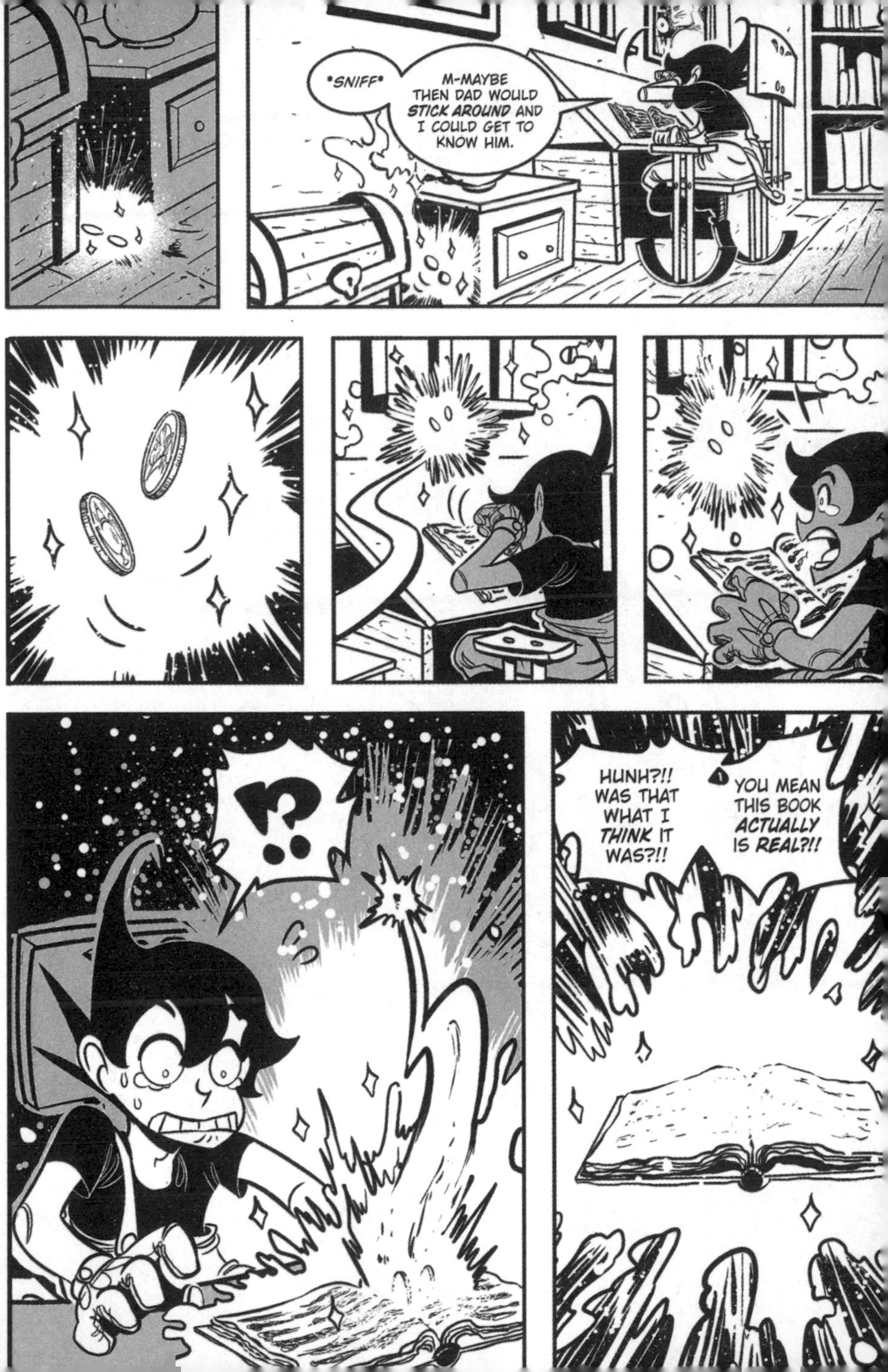
SNIFF
M-MAYBE THEN DAD WOULD STICK AROUND AND I COULD GET TO KNOW HIM.
?!
HUNH?!! WAS THAT WHAT I THINK IT WAS?!!
YOU MEAN THIS BOOK ACTUALLY IS REAL?!!

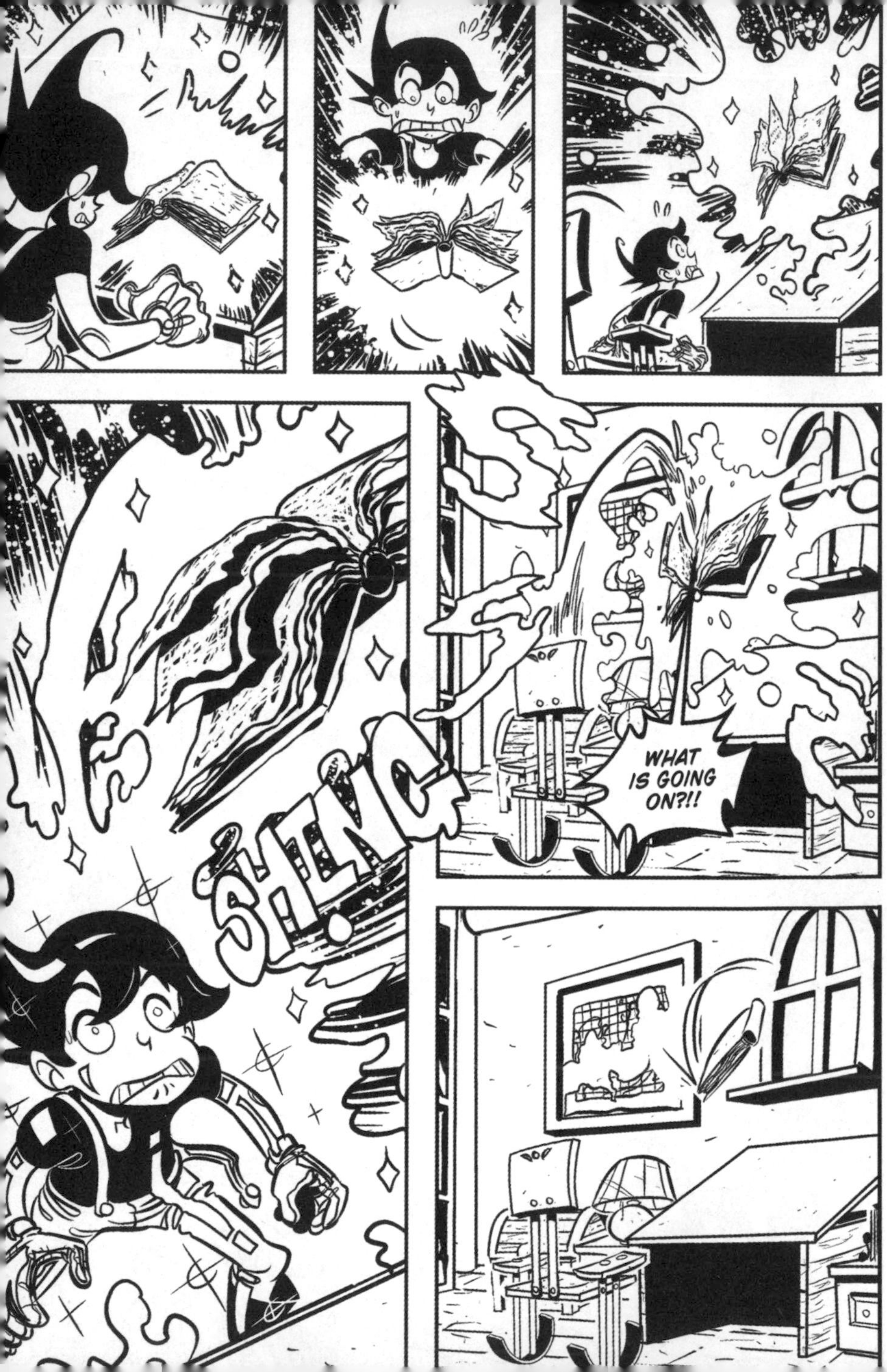
SHING
WHAT IS GOING ON?!!

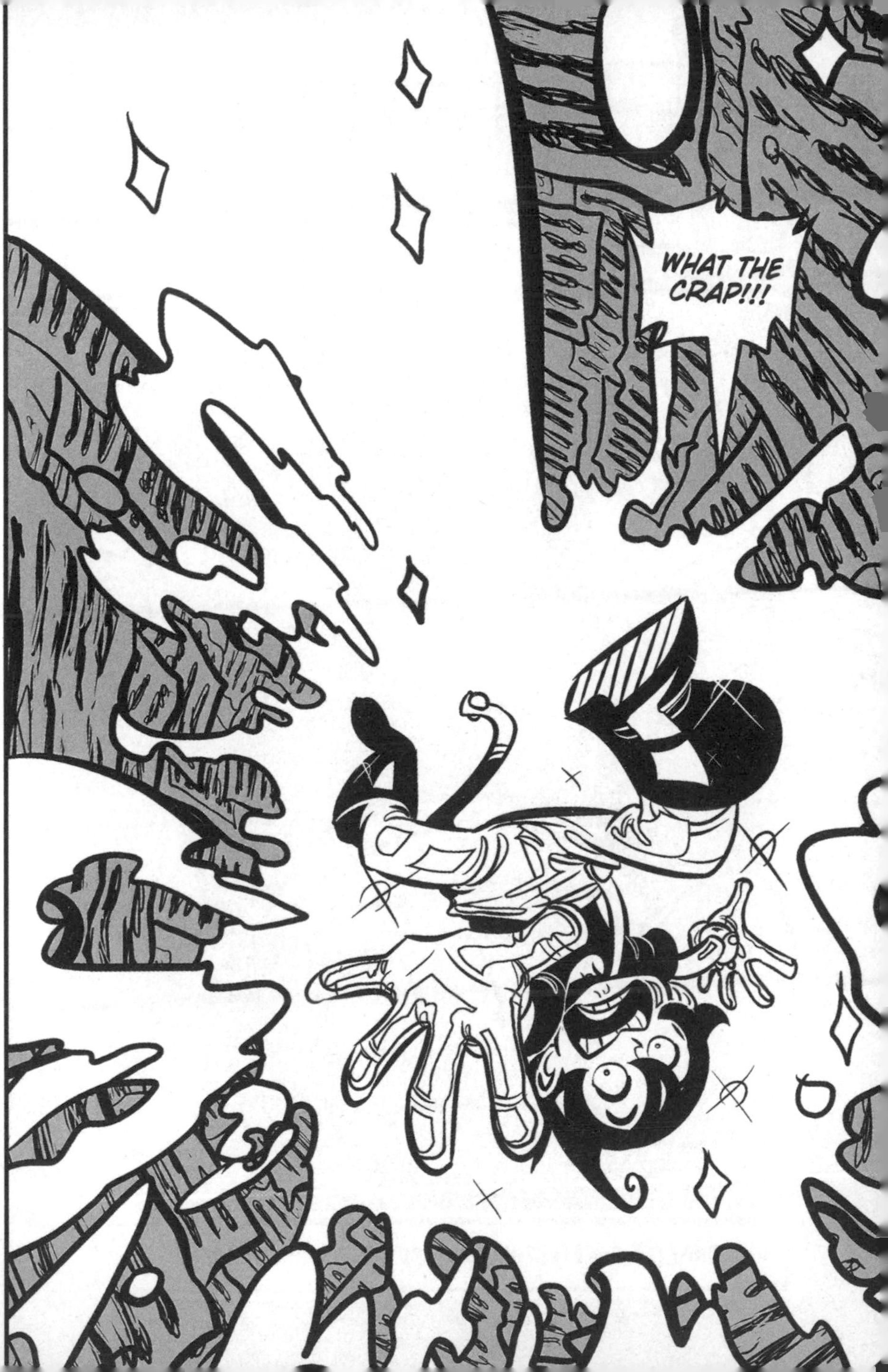
WHAT THE CRAP!!!

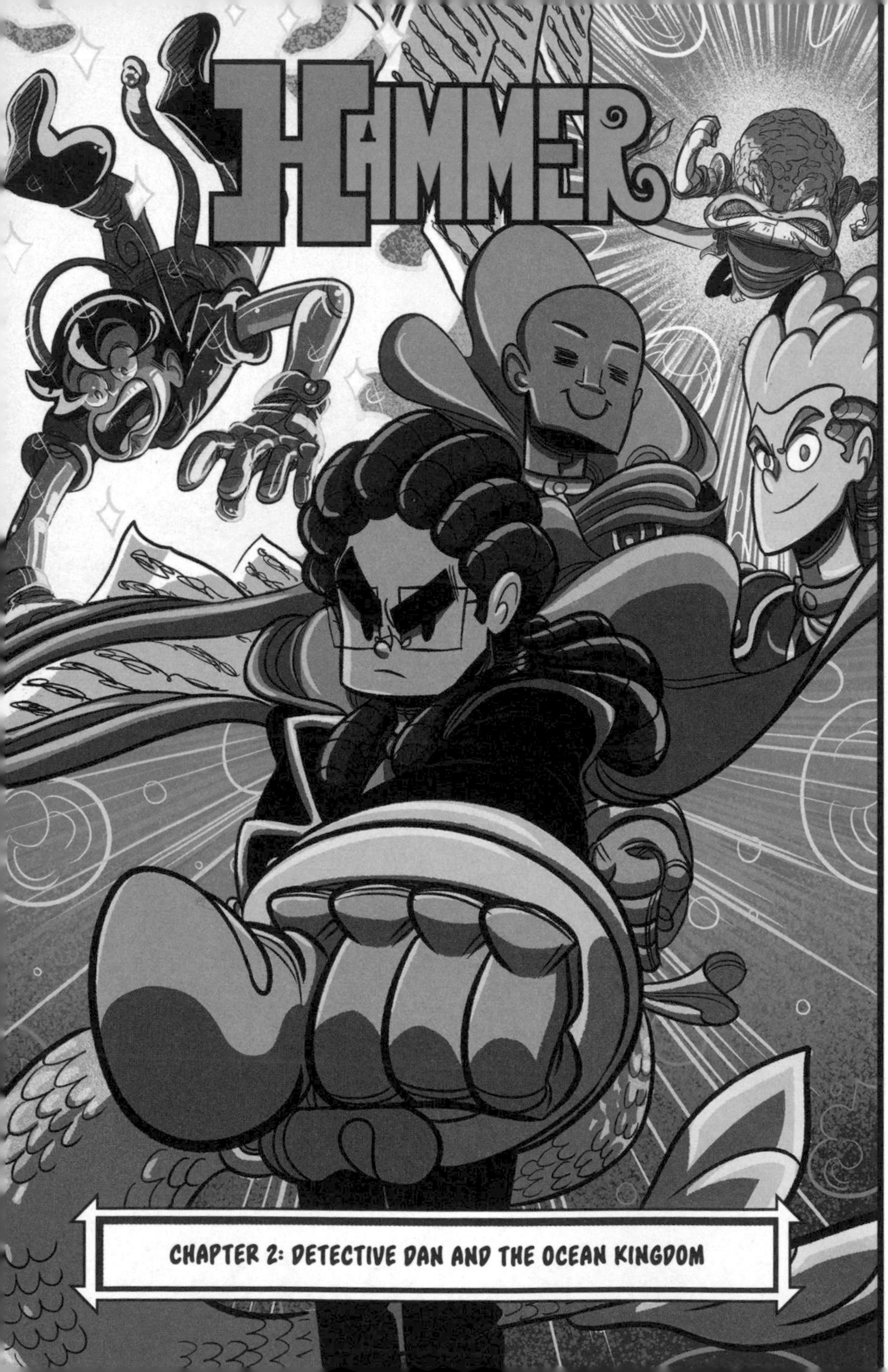
HAMMER
CHAPTER 2: DETECTIVE DAN AND THE OCEAN KINGDOM

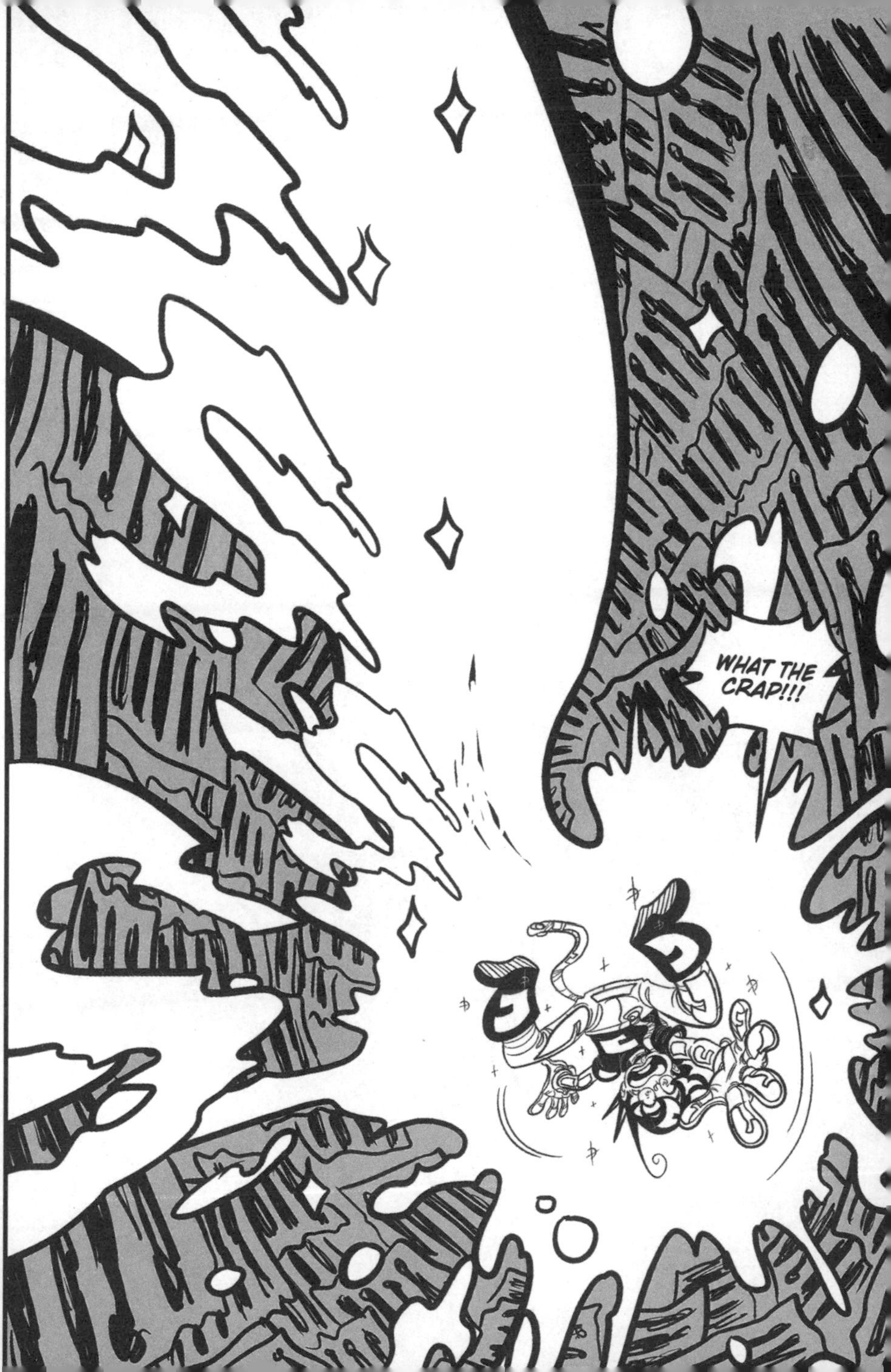
WHAT THE CRAP!!!

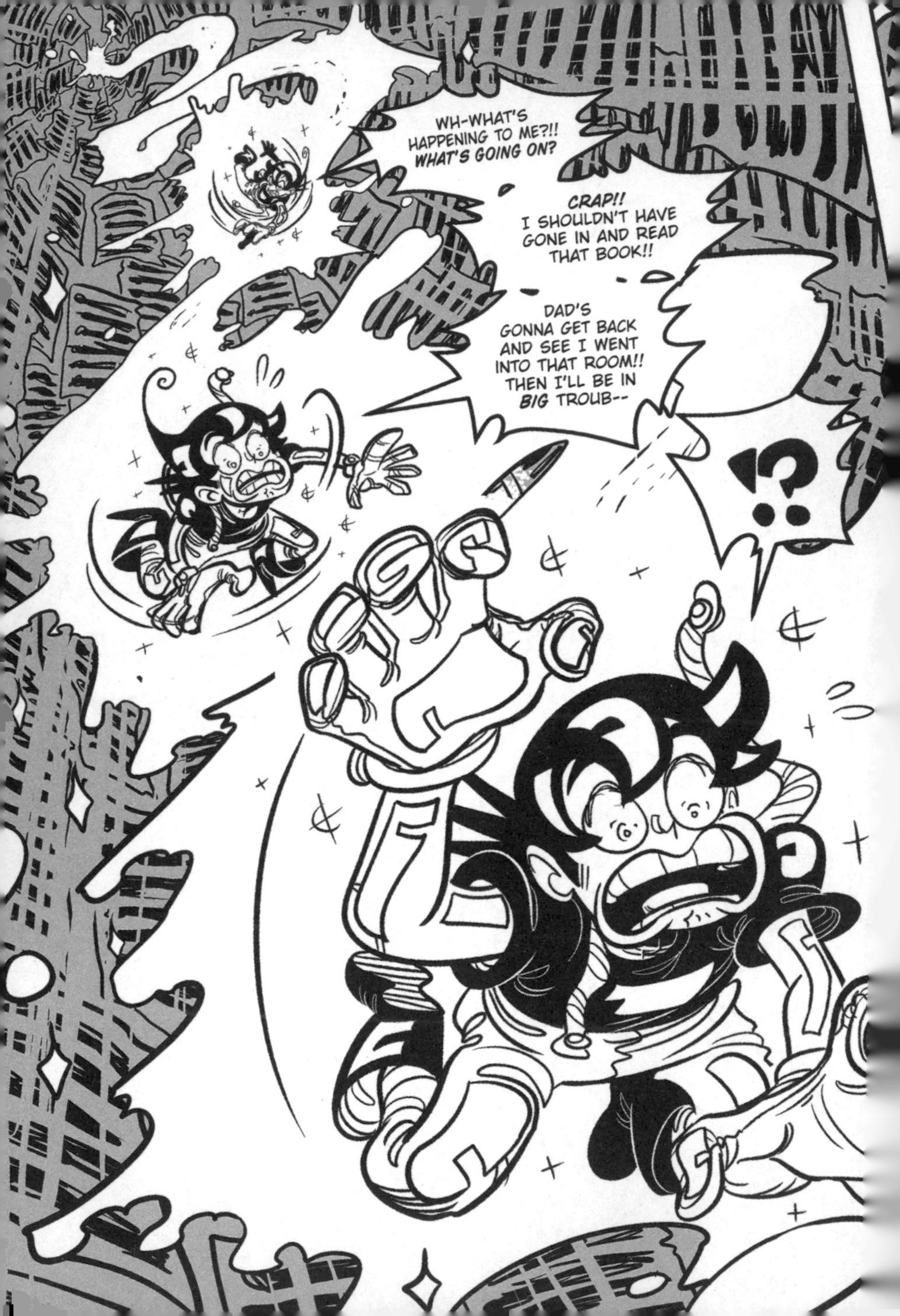

WH-WHAT'S HAPPENING TO ME?!! *WHAT'S GOING ON?*
CRAP!! I SHOULDN'T HAVE GONE IN AND READ THAT BOOK!!
DAD'S GONNA GET BACK AND SEE I WENT INTO THAT ROOM!! THEN I'LL BE IN *BIG* TROUB--
!?

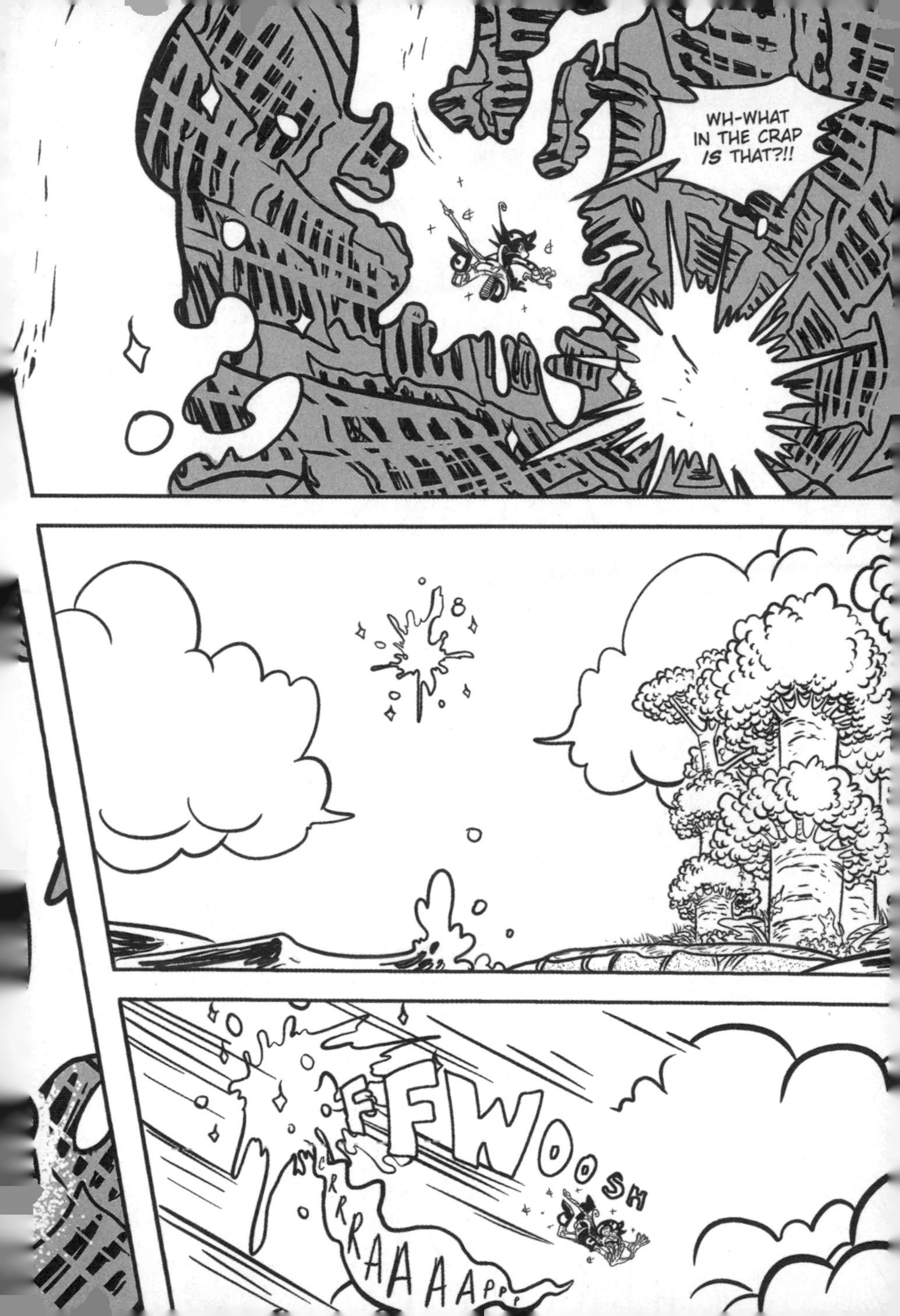
WH-WHAT IN THE CRAP IS THAT?!!
FFWOOSH
SCRRRRAAAAAPPP

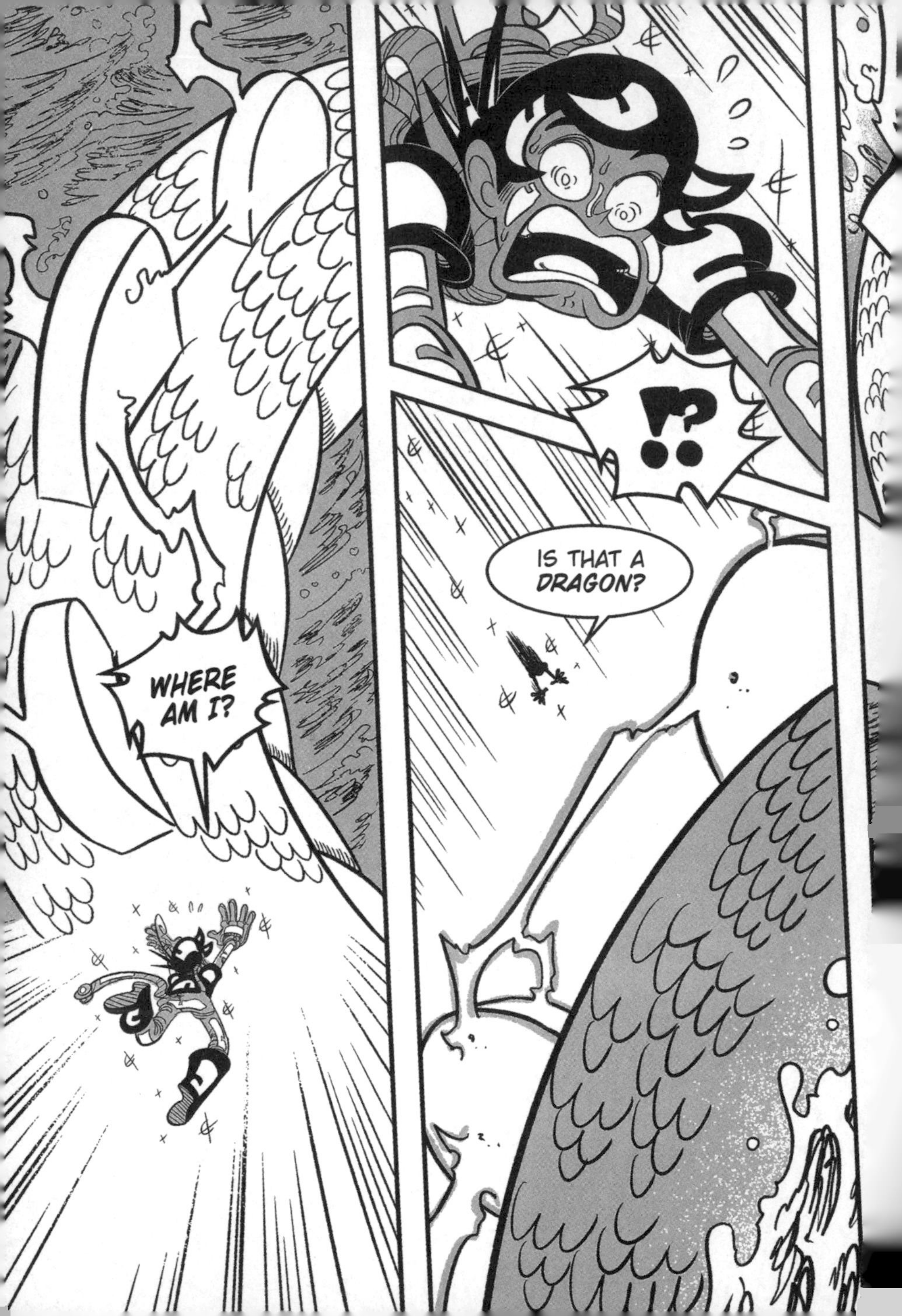
WHERE AM I?
!?
IS THAT A DRAGON?

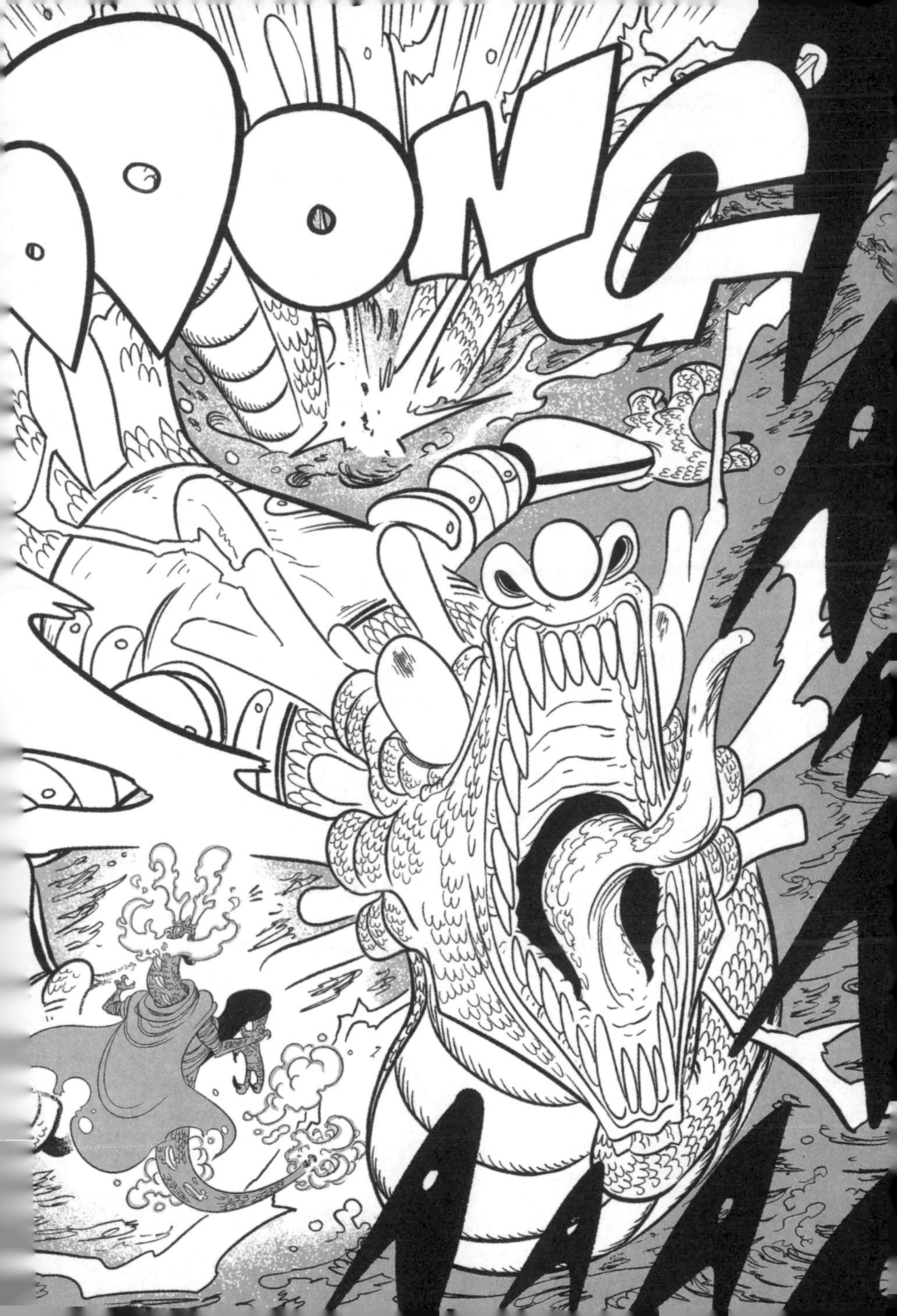
DONG!

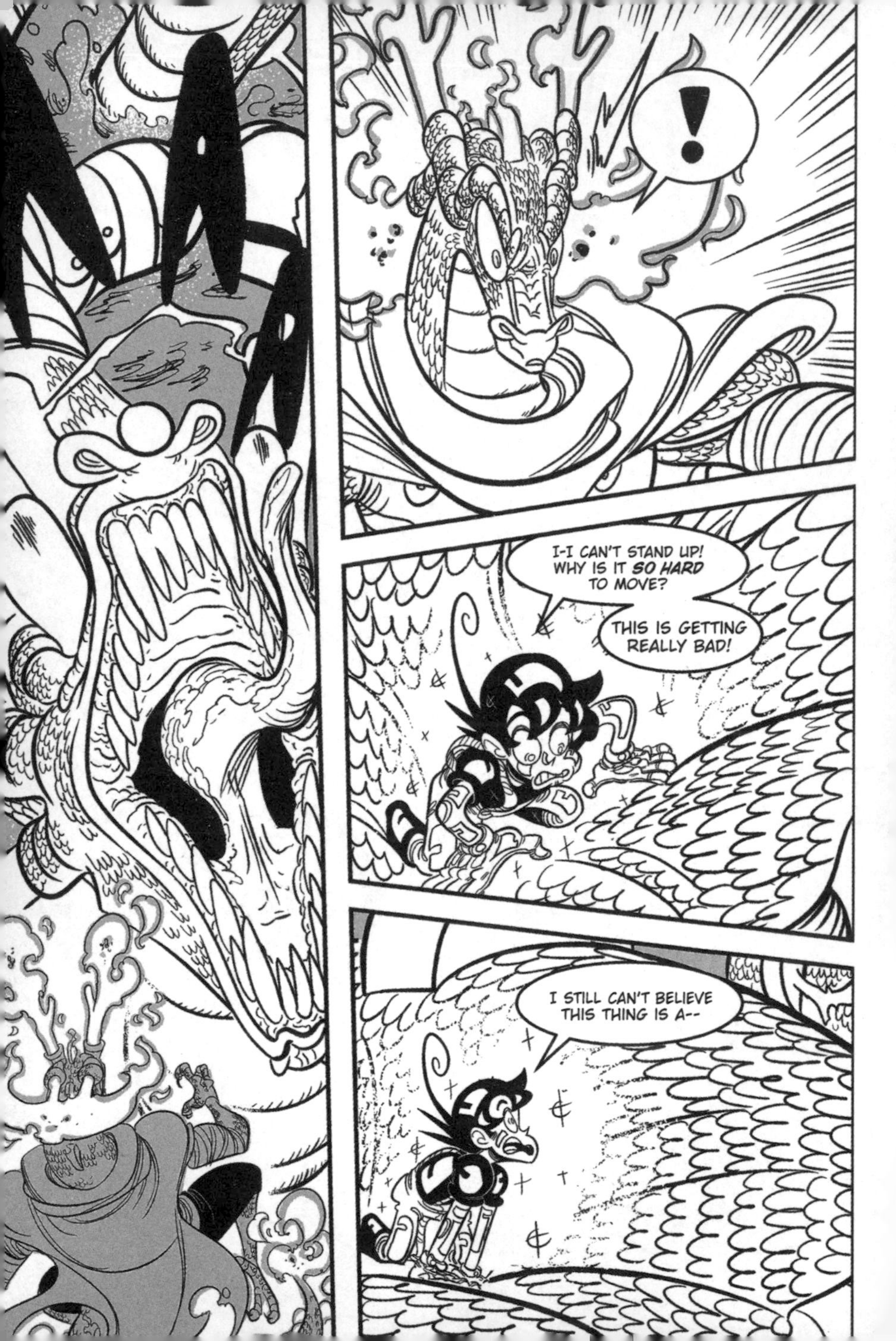
!
I-I CAN'T STAND UP! WHY IS IT SO HARD TO MOVE?
THIS IS GETTING REALLY BAD!
I STILL CAN'T BELIEVE THIS THING IS A--

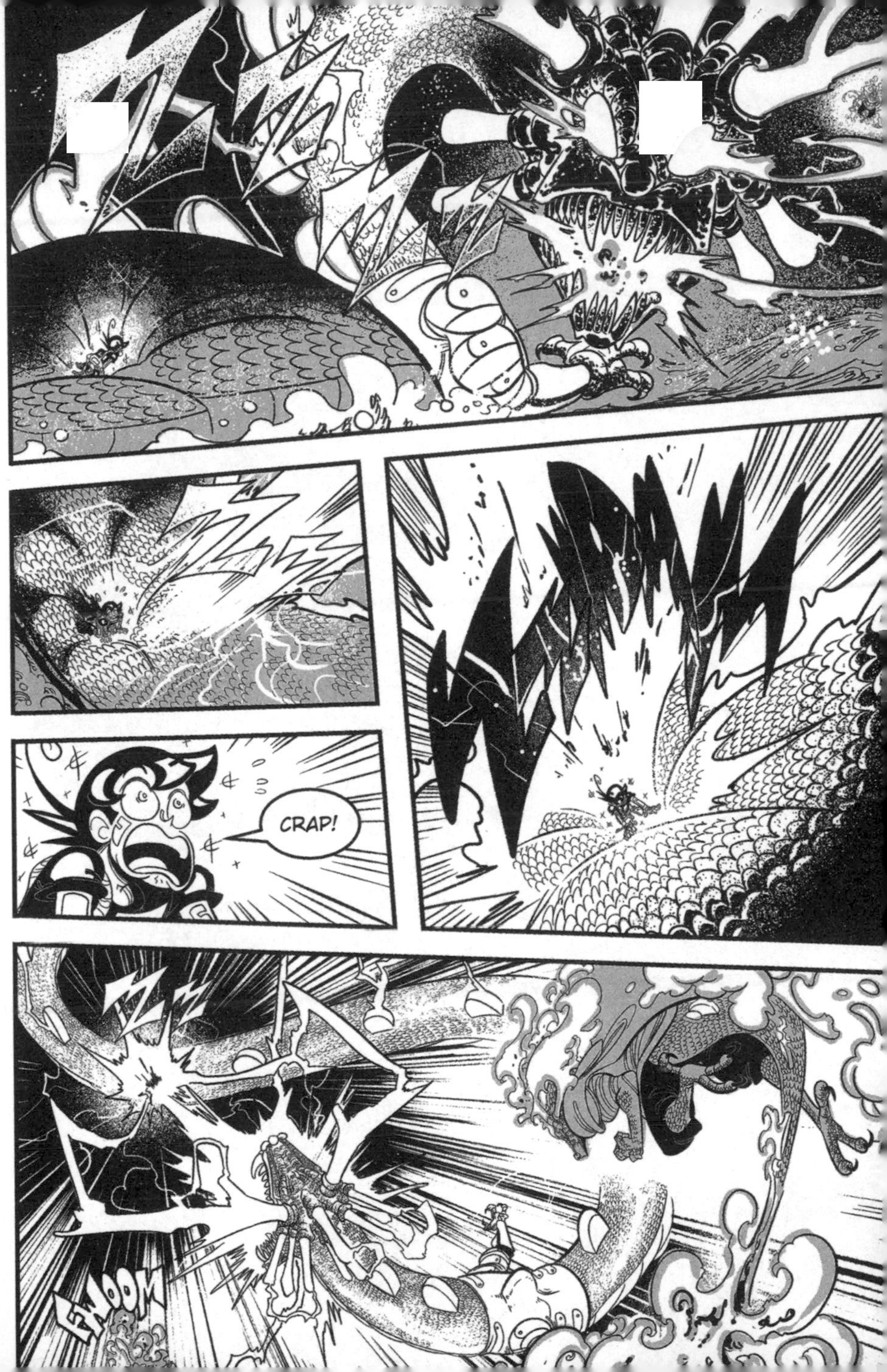
CRAP!
FWOOM

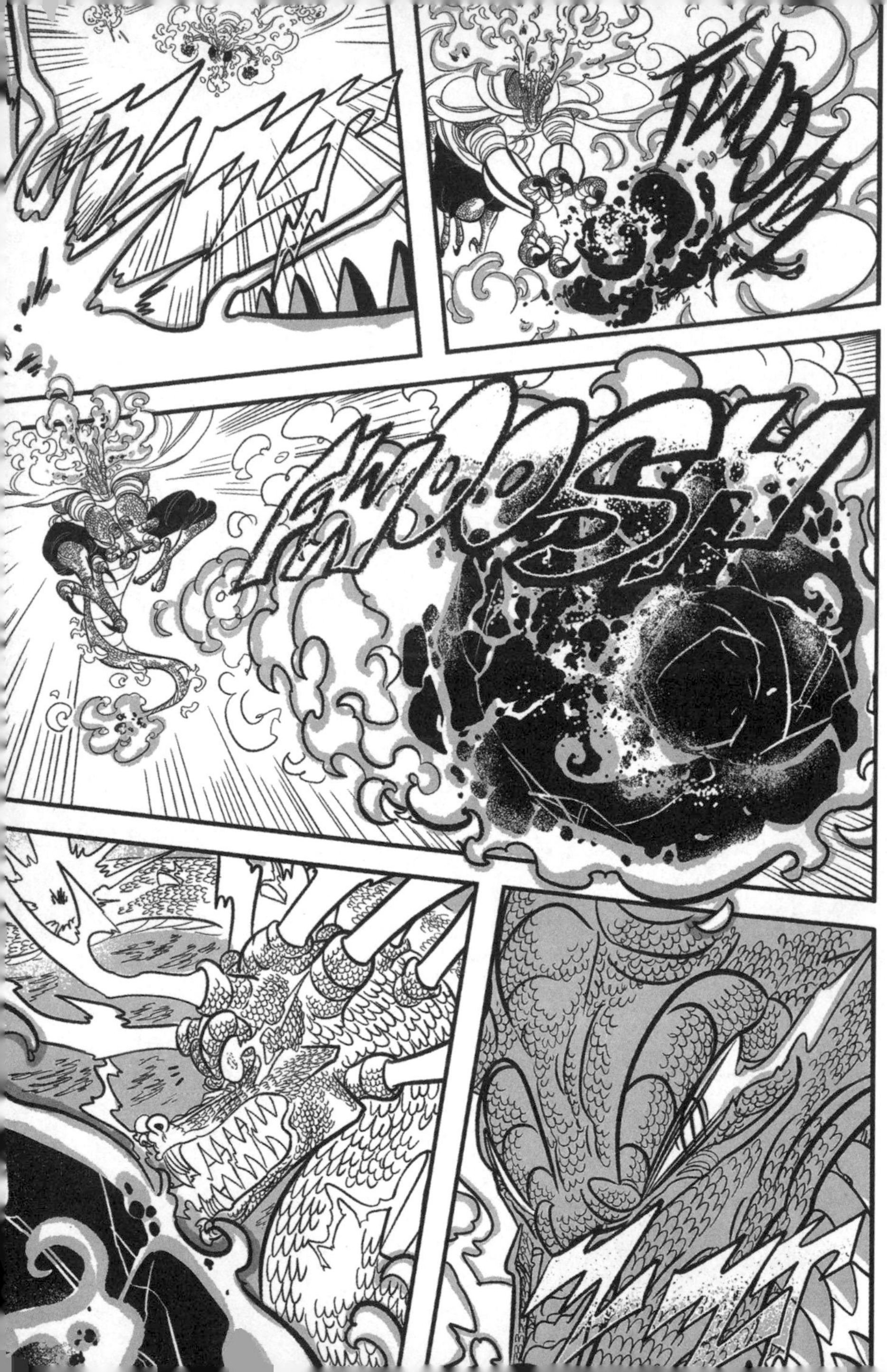
FWOOM
WHOOSH

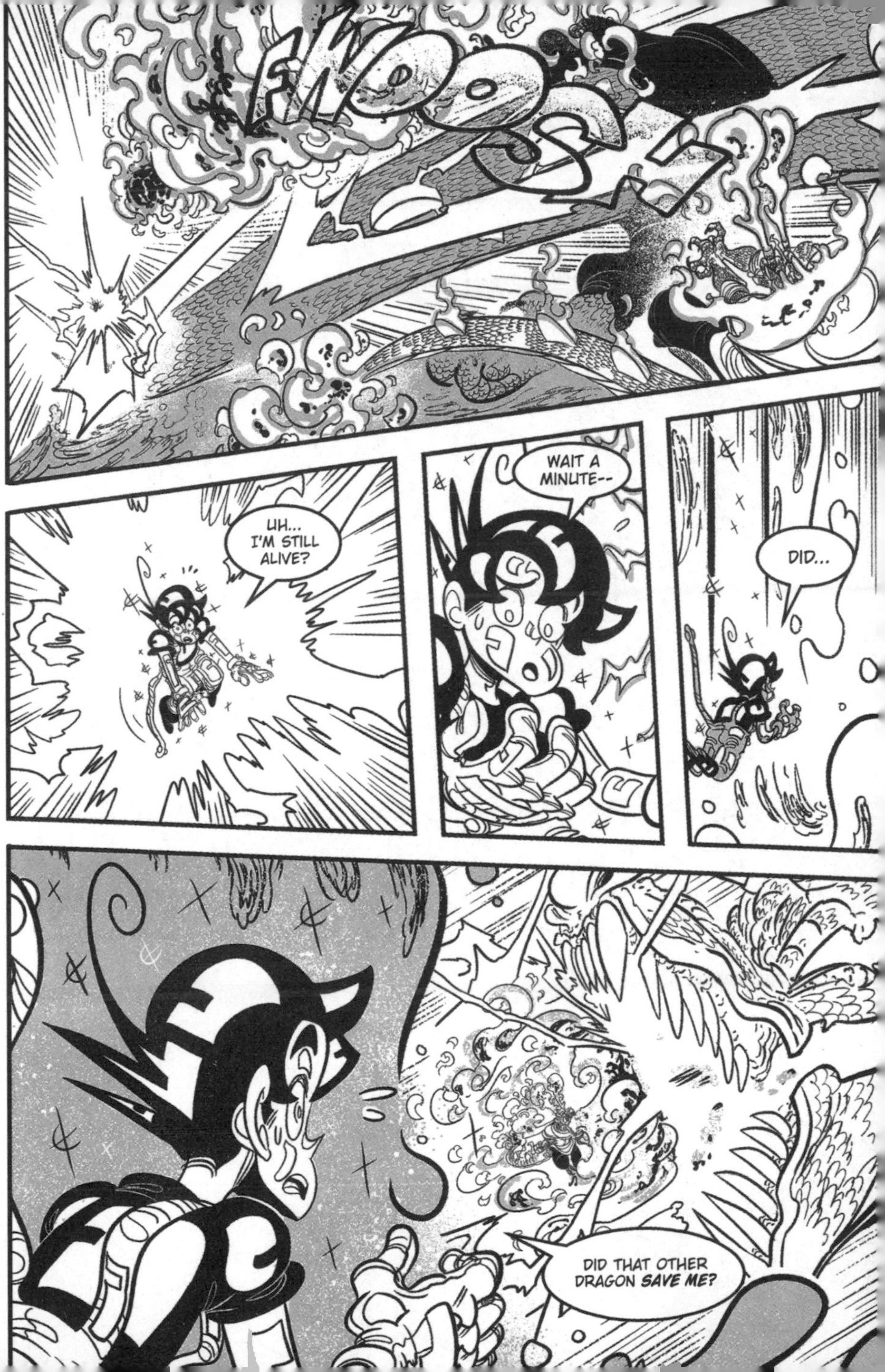
FWOOSH
UH... I'M STILL ALIVE?
WAIT A MINUTE--
DID...
DID THAT OTHER DRAGON **SAVE ME?**

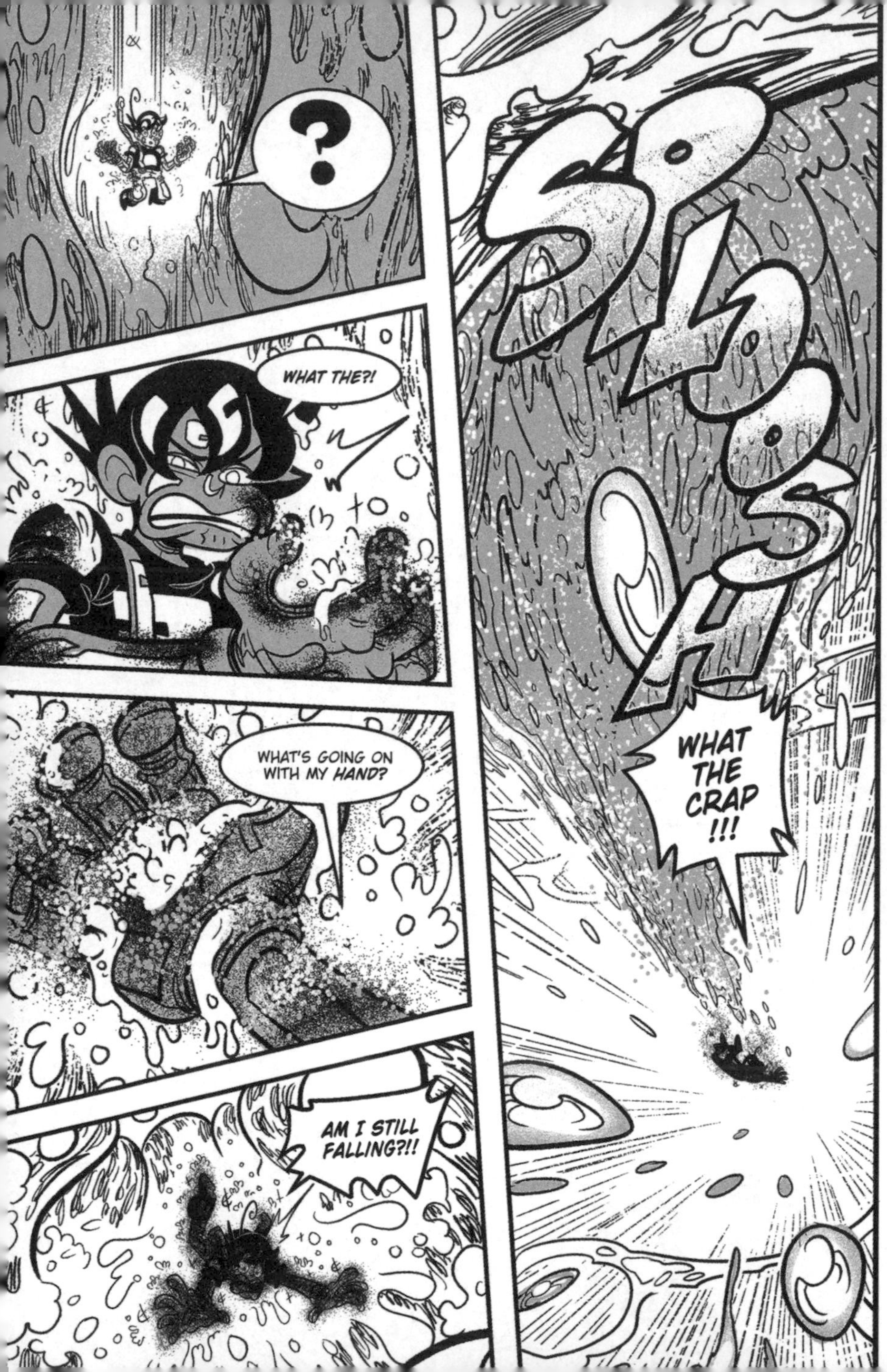
?
WHAT THE?!
WHAT'S GOING ON WITH MY HAND?
AM I STILL FALLING?!!
SPLOOSH
WHAT THE CRAP !!!

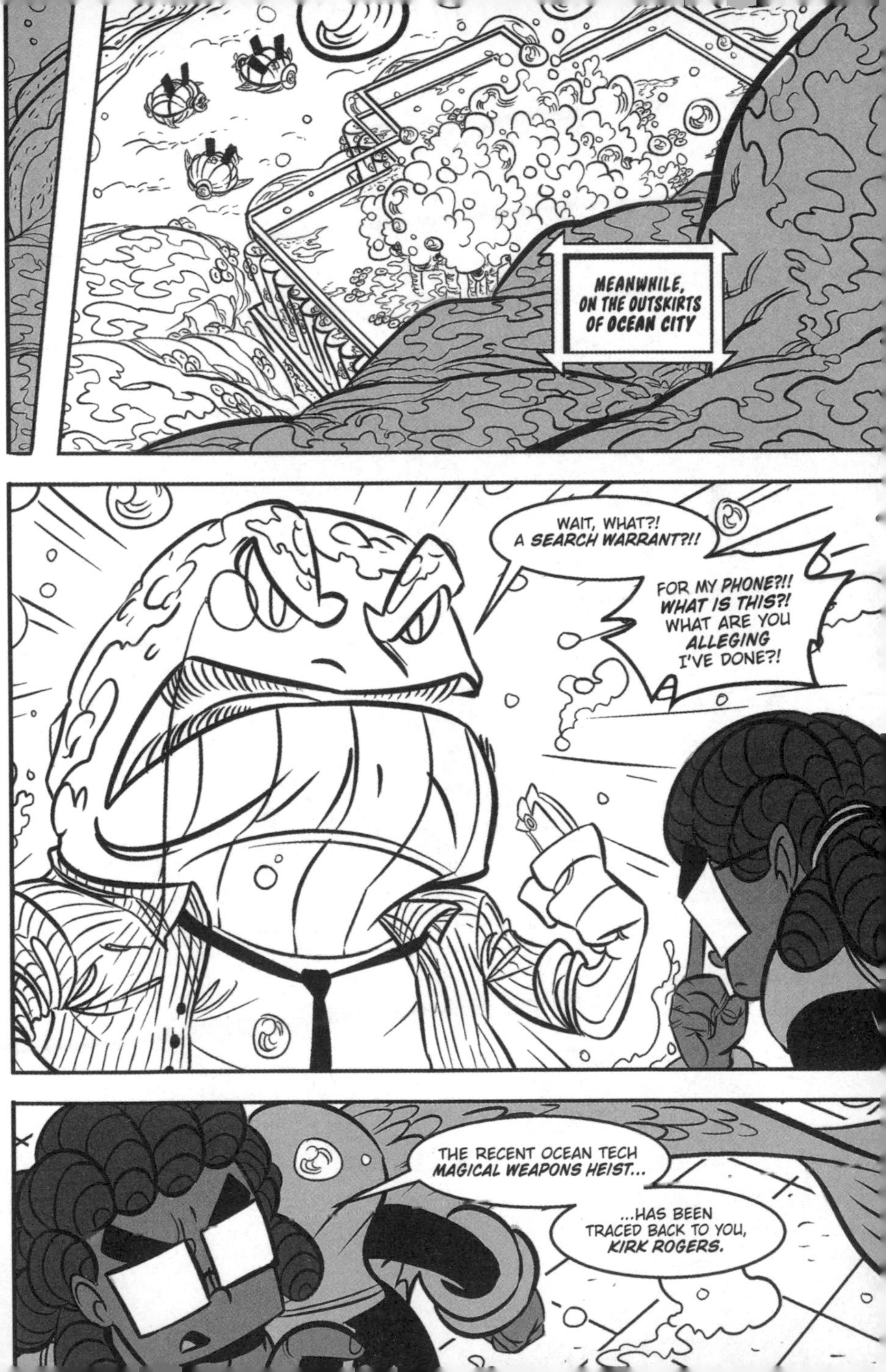
MEANWHILE, ON THE OUTSKIRTS OF OCEAN CITY
WAIT, WHAT?! A SEARCH WARRANT?!!
FOR MY PHONE?!! WHAT IS THIS?! WHAT ARE YOU ALLEGING I'VE DONE?!
THE RECENT OCEAN TECH MAGICAL WEAPONS HEIST...
...HAS BEEN TRACED BACK TO YOU, KIRK ROGERS.

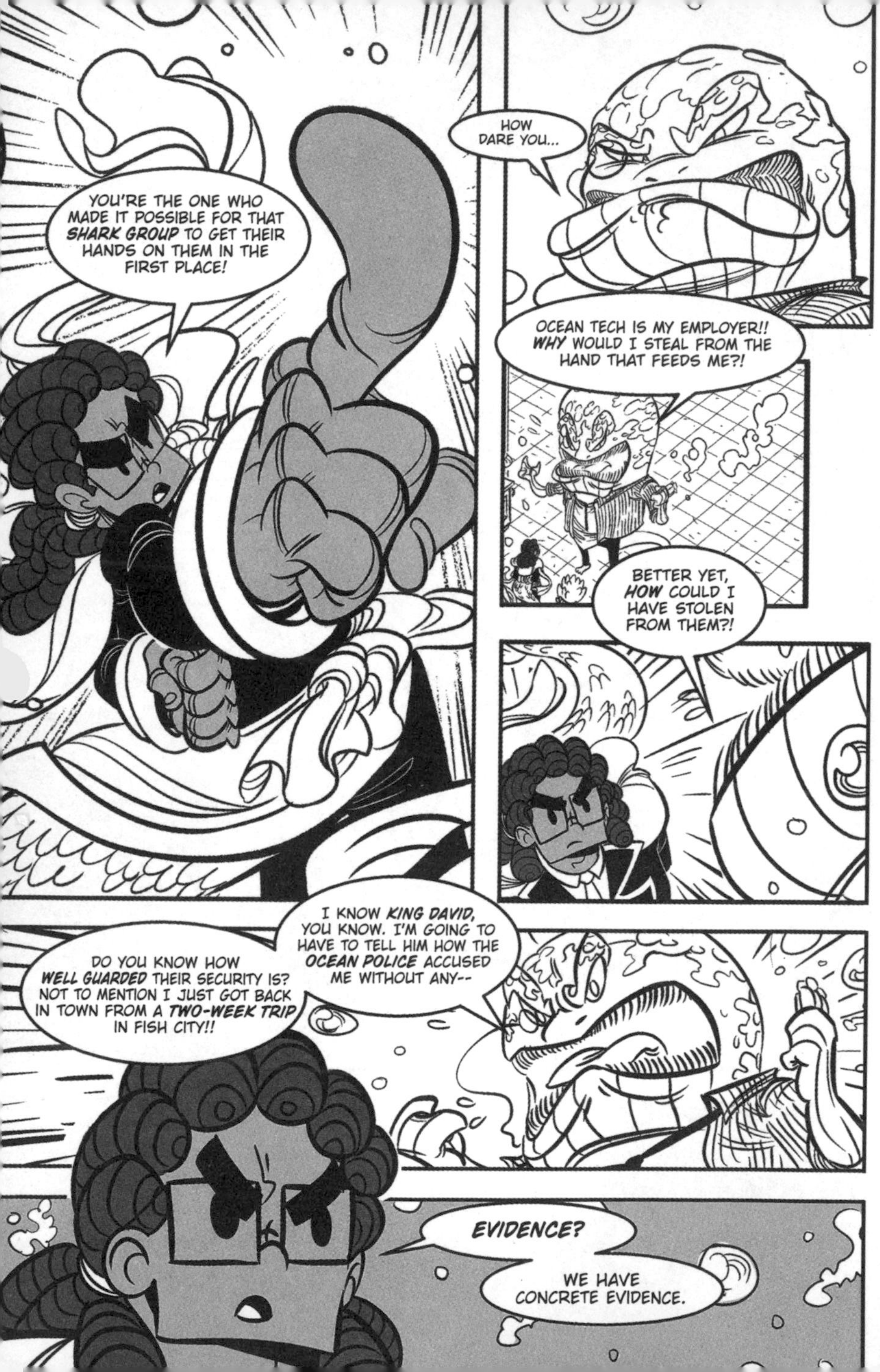
YOU'RE THE ONE WHO MADE IT POSSIBLE FOR THAT SHARK GROUP TO GET THEIR HANDS ON THEM IN THE FIRST PLACE!
HOW DARE YOU...
OCEAN TECH IS MY EMPLOYER!! WHY WOULD I STEAL FROM THE HAND THAT FEEDS ME?!
BETTER YET, HOW COULD I HAVE STOLEN FROM THEM?!
DO YOU KNOW HOW WELL GUARDED THEIR SECURITY IS? NOT TO MENTION I JUST GOT BACK IN TOWN FROM A TWO-WEEK TRIP IN FISH CITY!!
I KNOW KING DAVID, YOU KNOW. I'M GOING TO HAVE TO TELL HIM HOW THE OCEAN POLICE ACCUSED ME WITHOUT ANY--
EVIDENCE?
WE HAVE CONCRETE EVIDENCE.

OCEAN TECH INDUSTRIES keeps both the magical weapons and a few MAGIC STONES in the same laboratory.

EVEN IF THE GUARDS IN THE FACILITY WEREN'T AN ISSUE, THE ROOM ITSELF IS GUARDED BY SECRET PASS CODES.

HAVING SUCH A HIGH POSITION THERE, I'M SURE YOU KNOW EXACTLY HOW SECURELY THAT ROOM IS GUARDED.

DURING THIS INVESTIGATION...

I LEARNED OCEAN TECH CHANGES THESE PASS CODES THREE TIMES A DAY, EVERY DAY.

AND THEY SEND THE NEW ASSIGNED UPDATED CODES TO THE PEOPLE WHO HAVE ACCESS TO THAT ROOM WHENEVER THEY DO.

WHAT'S THAT SUPPOSED TO MEAN TO ME, HUNH?!

ARE YOU SAYING THE CODE ENTERED WAS MINE?

THINK BACK, KID. I TOLD YOU I JUST GOT BACK THIS MORNING.

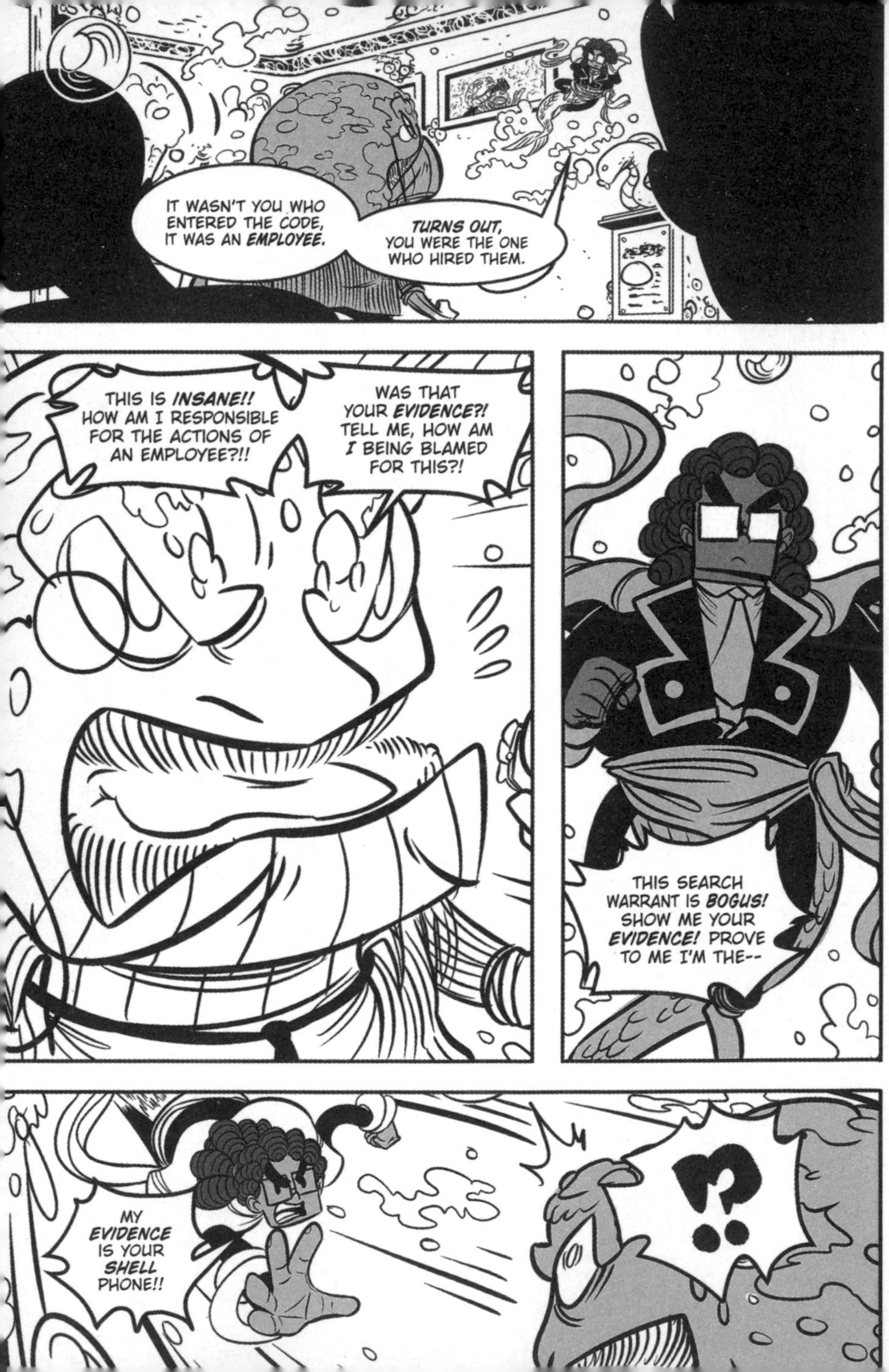
IT WASN'T YOU WHO ENTERED THE CODE, IT WAS AN *EMPLOYEE.*
TURNS OUT, YOU WERE THE ONE WHO HIRED THEM.
THIS IS *INSANE!!* HOW AM I RESPONSIBLE FOR THE ACTIONS OF AN EMPLOYEE?!!
WAS THAT YOUR *EVIDENCE?!* TELL ME, HOW AM *I* BEING BLAMED FOR THIS?!
THIS SEARCH WARRANT IS *BOGUS!* SHOW ME YOUR *EVIDENCE!* PROVE TO ME I'M THE--
MY *EVIDENCE* IS YOUR *SHELL* PHONE!!
?!

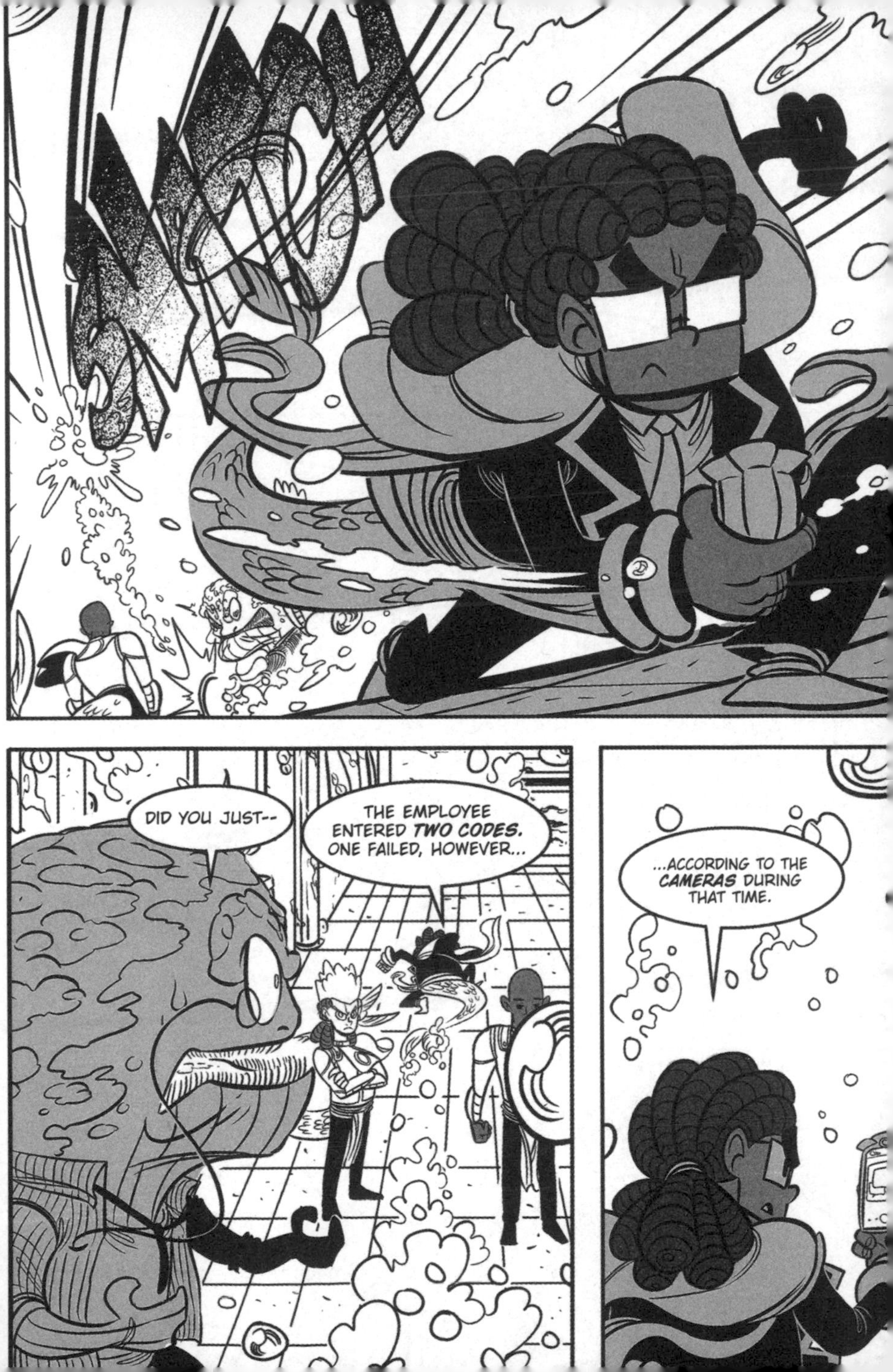
DID YOU JUST--
THE EMPLOYEE ENTERED TWO CODES. ONE FAILED, HOWEVER...
...ACCORDING TO THE CAMERAS DURING THAT TIME.

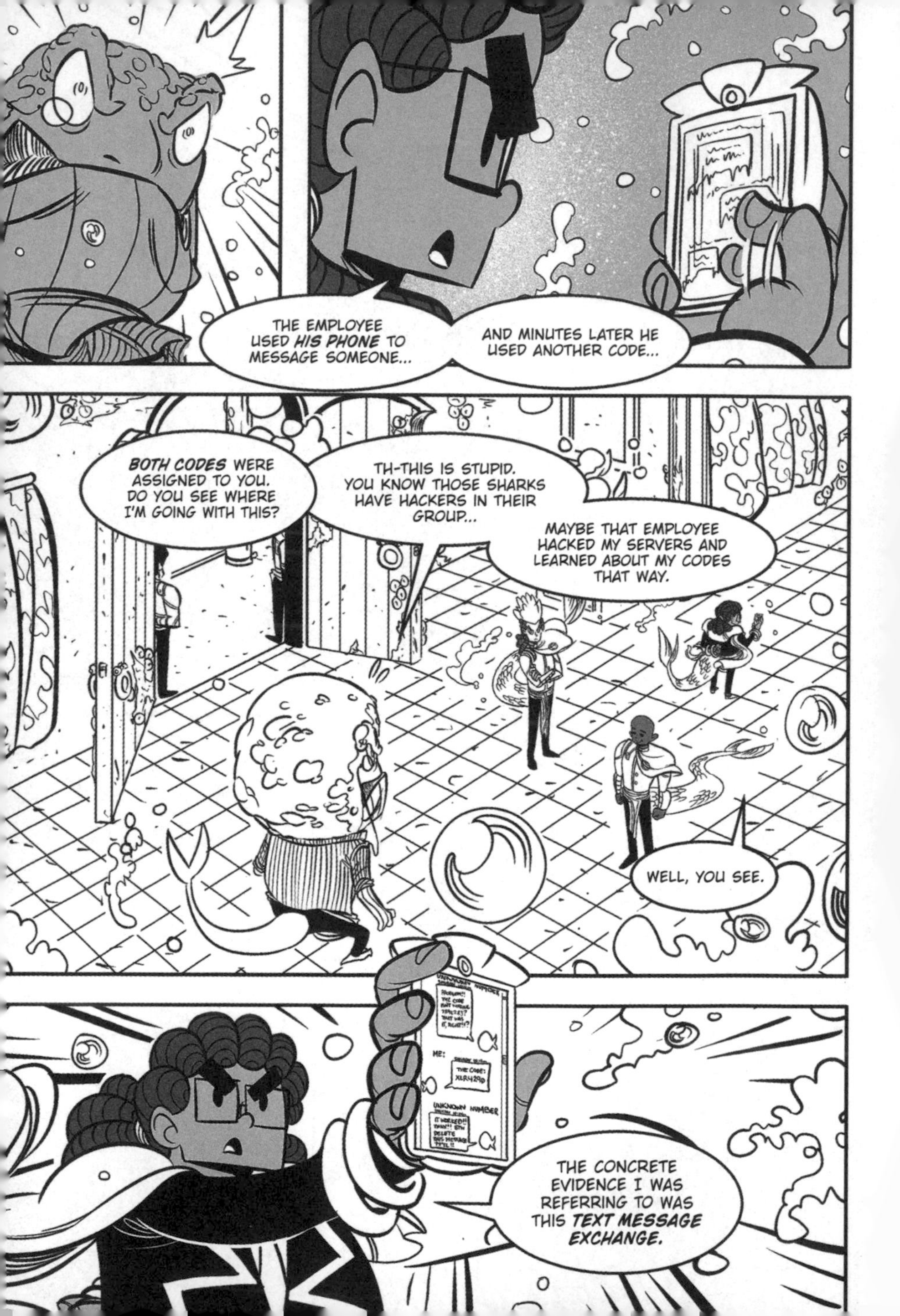
THE EMPLOYEE USED *HIS PHONE* TO MESSAGE SOMEONE...
AND MINUTES LATER HE USED ANOTHER CODE...
BOTH CODES WERE ASSIGNED TO YOU. DO YOU SEE WHERE I'M GOING WITH THIS?
TH-THIS IS STUPID. YOU KNOW THOSE SHARKS HAVE HACKERS IN THEIR GROUP...
MAYBE THAT EMPLOYEE HACKED MY SERVERS AND LEARNED ABOUT MY CODES THAT WAY.
WELL, YOU SEE.
ME:
THE CODE: XLR4290
UNKNOWN NUMBER
IT WORKED!!
THE CONCRETE EVIDENCE I WAS REFERRING TO WAS THIS *TEXT MESSAGE EXCHANGE.*

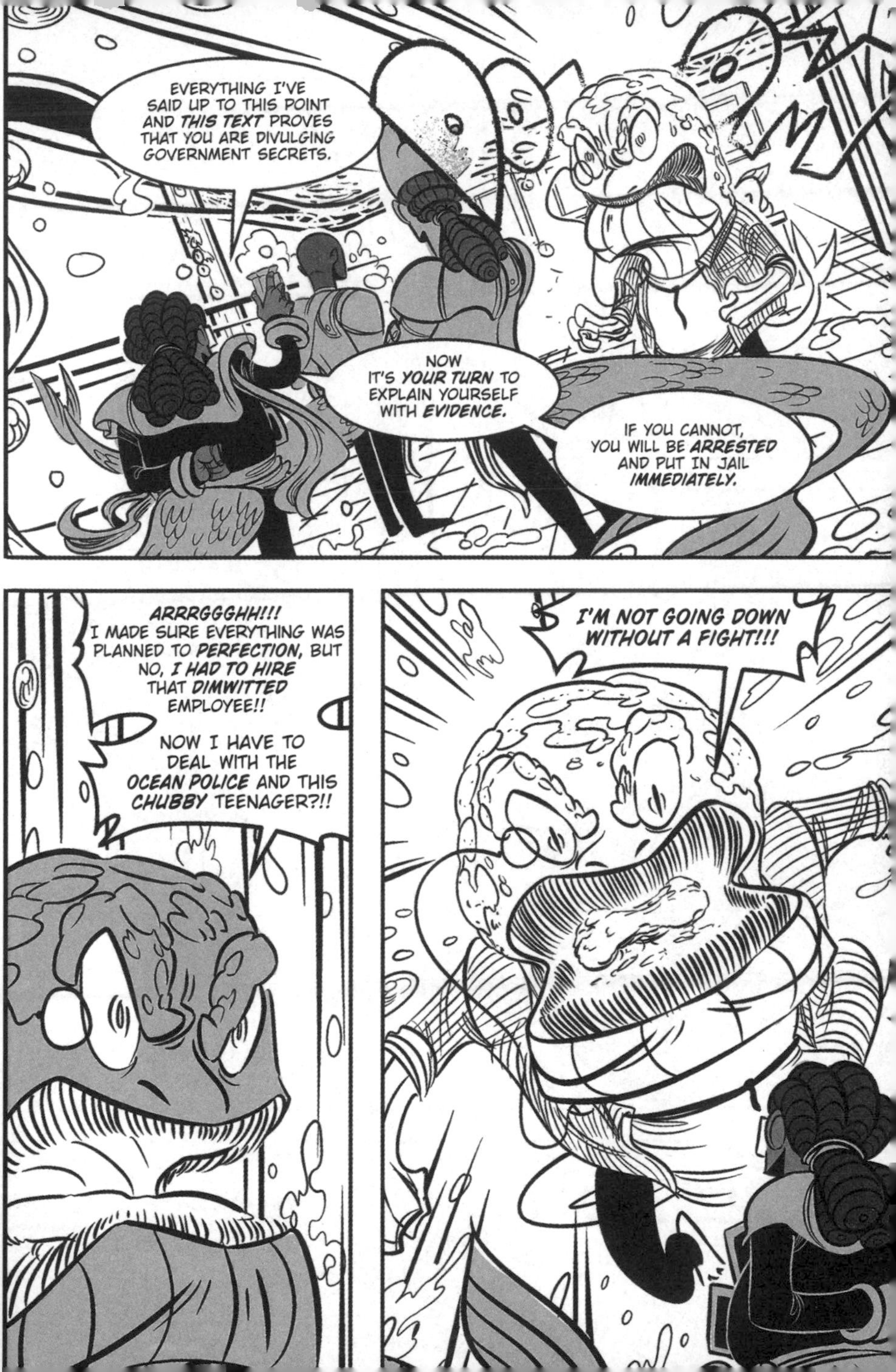
EVERYTHING I'VE SAID UP TO THIS POINT AND *THIS TEXT* PROVES THAT YOU ARE DIVULGING GOVERNMENT SECRETS.
NOW IT'S *YOUR TURN* TO EXPLAIN YOURSELF WITH *EVIDENCE.*
IF YOU CANNOT, YOU WILL BE *ARRESTED* AND PUT IN JAIL *IMMEDIATELY.*
ARRRGGGHH!!! I MADE SURE EVERYTHING WAS PLANNED TO *PERFECTION,* BUT NO, *I HAD TO HIRE* THAT *DIMWITTED* EMPLOYEE!!
NOW I HAVE TO DEAL WITH THE *OCEAN POLICE* AND THIS *CHUBBY* TEENAGER?!!
I'M NOT GOING DOWN WITHOUT A FIGHT!!!

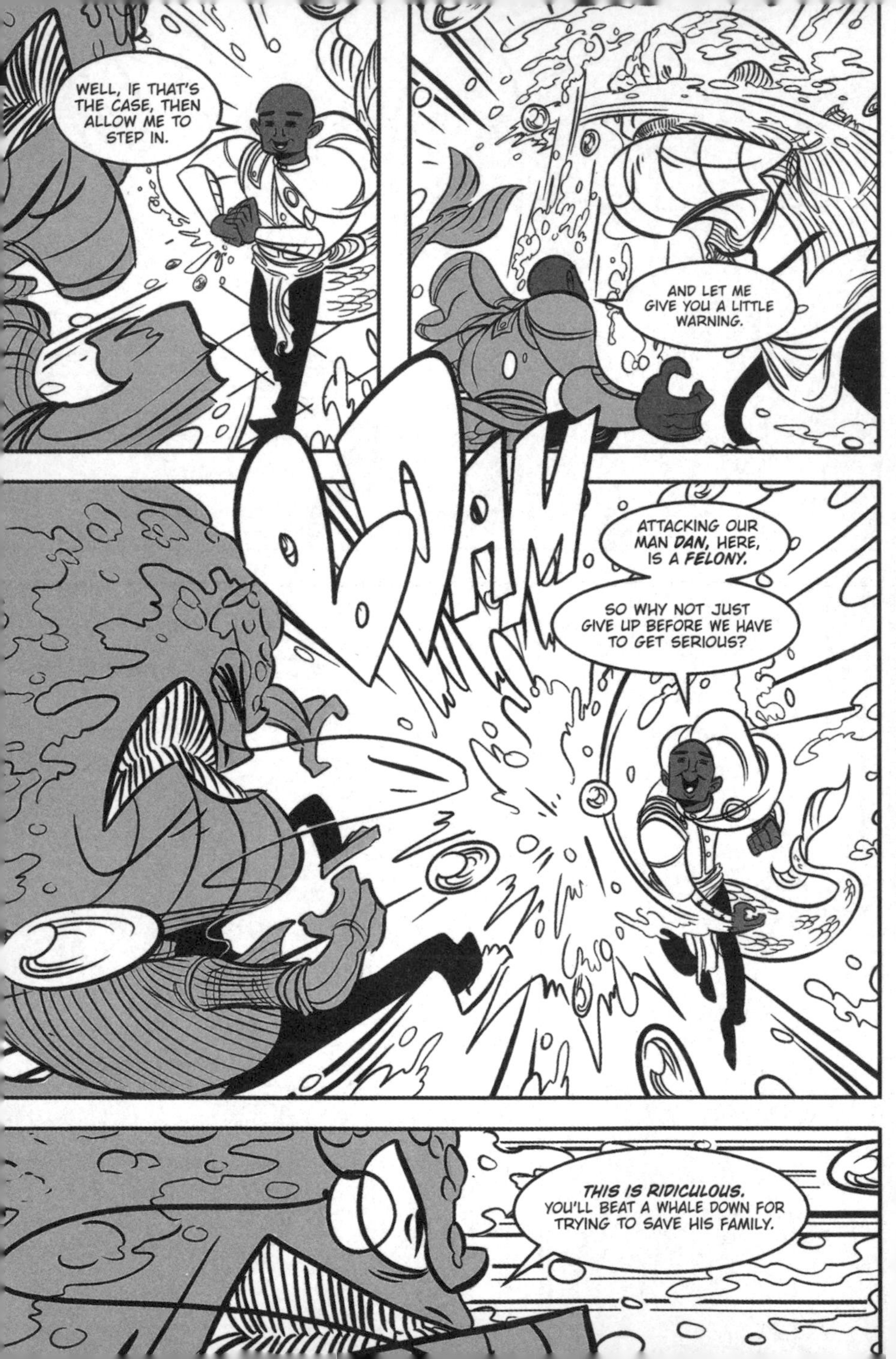
WELL, IF THAT'S THE CASE, THEN ALLOW ME TO STEP IN.
AND LET ME GIVE YOU A LITTLE WARNING.
ATTACKING OUR MAN *DAN,* HERE, IS A *FELONY.*
SO WHY NOT JUST GIVE UP BEFORE WE HAVE TO GET SERIOUS?
THIS IS RIDICULOUS. YOU'LL BEAT A WHALE DOWN FOR TRYING TO SAVE HIS FAMILY.

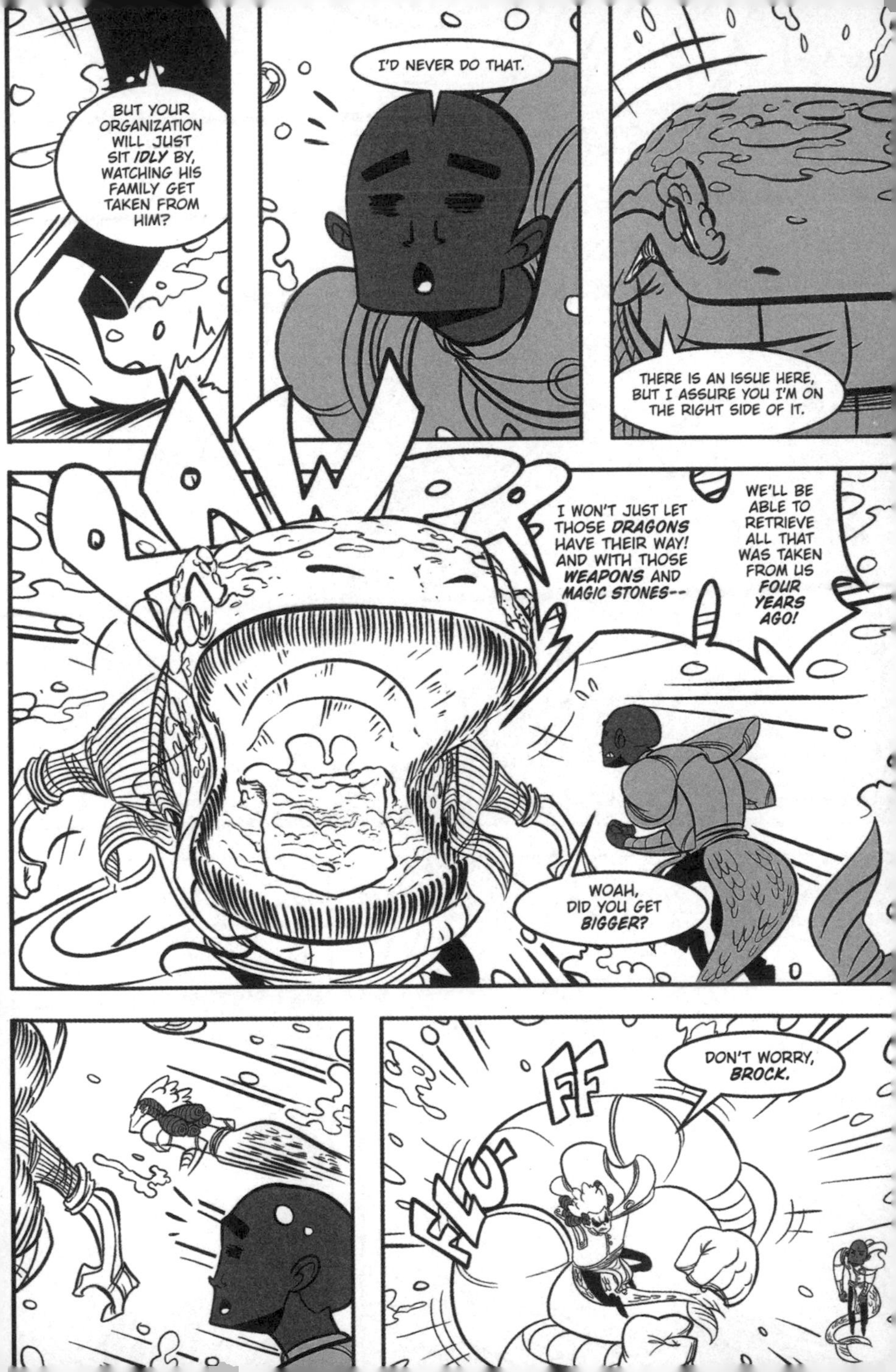
BUT YOUR ORGANIZATION WILL JUST SIT *IDLY* BY, WATCHING HIS FAMILY GET TAKEN FROM HIM?
I'D NEVER DO THAT.
THERE IS AN ISSUE HERE, BUT I ASSURE YOU I'M ON THE RIGHT SIDE OF IT.
I WON'T JUST LET THOSE *DRAGONS* HAVE THEIR WAY! AND WITH THOSE *WEAPONS* AND *MAGIC STONES*--
WE'LL BE ABLE TO RETRIEVE ALL THAT WAS TAKEN FROM US *FOUR YEARS AGO!*
WOAH, DID YOU GET *BIGGER?*
FLU-FF
DON'T WORRY, *BROCK.*

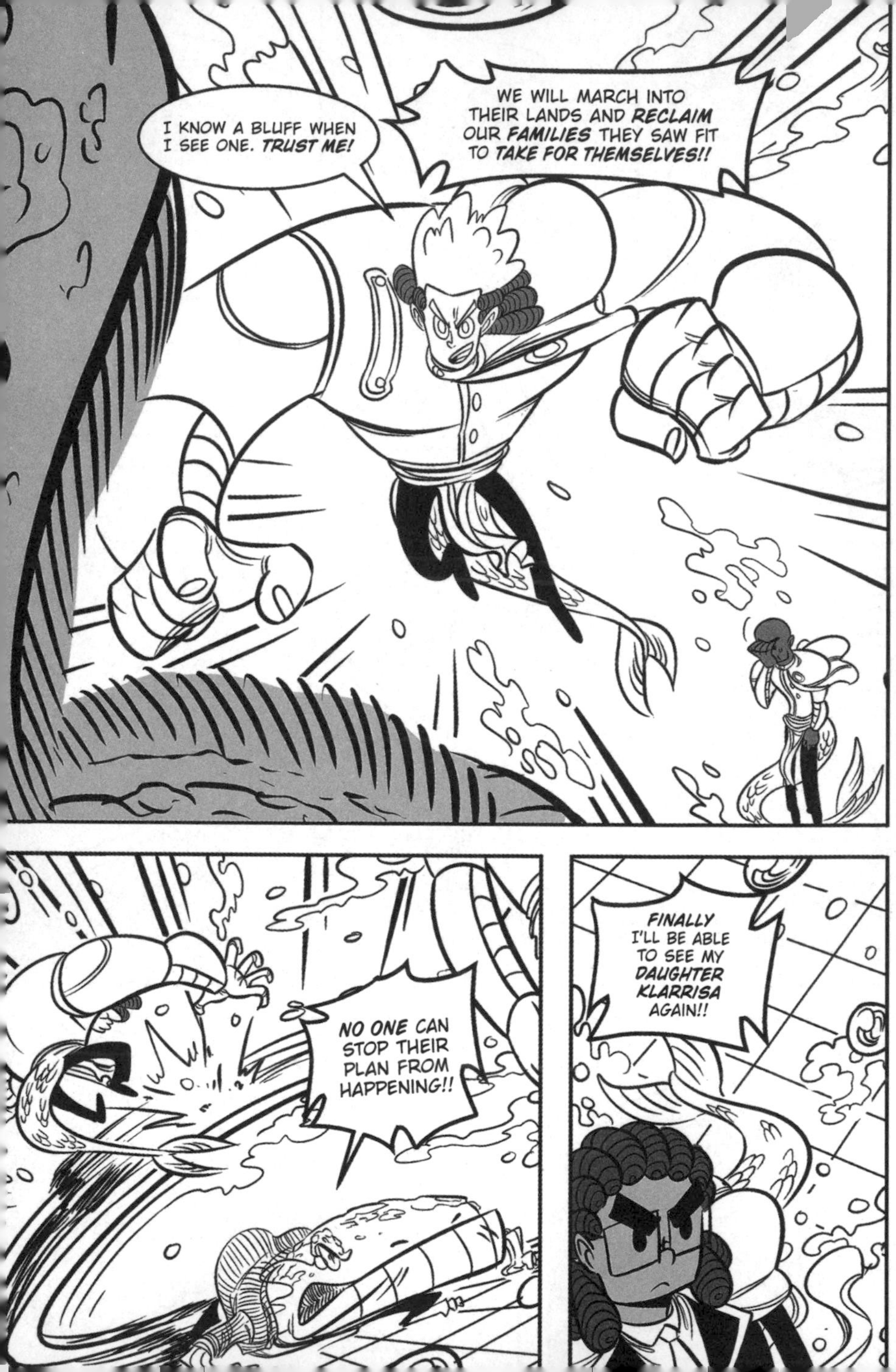

I KNOW A BLUFF WHEN I SEE ONE. TRUST ME!
WE WILL MARCH INTO THEIR LANDS AND RECLAIM OUR FAMILIES THEY SAW FIT TO TAKE FOR THEMSELVES!!
NO ONE CAN STOP THEIR PLAN FROM HAPPENING!!
FINALLY I'LL BE ABLE TO SEE MY DAUGHTER KLARRISA AGAIN!!

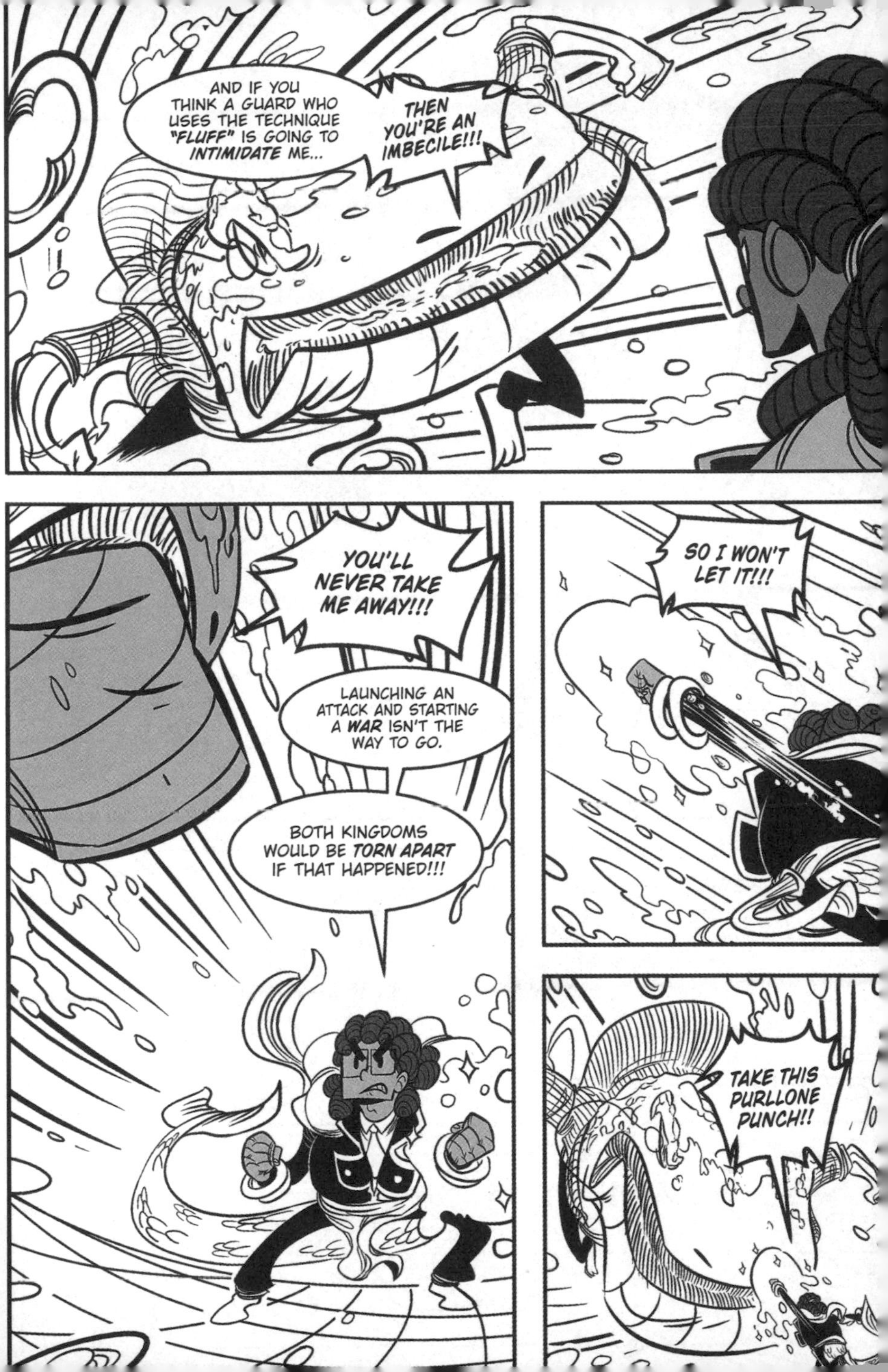
AND IF YOU THINK A GUARD WHO USES THE TECHNIQUE "FLUFF" IS GOING TO INTIMIDATE ME...
THEN YOU'RE AN IMBECILE!!!
!
YOU'LL NEVER TAKE ME AWAY!!!
LAUNCHING AN ATTACK AND STARTING A WAR ISN'T THE WAY TO GO.
BOTH KINGDOMS WOULD BE TORN APART IF THAT HAPPENED!!!
SO I WON'T LET IT!!!
TAKE THIS PURLLONE PUNCH!!

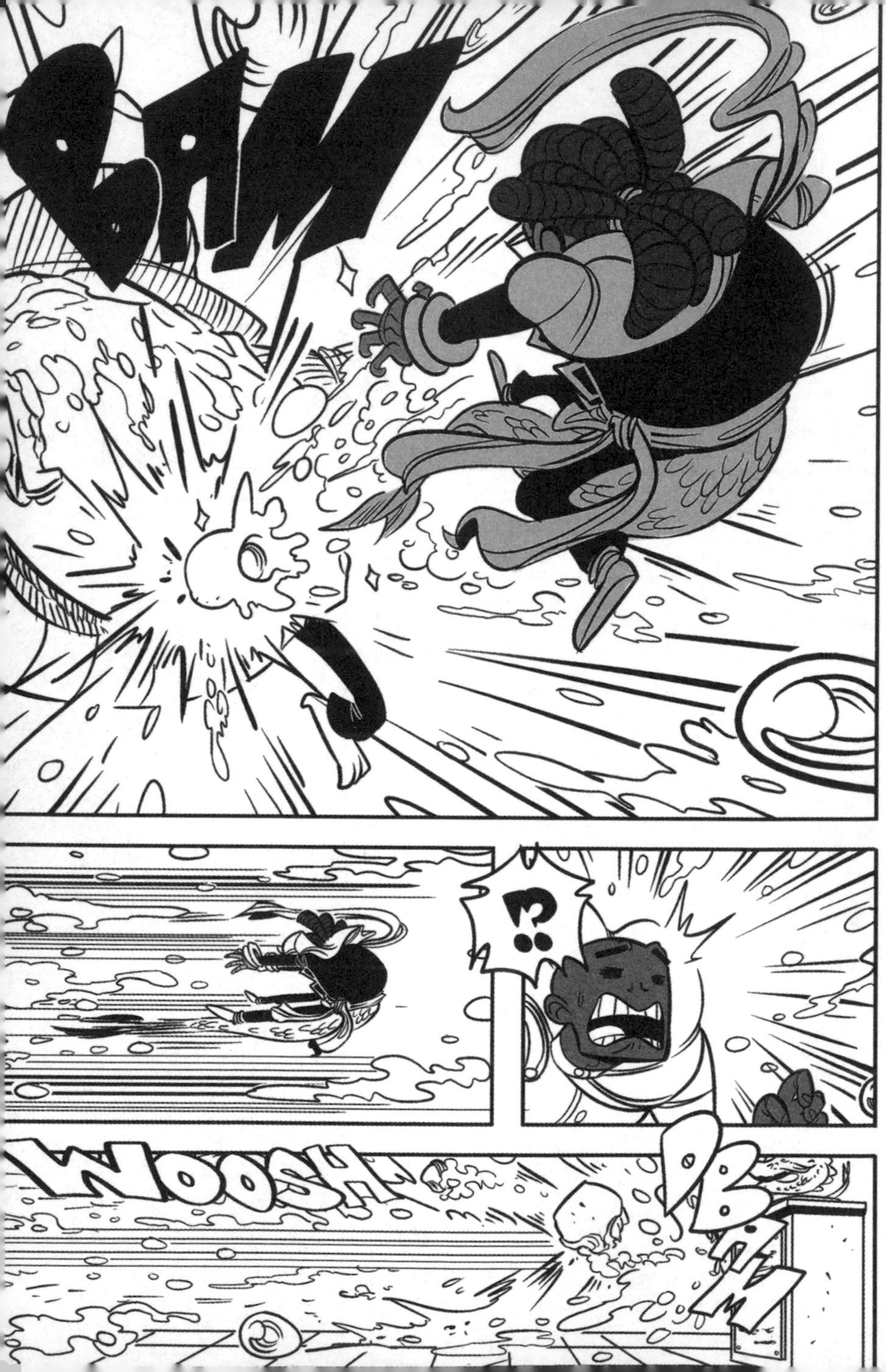
BAM
!?
WOOSH!

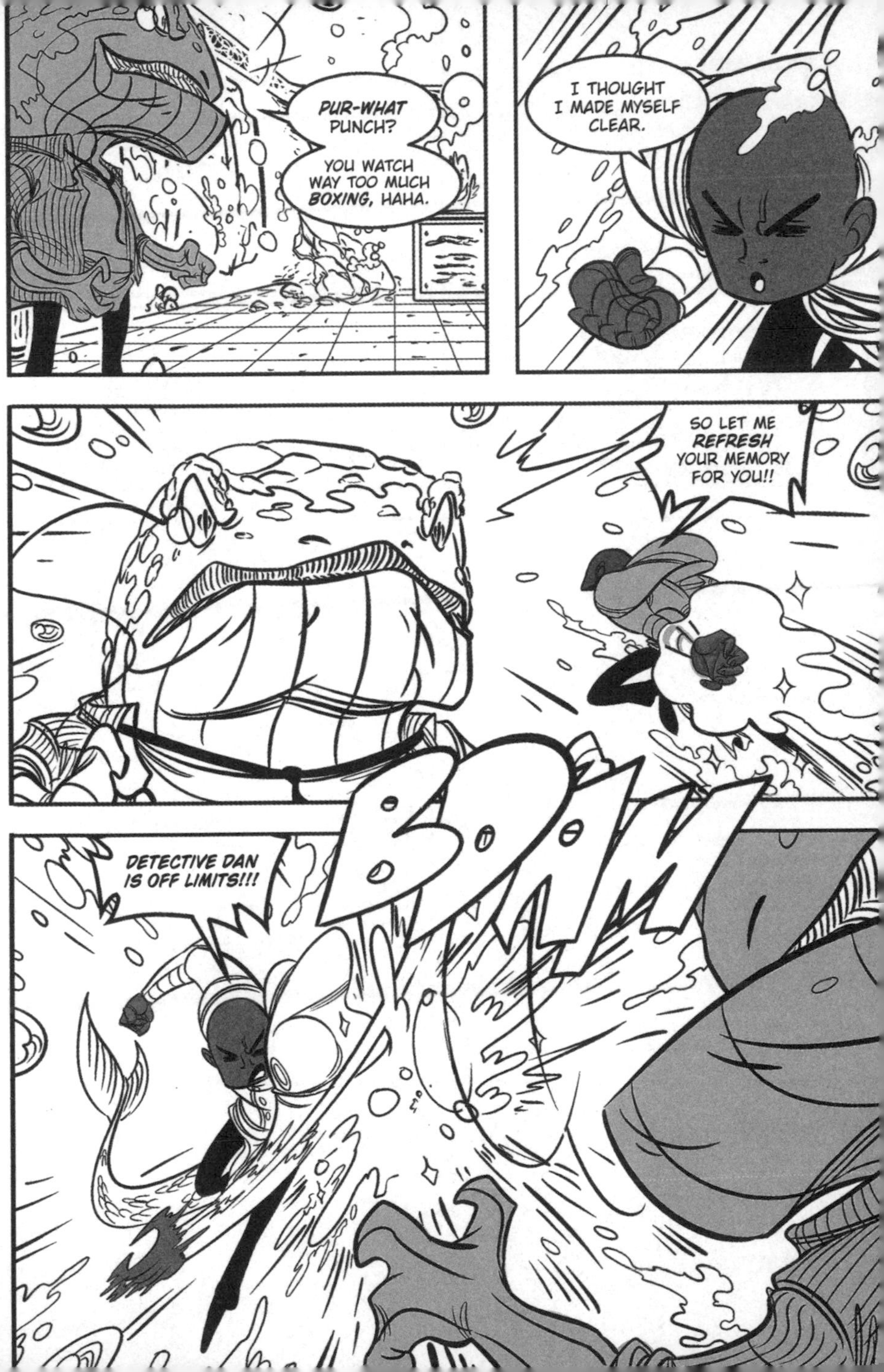
PUR-WHAT PUNCH?
YOU WATCH WAY TOO MUCH BOXING, HAHA.
I THOUGHT I MADE MYSELF CLEAR.
SO LET ME REFRESH YOUR MEMORY FOR YOU!!
BOOM
DETECTIVE DAN IS OFF LIMITS!!!

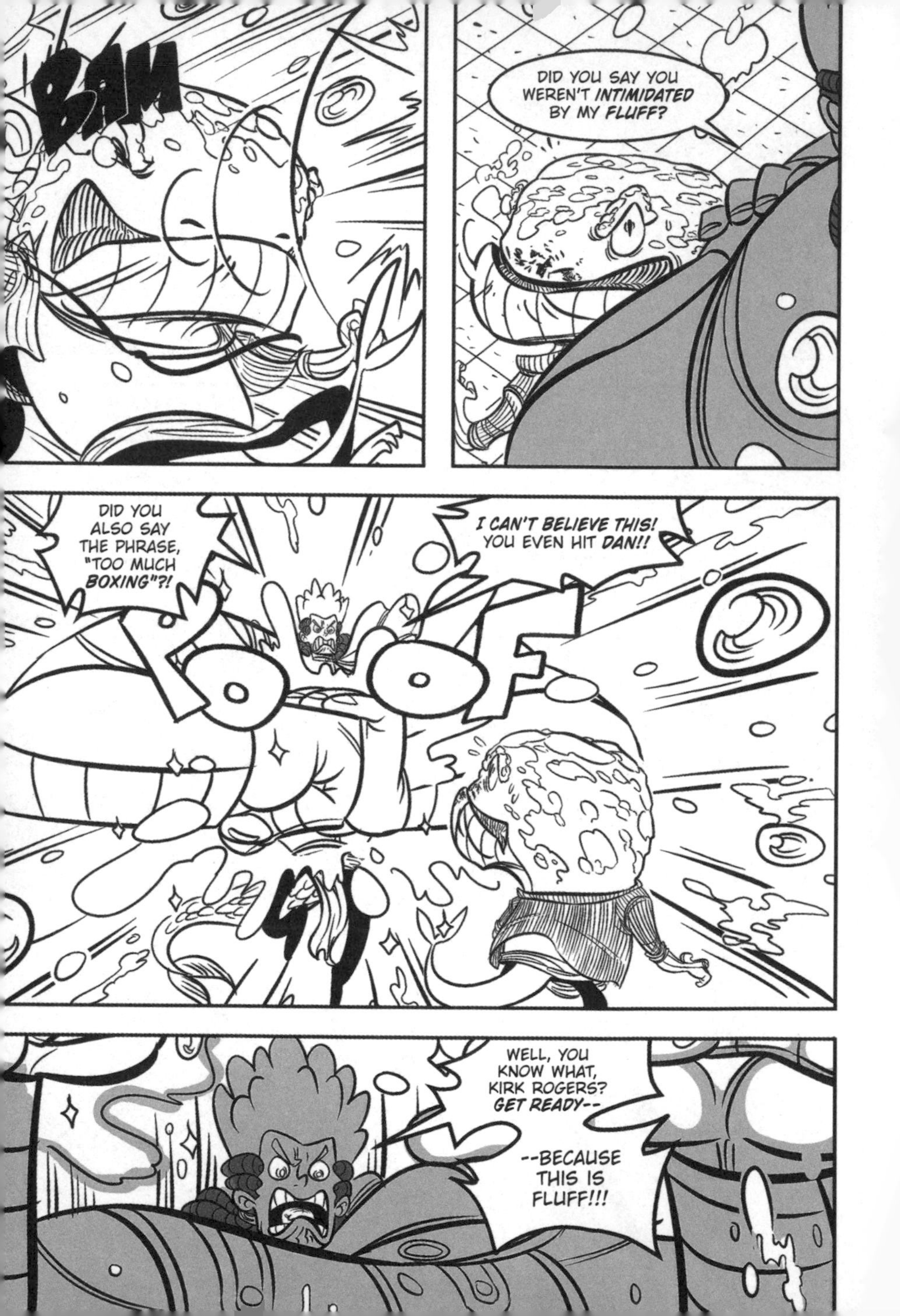
BAM
DID YOU SAY YOU WEREN'T *INTIMIDATED* BY MY *FLUFF?*
DID YOU ALSO SAY THE PHRASE, "TOO MUCH *BOXING*"?!
I CAN'T BELIEVE THIS! YOU EVEN HIT *DAN!!*
WOOF
WELL, YOU KNOW WHAT, KIRK ROGERS? *GET READY--*
--BECAUSE THIS IS FLUFF!!!

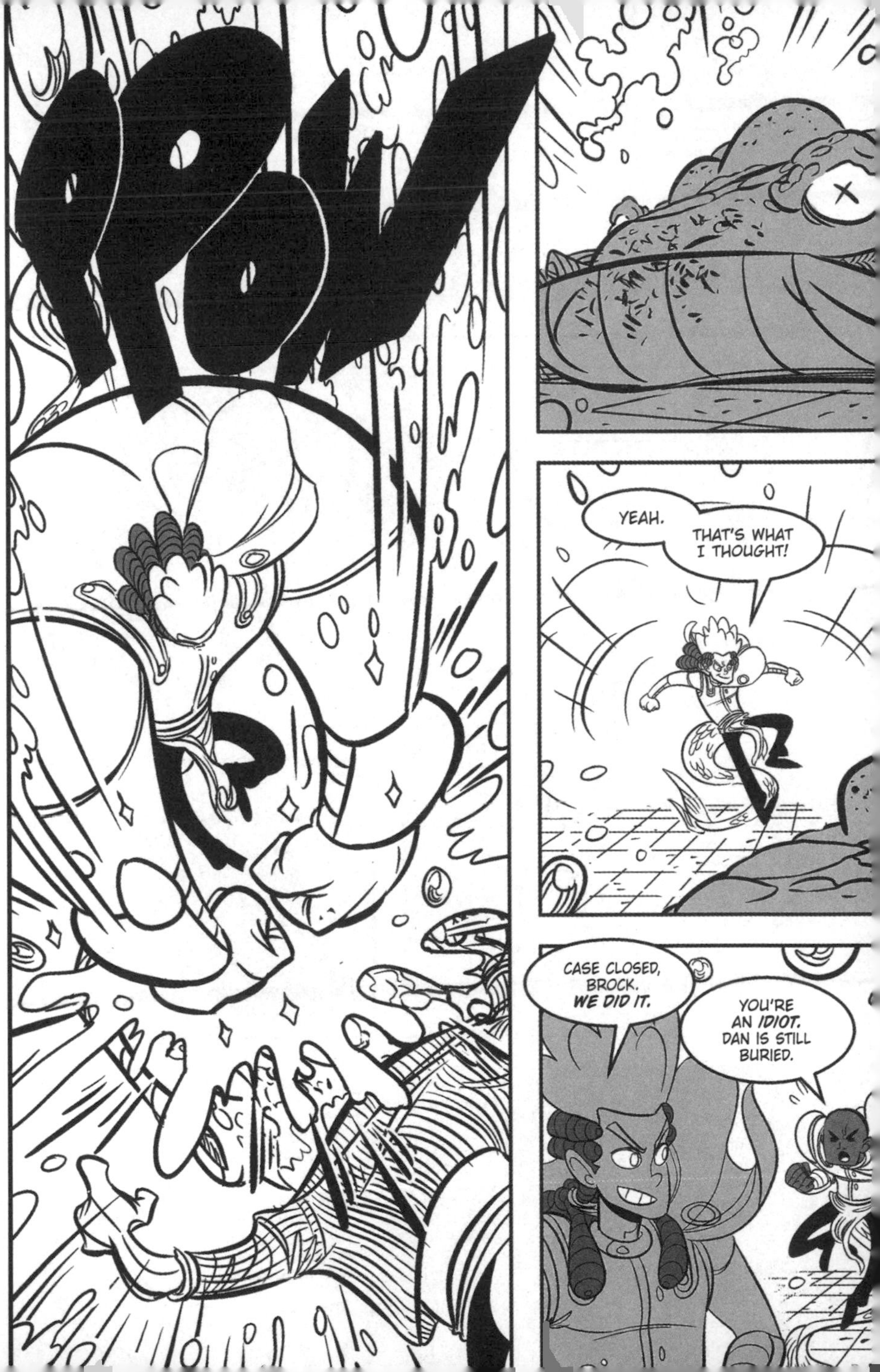
POW!
YEAH.
THAT'S WHAT I THOUGHT!
CASE CLOSED, BROCK. **WE DID IT.**
YOU'RE AN *IDIOT.* DAN IS STILL BURIED.

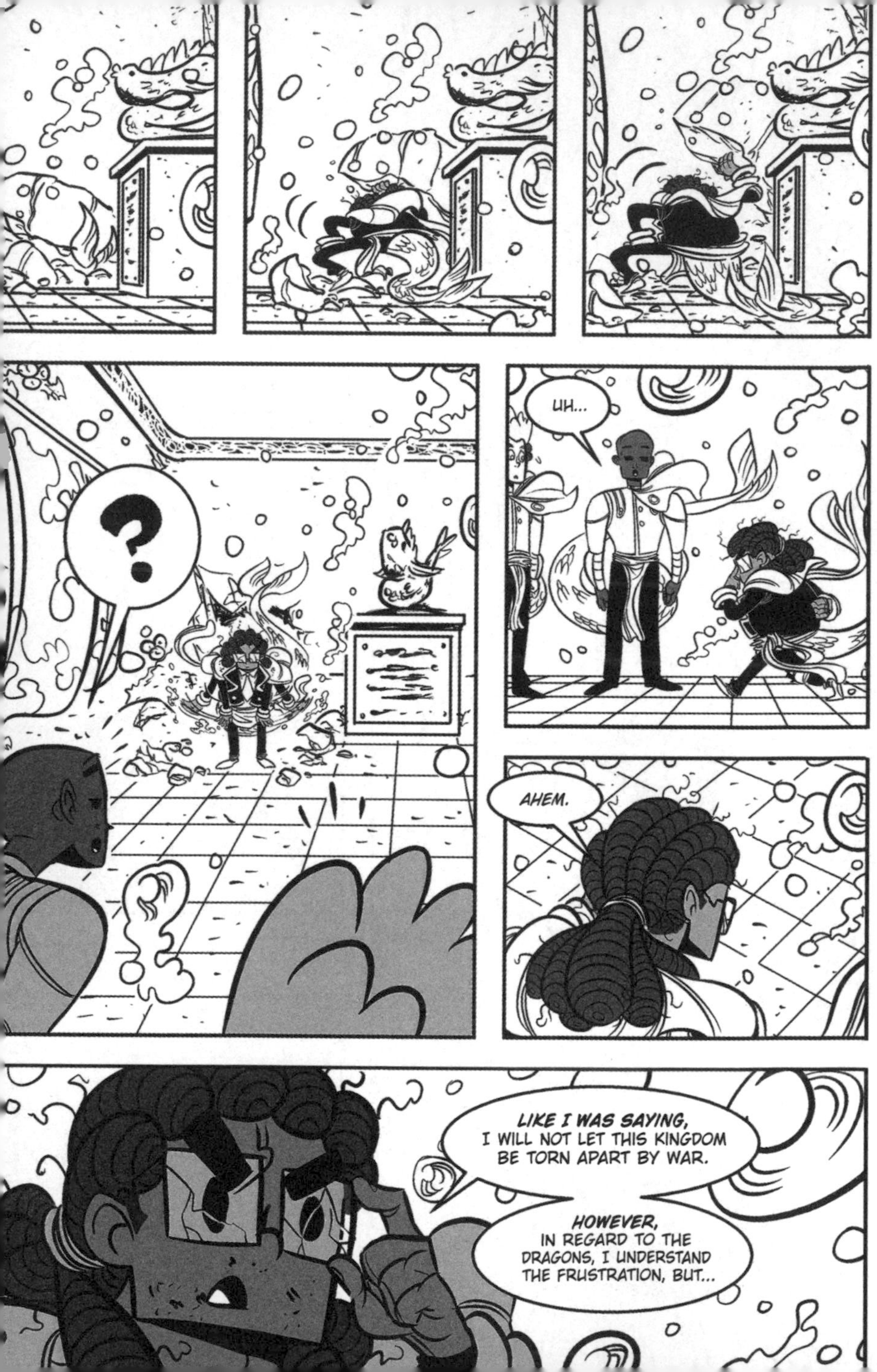
?
UH...
AHEM.
LIKE I WAS SAYING, I WILL NOT LET THIS KINGDOM BE TORN APART BY WAR.
HOWEVER, IN REGARD TO THE DRAGONS, I UNDERSTAND THE FRUSTRATION, BUT...

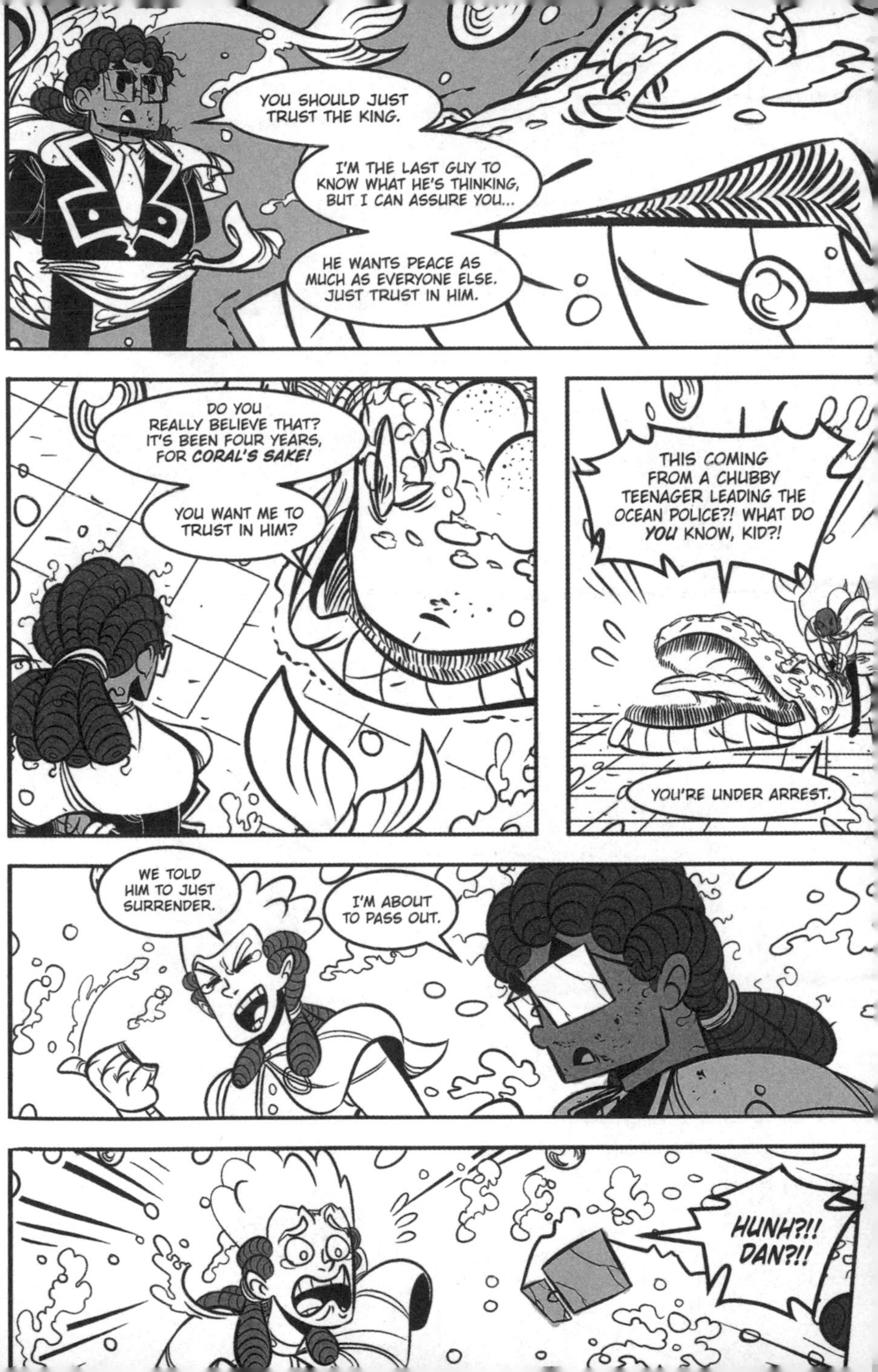
YOU SHOULD JUST TRUST THE KING.
I'M THE LAST GUY TO KNOW WHAT HE'S THINKING, BUT I CAN ASSURE YOU...
HE WANTS PEACE AS MUCH AS EVERYONE ELSE. JUST TRUST IN HIM.
DO YOU REALLY BELIEVE THAT? IT'S BEEN FOUR YEARS, FOR ***CORAL'S SAKE!***
YOU WANT ME TO TRUST IN HIM?
THIS COMING FROM A CHUBBY TEENAGER LEADING THE OCEAN POLICE?! WHAT DO ***YOU*** KNOW, KID?!
YOU'RE UNDER ARREST.
WE TOLD HIM TO JUST SURRENDER.
I'M ABOUT TO PASS OUT.
HUNH?!! DAN?!!

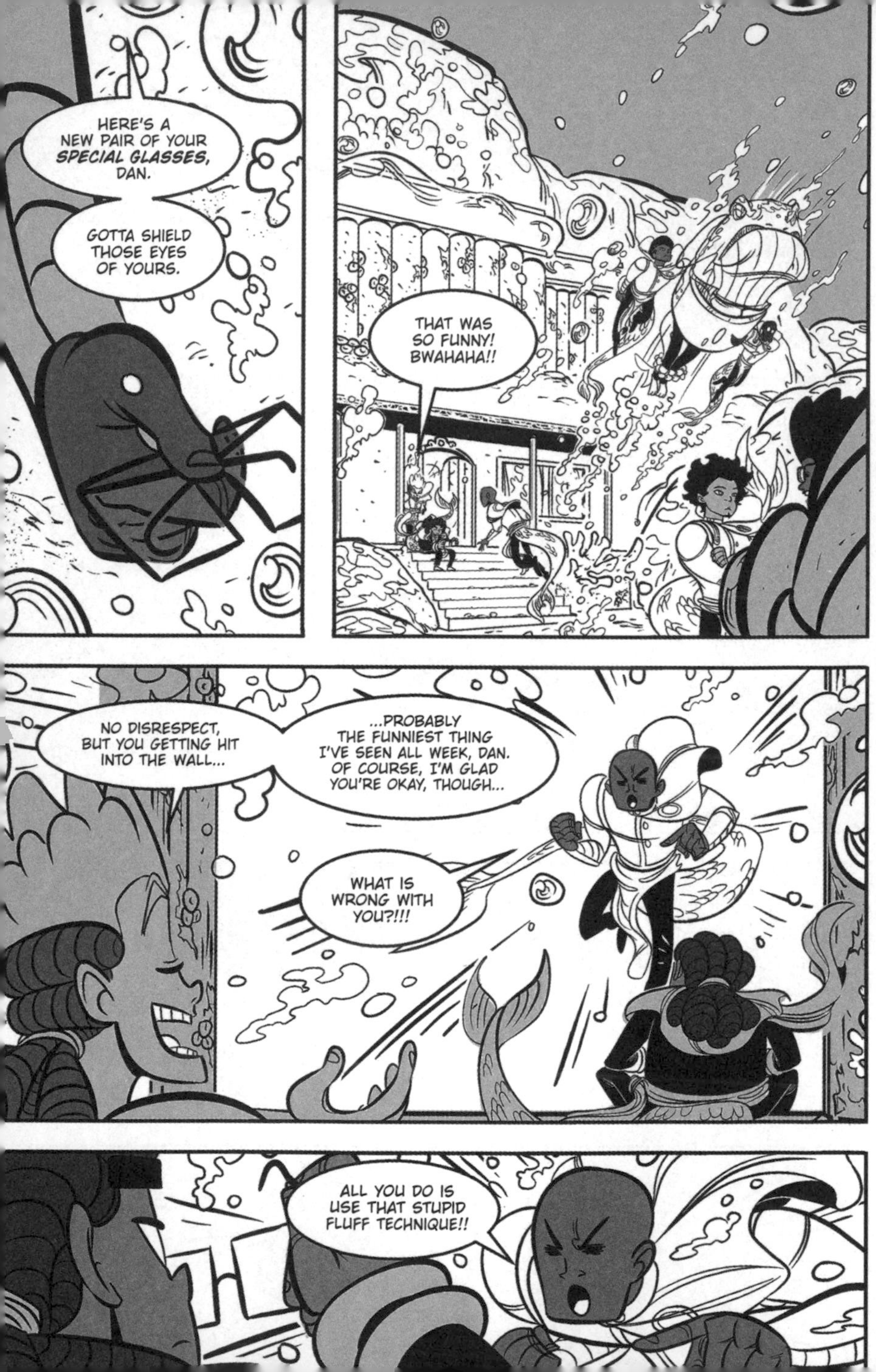
HERE'S A NEW PAIR OF YOUR *SPECIAL GLASSES,* DAN.
GOTTA SHIELD THOSE EYES OF YOURS.
THAT WAS SO FUNNY! BWAHAHA!!
NO DISRESPECT, BUT YOU GETTING HIT INTO THE WALL...
...PROBABLY THE FUNNIEST THING I'VE SEEN ALL WEEK, DAN. OF COURSE, I'M GLAD YOU'RE OKAY, THOUGH...
WHAT IS WRONG WITH YOU?!!!
ALL YOU DO IS USE THAT STUPID FLUFF TECHNIQUE!!

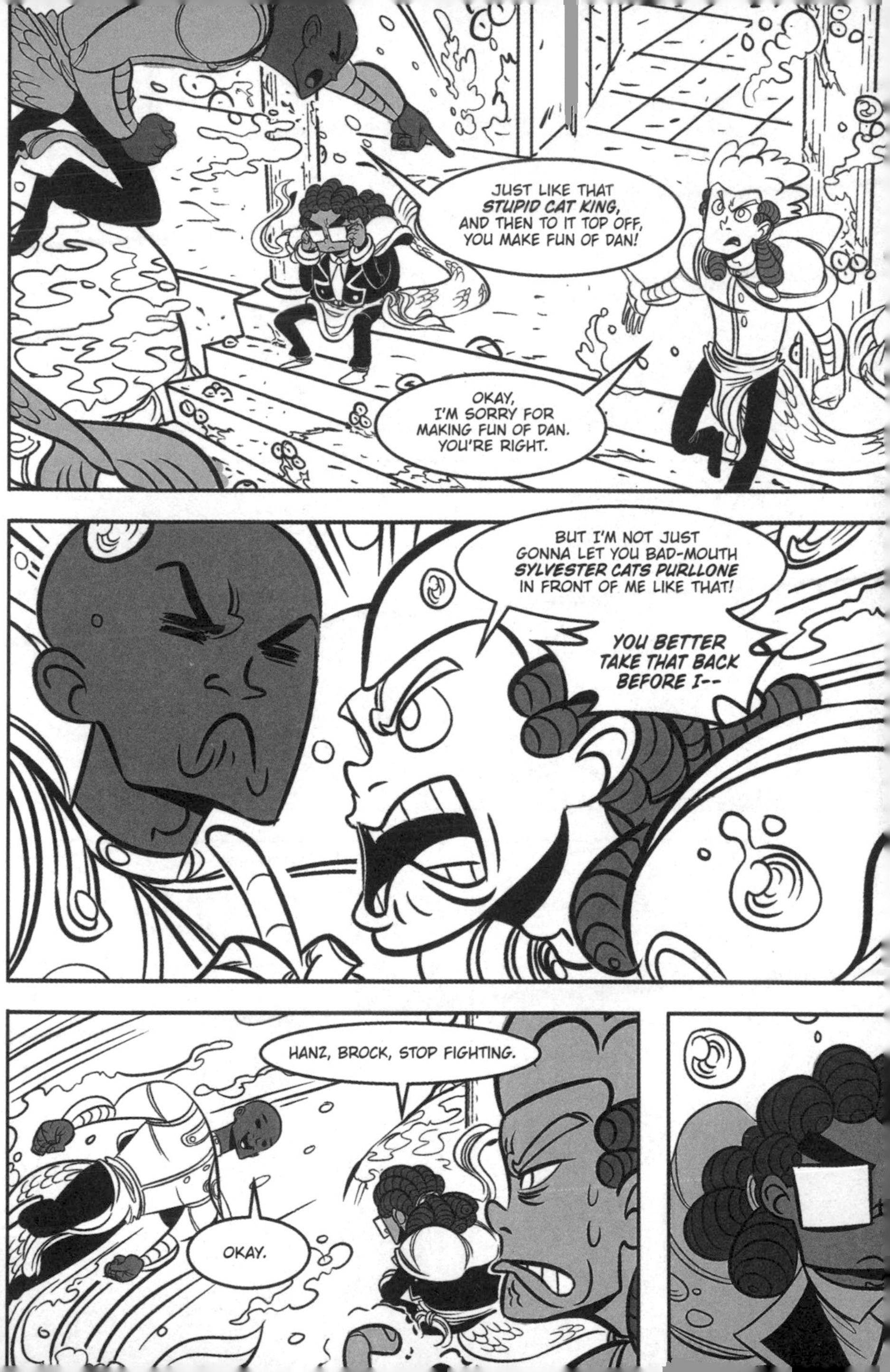
JUST LIKE THAT STUPID CAT KING, AND THEN TO IT TOP OFF, YOU MAKE FUN OF DAN!
OKAY, I'M SORRY FOR MAKING FUN OF DAN. YOU'RE RIGHT.
BUT I'M NOT JUST GONNA LET YOU BAD-MOUTH SYLVESTER CATS PURLLONE IN FRONT OF ME LIKE THAT!
YOU BETTER TAKE THAT BACK BEFORE I--
HANZ, BROCK, STOP FIGHTING.
OKAY.

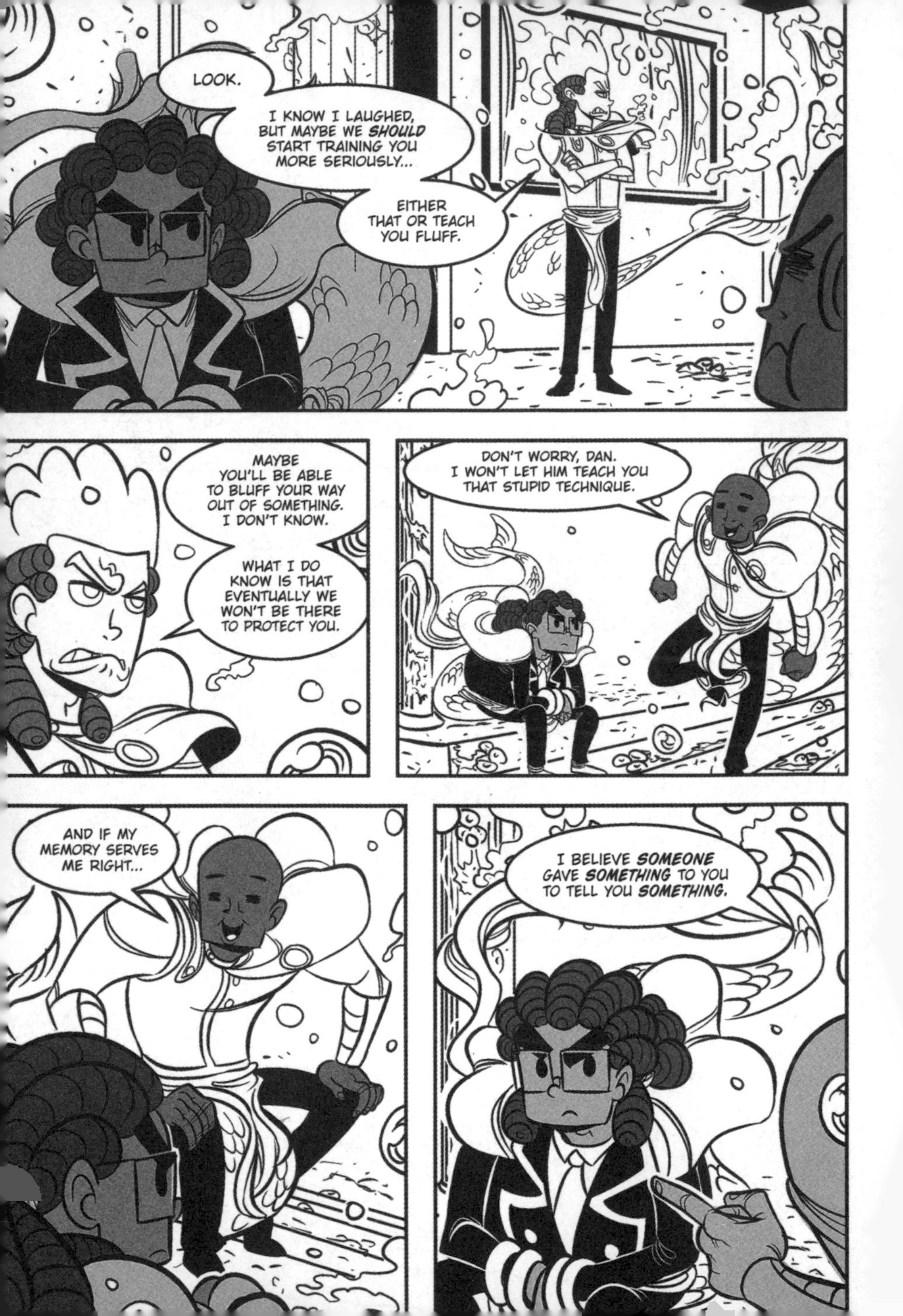
LOOK.
I KNOW I LAUGHED, BUT MAYBE WE SHOULD START TRAINING YOU MORE SERIOUSLY...
EITHER THAT OR TEACH YOU FLUFF.
MAYBE YOU'LL BE ABLE TO BLUFF YOUR WAY OUT OF SOMETHING. I DON'T KNOW.
WHAT I DO KNOW IS THAT EVENTUALLY WE WON'T BE THERE TO PROTECT YOU.
DON'T WORRY, DAN. I WON'T LET HIM TEACH YOU THAT STUPID TECHNIQUE.
AND IF MY MEMORY SERVES ME RIGHT...
I BELIEVE SOMEONE GAVE SOMETHING TO YOU TO TELL YOU SOMETHING.

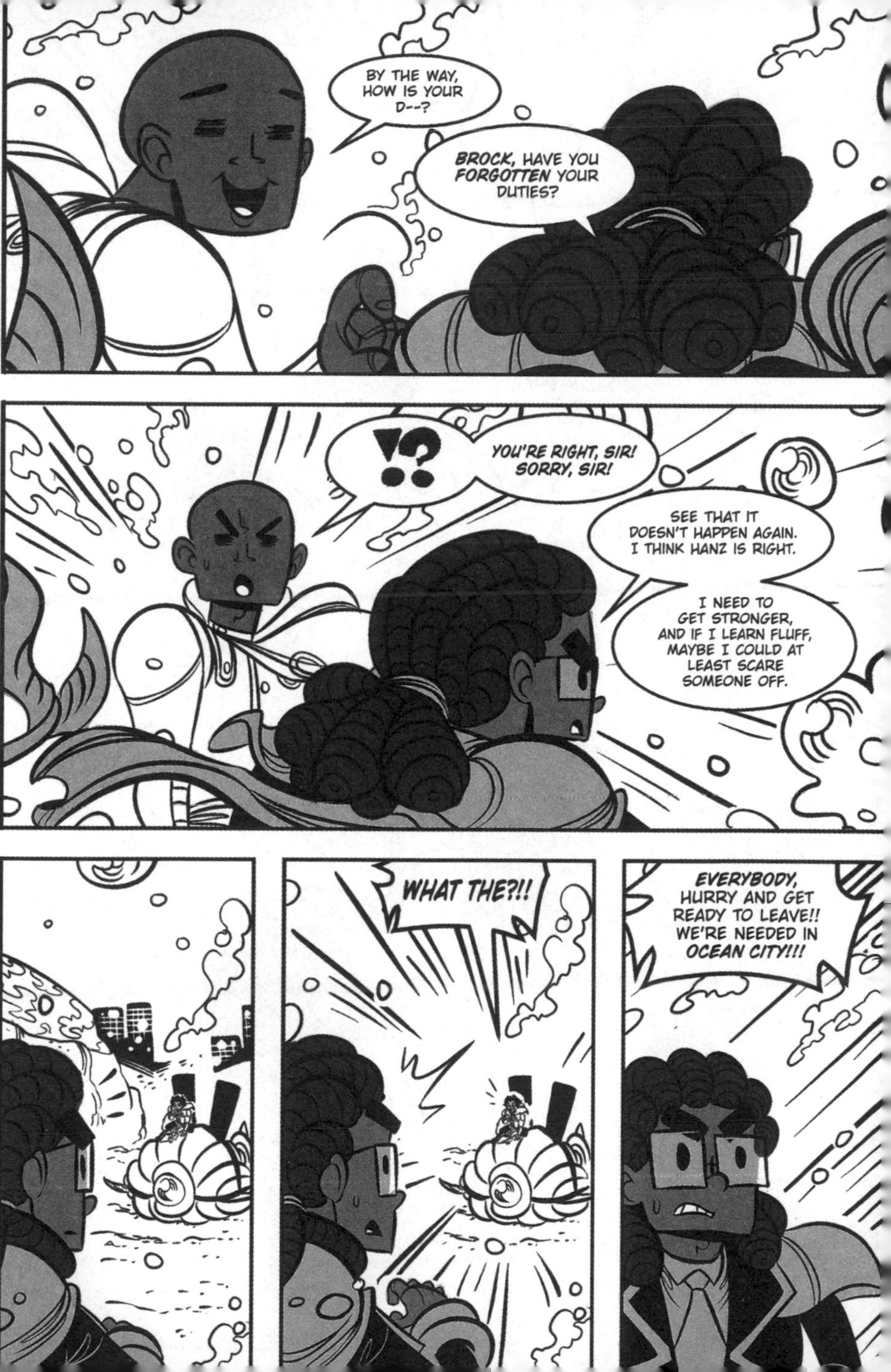
BY THE WAY, HOW IS YOUR D--?
BROCK, HAVE YOU FORGOTTEN YOUR DUTIES?
!?
YOU'RE RIGHT, SIR! SORRY, SIR!
SEE THAT IT DOESN'T HAPPEN AGAIN. I THINK HANZ IS RIGHT.
I NEED TO GET STRONGER, AND IF I LEARN FLUFF, MAYBE I COULD AT LEAST SCARE SOMEONE OFF.
WHAT THE?!!
EVERYBODY, HURRY AND GET READY TO LEAVE!! WE'RE NEEDED IN OCEAN CITY!!!

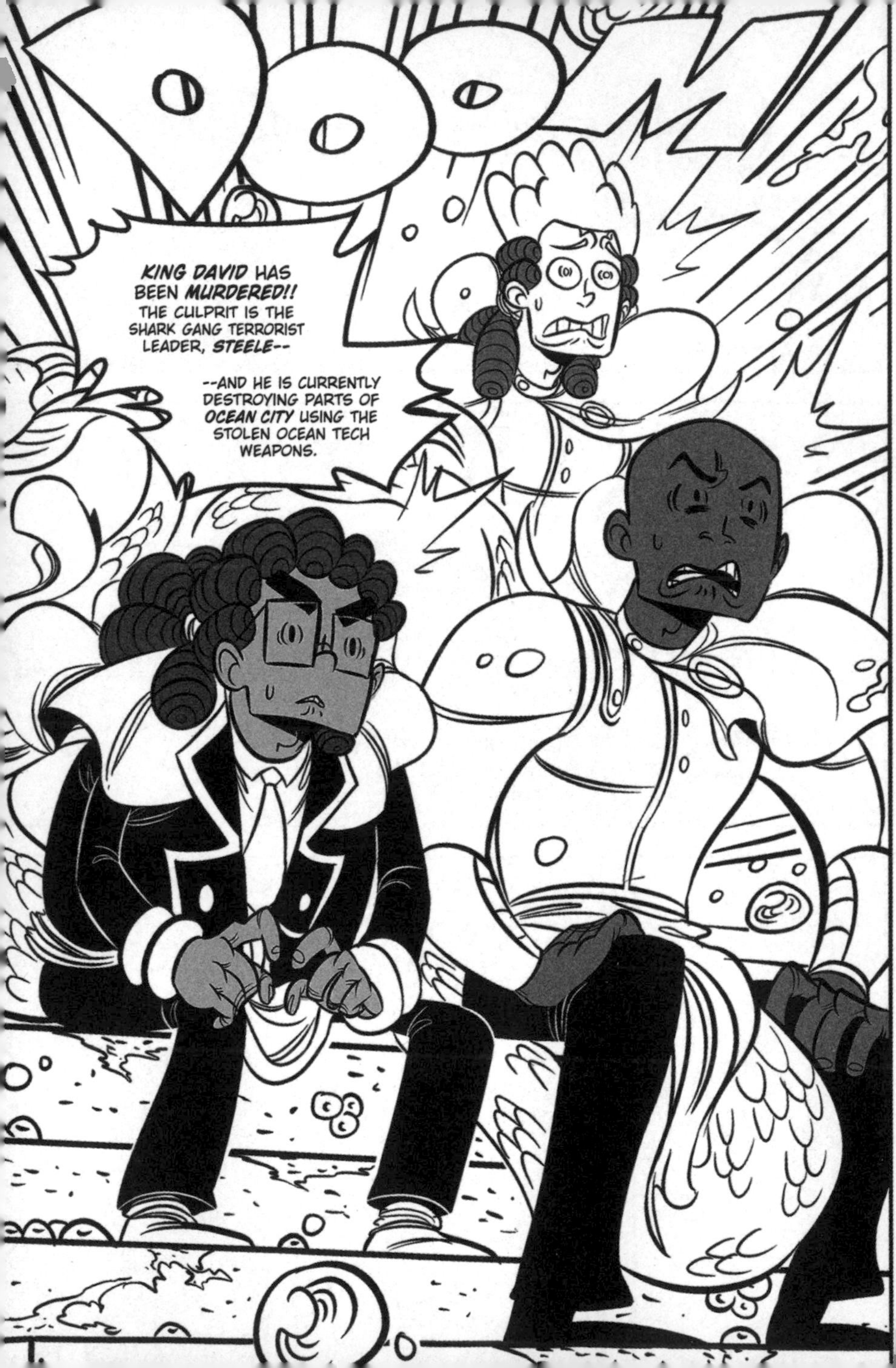
DOOM!
KING DAVID HAS BEEN MURDERED!! THE CULPRIT IS THE SHARK GANG TERRORIST LEADER, STEELE--
--AND HE IS CURRENTLY DESTROYING PARTS OF OCEAN CITY USING THE STOLEN OCEAN TECH WEAPONS.

HAMMER

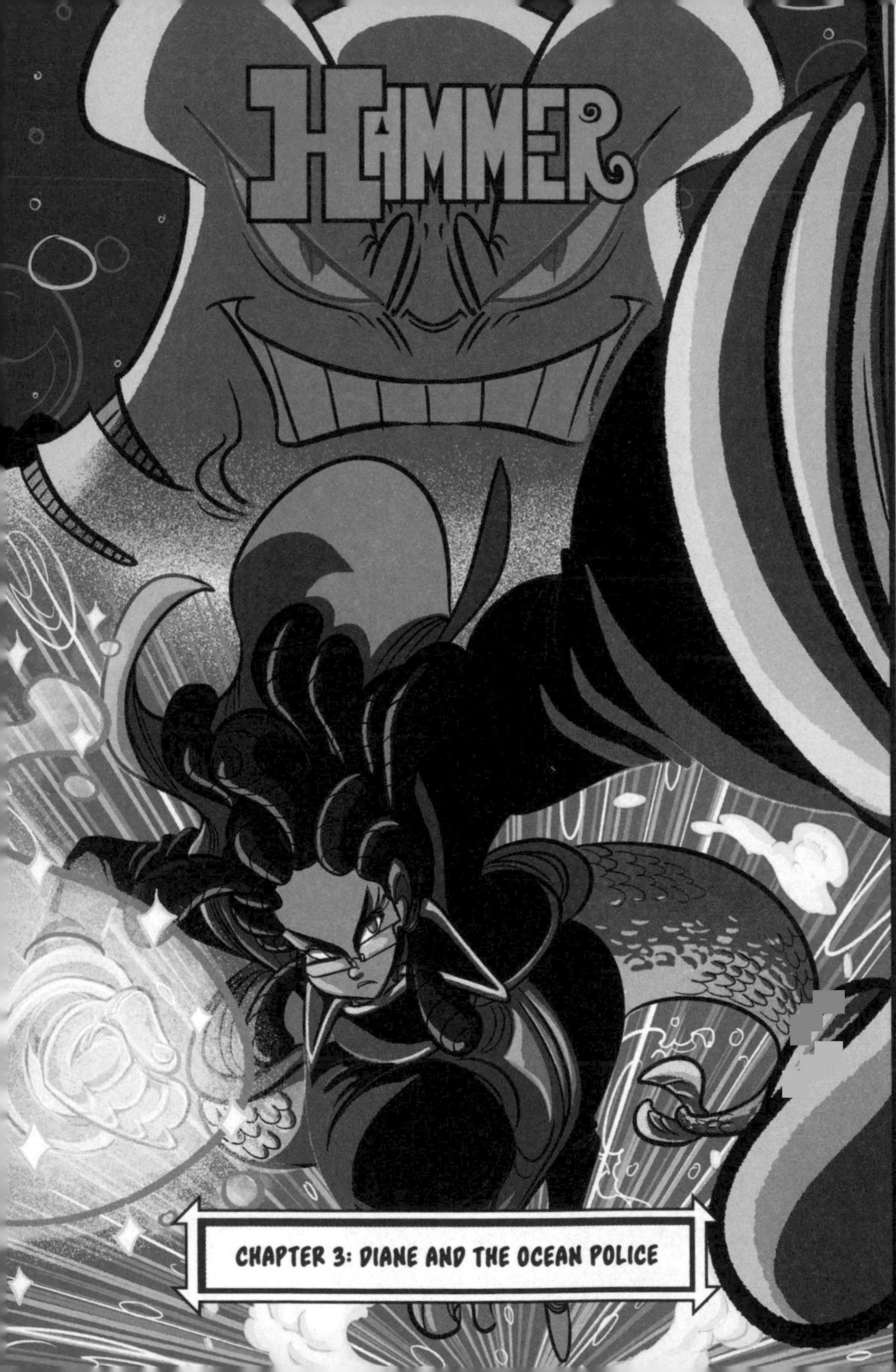
HAMMER
CHAPTER 3: DIANE AND THE OCEAN POLICE

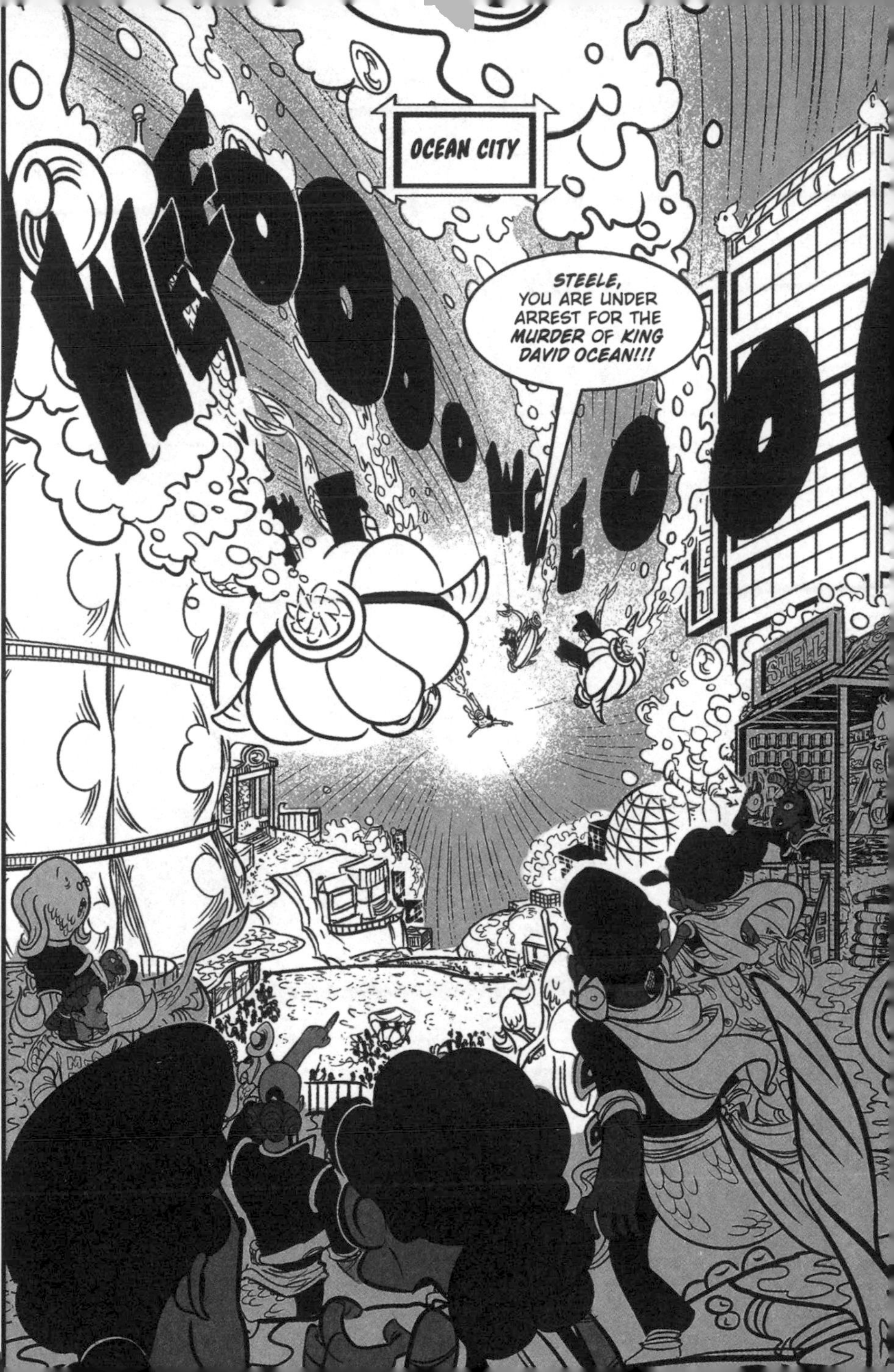
OCEAN CITY
STEELE, YOU ARE UNDER ARREST FOR THE MURDER OF KING DAVID OCEAN!!!
SHELL

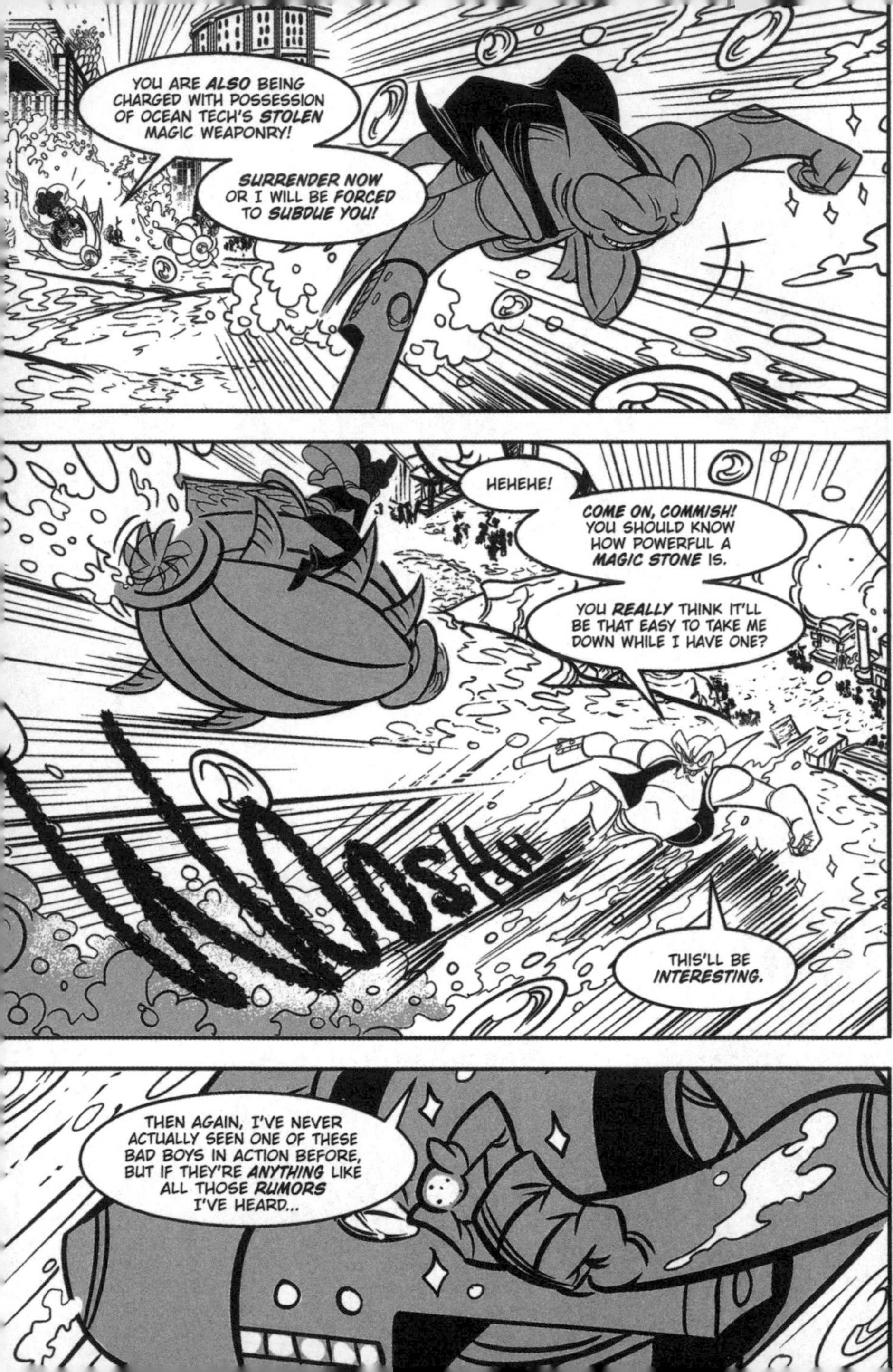
YOU ARE **ALSO** BEING CHARGED WITH POSSESSION OF OCEAN TECH'S **STOLEN** MAGIC WEAPONRY!
SURRENDER NOW OR I WILL BE **FORCED** TO **SUBDUE YOU!**
HEHEHE!
COME ON, COMMISH! YOU SHOULD KNOW HOW POWERFUL A **MAGIC STONE** IS.
YOU **REALLY** THINK IT'LL BE THAT EASY TO TAKE ME DOWN WHILE I HAVE ONE?
WHOOSHH
THIS'LL BE **INTERESTING.**
THEN AGAIN, I'VE NEVER ACTUALLY SEEN ONE OF THESE BAD BOYS IN ACTION BEFORE, BUT IF THEY'RE **ANYTHING** LIKE ALL THOSE **RUMORS** I'VE HEARD...

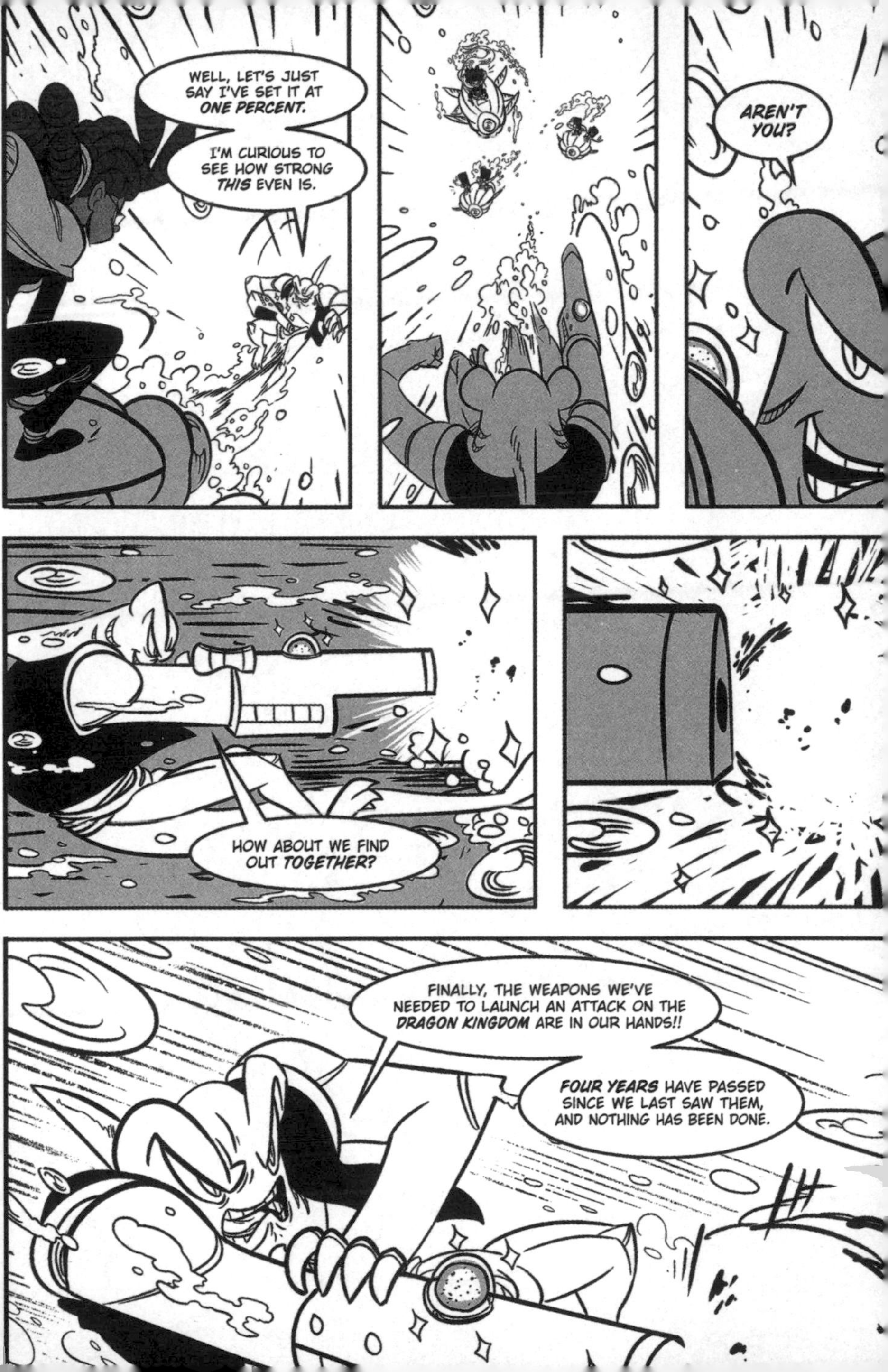
WELL, LET'S JUST SAY I'VE SET IT AT ONE PERCENT.
I'M CURIOUS TO SEE HOW STRONG THIS EVEN IS.
AREN'T YOU?
HOW ABOUT WE FIND OUT TOGETHER?
FINALLY, THE WEAPONS WE'VE NEEDED TO LAUNCH AN ATTACK ON THE DRAGON KINGDOM ARE IN OUR HANDS!!
FOUR YEARS HAVE PASSED SINCE WE LAST SAW THEM, AND NOTHING HAS BEEN DONE.

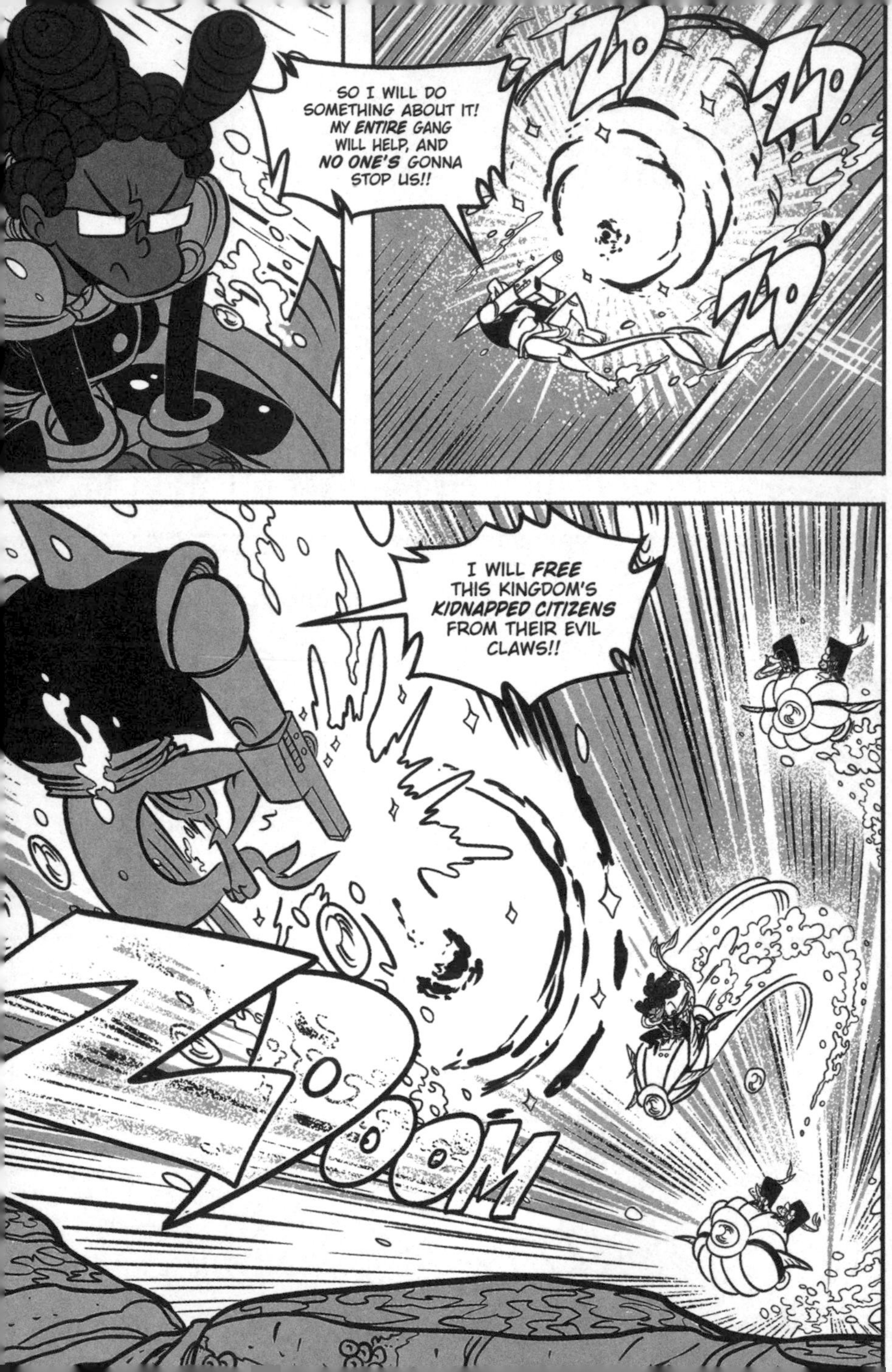
SO I WILL DO SOMETHING ABOUT IT! MY ENTIRE GANG WILL HELP, AND NO ONE'S GONNA STOP US!!
I WILL FREE THIS KINGDOM'S KIDNAPPED CITIZENS FROM THEIR EVIL CLAWS!!

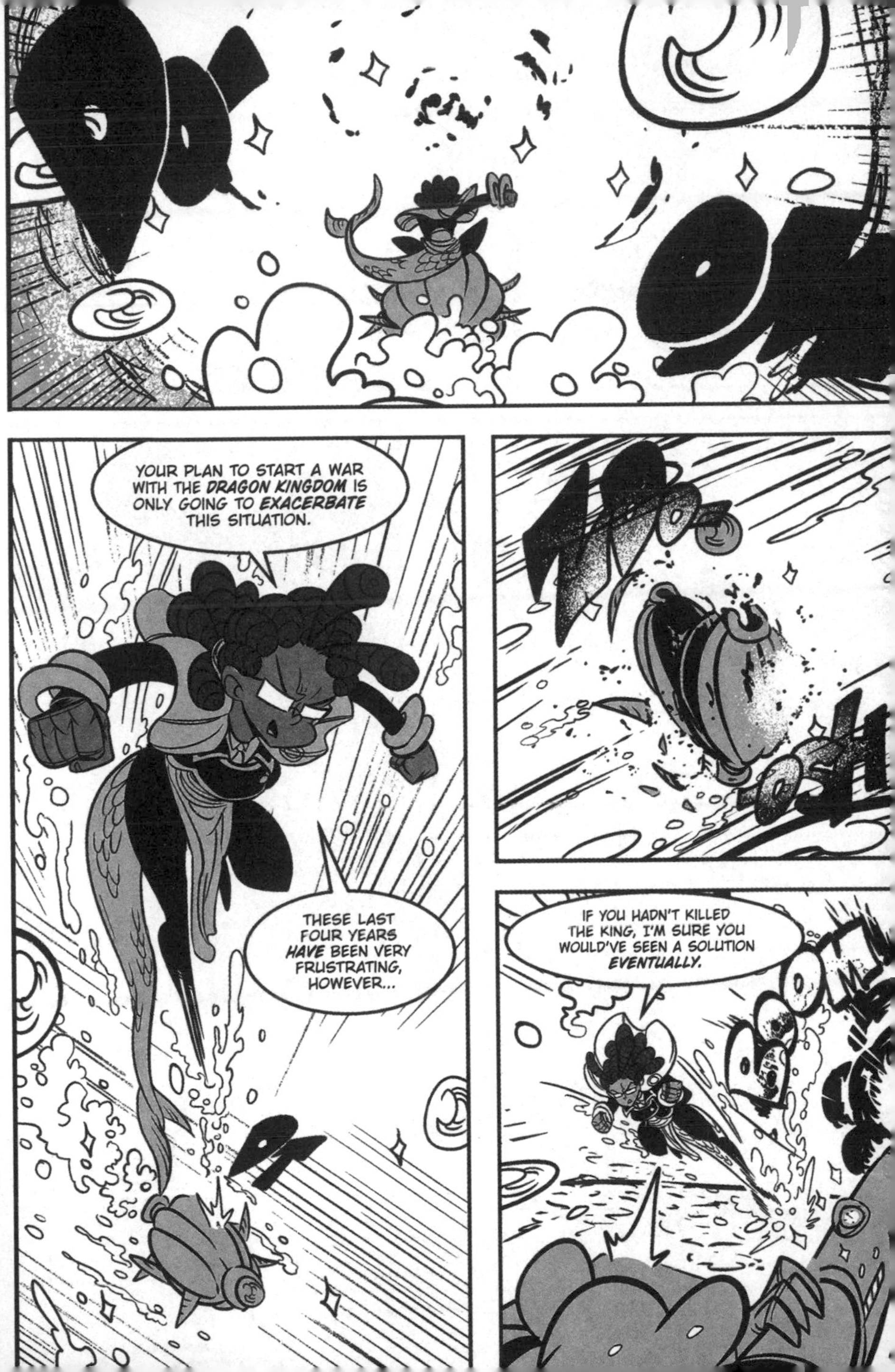
YOUR PLAN TO START A WAR WITH THE DRAGON KINGDOM IS ONLY GOING TO EXACERBATE THIS SITUATION.
THESE LAST FOUR YEARS HAVE BEEN VERY FRUSTRATING, HOWEVER...
IF YOU HADN'T KILLED THE KING, I'M SURE YOU WOULD'VE SEEN A SOLUTION EVENTUALLY.

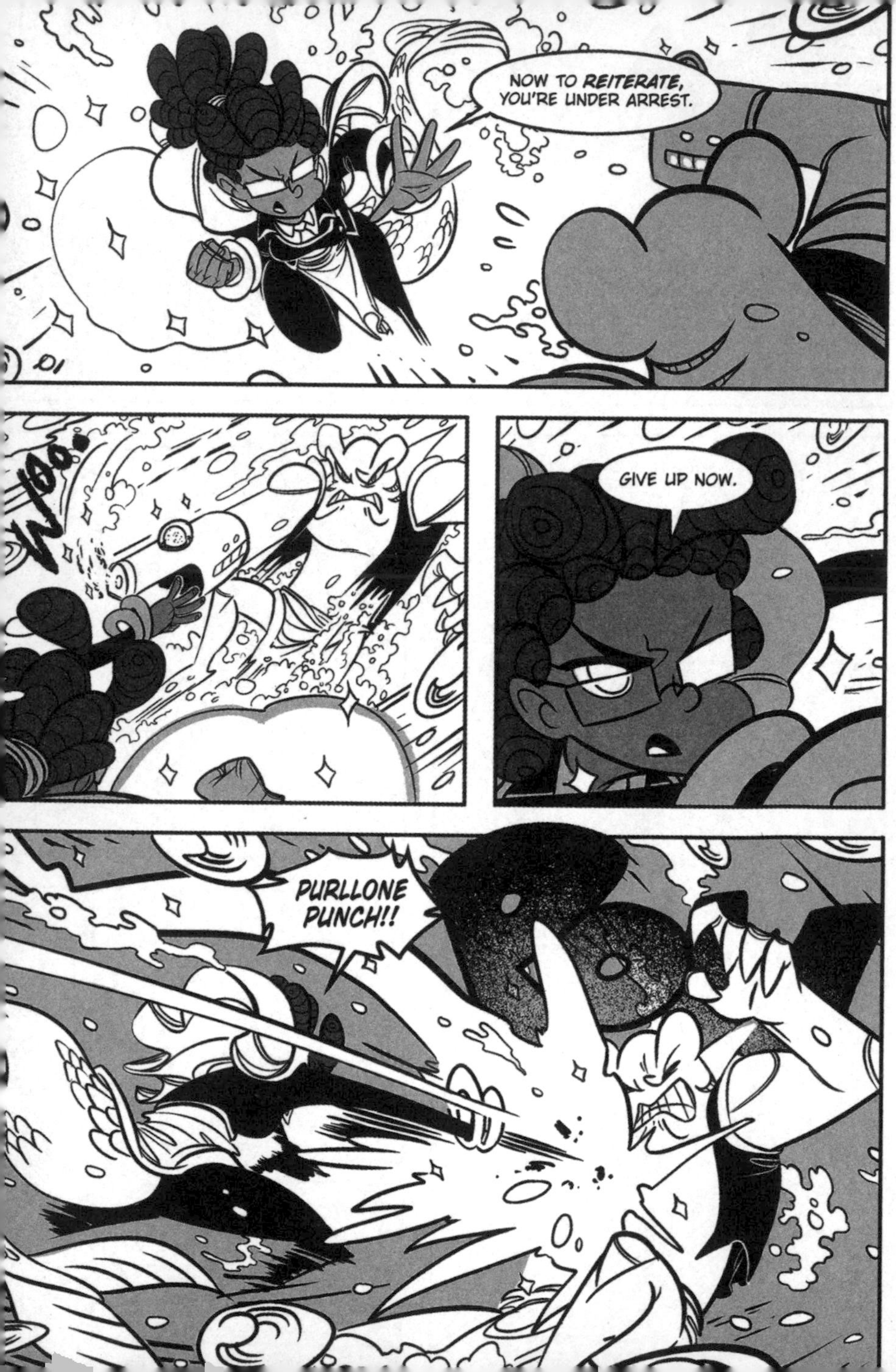
NOW TO *REITERATE*, YOU'RE UNDER ARREST.
WOO
GIVE UP NOW.
PURLLONE PUNCH!!

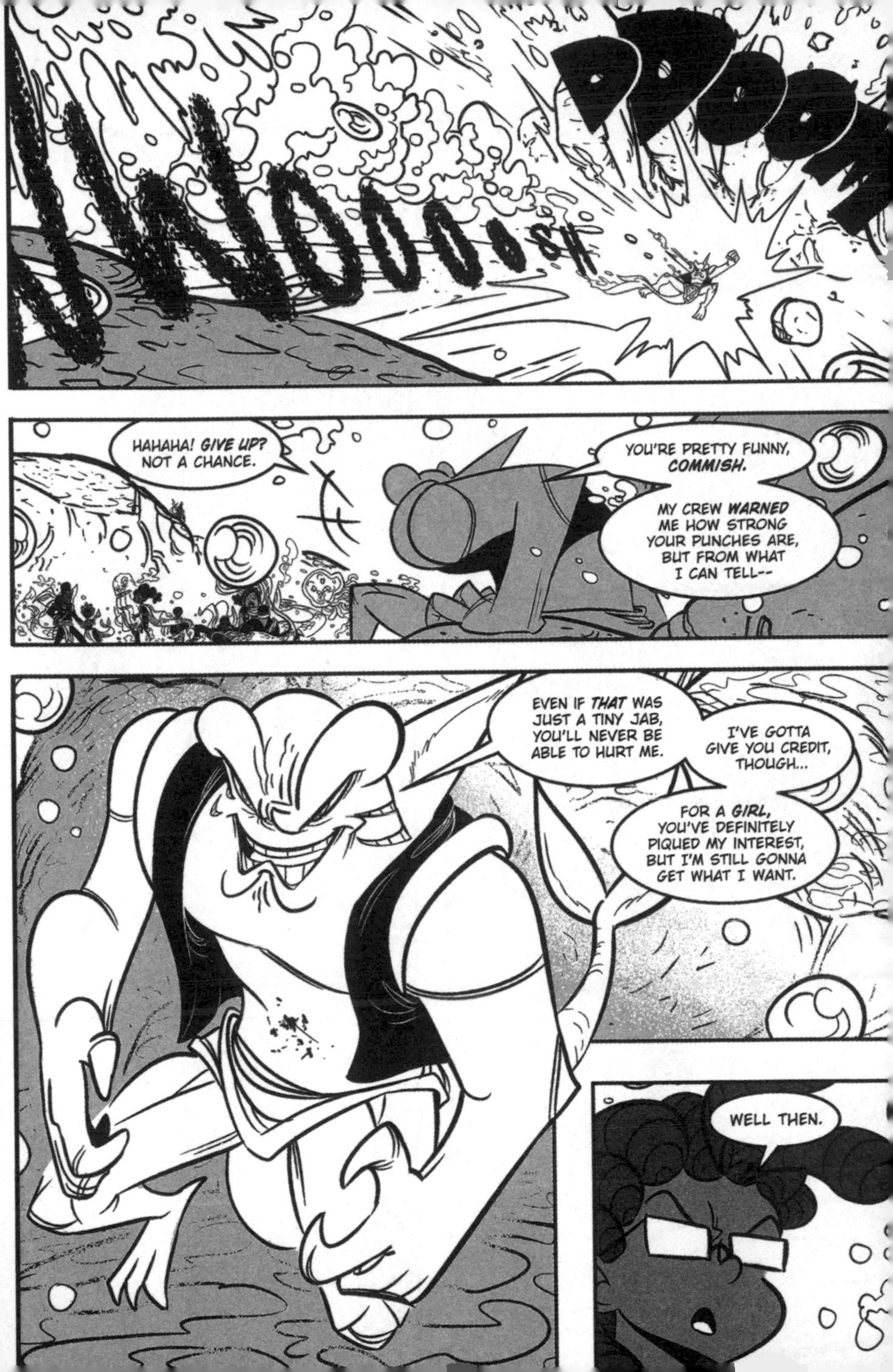
WHOOOOOSH
DDOOM
HAHAHA! GIVE UP? NOT A CHANCE.
YOU'RE PRETTY FUNNY, COMMISH.
MY CREW WARNED ME HOW STRONG YOUR PUNCHES ARE, BUT FROM WHAT I CAN TELL--
EVEN IF THAT WAS JUST A TINY JAB, YOU'LL NEVER BE ABLE TO HURT ME.
I'VE GOTTA GIVE YOU CREDIT, THOUGH...
FOR A GIRL, YOU'VE DEFINITELY PIQUED MY INTEREST, BUT I'M STILL GONNA GET WHAT I WANT.
WELL THEN.

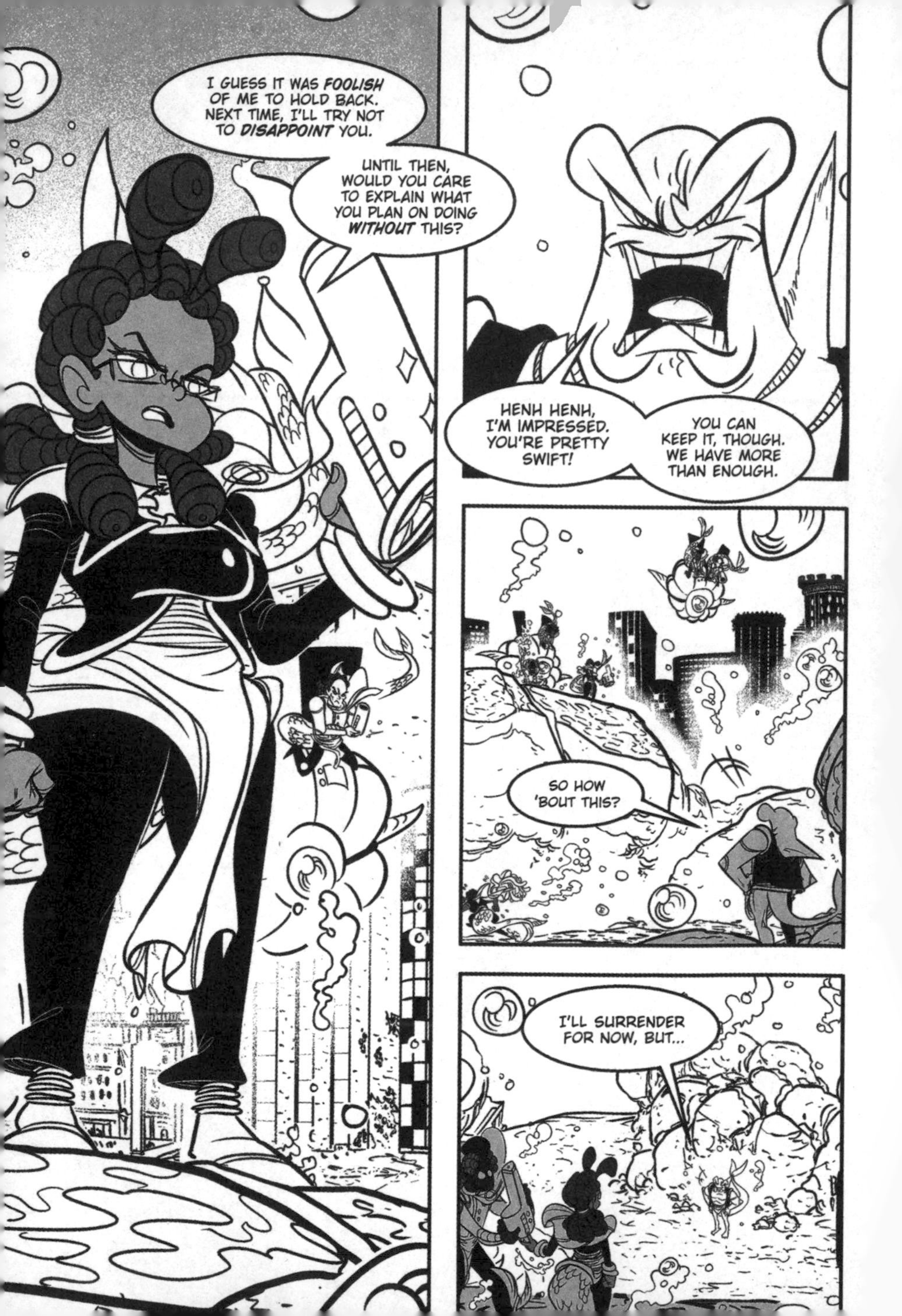
I GUESS IT WAS *FOOLISH* OF ME TO HOLD BACK. NEXT TIME, I'LL TRY NOT TO *DISAPPOINT* YOU.
UNTIL THEN, WOULD YOU CARE TO EXPLAIN WHAT YOU PLAN ON DOING *WITHOUT* THIS?
HENH HENH, I'M IMPRESSED. YOU'RE PRETTY SWIFT!
YOU CAN KEEP IT, THOUGH. WE HAVE MORE THAN ENOUGH.
SO HOW 'BOUT THIS?
I'LL SURRENDER FOR NOW, BUT...

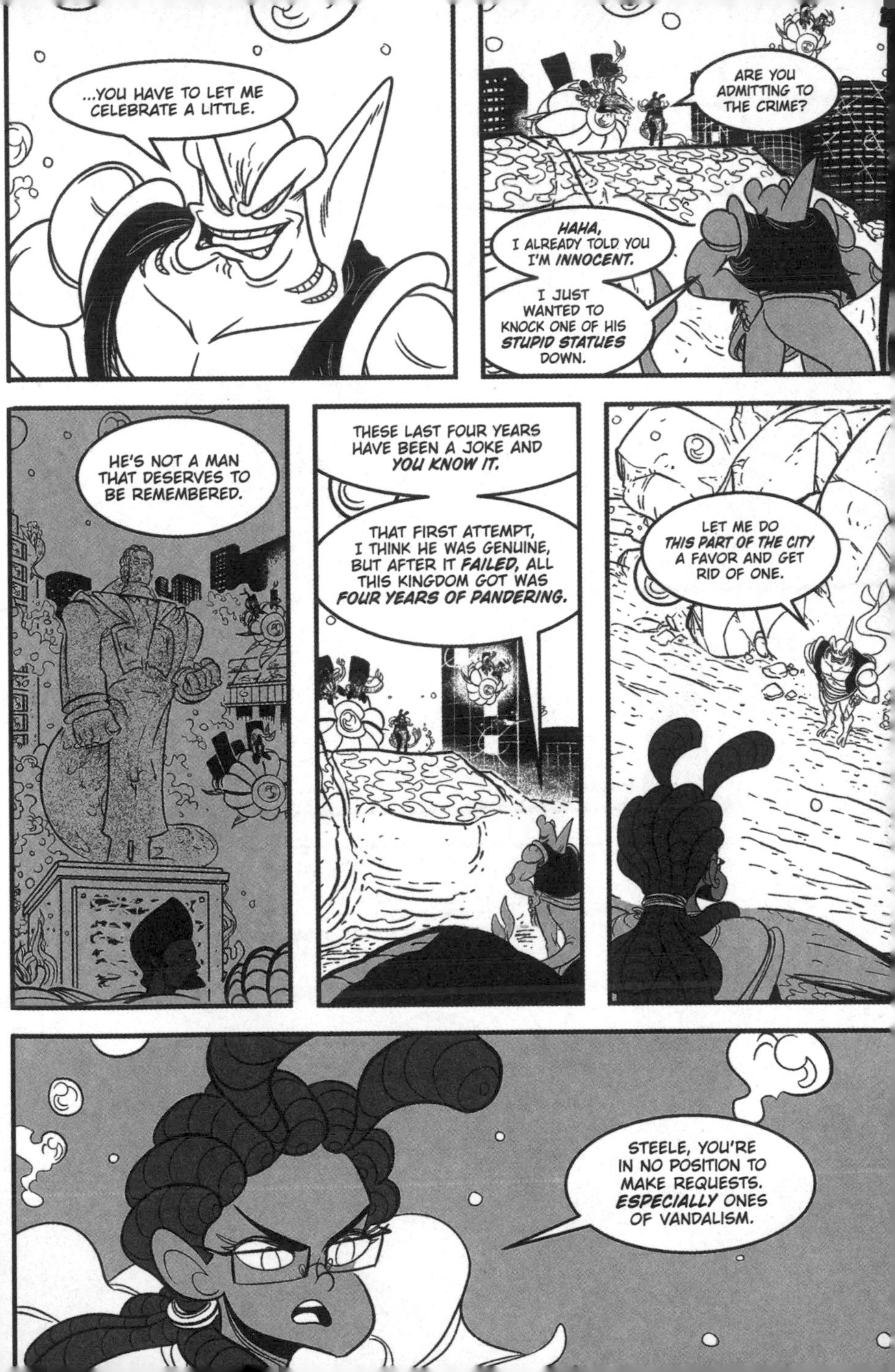
...YOU HAVE TO LET ME CELEBRATE A LITTLE.
ARE YOU ADMITTING TO THE CRIME?
HAHA, I ALREADY TOLD YOU I'M INNOCENT.
I JUST WANTED TO KNOCK ONE OF HIS STUPID STATUES DOWN.
HE'S NOT A MAN THAT DESERVES TO BE REMEMBERED.
THESE LAST FOUR YEARS HAVE BEEN A JOKE AND YOU KNOW IT.
THAT FIRST ATTEMPT, I THINK HE WAS GENUINE, BUT AFTER IT FAILED, ALL THIS KINGDOM GOT WAS FOUR YEARS OF PANDERING.
LET ME DO THIS PART OF THE CITY A FAVOR AND GET RID OF ONE.
STEELE, YOU'RE IN NO POSITION TO MAKE REQUESTS. ESPECIALLY ONES OF VANDALISM.

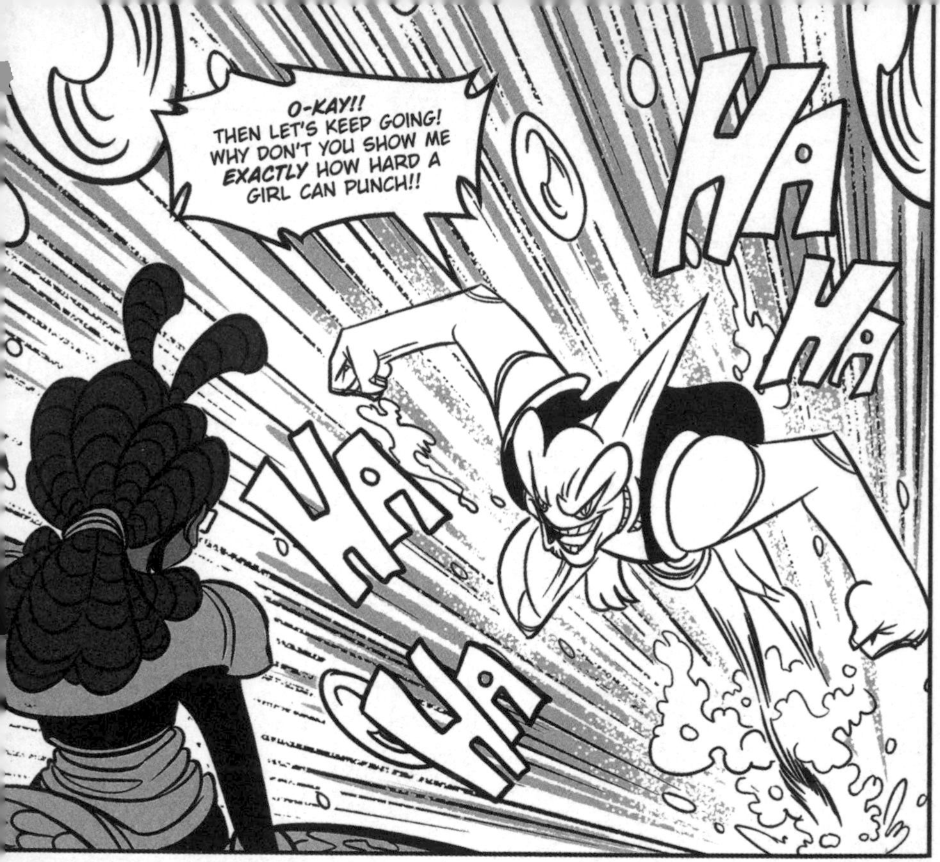
O-KAY!! THEN LET'S KEEP GOING! WHY DON'T YOU SHOW ME EXACTLY HOW HARD A GIRL CAN PUNCH!!
HA
HA
HA
HA
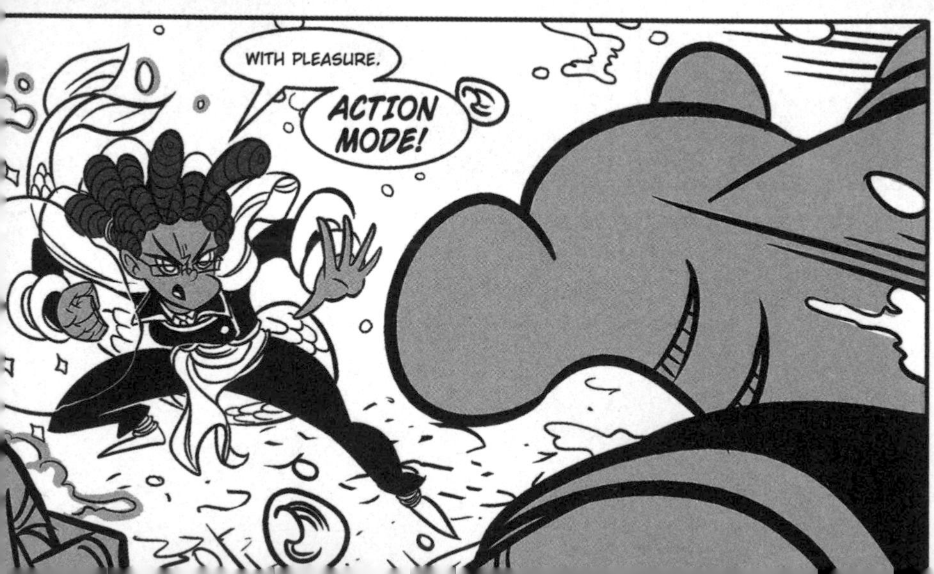
WITH PLEASURE.
ACTION MODE!

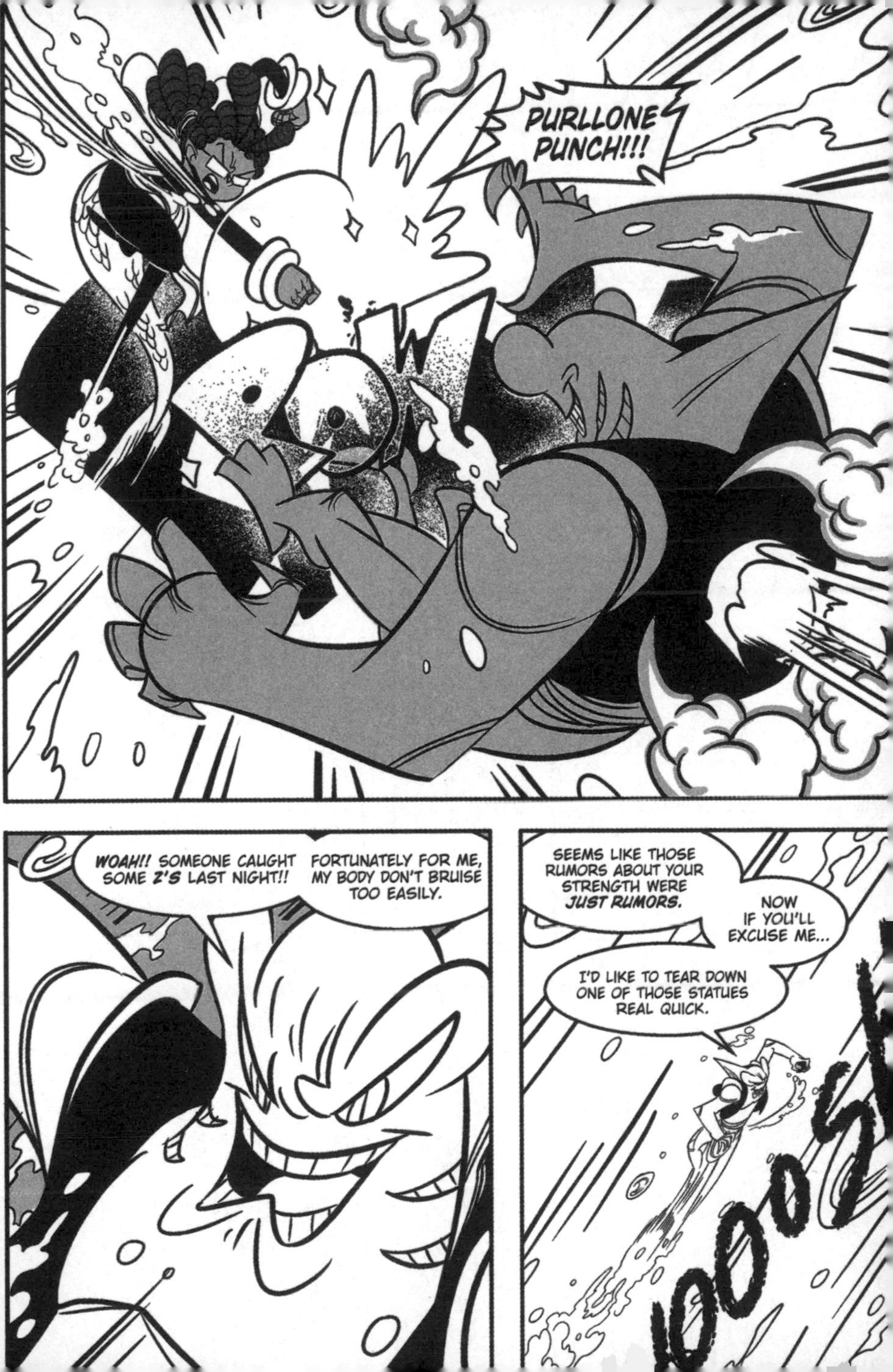
PURLLONE PUNCH!!!
WOAH!! SOMEONE CAUGHT SOME Z'S LAST NIGHT!!
FORTUNATELY FOR ME, MY BODY DON'T BRUISE TOO EASILY.
SEEMS LIKE THOSE RUMORS ABOUT YOUR STRENGTH WERE JUST RUMORS.
NOW IF YOU'LL EXCUSE ME...
I'D LIKE TO TEAR DOWN ONE OF THOSE STATUES REAL QUICK.

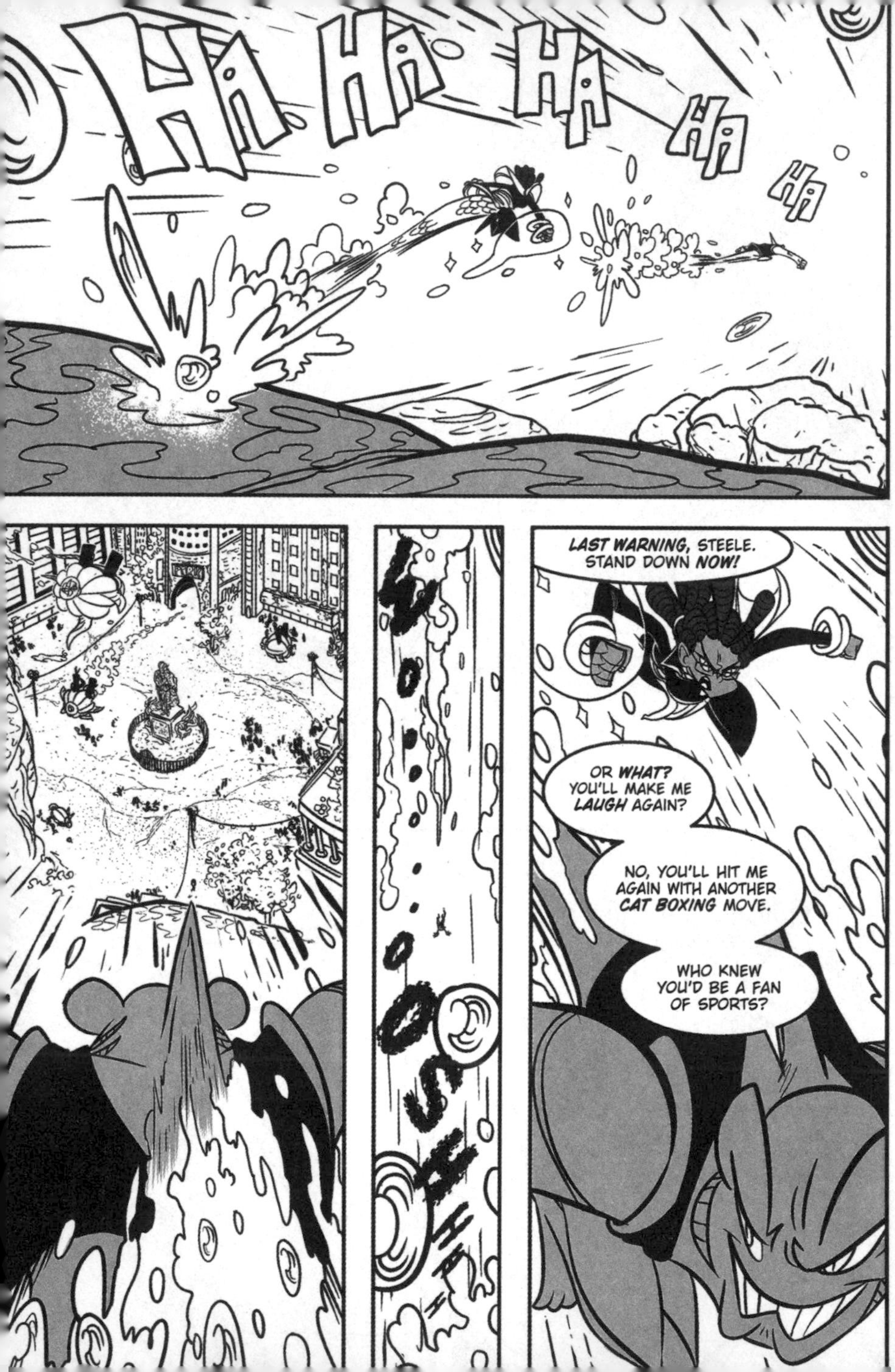
HA HA HA HA HA HA
LAST WARNING, STEELE. STAND DOWN NOW!
OR WHAT? YOU'LL MAKE ME LAUGH AGAIN?
NO, YOU'LL HIT ME AGAIN WITH ANOTHER CAT BOXING MOVE.
WHO KNEW YOU'D BE A FAN OF SPORTS?

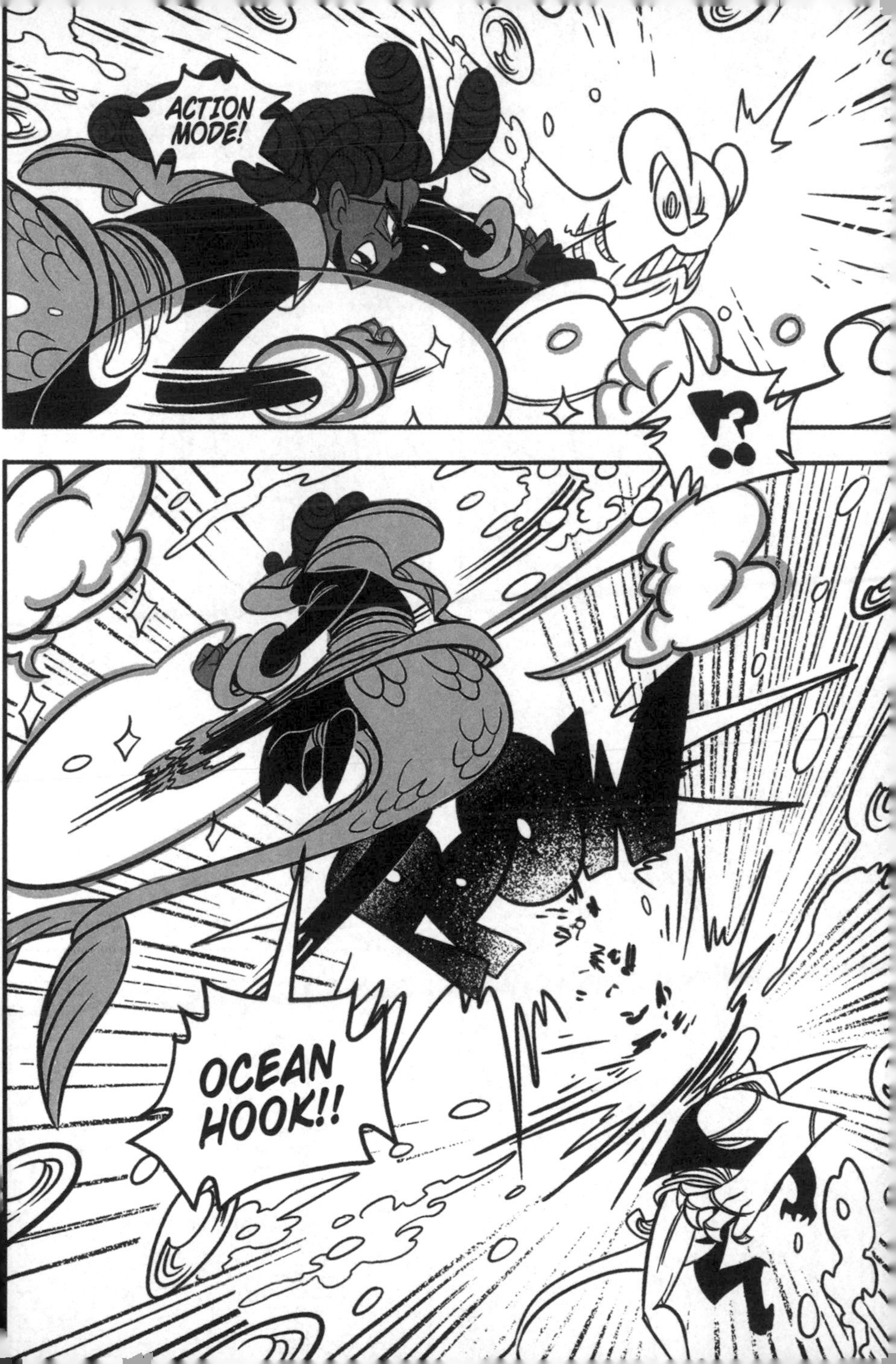
ACTION MODE!
!?
OCEAN HOOK!!

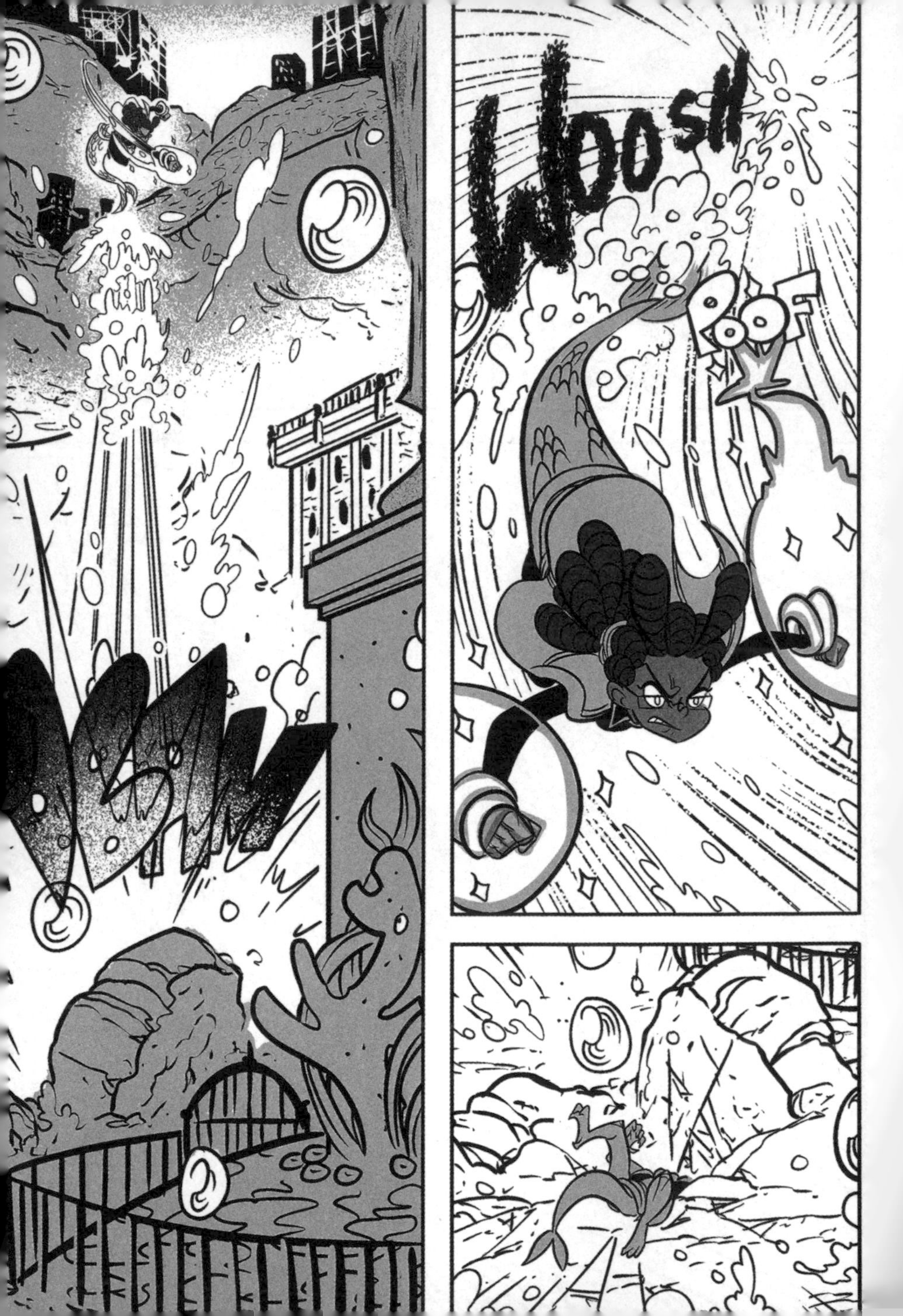
WOOSH
POOF

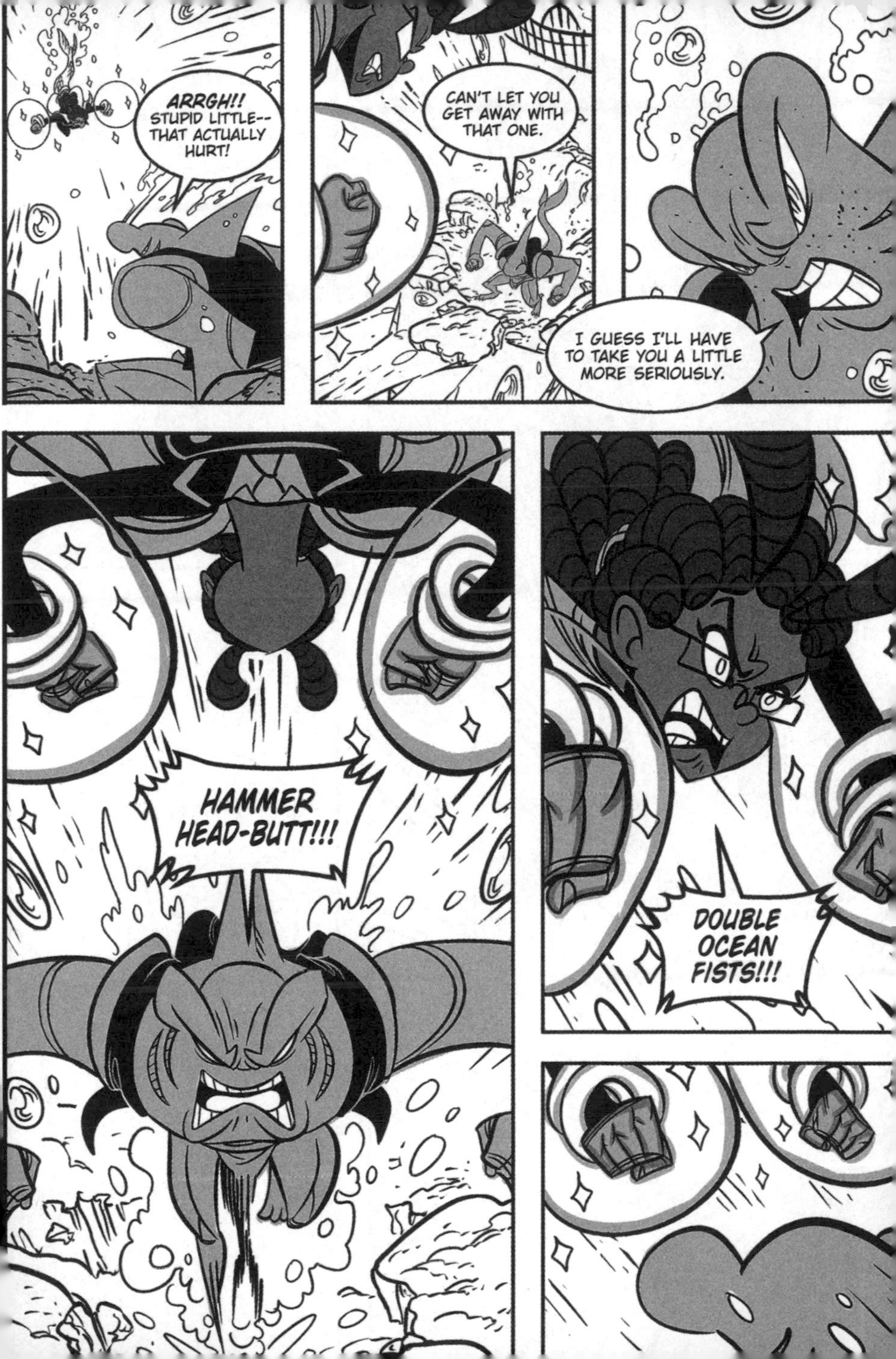
ARRGH!! STUPID LITTLE-- THAT ACTUALLY HURT!
CAN'T LET YOU GET AWAY WITH THAT ONE.
I GUESS I'LL HAVE TO TAKE YOU A LITTLE MORE SERIOUSLY.
HAMMER HEAD-BUTT!!!
DOUBLE OCEAN FISTS!!!

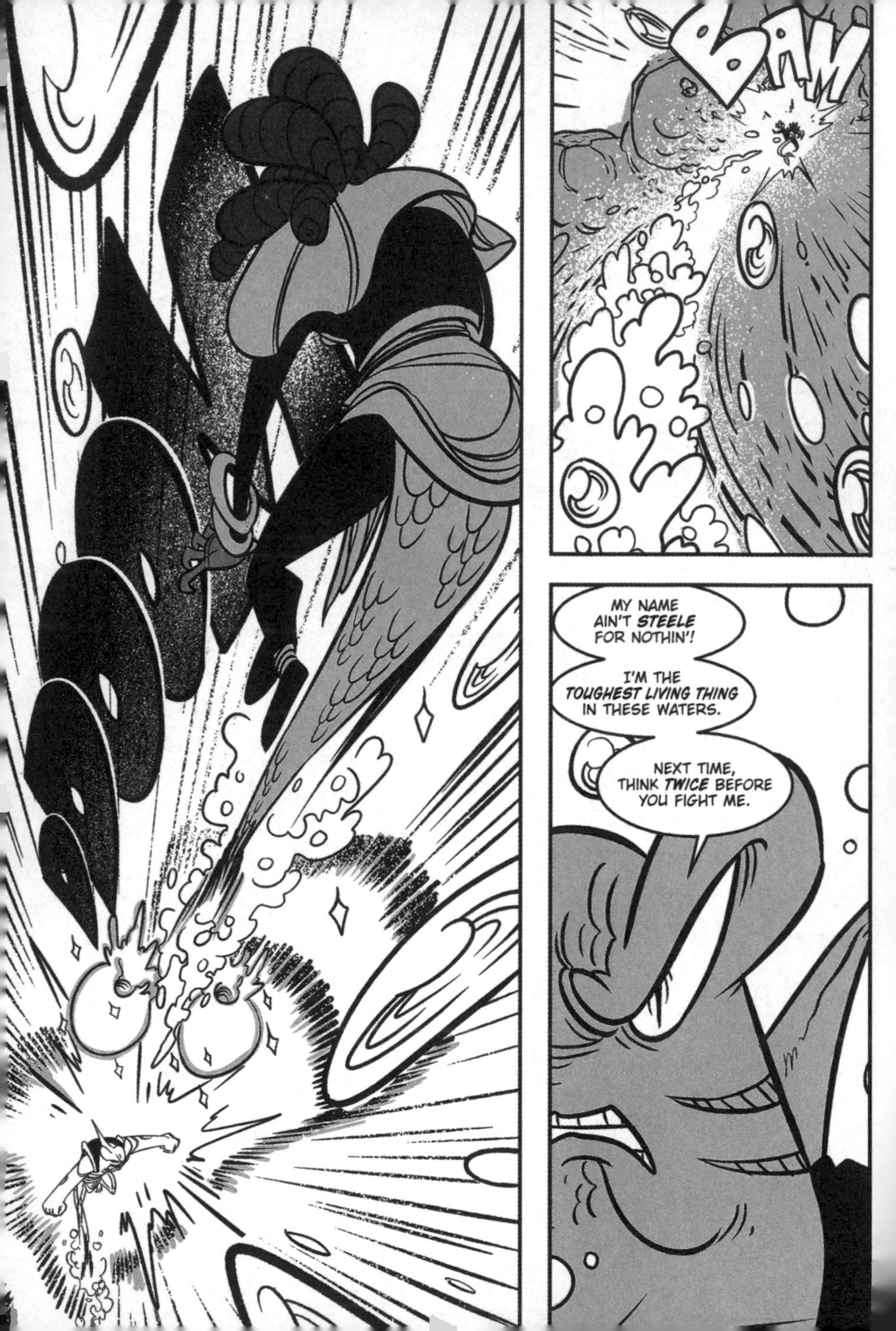
BAM
MY NAME AIN'T **STEELE** FOR NOTHIN'!
I'M THE ***TOUGHEST LIVING THING*** IN THESE WATERS.
NEXT TIME, THINK ***TWICE*** BEFORE YOU FIGHT ME.

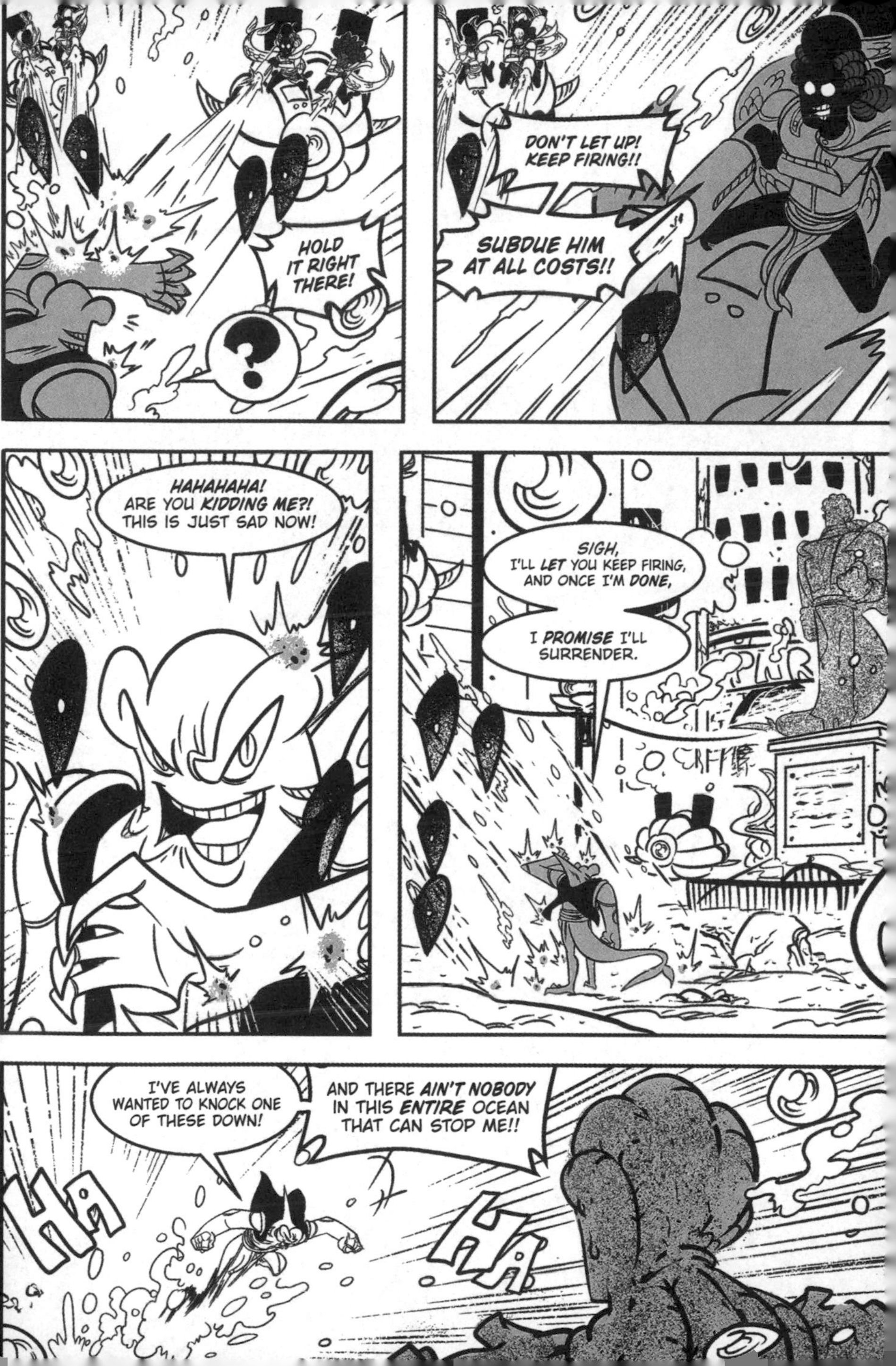
HOLD IT RIGHT THERE!
?
DON'T LET UP! KEEP FIRING!!
SUBDUE HIM AT ALL COSTS!!
HAHAHAHA! ARE YOU KIDDING ME?! THIS IS JUST SAD NOW!
SIGH, I'LL LET YOU KEEP FIRING, AND ONCE I'M DONE,
I PROMISE I'LL SURRENDER.
I'VE ALWAYS WANTED TO KNOCK ONE OF THESE DOWN!
AND THERE AIN'T NOBODY IN THIS ENTIRE OCEAN THAT CAN STOP ME!!
HA
HA

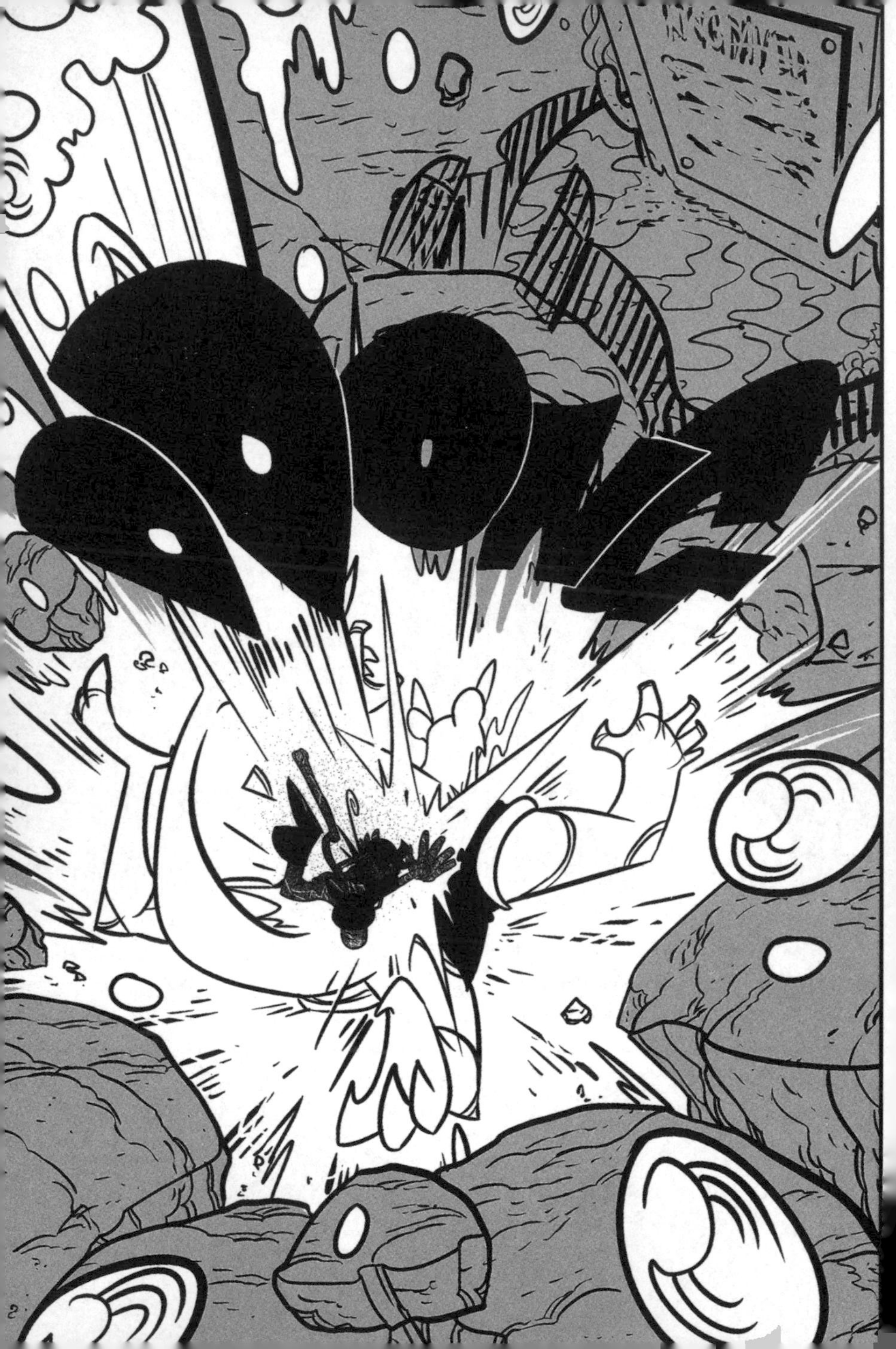

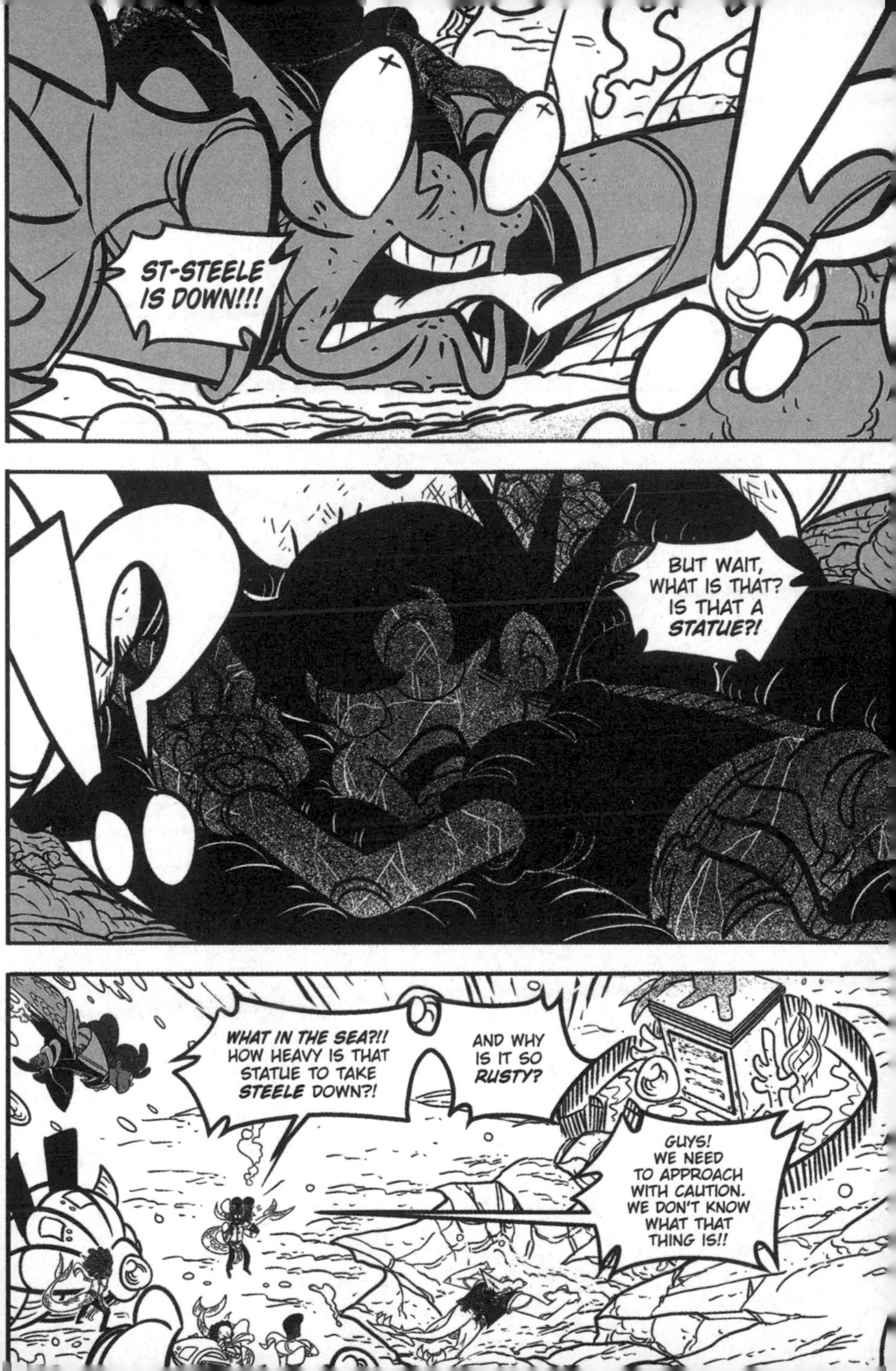
ST-STEELE IS DOWN!!!
BUT WAIT, WHAT IS THAT? IS THAT A *STATUE?!*
WHAT IN THE SEA?!! HOW HEAVY IS THAT STATUE TO TAKE *STEELE* DOWN?!
AND WHY IS IT SO *RUSTY?*
GUYS! WE NEED TO APPROACH WITH CAUTION. WE DON'T KNOW WHAT THAT THING IS!!

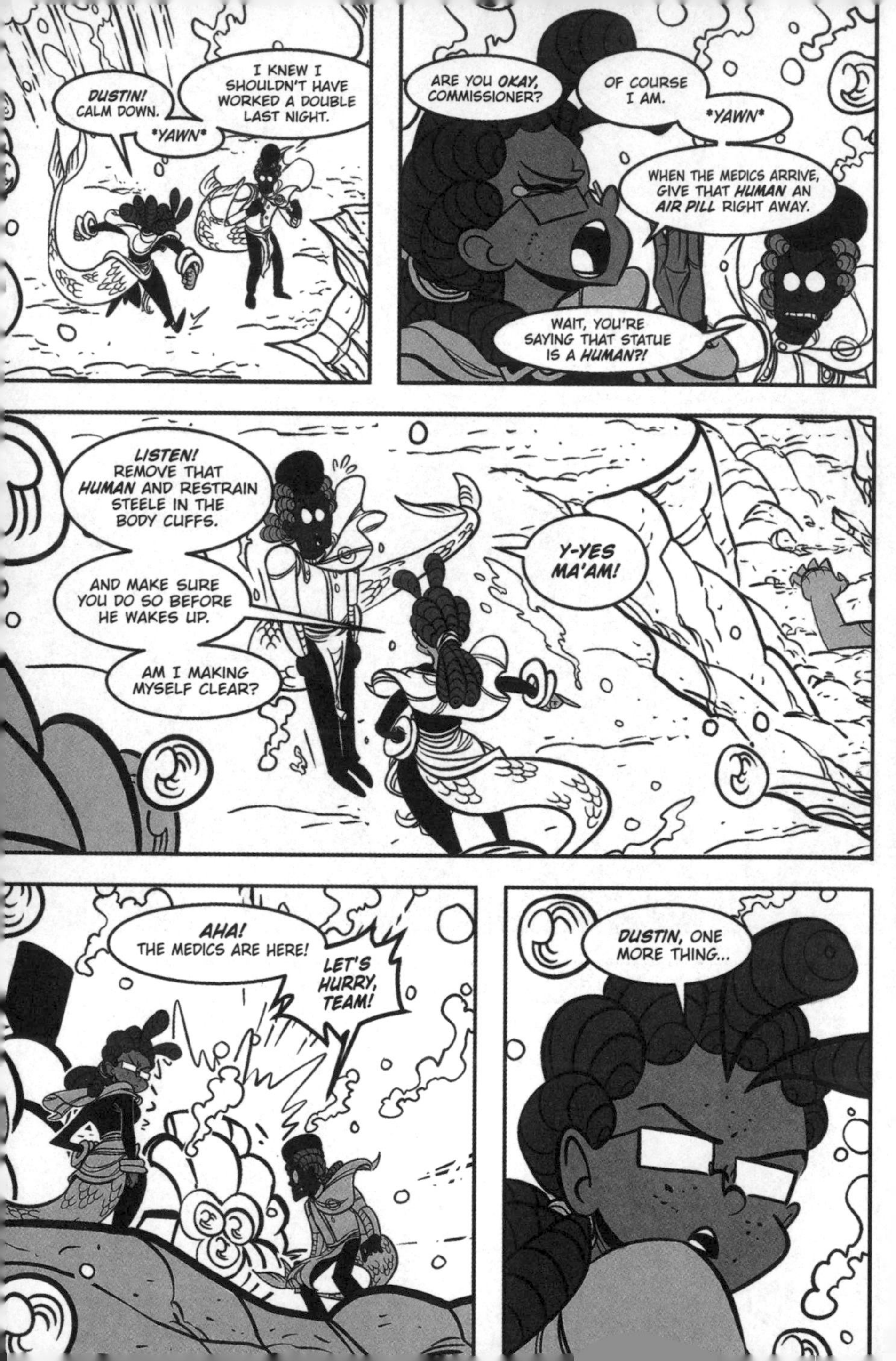
DUSTIN! CALM DOWN.
I KNEW I SHOULDN'T HAVE WORKED A DOUBLE LAST NIGHT.
YAWN
ARE YOU OKAY, COMMISSIONER?
OF COURSE I AM.
YAWN
WHEN THE MEDICS ARRIVE, GIVE THAT HUMAN AN AIR PILL RIGHT AWAY.
WAIT, YOU'RE SAYING THAT STATUE IS A HUMAN?!
LISTEN! REMOVE THAT HUMAN AND RESTRAIN STEELE IN THE BODY CUFFS.
AND MAKE SURE YOU DO SO BEFORE HE WAKES UP.
AM I MAKING MYSELF CLEAR?
Y-YES MA'AM!
AHA! THE MEDICS ARE HERE!
LET'S HURRY, TEAM!
DUSTIN, ONE MORE THING...

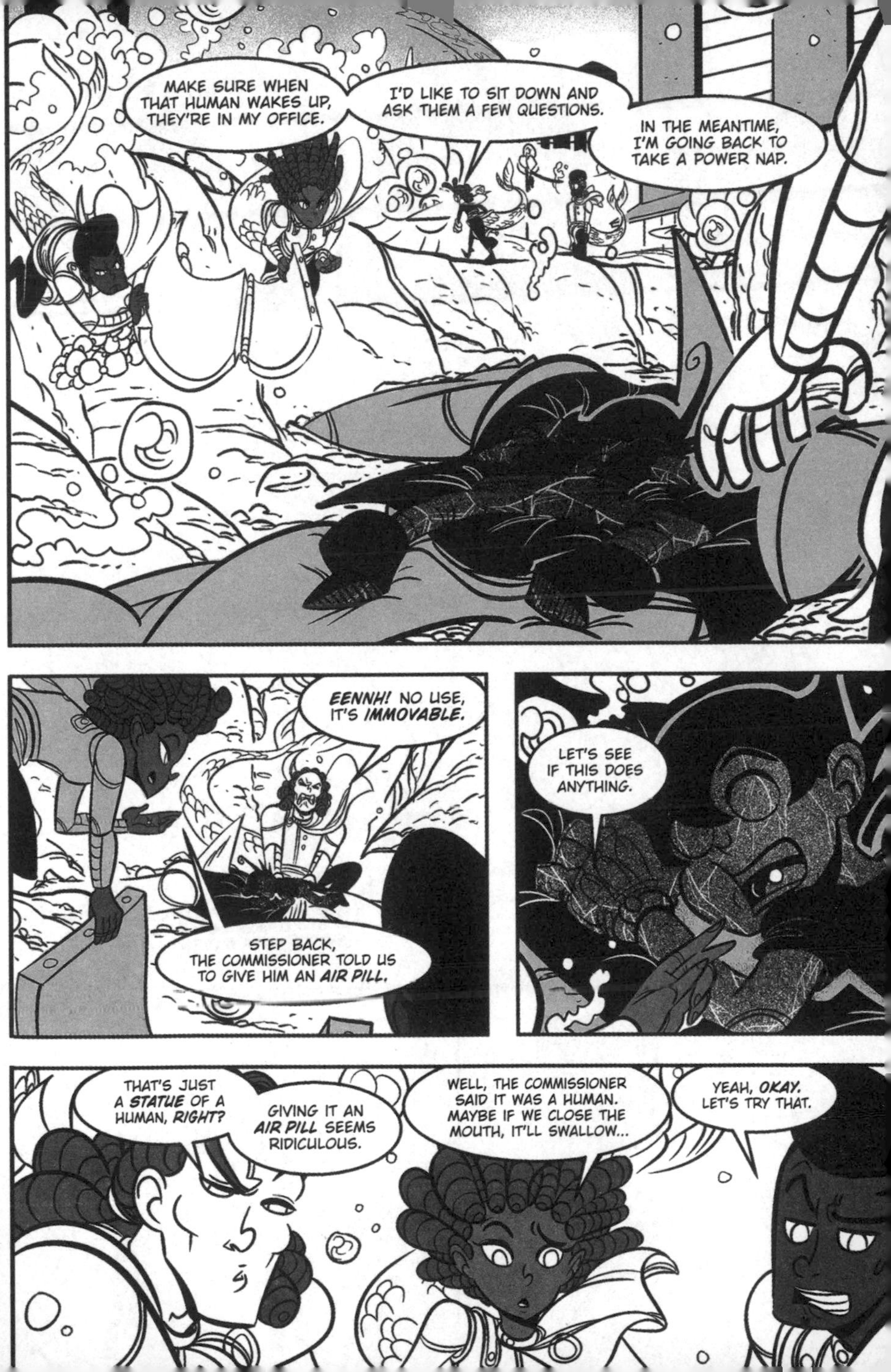
MAKE SURE WHEN THAT HUMAN WAKES UP, THEY'RE IN MY OFFICE.
I'D LIKE TO SIT DOWN AND ASK THEM A FEW QUESTIONS.
IN THE MEANTIME, I'M GOING BACK TO TAKE A POWER NAP.
EENNH! NO USE, IT'S *IMMOVABLE.*
STEP BACK, THE COMMISSIONER TOLD US TO GIVE HIM AN *AIR PILL.*
LET'S SEE IF THIS DOES ANYTHING.
THAT'S JUST A *STATUE* OF A HUMAN, *RIGHT?*
GIVING IT AN *AIR PILL* SEEMS RIDICULOUS.
WELL, THE COMMISSIONER SAID IT WAS A HUMAN. MAYBE IF WE CLOSE THE MOUTH, IT'LL SWALLOW...
YEAH, *OKAY.* LET'S TRY THAT.

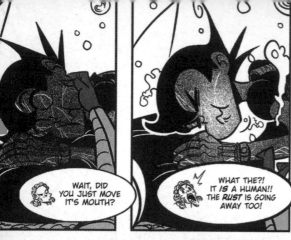

WAIT, DID YOU JUST MOVE IT'S MOUTH?

WHAT THE?! IT *IS* A HUMAN!! THE *RUST* IS GOING AWAY TOO!

SO, UM, WHAT?

DUDE, IT DOESN'T LOOK LIKE HE'S HEAVY ANYMORE.

WELL YEAH, IF YOU *MAGICALLY* MAKE HIM NOT A *STATUE* ANYMORE, I'M SURE HE *WOULD* BE LIGHTER.

HE'S A LOT HEAVIER THAN YOU'D THINK, BUT HE ISN'T *IMMOVABLE*, HAHA.

I'LL TAKE CARE OF THIS. YOU TWO CUFF UP STEELE BEFORE HE WAKES UP.

THAT *STATUE* WAS IMMOVABLE.

THAT WAS KINDA FUNNY, HAHA.

SH-SHUT UP!

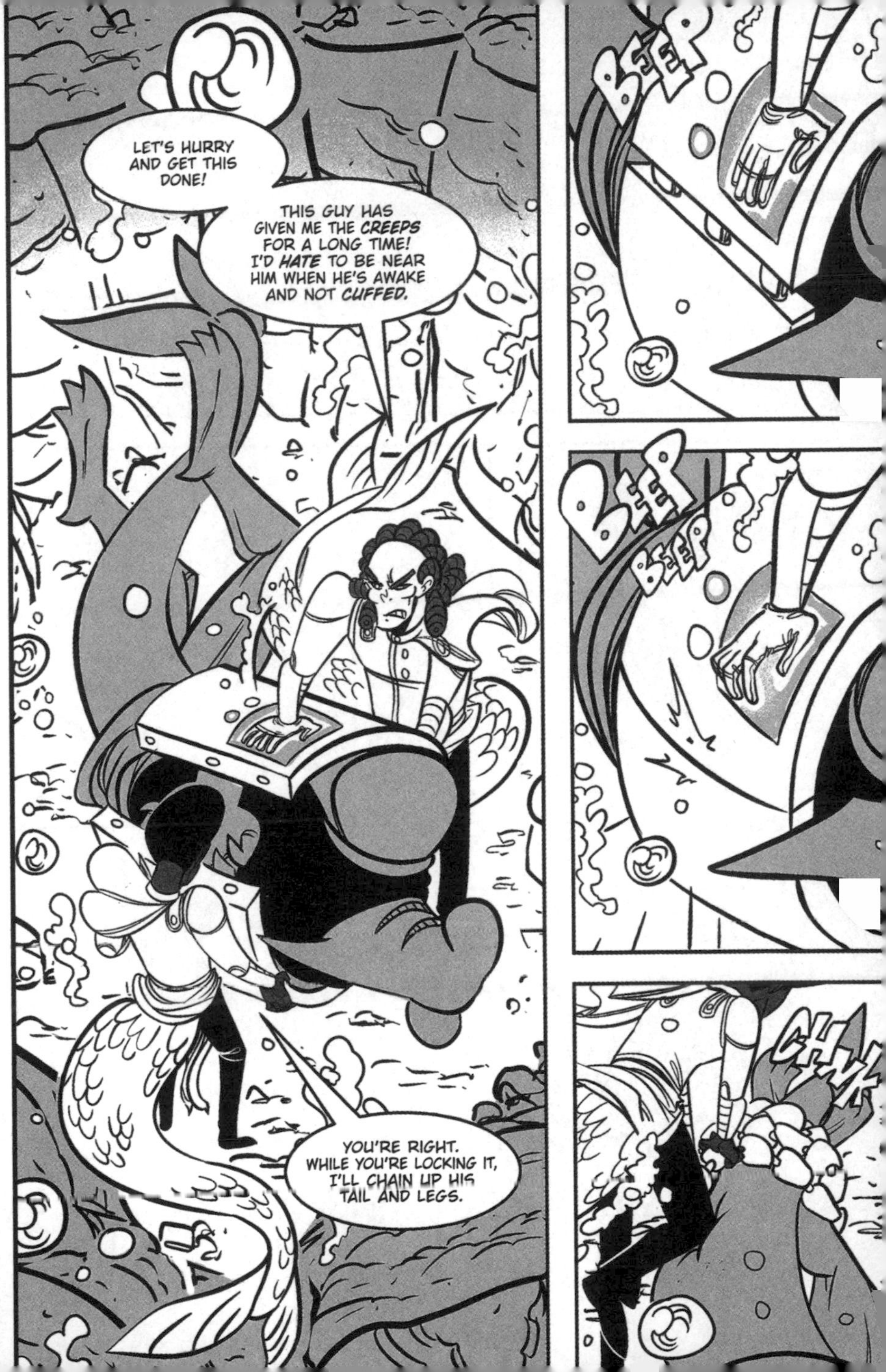
LET'S HURRY AND GET THIS DONE!
THIS GUY HAS GIVEN ME THE *CREEPS* FOR A LONG TIME! I'D *HATE* TO BE NEAR HIM WHEN HE'S AWAKE AND NOT *CUFFED.*
YOU'RE RIGHT. WHILE YOU'RE LOCKING IT, I'LL CHAIN UP HIS TAIL AND LEGS.
BEEP
BEEP
BEEP
CHNK

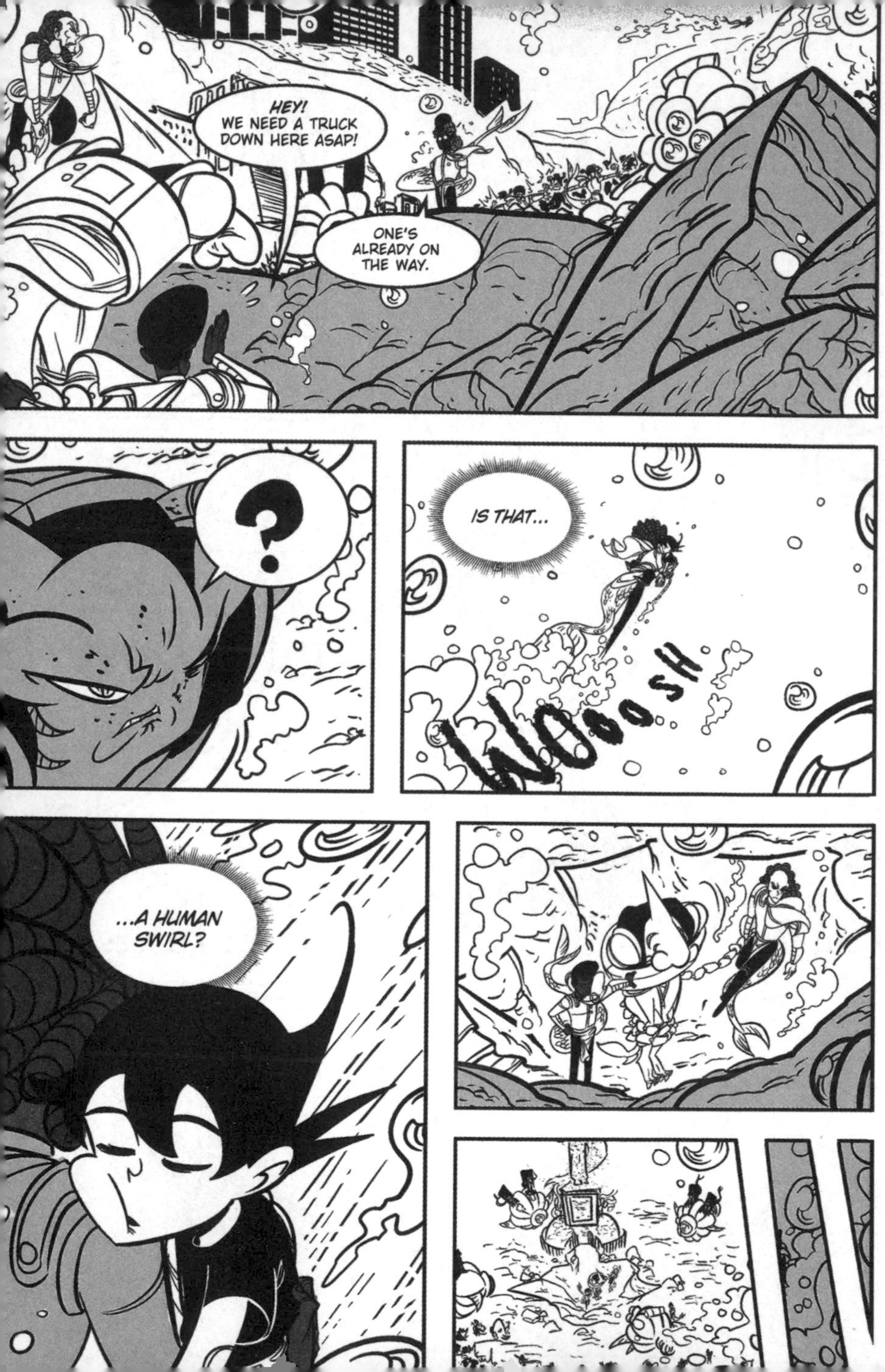
HEY! WE NEED A TRUCK DOWN HERE ASAP!
ONE'S ALREADY ON THE WAY.
?
IS THAT...
WOOOOSH
...A HUMAN SWIRL?

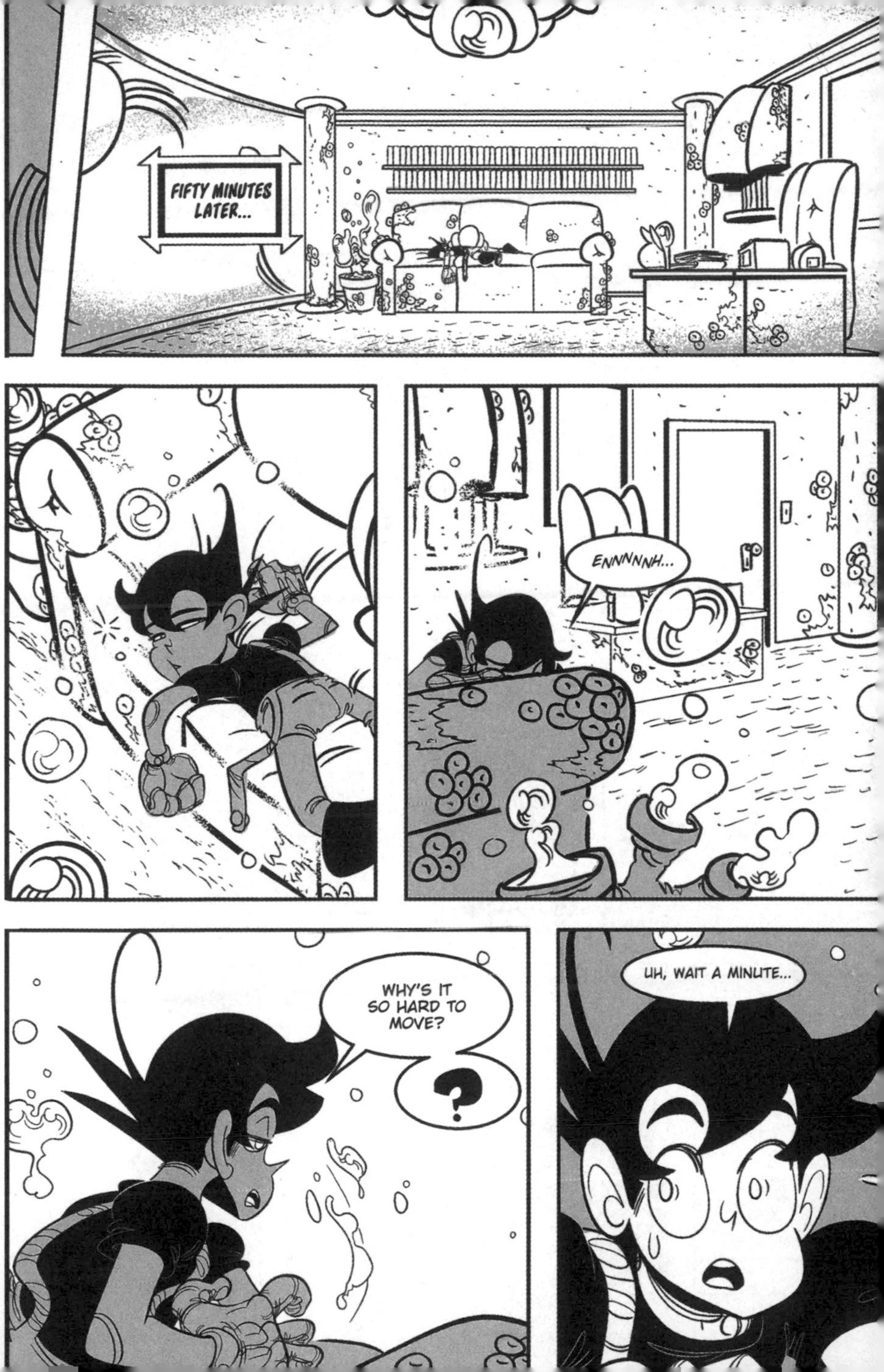
FIFTY MINUTES LATER...
ENNNNNH...
WHY'S IT SO HARD TO MOVE?
?
UH, WAIT A MINUTE...

WHERE THE CRAP AM I?

WHAT IS THIS PLACE?!!

AM I SEEING THINGS?

OR IS THAT REALLY A GIANT BUBBLE WINDOW?!!

OKAY, STUD.

CALM DOWN AND THINK ABOUT WHAT HAPPENED.

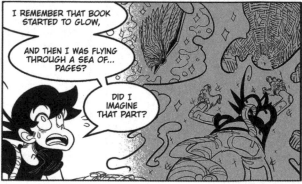

I REMEMBER THAT BOOK STARTED TO GLOW,

AND THEN I WAS FLYING THROUGH A SEA OF... PAGES?

DID I IMAGINE THAT PART?

?

CRAP! THIS IS BAD!!

I HAVE TO GET BACK HOME!!

IF DAD FINDS OUT I WENT INTO THE STUDY AND READ THAT BOOK, I'LL GET IN TROUBLE!

HUNH? WAIT A MINUTE...

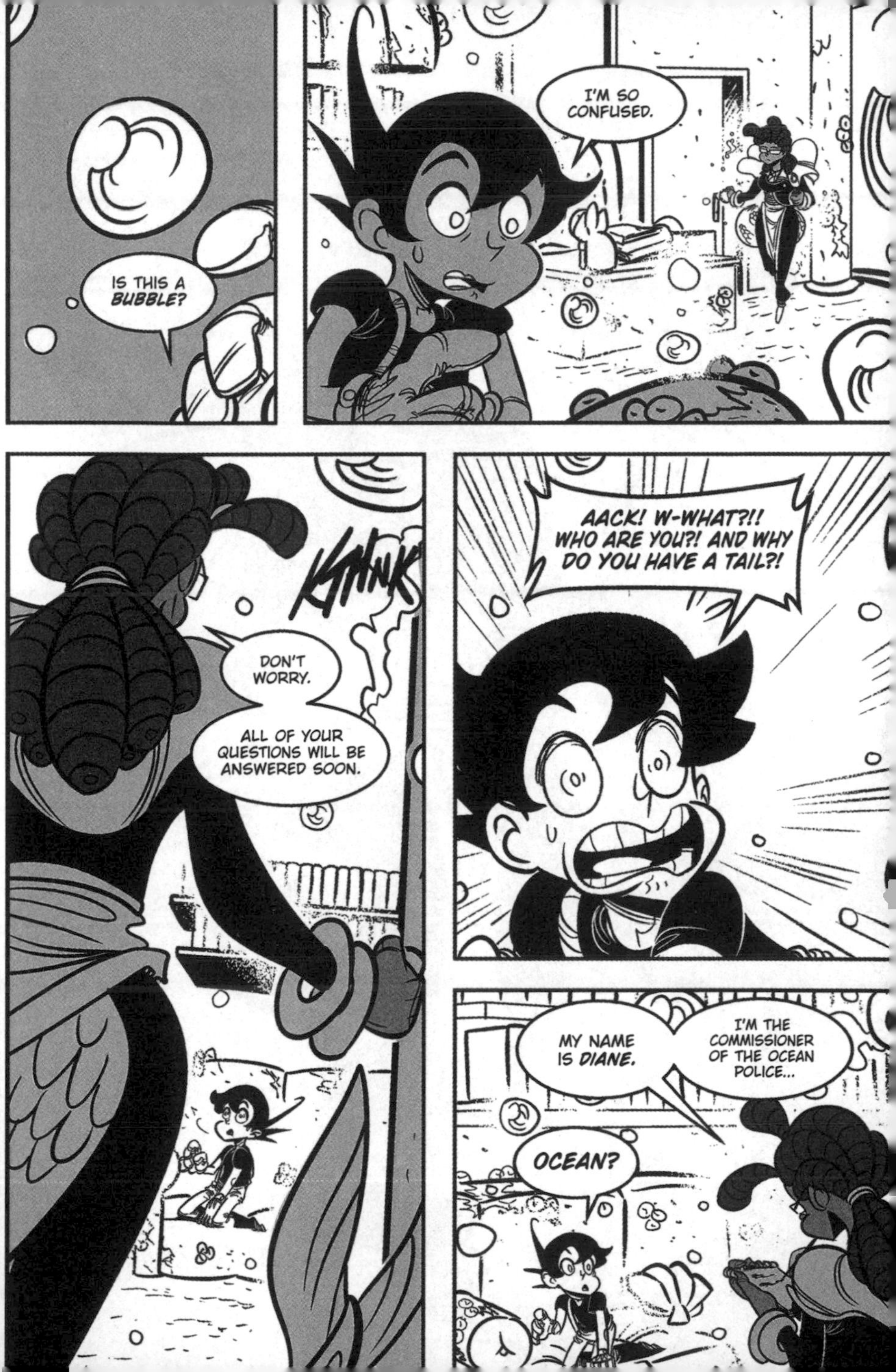
IS THIS A BUBBLE?
I'M SO CONFUSED.
KSHNK
DON'T WORRY.
ALL OF YOUR QUESTIONS WILL BE ANSWERED SOON.
AACK! W-WHAT?!! WHO ARE YOU?! AND WHY DO YOU HAVE A TAIL?!
MY NAME IS DIANE.
I'M THE COMMISSIONER OF THE OCEAN POLICE...
OCEAN?

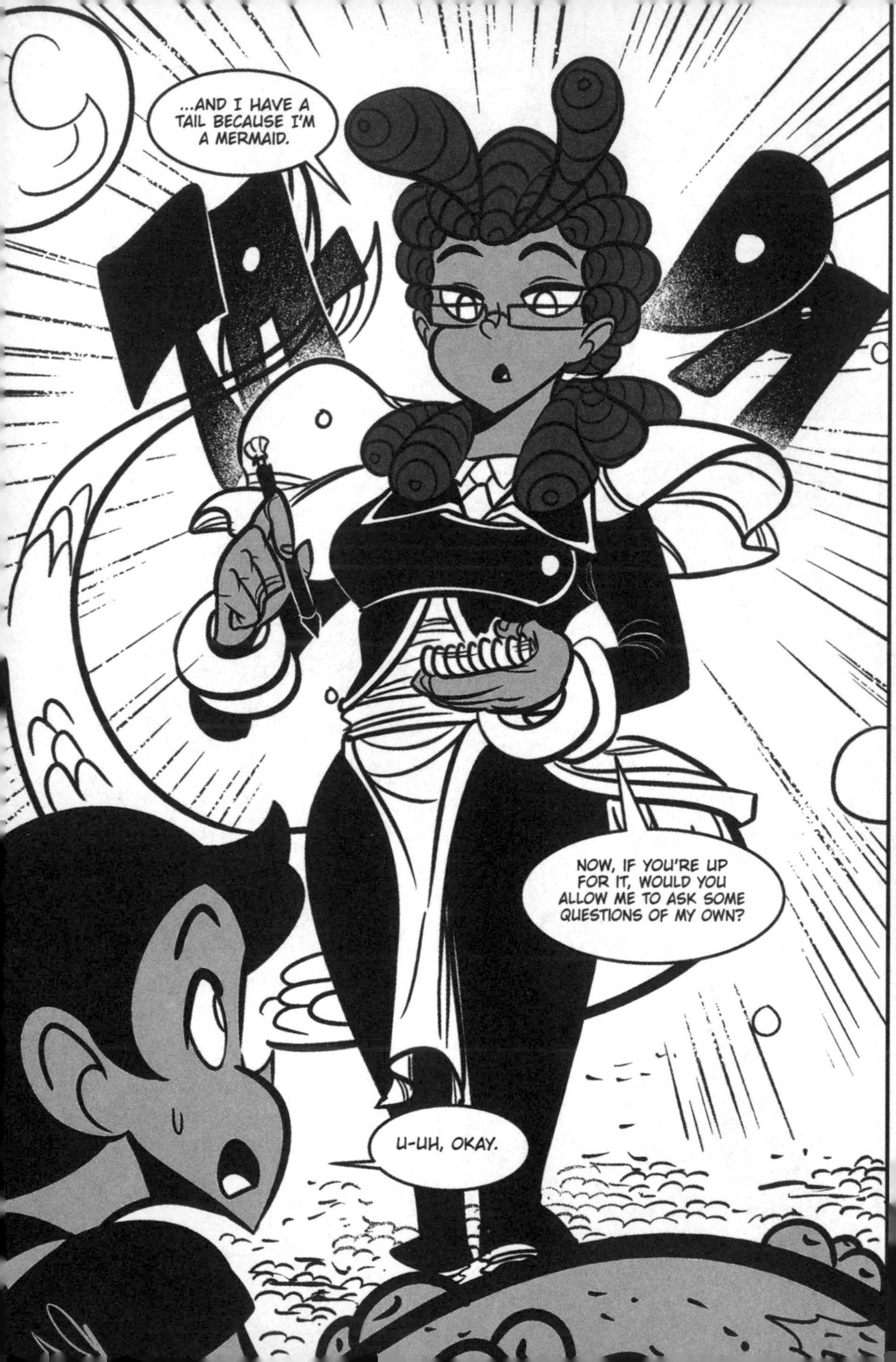
...AND I HAVE A TAIL BECAUSE I'M A MERMAID.
NOW, IF YOU'RE UP FOR IT, WOULD YOU ALLOW ME TO ASK SOME QUESTIONS OF MY OWN?
U-UH, OKAY.

HAMMER

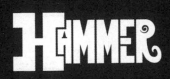

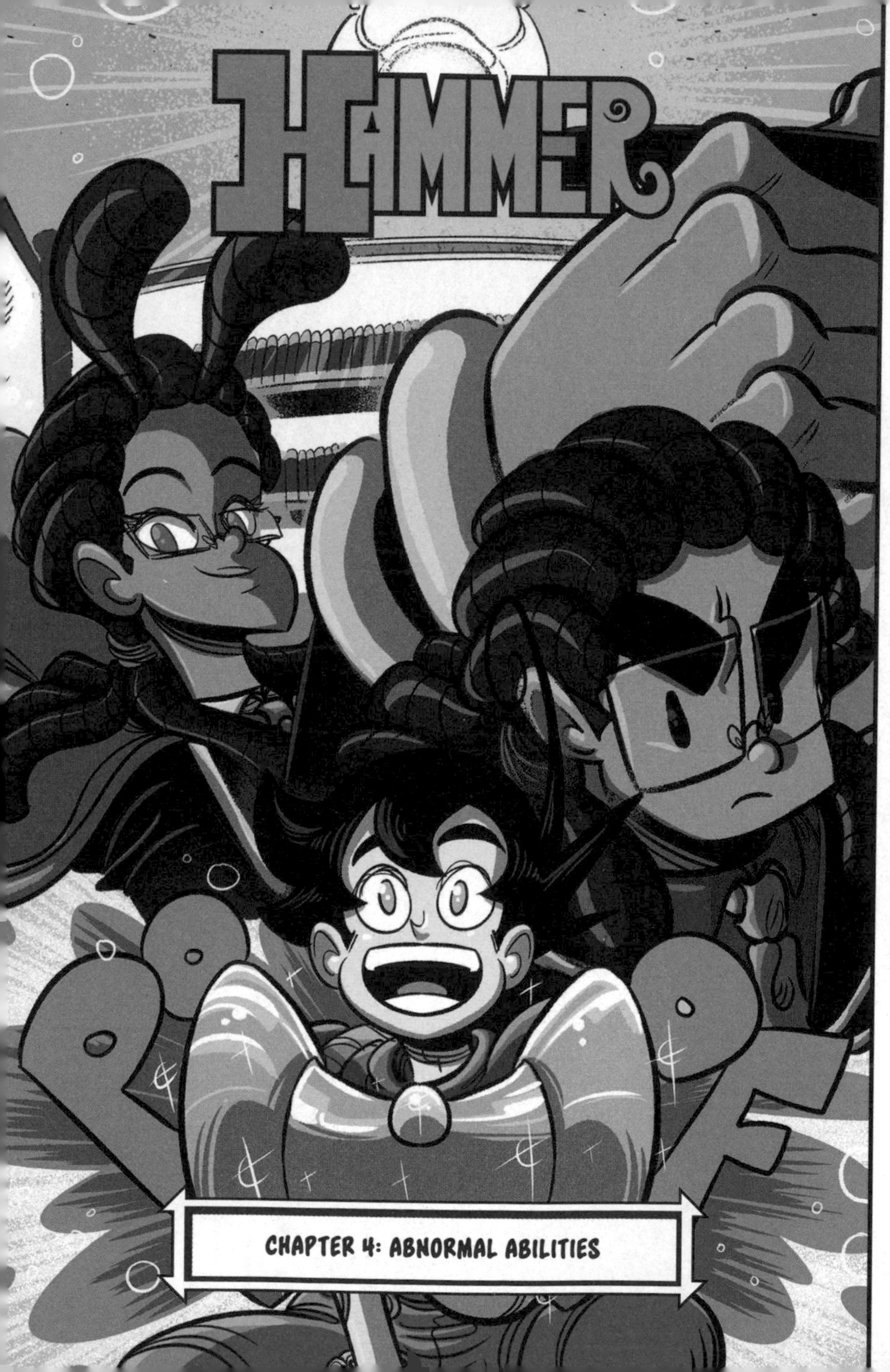
HAMMER
CHAPTER 4: ABNORMAL ABILITIES

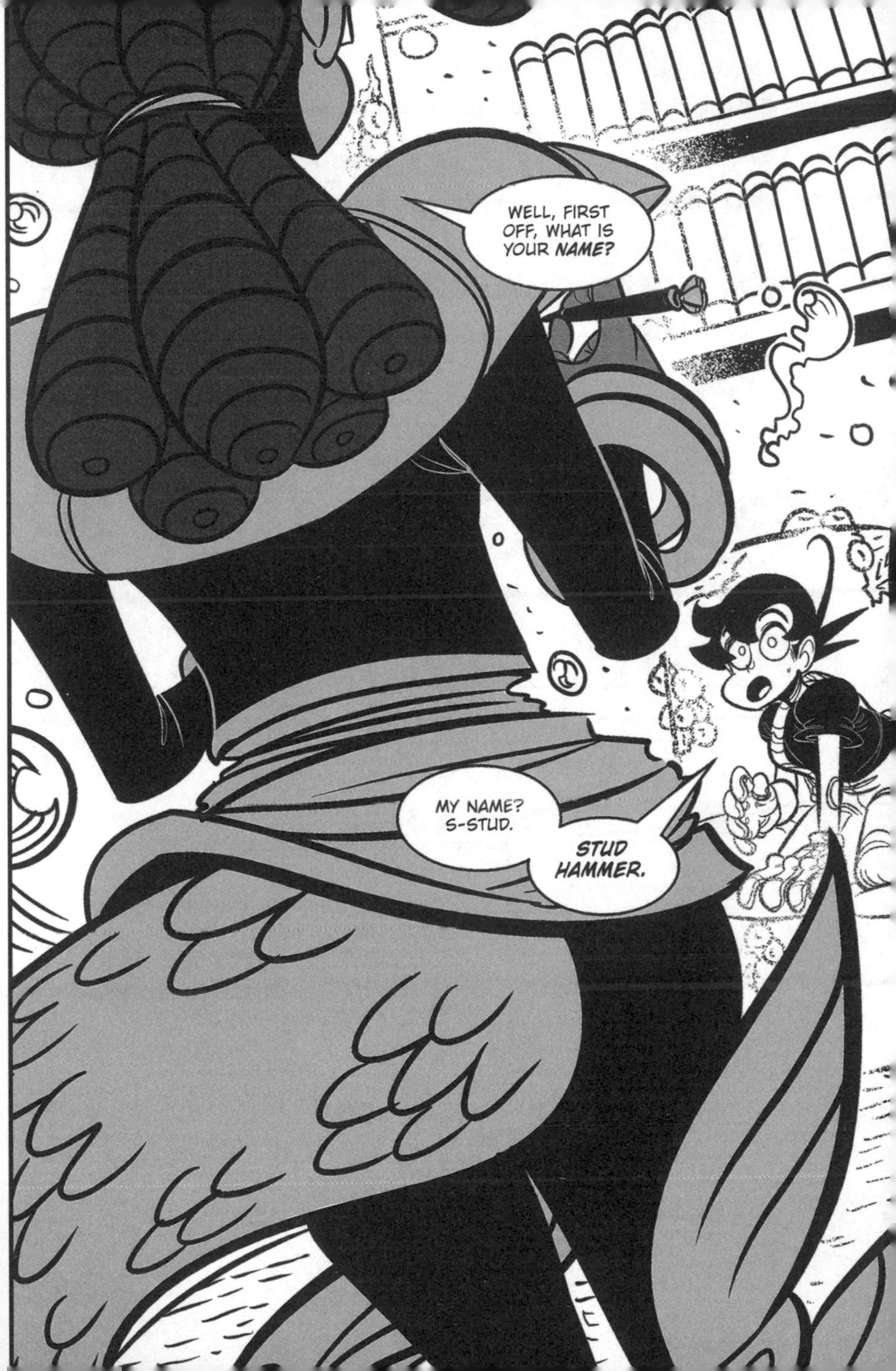
WELL, FIRST OFF, WHAT IS YOUR *NAME?*
MY NAME? S-STUD.
STUD HAMMER.

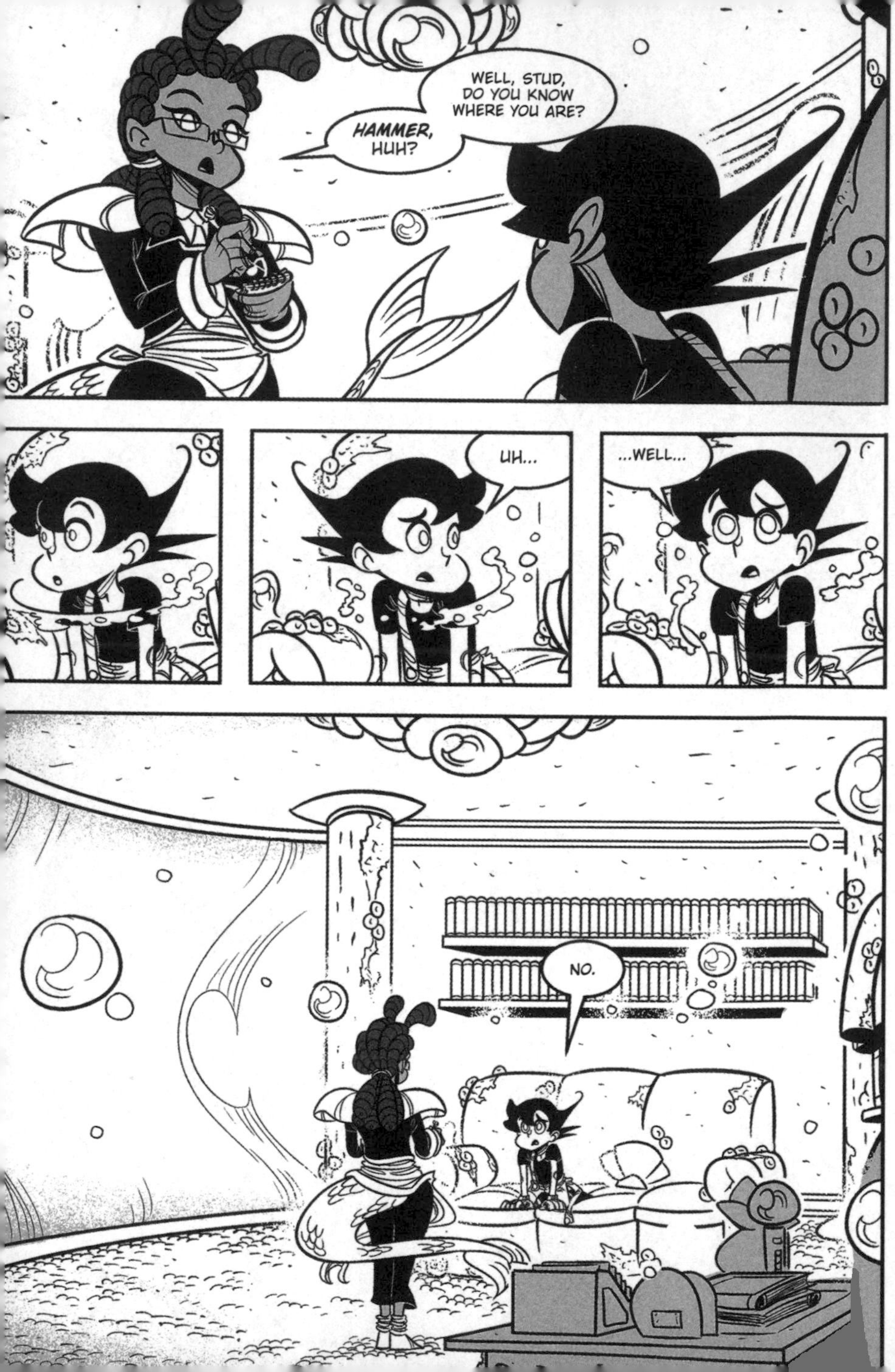
WELL, STUD, DO YOU KNOW WHERE YOU ARE?
HAMMER, HUH?
UH...
...WELL...
NO.

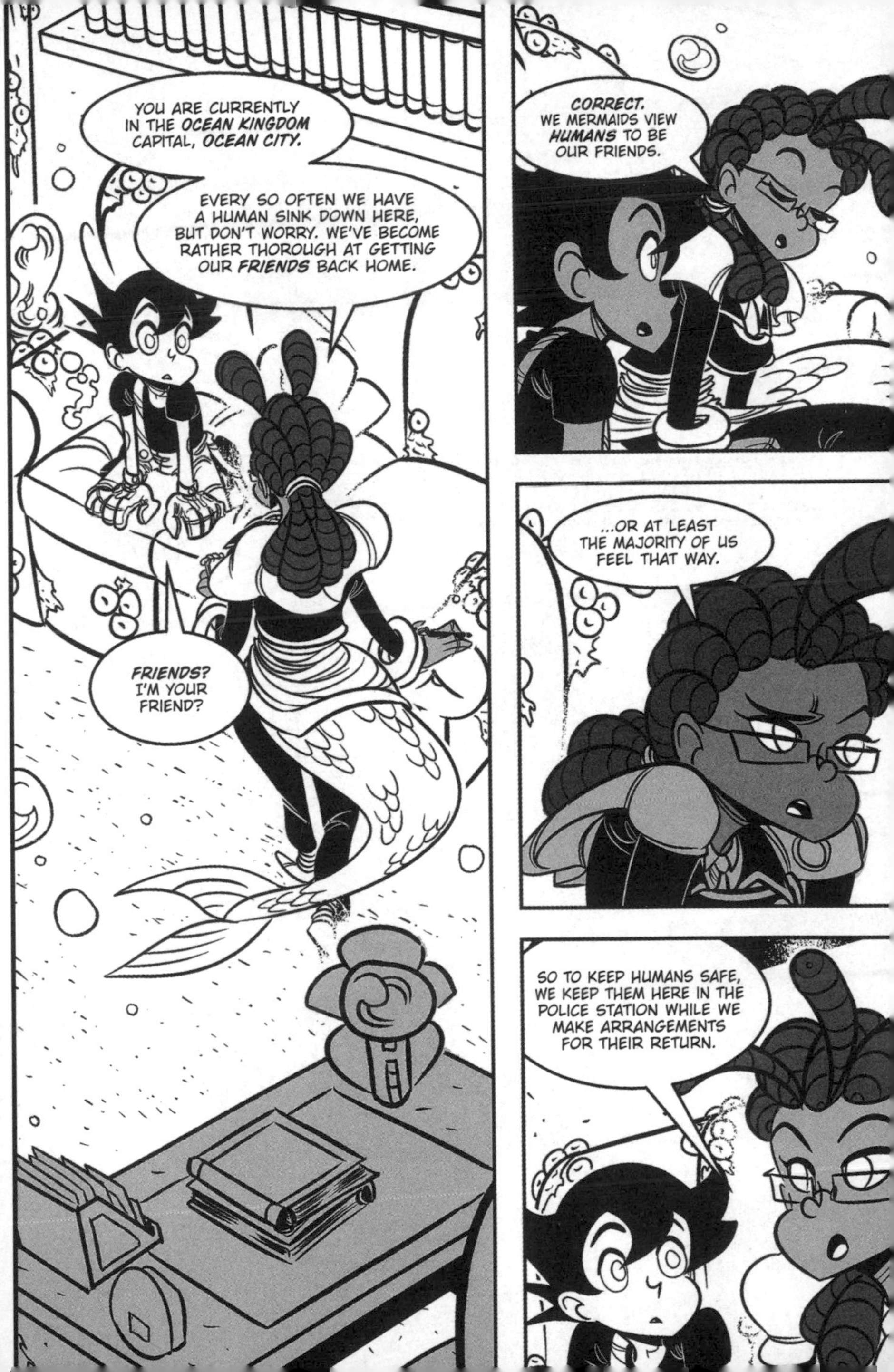
YOU ARE CURRENTLY IN THE OCEAN KINGDOM CAPITAL, OCEAN CITY.
EVERY SO OFTEN WE HAVE A HUMAN SINK DOWN HERE, BUT DON'T WORRY. WE'VE BECOME RATHER THOROUGH AT GETTING OUR FRIENDS BACK HOME.
FRIENDS? I'M YOUR FRIEND?
CORRECT. WE MERMAIDS VIEW HUMANS TO BE OUR FRIENDS.
...OR AT LEAST THE MAJORITY OF US FEEL THAT WAY.
SO TO KEEP HUMANS SAFE, WE KEEP THEM HERE IN THE POLICE STATION WHILE WE MAKE ARRANGEMENTS FOR THEIR RETURN.

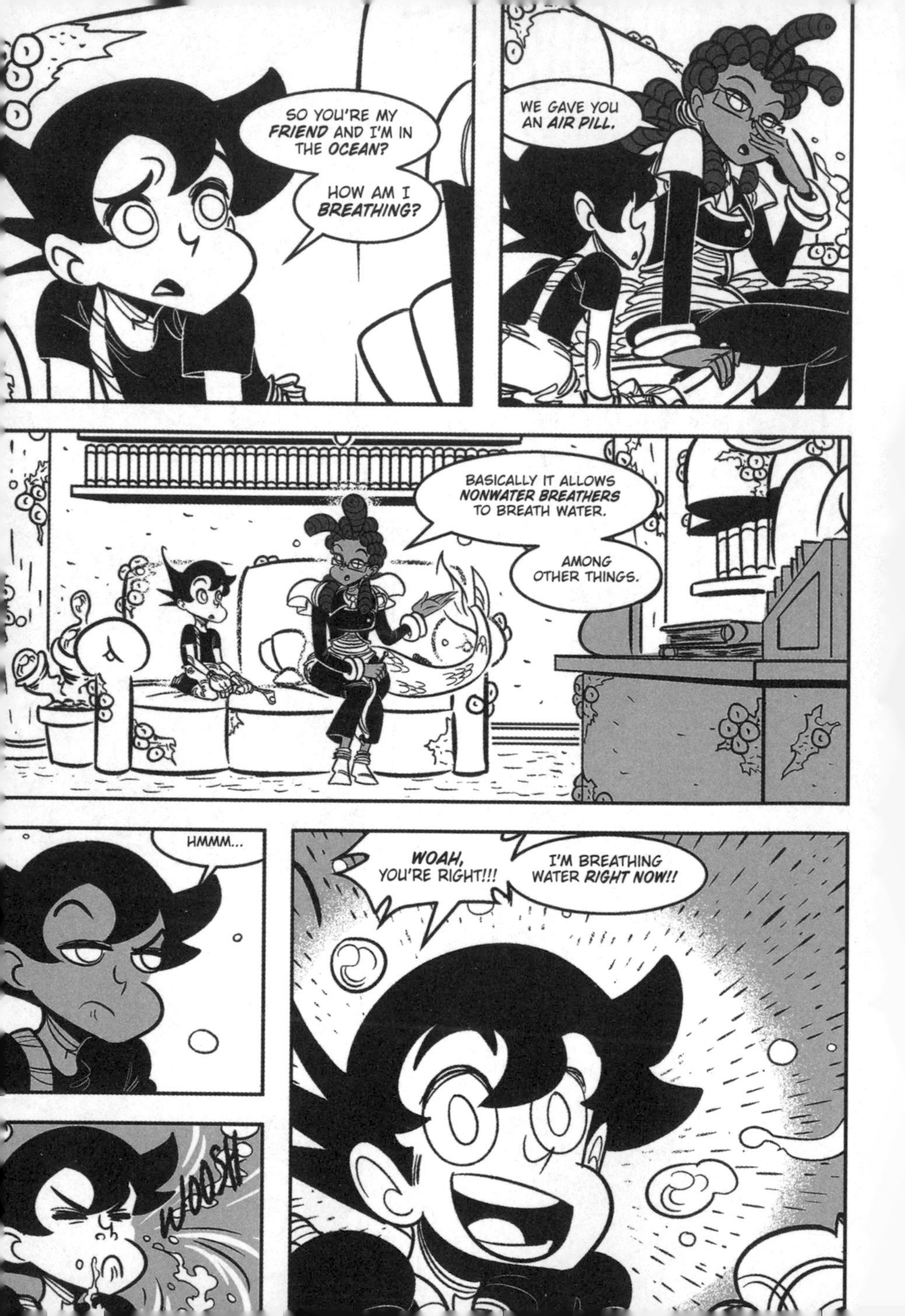
SO YOU'RE MY FRIEND AND I'M IN THE OCEAN?
HOW AM I BREATHING?
WE GAVE YOU AN AIR PILL.
BASICALLY IT ALLOWS NONWATER BREATHERS TO BREATH WATER.
AMONG OTHER THINGS.
HMMM...
WOOSH
WOAH, YOU'RE RIGHT!!!
I'M BREATHING WATER RIGHT NOW!!

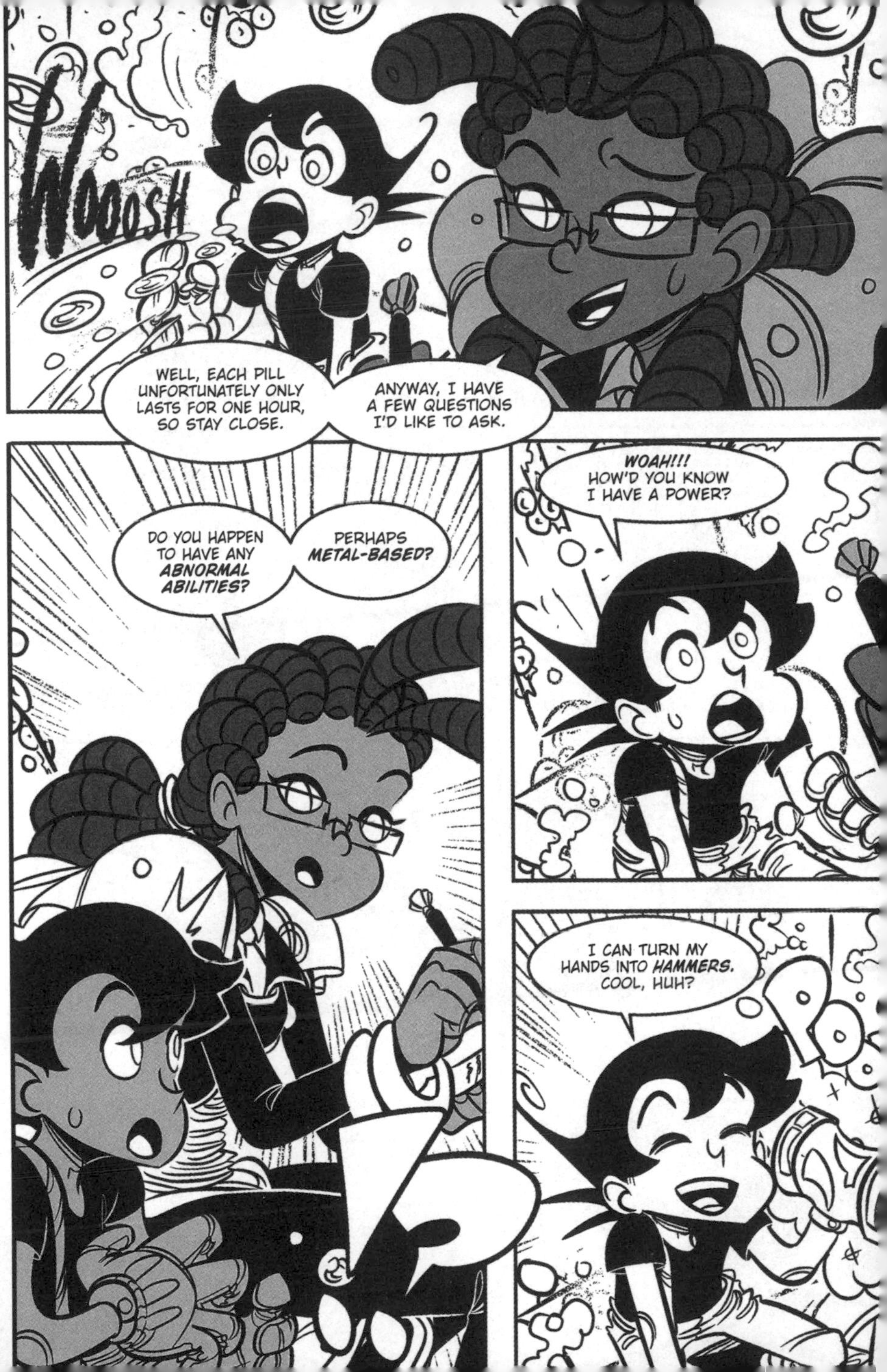
WOOOSH
WELL, EACH PILL UNFORTUNATELY ONLY LASTS FOR ONE HOUR, SO STAY CLOSE.
ANYWAY, I HAVE A FEW QUESTIONS I'D LIKE TO ASK.
DO YOU HAPPEN TO HAVE ANY ABNORMAL ABILITIES?
PERHAPS METAL-BASED?
WOAH!!! HOW'D YOU KNOW I HAVE A POWER?
I CAN TURN MY HANDS INTO HAMMERS. COOL, HUH?

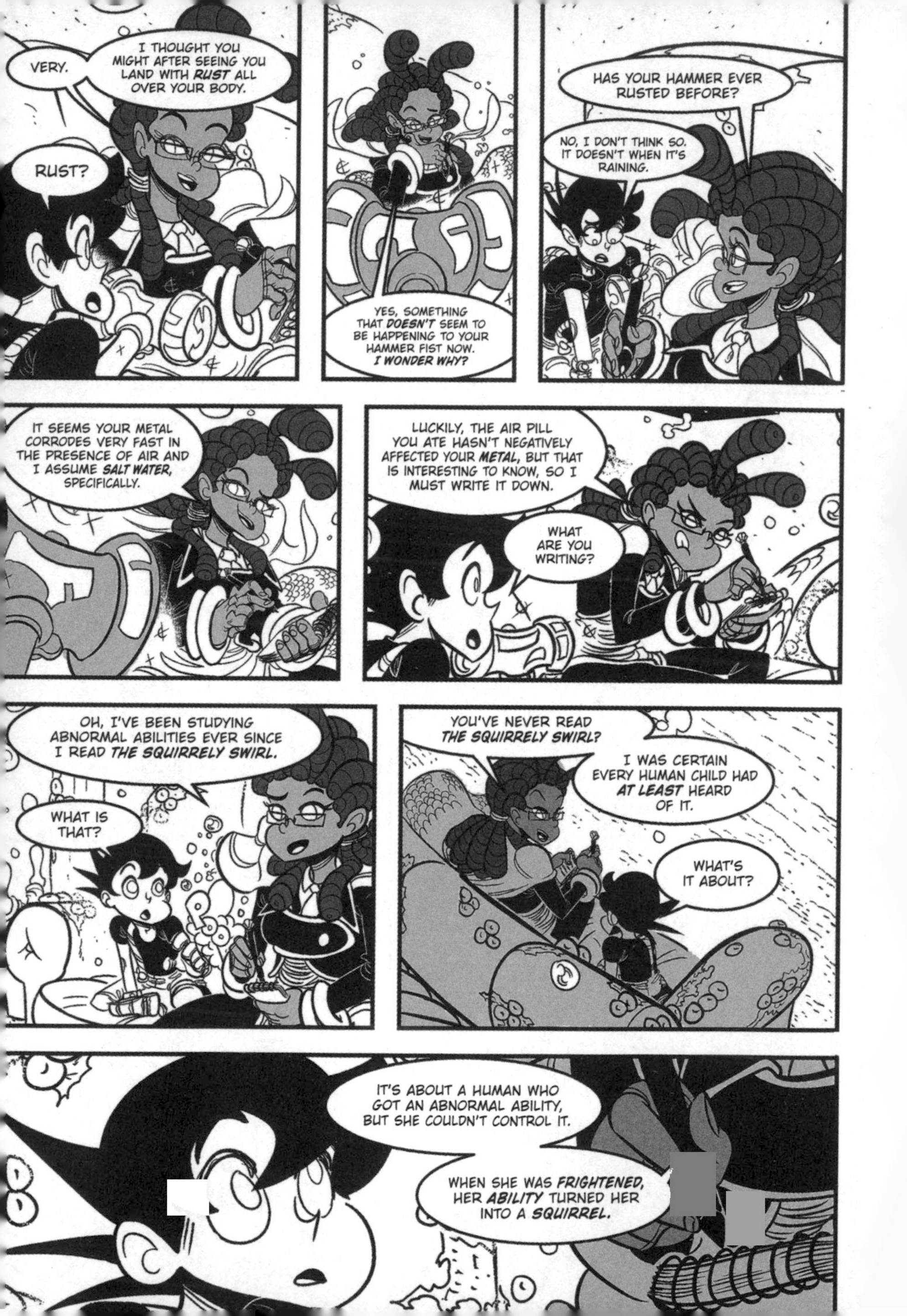
VERY.
I THOUGHT YOU MIGHT AFTER SEEING YOU LAND WITH ***RUST*** ALL OVER YOUR BODY.
RUST?
YES, SOMETHING THAT ***DOESN'T*** SEEM TO BE HAPPENING TO YOUR HAMMER FIST NOW. ***I WONDER WHY?***
HAS YOUR HAMMER EVER RUSTED BEFORE?
NO, I DON'T THINK SO. IT DOESN'T WHEN IT'S RAINING.
IT SEEMS YOUR METAL CORRODES VERY FAST IN THE PRESENCE OF AIR AND I ASSUME ***SALT WATER***, SPECIFICALLY.
LUCKILY, THE AIR PILL YOU ATE HASN'T NEGATIVELY AFFECTED YOUR ***METAL***, BUT THAT IS INTERESTING TO KNOW, SO I MUST WRITE IT DOWN.
WHAT ARE YOU WRITING?
OH, I'VE BEEN STUDYING ABNORMAL ABILITIES EVER SINCE I READ ***THE SQUIRRELY SWIRL.***
WHAT IS THAT?
YOU'VE NEVER READ ***THE SQUIRRELY SWIRL?***
I WAS CERTAIN EVERY HUMAN CHILD HAD ***AT LEAST*** HEARD OF IT.
WHAT'S IT ABOUT?
IT'S ABOUT A HUMAN WHO GOT AN ABNORMAL ABILITY, BUT SHE COULDN'T CONTROL IT.
WHEN SHE WAS ***FRIGHTENED***, HER ***ABILITY*** TURNED HER INTO A ***SQUIRREL.***

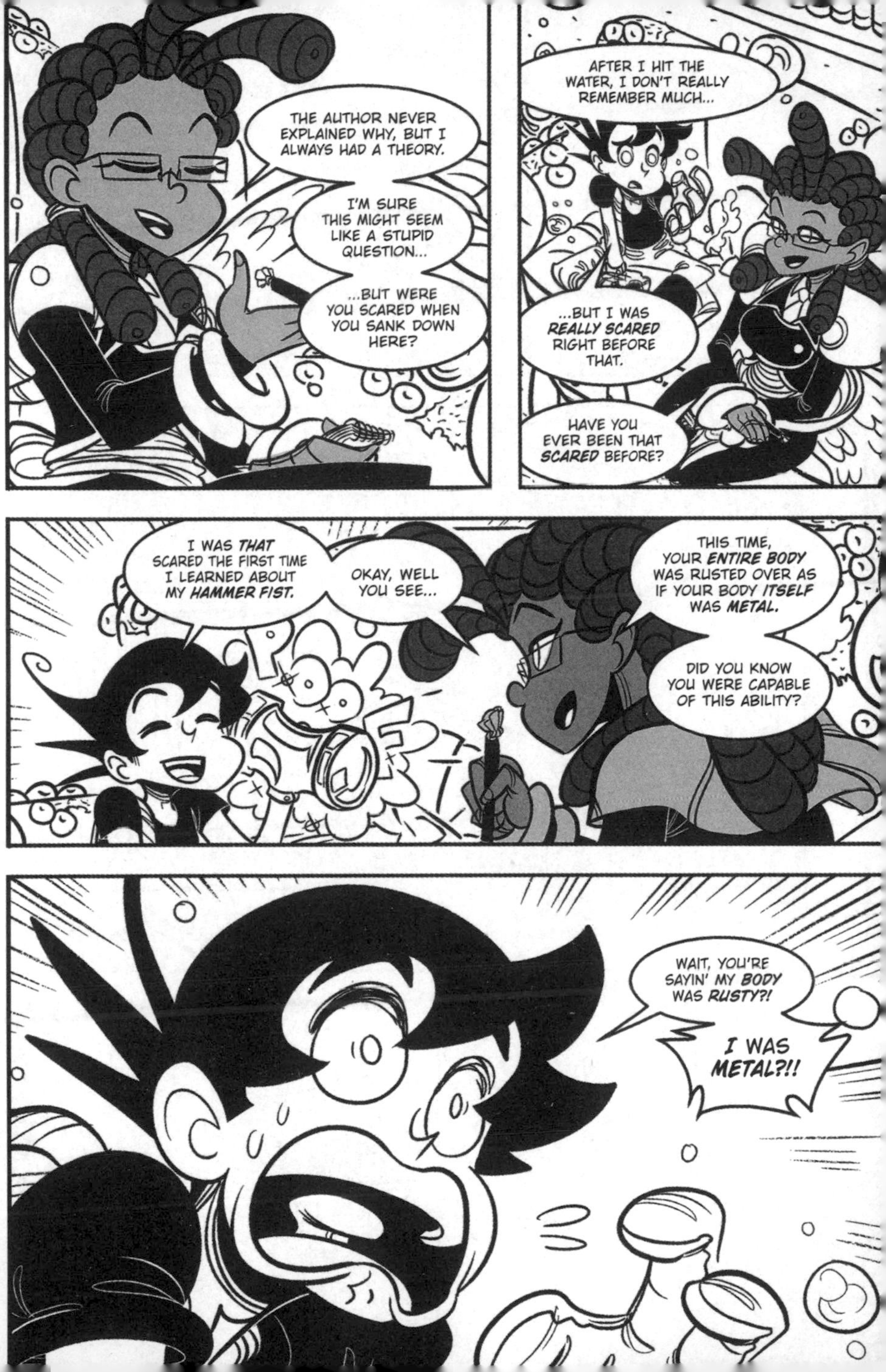
THE AUTHOR NEVER EXPLAINED WHY, BUT I ALWAYS HAD A THEORY.
I'M SURE THIS MIGHT SEEM LIKE A STUPID QUESTION...
...BUT WERE YOU SCARED WHEN YOU SANK DOWN HERE?
AFTER I HIT THE WATER, I DON'T REALLY REMEMBER MUCH...
...BUT I WAS REALLY SCARED RIGHT BEFORE THAT.
HAVE YOU EVER BEEN THAT SCARED BEFORE?
I WAS THAT SCARED THE FIRST TIME I LEARNED ABOUT MY HAMMER FIST.
POOF
OKAY, WELL YOU SEE...
THIS TIME, YOUR ENTIRE BODY WAS RUSTED OVER AS IF YOUR BODY ITSELF WAS METAL.
DID YOU KNOW YOU WERE CAPABLE OF THIS ABILITY?
WAIT, YOU'RE SAYIN' MY BODY WAS RUSTY?!
I WAS METAL?!!

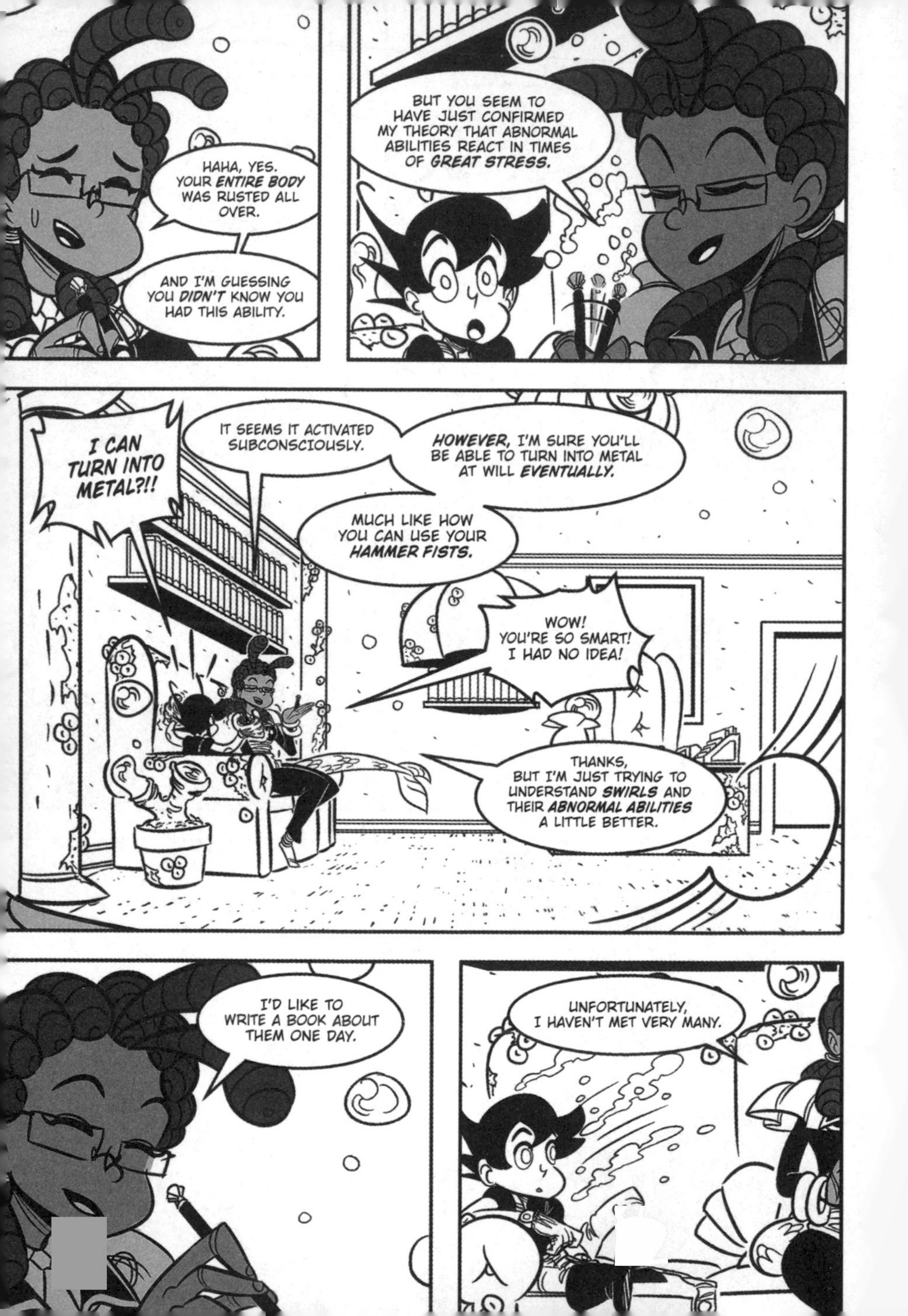
HAHA, YES. YOUR ENTIRE BODY WAS RUSTED ALL OVER.
AND I'M GUESSING YOU DIDN'T KNOW YOU HAD THIS ABILITY.
BUT YOU SEEM TO HAVE JUST CONFIRMED MY THEORY THAT ABNORMAL ABILITIES REACT IN TIMES OF GREAT STRESS.
I CAN TURN INTO METAL?!!
IT SEEMS IT ACTIVATED SUBCONSCIOUSLY.
HOWEVER, I'M SURE YOU'LL BE ABLE TO TURN INTO METAL AT WILL EVENTUALLY.
MUCH LIKE HOW YOU CAN USE YOUR HAMMER FISTS.
WOW! YOU'RE SO SMART! I HAD NO IDEA!
THANKS, BUT I'M JUST TRYING TO UNDERSTAND SWIRLS AND THEIR ABNORMAL ABILITIES A LITTLE BETTER.
I'D LIKE TO WRITE A BOOK ABOUT THEM ONE DAY.
UNFORTUNATELY, I HAVEN'T MET VERY MANY.

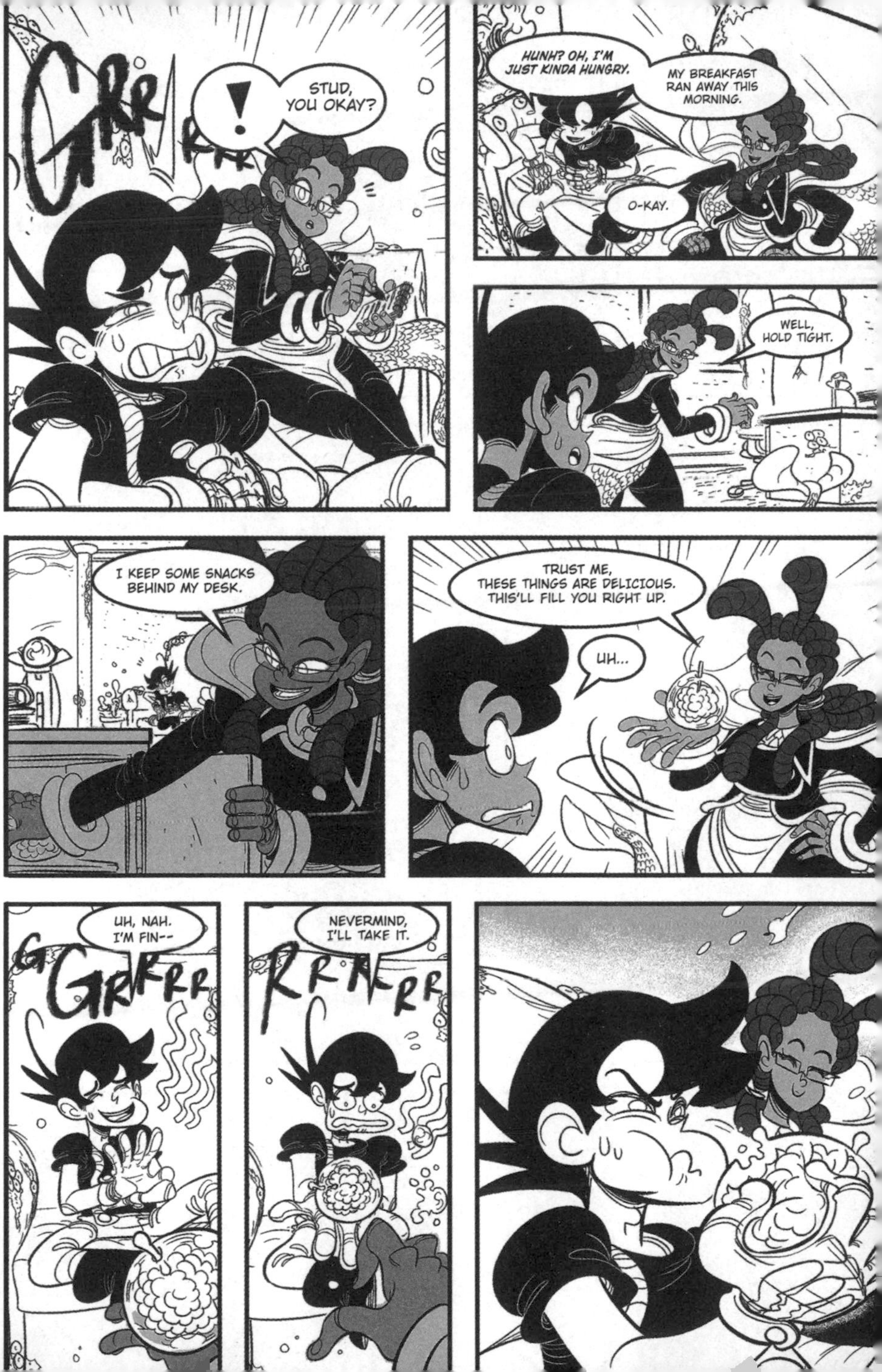
GRRRRR
!
STUD, YOU OKAY?
HUNH? OH, I'M JUST KINDA HUNGRY.
MY BREAKFAST RAN AWAY THIS MORNING.
O-KAY.
WELL, HOLD TIGHT.
I KEEP SOME SNACKS BEHIND MY DESK.
TRUST ME, THESE THINGS ARE DELICIOUS. THIS'LL FILL YOU RIGHT UP.
UH...
UH, NAH. I'M FIN--
GGRRRRR
NEVERMIND, I'LL TAKE IT.
RRRRRR

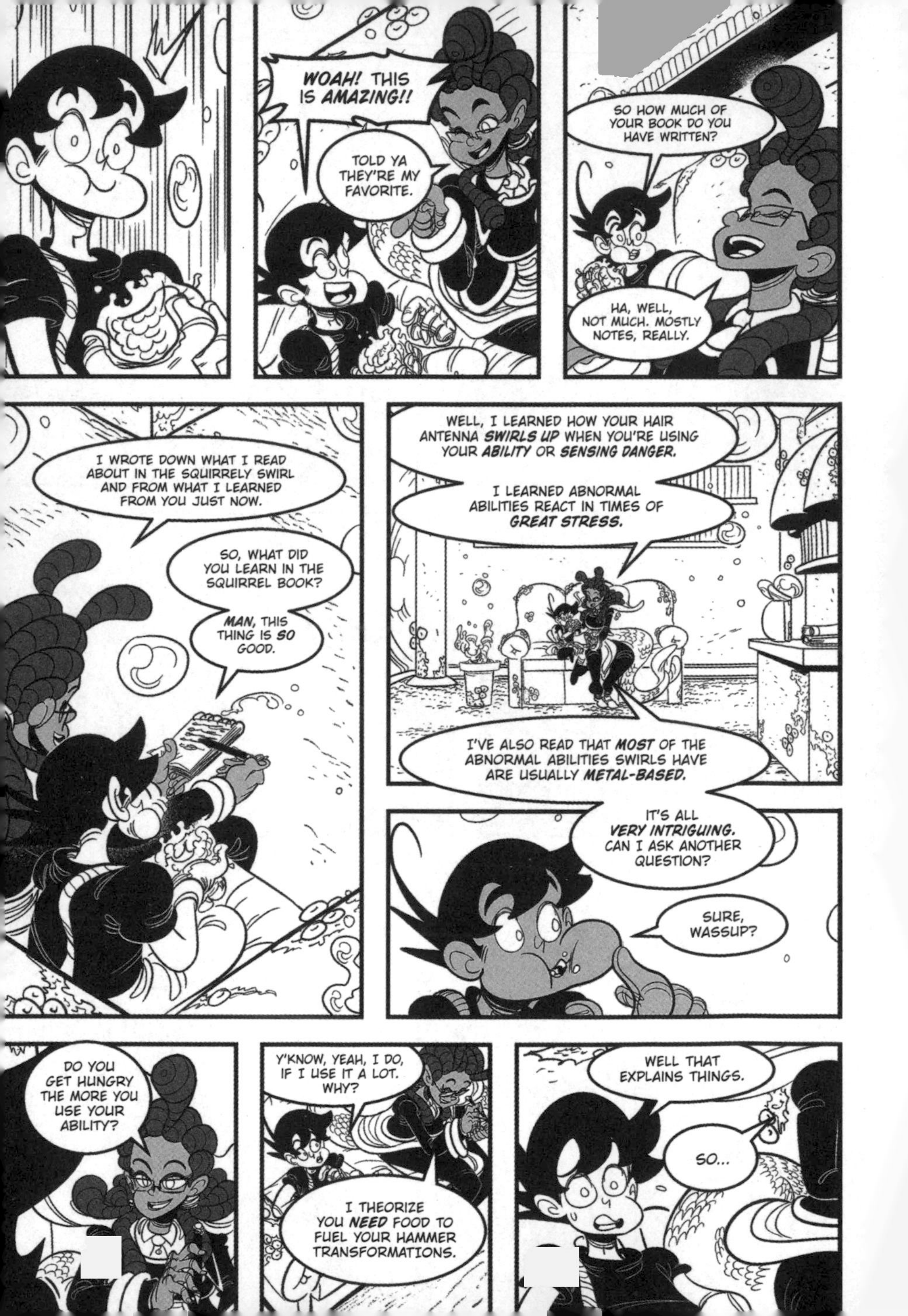
WOAH! THIS IS AMAZING!!
TOLD YA THEY'RE MY FAVORITE.
SO HOW MUCH OF YOUR BOOK DO YOU HAVE WRITTEN?
HA, WELL, NOT MUCH. MOSTLY NOTES, REALLY.
I WROTE DOWN WHAT I READ ABOUT IN THE SQUIRRELY SWIRL AND FROM WHAT I LEARNED FROM YOU JUST NOW.
SO, WHAT DID YOU LEARN IN THE SQUIRREL BOOK?
MAN, THIS THING IS SO GOOD.
WELL, I LEARNED HOW YOUR HAIR ANTENNA SWIRLS UP WHEN YOU'RE USING YOUR ABILITY OR SENSING DANGER.
I LEARNED ABNORMAL ABILITIES REACT IN TIMES OF GREAT STRESS.
I'VE ALSO READ THAT MOST OF THE ABNORMAL ABILITIES SWIRLS HAVE ARE USUALLY METAL-BASED.
IT'S ALL VERY INTRIGUING. CAN I ASK ANOTHER QUESTION?
SURE, WASSUP?
DO YOU GET HUNGRY THE MORE YOU USE YOUR ABILITY?
Y'KNOW, YEAH, I DO, IF I USE IT A LOT. WHY?
I THEORIZE YOU NEED FOOD TO FUEL YOUR HAMMER TRANSFORMATIONS.
WELL THAT EXPLAINS THINGS.
SO...

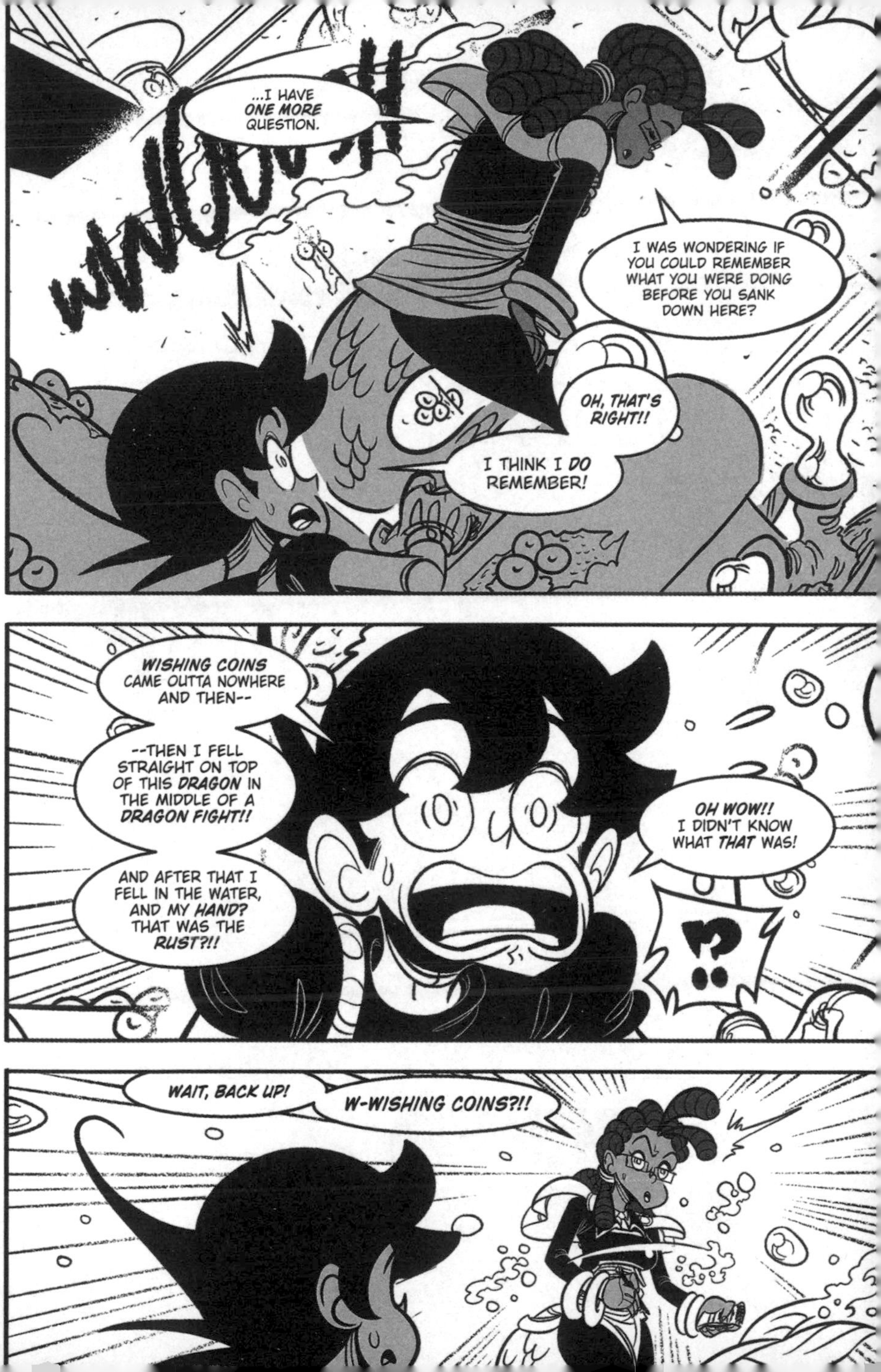
...I HAVE ONE MORE QUESTION.
WHOOOSH
I WAS WONDERING IF YOU COULD REMEMBER WHAT YOU WERE DOING BEFORE YOU SANK DOWN HERE?
OH, THAT'S RIGHT!!
I THINK I DO REMEMBER!
WISHING COINS CAME OUTTA NOWHERE AND THEN--
--THEN I FELL STRAIGHT ON TOP OF THIS DRAGON IN THE MIDDLE OF A DRAGON FIGHT!!
AND AFTER THAT I FELL IN THE WATER, AND MY HAND? THAT WAS THE RUST?!!
OH WOW!! I DIDN'T KNOW WHAT THAT WAS!
!?
WAIT, BACK UP!
W-WISHING COINS?!!

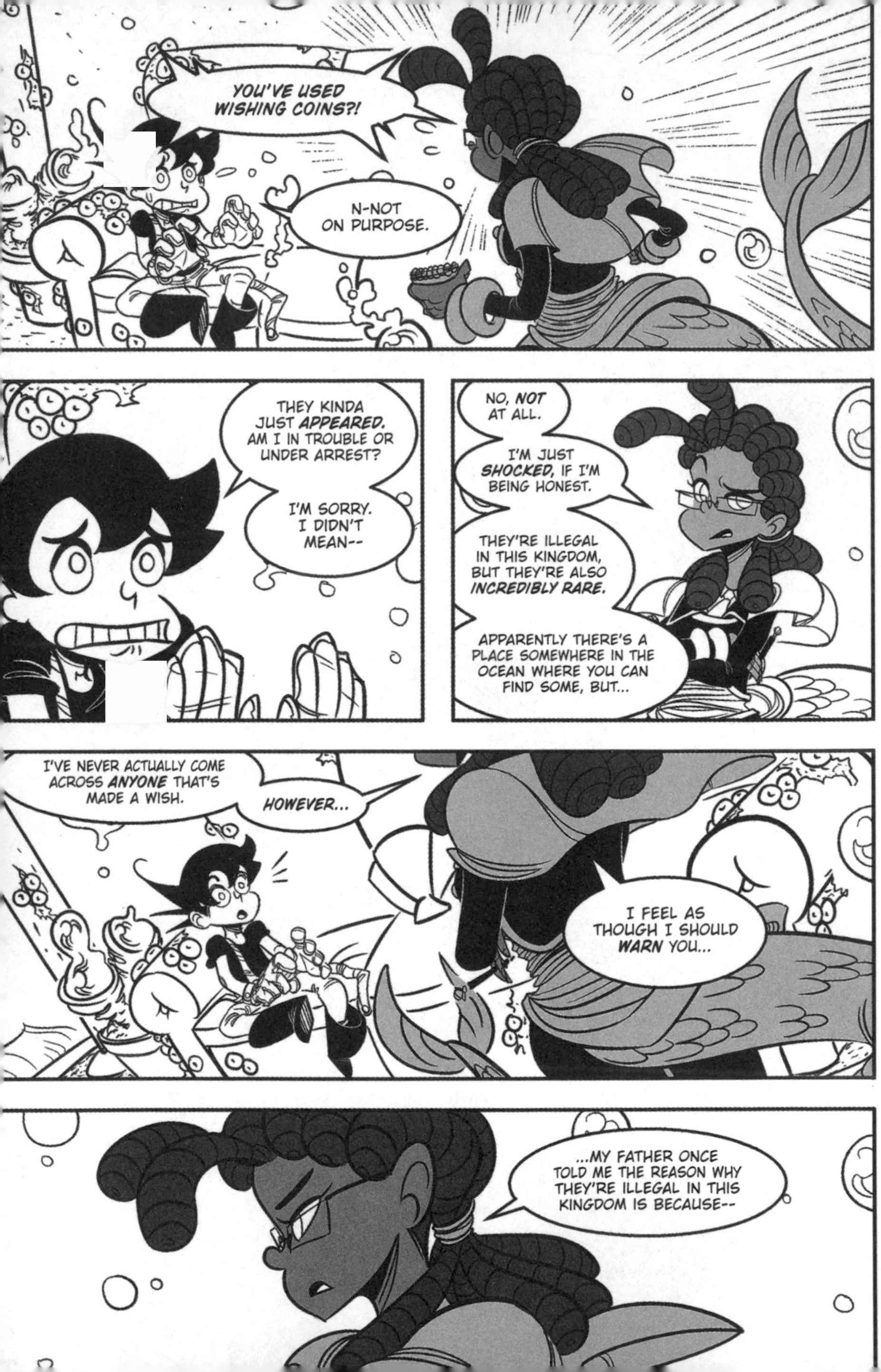
YOU'VE USED WISHING COINS?!
N-NOT ON PURPOSE.
THEY KINDA JUST APPEARED. AM I IN TROUBLE OR UNDER ARREST?
I'M SORRY. I DIDN'T MEAN--
NO, NOT AT ALL.
I'M JUST SHOCKED, IF I'M BEING HONEST.
THEY'RE ILLEGAL IN THIS KINGDOM, BUT THEY'RE ALSO INCREDIBLY RARE.
APPARENTLY THERE'S A PLACE SOMEWHERE IN THE OCEAN WHERE YOU CAN FIND SOME, BUT...
I'VE NEVER ACTUALLY COME ACROSS ANYONE THAT'S MADE A WISH.
HOWEVER...
I FEEL AS THOUGH I SHOULD WARN YOU...
...MY FATHER ONCE TOLD ME THE REASON WHY THEY'RE ILLEGAL IN THIS KINGDOM IS BECAUSE--

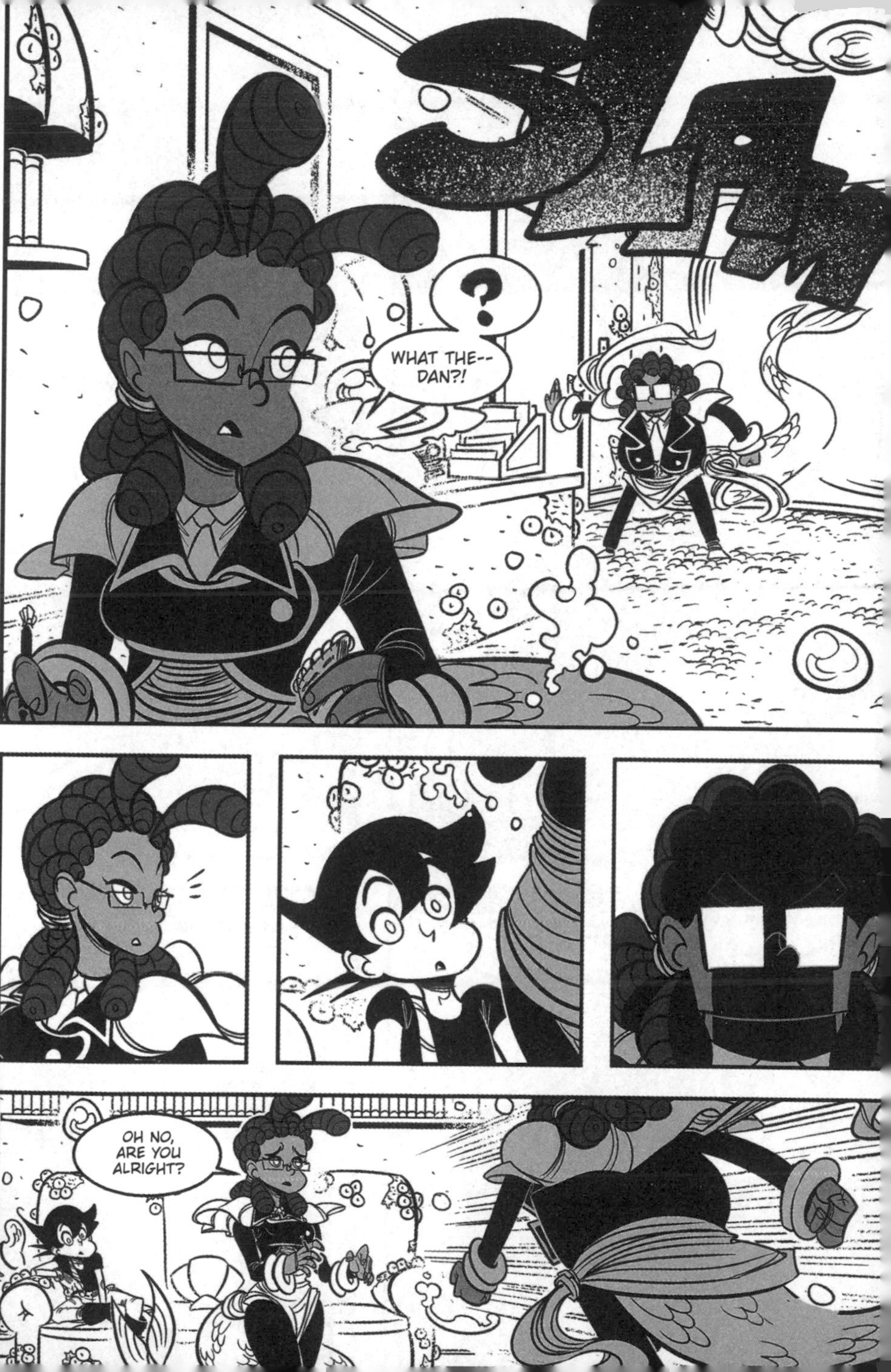
SLAM
?
WHAT THE-- DAN?!
OH NO, ARE YOU ALRIGHT?

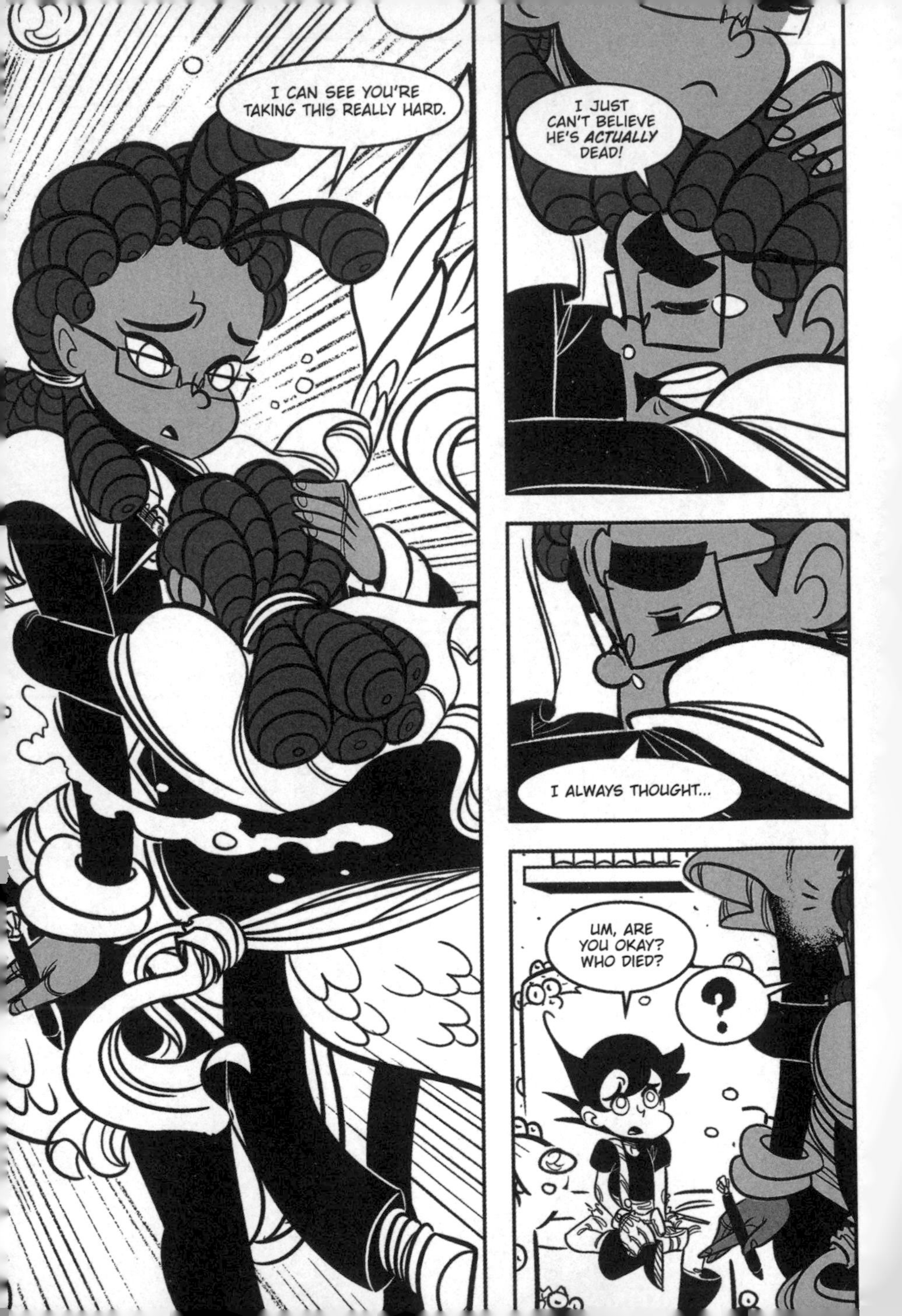
I CAN SEE YOU'RE TAKING THIS REALLY HARD.
I JUST CAN'T BELIEVE HE'S *ACTUALLY* DEAD!
I ALWAYS THOUGHT...
UM, ARE YOU OKAY? WHO DIED?
?

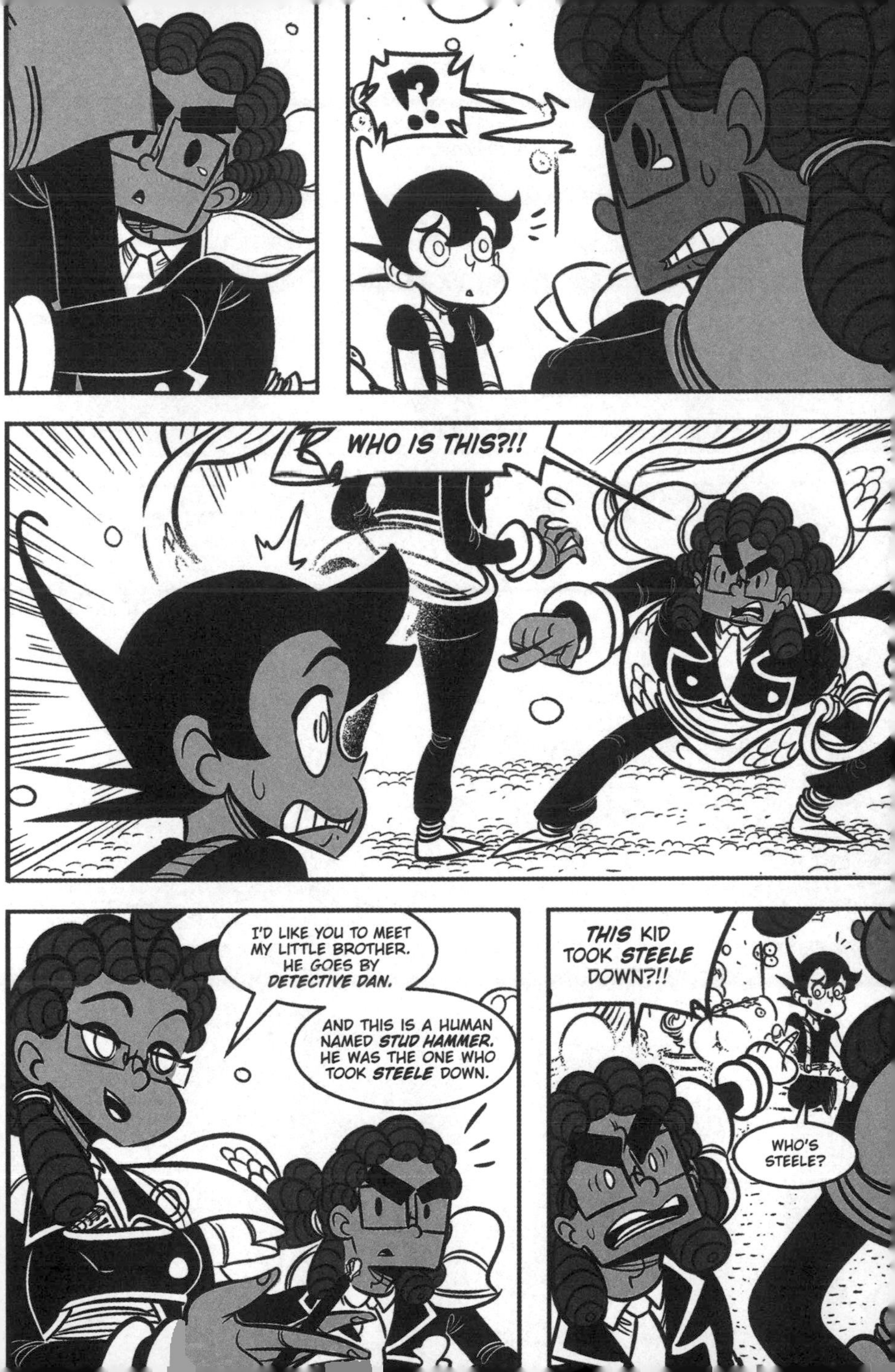
!?
WHO IS THIS?!!
I'D LIKE YOU TO MEET MY LITTLE BROTHER. HE GOES BY DETECTIVE DAN.
AND THIS IS A HUMAN NAMED STUD HAMMER. HE WAS THE ONE WHO TOOK STEELE DOWN.
THIS KID TOOK STEELE DOWN?!!
WHO'S STEELE?

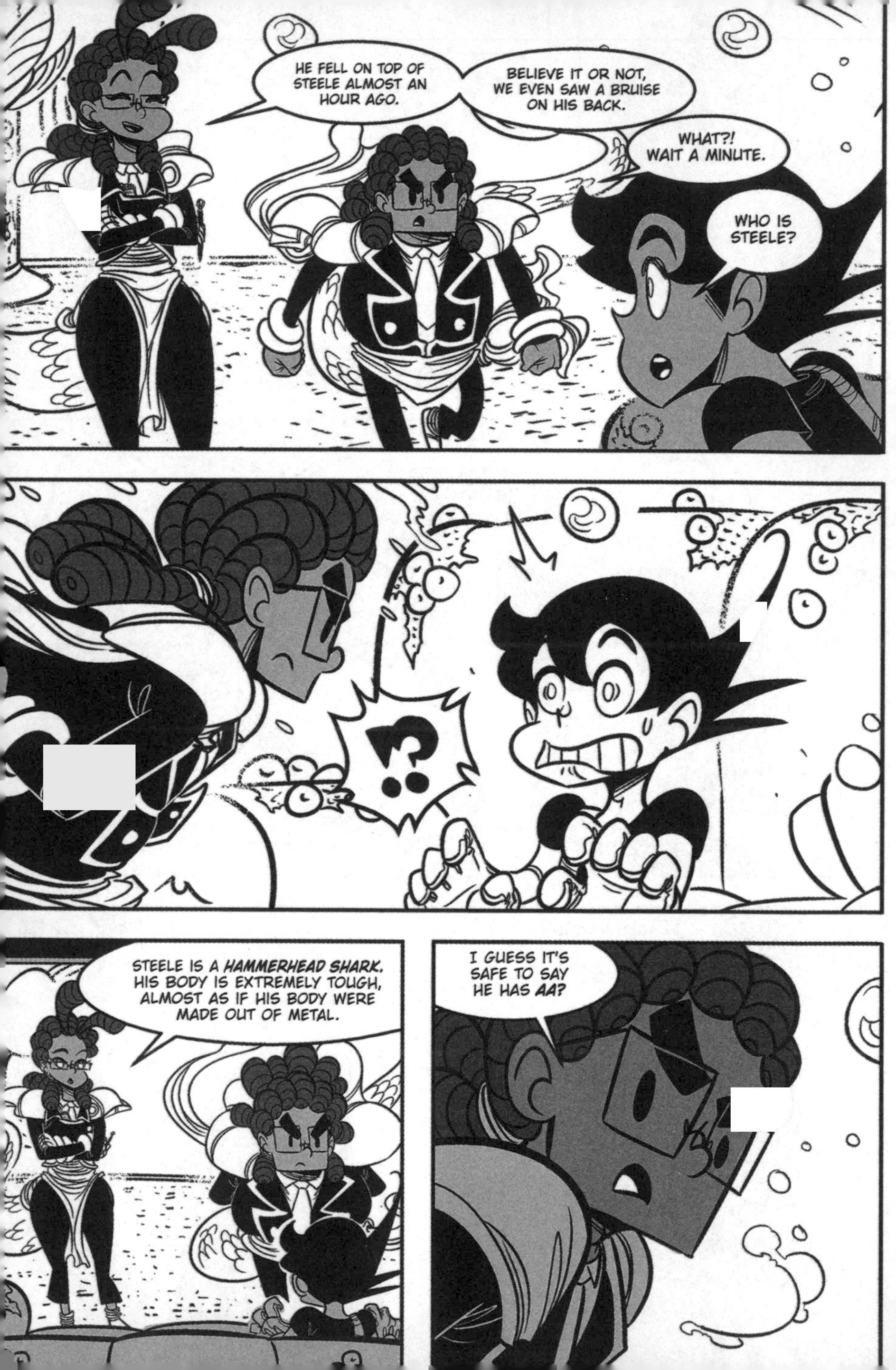
HE FELL ON TOP OF STEELE ALMOST AN HOUR AGO.
BELIEVE IT OR NOT, WE EVEN SAW A BRUISE ON HIS BACK.
WHAT?! WAIT A MINUTE.
WHO IS STEELE?
!?
STEELE IS A *HAMMERHEAD SHARK.* HIS BODY IS EXTREMELY TOUGH, ALMOST AS IF HIS BODY WERE MADE OUT OF METAL.
I GUESS IT'S SAFE TO SAY HE HAS *AA?*

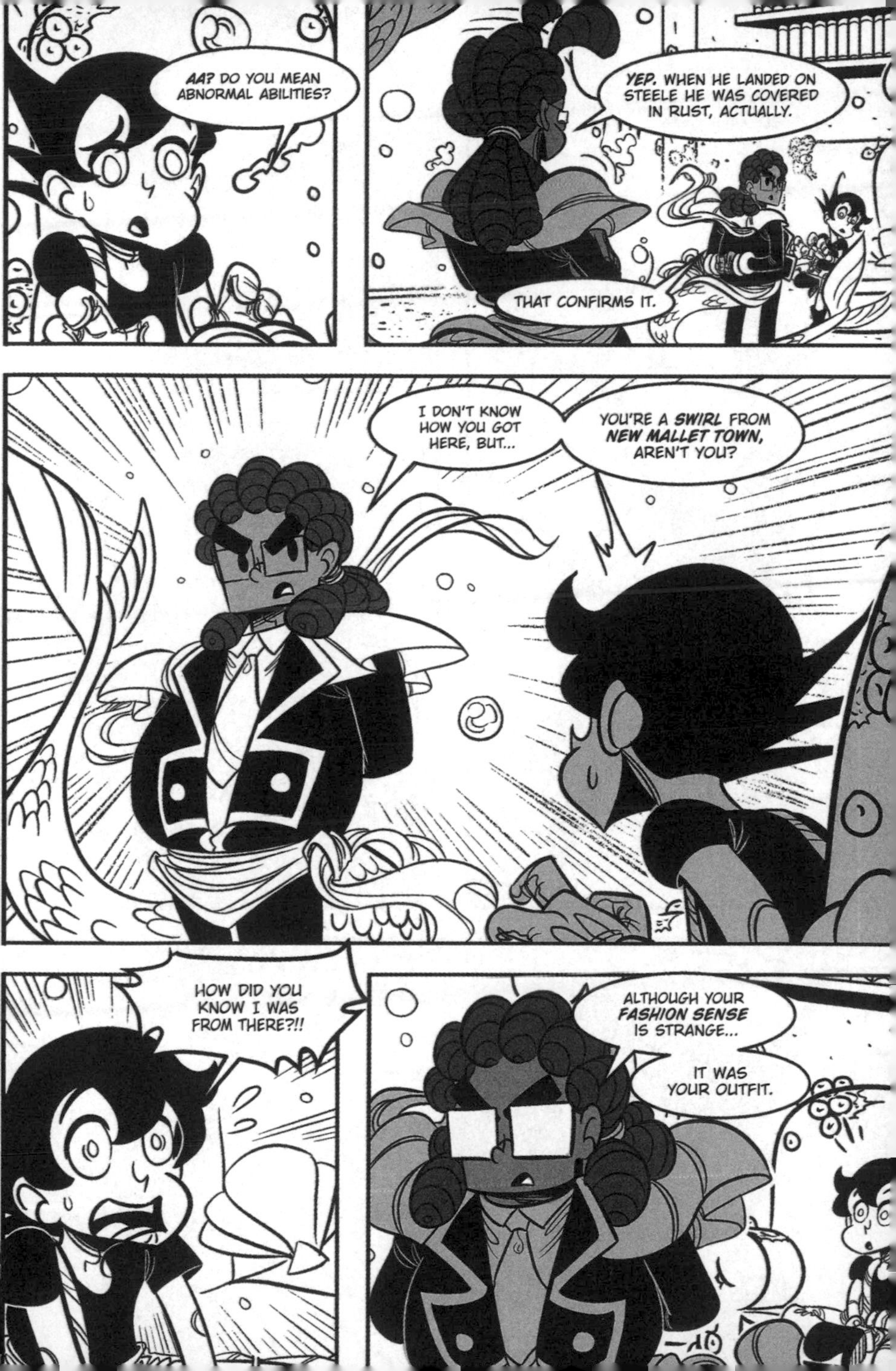

AA? DO YOU MEAN ABNORMAL ABILITIES?
YEP. WHEN HE LANDED ON STEELE HE WAS COVERED IN RUST, ACTUALLY.
THAT CONFIRMS IT.
I DON'T KNOW HOW YOU GOT HERE, BUT...
YOU'RE A SWIRL FROM NEW MALLET TOWN, AREN'T YOU?
HOW DID YOU KNOW I WAS FROM THERE?!!
ALTHOUGH YOUR FASHION SENSE IS STRANGE...
IT WAS YOUR OUTFIT.

YOUR OVERALLS, BOOTS, AND EVEN THE MAKE OF THOSE BRIGHT YELLOW GLOVES...

THEY ALL SCREAM, *"I'M FROM NEW MALLET TOWN."* MY ONLY QUESTION IS WHY YOU ONLY HAVE ONE STRAP ON.

WELL THAT'S STUPID. IT DEFEATS THE PURPOSE OF WEARING OVERALLS.

HUH? BUT EVERYONE WEARS IT LIKE THIS.

IN FACT, THE *LAST* HUMAN I SAW HAD BOTH STRAPS ON, SO MAYBE YOU'RE JUST *WEIRD.*

I'M WEIRD?

YOU'RE WEIRD!!!

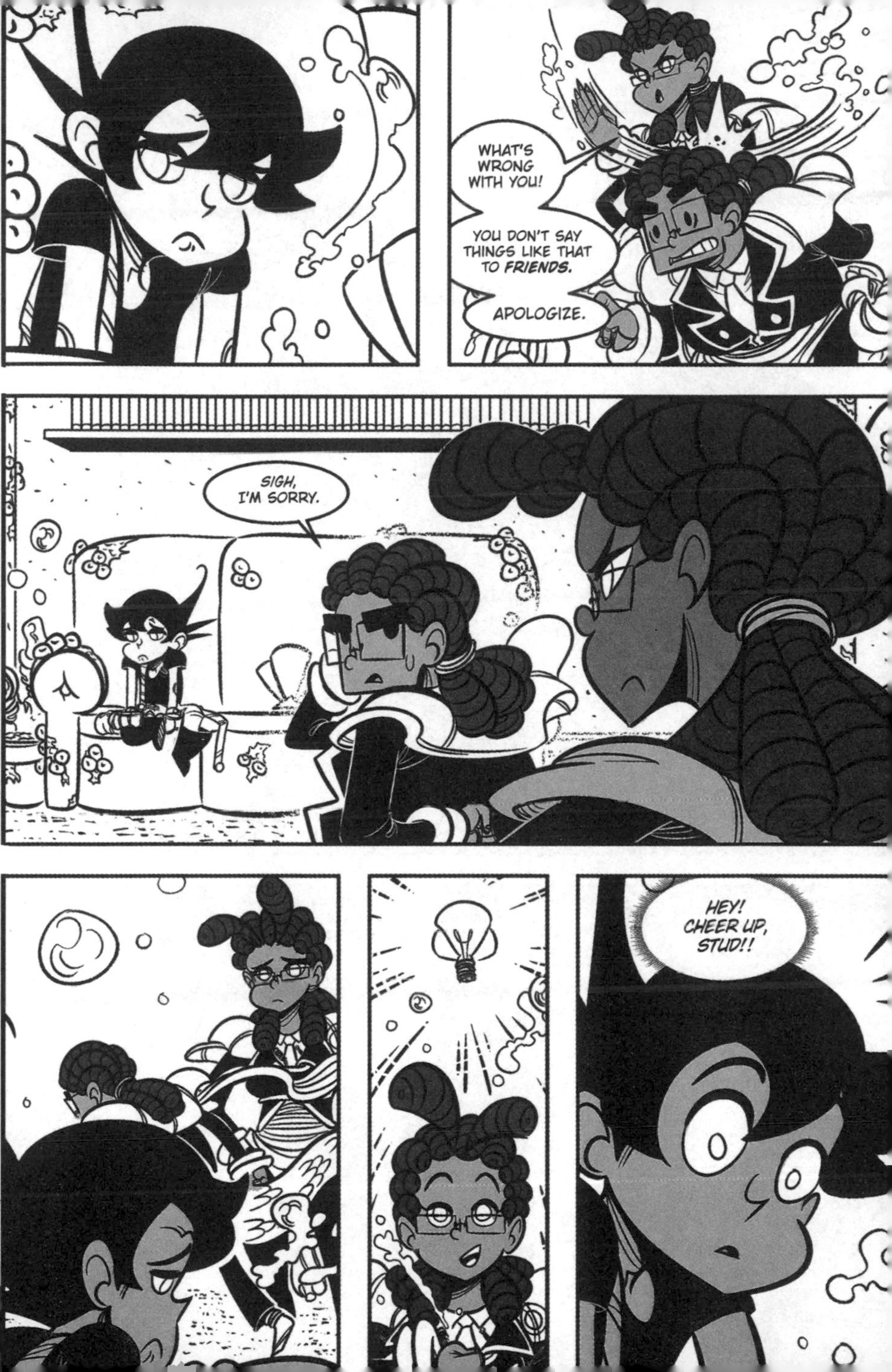
WHAT'S WRONG WITH YOU!
YOU DON'T SAY THINGS LIKE THAT TO FRIENDS.
APOLOGIZE.
SIGH, I'M SORRY.
HEY! CHEER UP, STUD!!

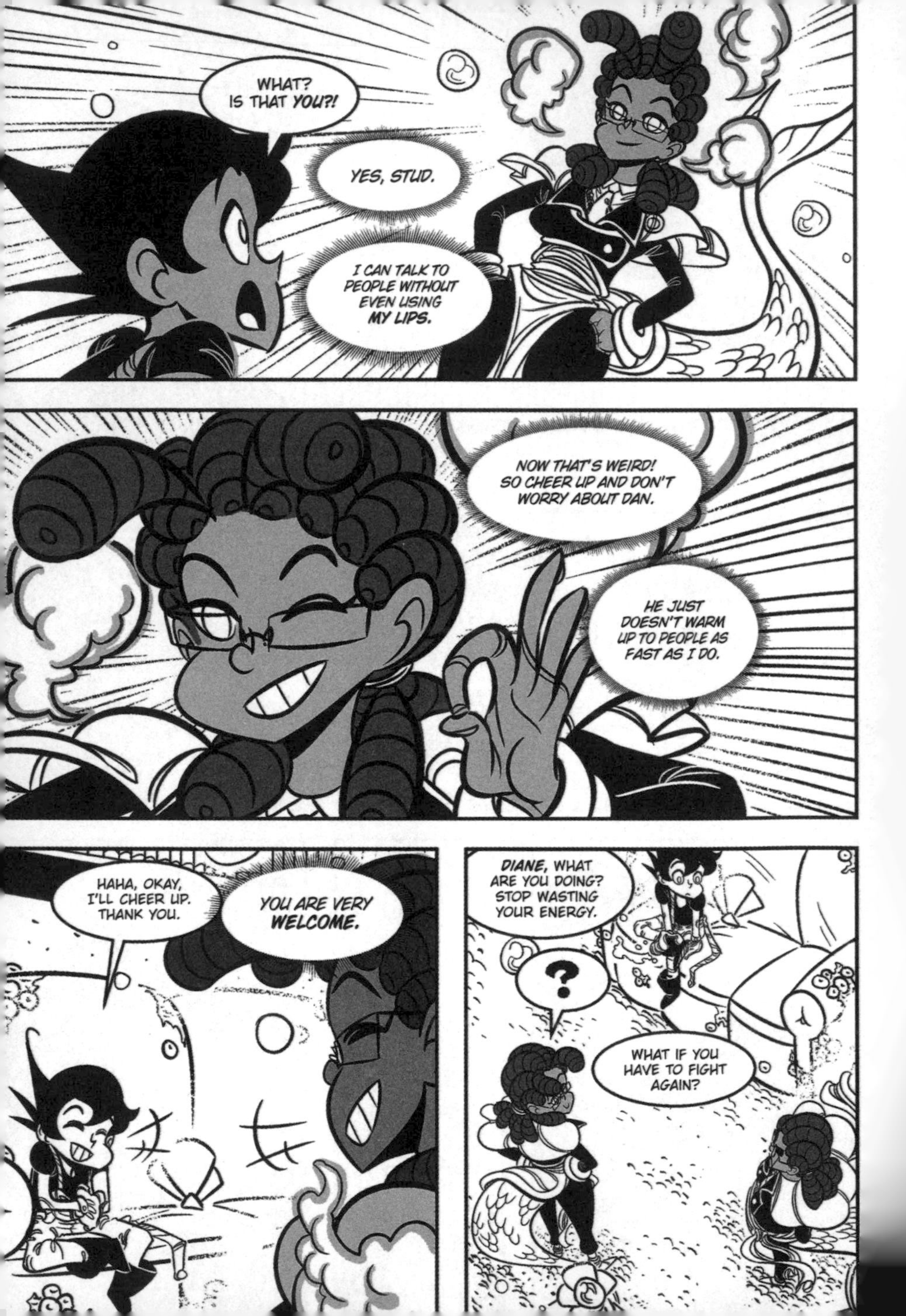
WHAT? IS THAT YOU?!
YES, STUD.
I CAN TALK TO PEOPLE WITHOUT EVEN USING MY LIPS.
NOW THAT'S WEIRD! SO CHEER UP AND DON'T WORRY ABOUT DAN.
HE JUST DOESN'T WARM UP TO PEOPLE AS FAST AS I DO.
HAHA, OKAY, I'LL CHEER UP. THANK YOU.
YOU ARE VERY WELCOME.
DIANE, WHAT ARE YOU DOING? STOP WASTING YOUR ENERGY.
?
WHAT IF YOU HAVE TO FIGHT AGAIN?

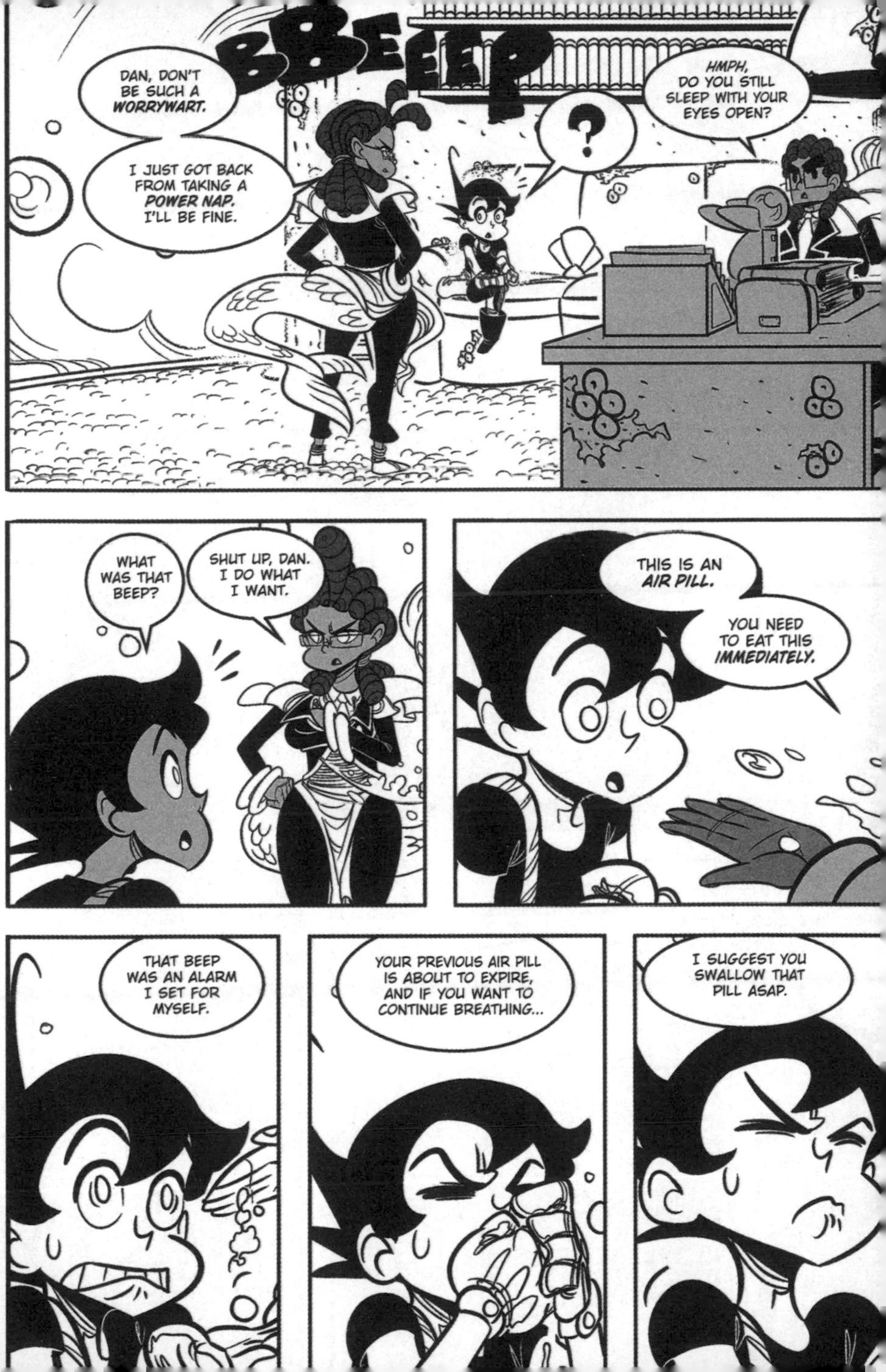
BBEEEP
DAN, DON'T BE SUCH A WORRYWART.
I JUST GOT BACK FROM TAKING A POWER NAP. I'LL BE FINE.
?
HMPH, DO YOU STILL SLEEP WITH YOUR EYES OPEN?
WHAT WAS THAT BEEP?
SHUT UP, DAN. I DO WHAT I WANT.
THIS IS AN AIR PILL.
YOU NEED TO EAT THIS IMMEDIATELY.
THAT BEEP WAS AN ALARM I SET FOR MYSELF.
YOUR PREVIOUS AIR PILL IS ABOUT TO EXPIRE, AND IF YOU WANT TO CONTINUE BREATHING...
I SUGGEST YOU SWALLOW THAT PILL ASAP.

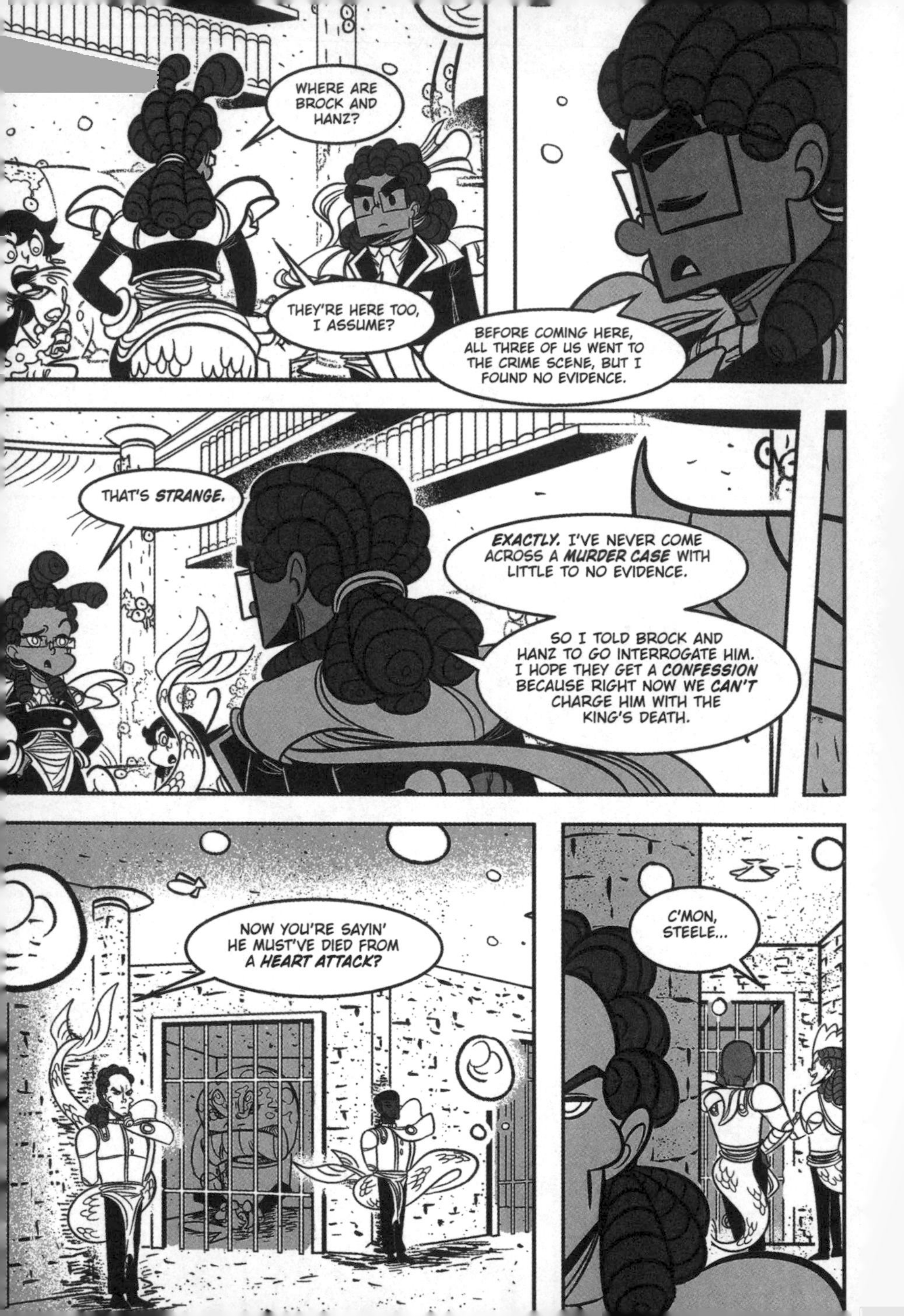

WHERE ARE BROCK AND HANZ?
THEY'RE HERE TOO, I ASSUME?
BEFORE COMING HERE, ALL THREE OF US WENT TO THE CRIME SCENE, BUT I FOUND NO EVIDENCE.
THAT'S STRANGE.
EXACTLY. I'VE NEVER COME ACROSS A MURDER CASE WITH LITTLE TO NO EVIDENCE.
SO I TOLD BROCK AND HANZ TO GO INTERROGATE HIM. I HOPE THEY GET A CONFESSION BECAUSE RIGHT NOW WE CAN'T CHARGE HIM WITH THE KING'S DEATH.
NOW YOU'RE SAYIN' HE MUST'VE DIED FROM A HEART ATTACK?
C'MON, STEELE...

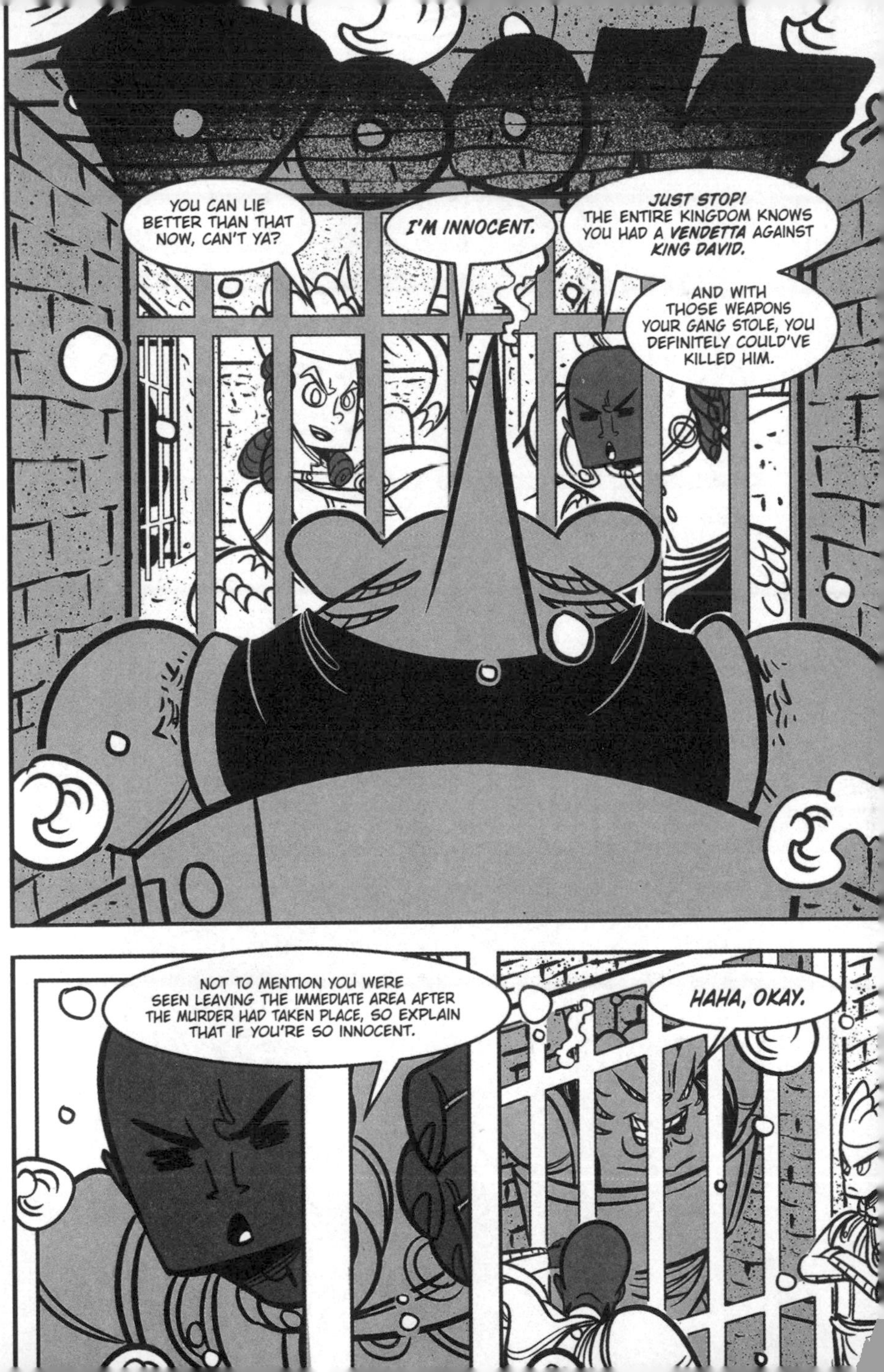
YOU CAN LIE BETTER THAN THAT NOW, CAN'T YA?
I'M INNOCENT.
JUST STOP! THE ENTIRE KINGDOM KNOWS YOU HAD A VENDETTA AGAINST KING DAVID.
AND WITH THOSE WEAPONS YOUR GANG STOLE, YOU DEFINITELY COULD'VE KILLED HIM.
NOT TO MENTION YOU WERE SEEN LEAVING THE IMMEDIATE AREA AFTER THE MURDER HAD TAKEN PLACE, SO EXPLAIN THAT IF YOU'RE SO INNOCENT.
HAHA, OKAY.

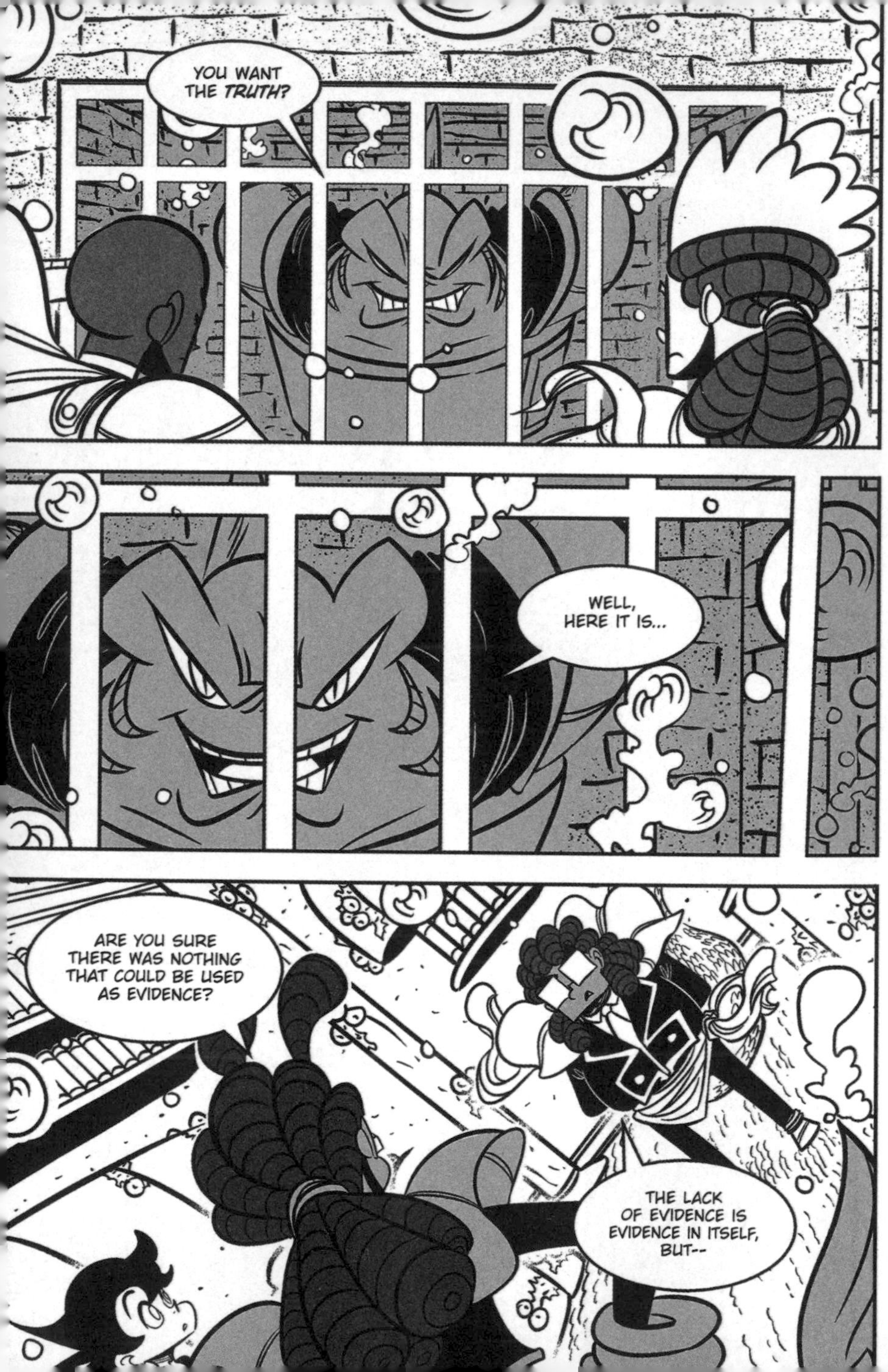
YOU WANT THE *TRUTH?*
WELL, HERE IT IS...
ARE YOU SURE THERE WAS NOTHING THAT COULD BE USED AS EVIDENCE?
THE LACK OF EVIDENCE IS EVIDENCE IN ITSELF, BUT--

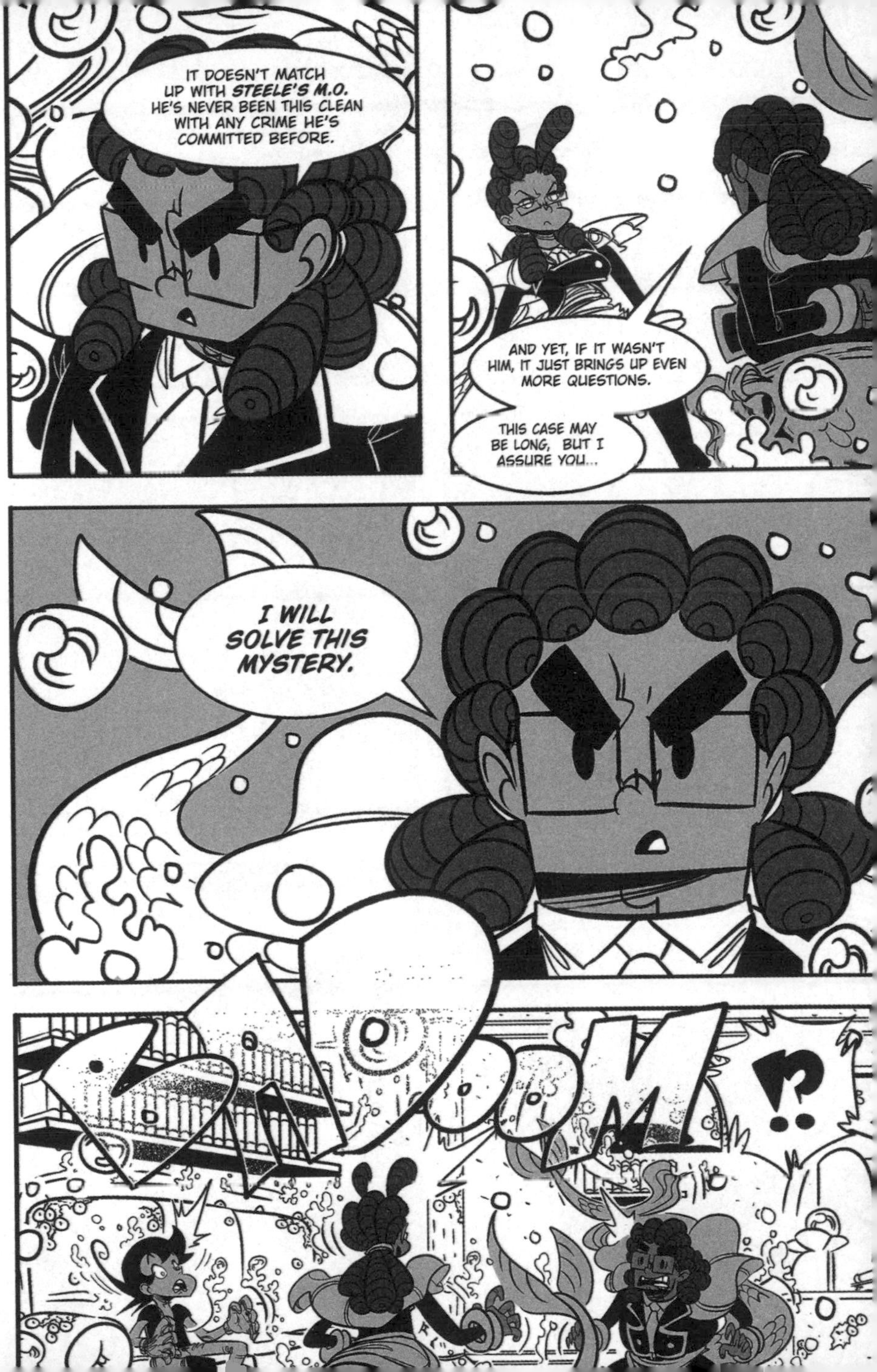
IT DOESN'T MATCH UP WITH **STEELE'S M.O.** HE'S NEVER BEEN THIS CLEAN WITH ANY CRIME HE'S COMMITTED BEFORE.
AND YET, IF IT WASN'T HIM, IT JUST BRINGS UP EVEN MORE QUESTIONS.
THIS CASE MAY BE LONG, BUT I ASSURE YOU...
I WILL SOLVE THIS MYSTERY.

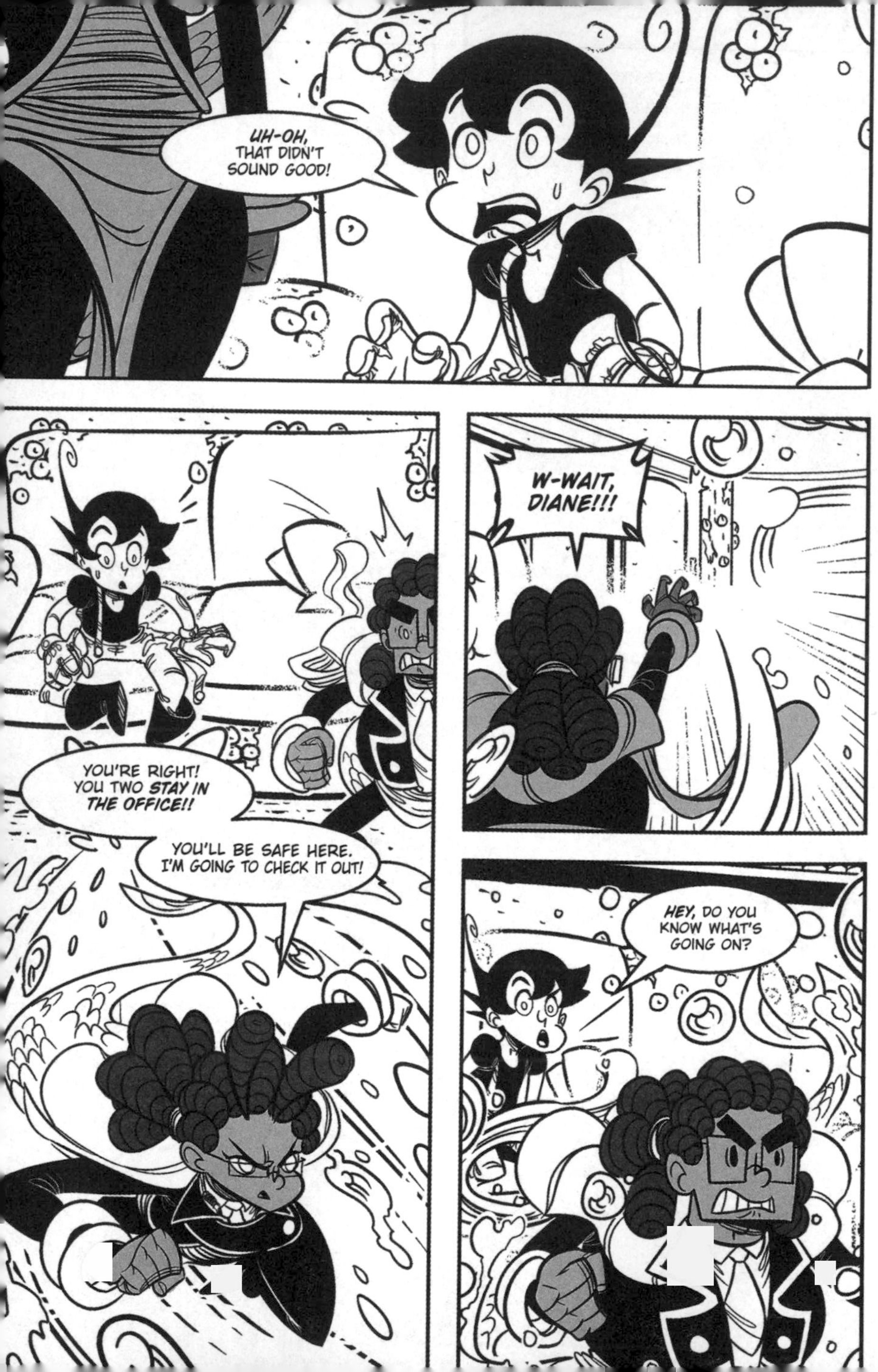
UH-OH, THAT DIDN'T SOUND GOOD!
YOU'RE RIGHT! YOU TWO STAY IN THE OFFICE!!
YOU'LL BE SAFE HERE. I'M GOING TO CHECK IT OUT!
W-WAIT, DIANE!!!
HEY, DO YOU KNOW WHAT'S GOING ON?

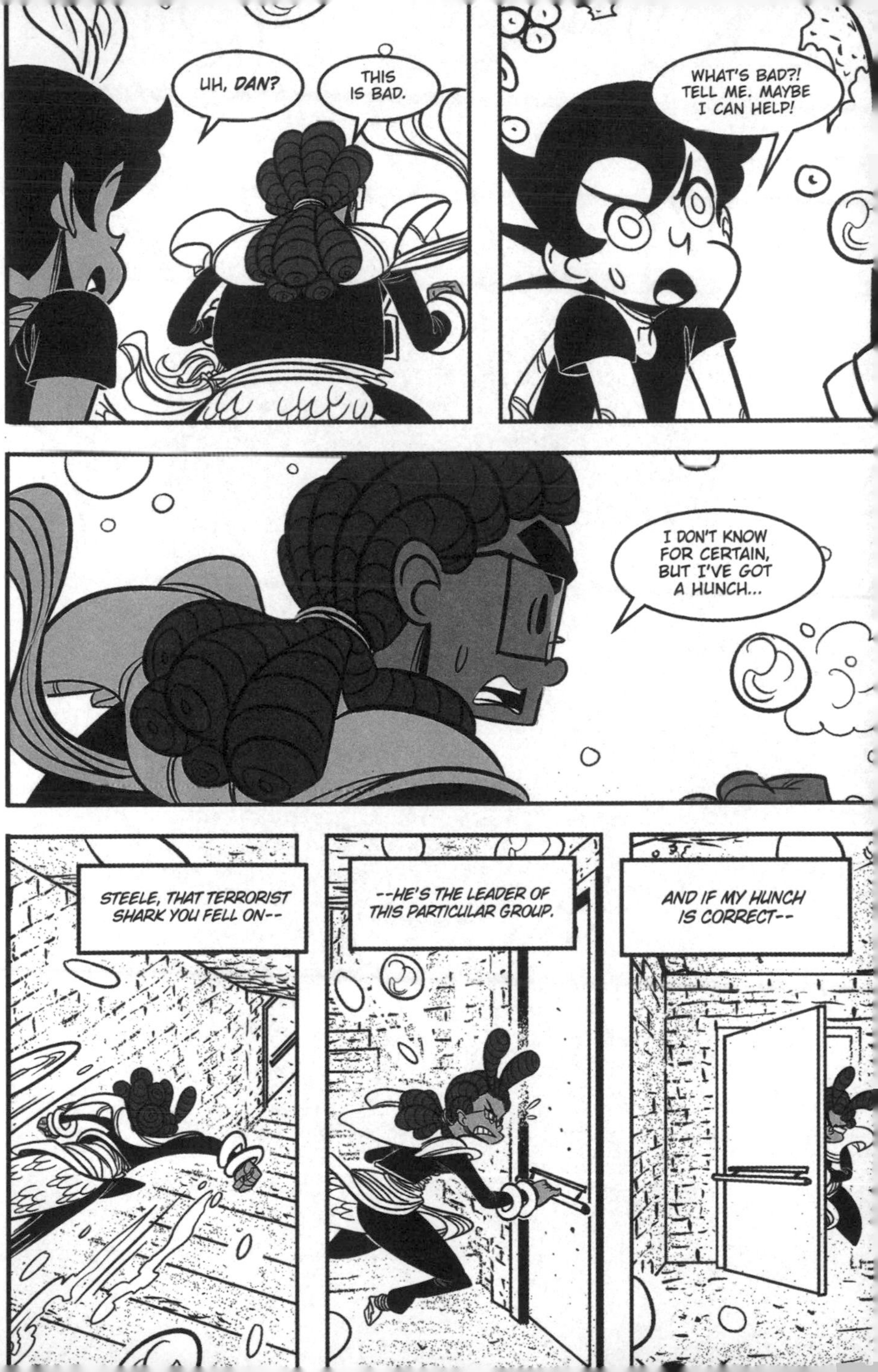
UH, DAN?
THIS IS BAD.
WHAT'S BAD?! TELL ME. MAYBE I CAN HELP!
I DON'T KNOW FOR CERTAIN, BUT I'VE GOT A HUNCH...
STEELE, THAT TERRORIST SHARK YOU FELL ON--
--HE'S THE LEADER OF THIS PARTICULAR GROUP.
AND IF MY HUNCH IS CORRECT--

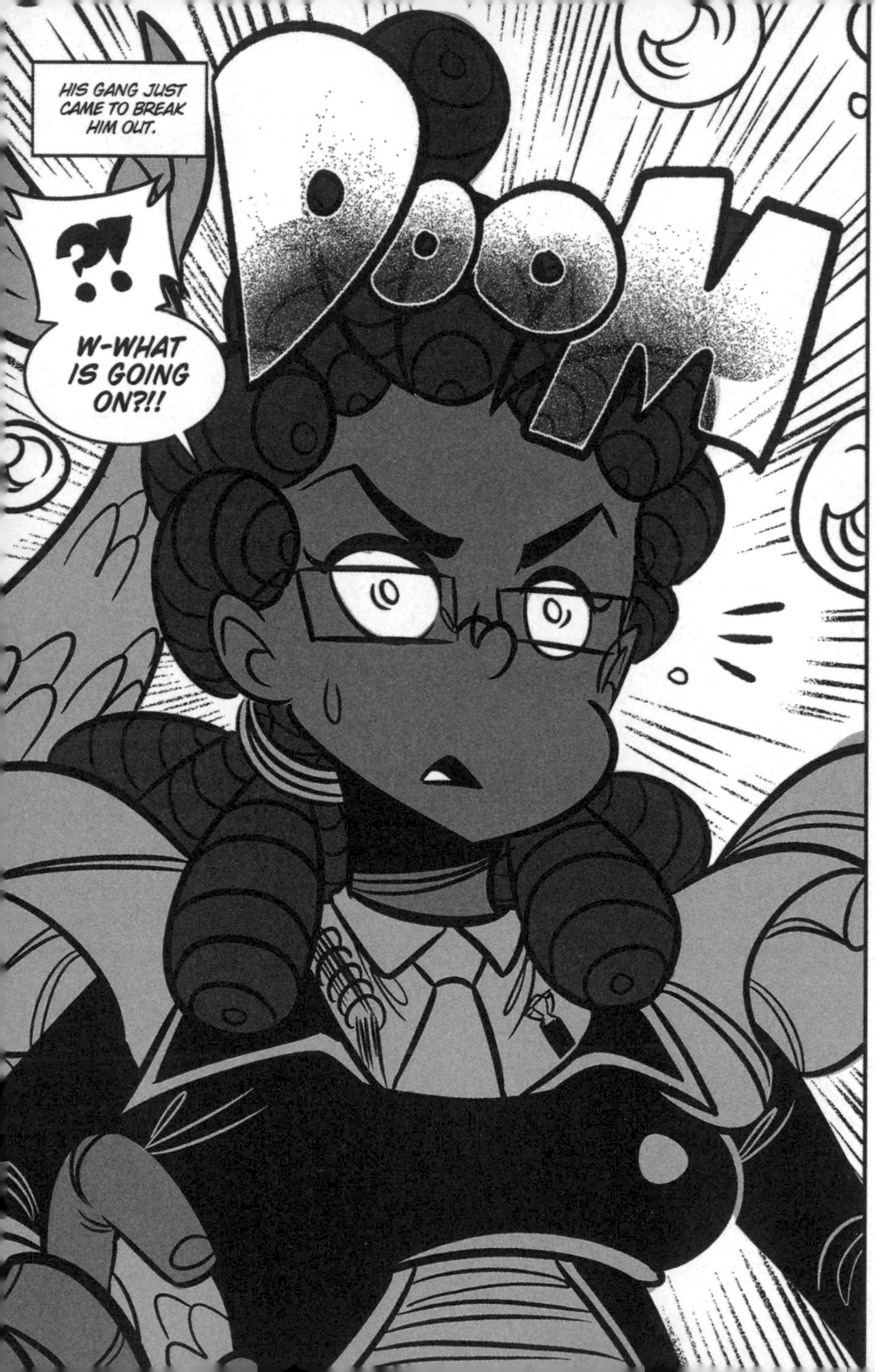
HIS GANG JUST CAME TO BREAK HIM OUT.
DOOM!
?!
W-WHAT IS GOING ON?!!

HAMMER

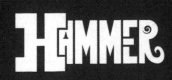

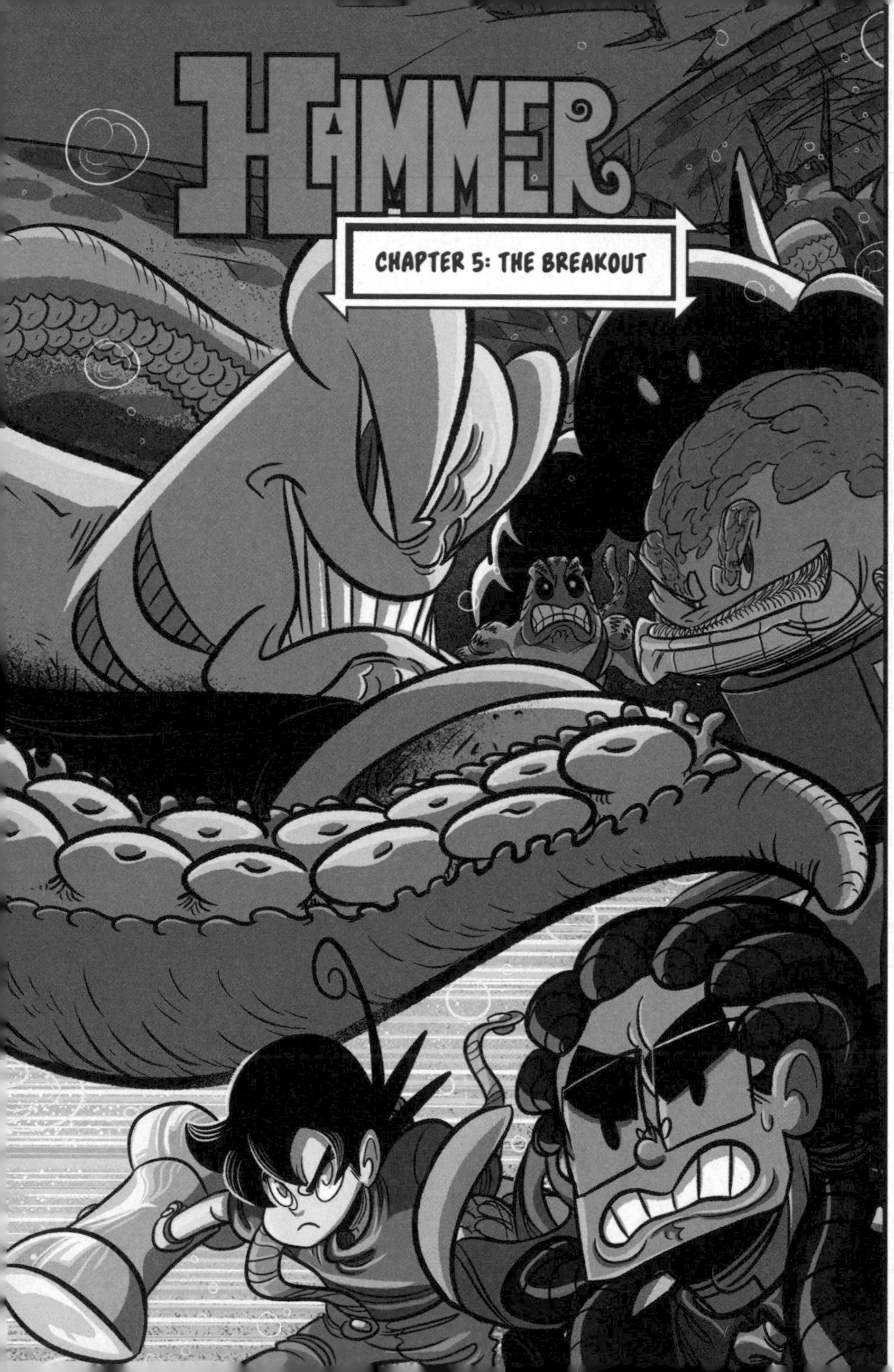
HAMMER
CHAPTER 5: THE BREAKOUT

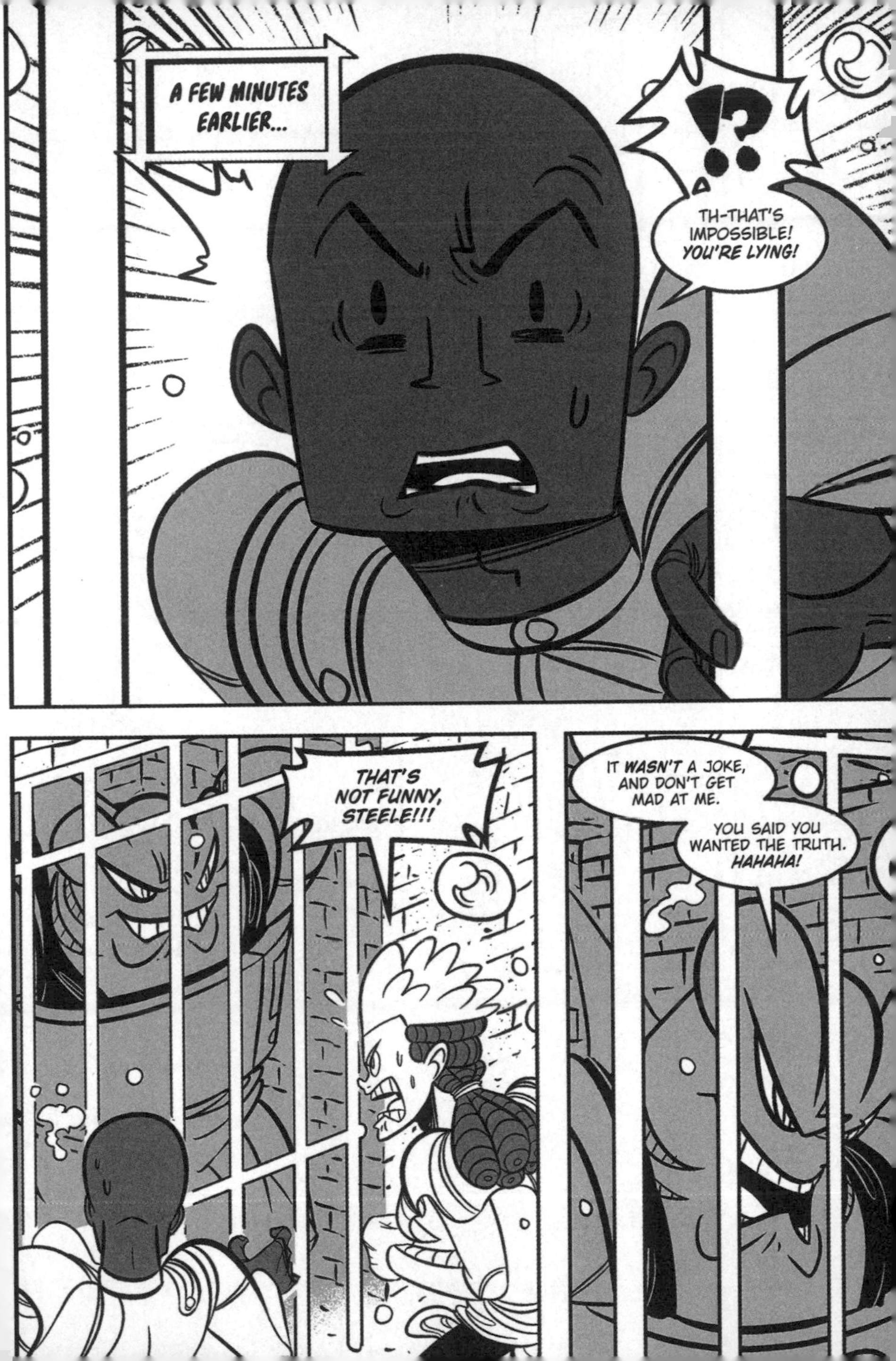
A FEW MINUTES EARLIER...
!?
TH-THAT'S IMPOSSIBLE! YOU'RE LYING!
THAT'S NOT FUNNY, STEELE!!!
IT WASN'T A JOKE, AND DON'T GET MAD AT ME.
YOU SAID YOU WANTED THE TRUTH. HAHAHA!

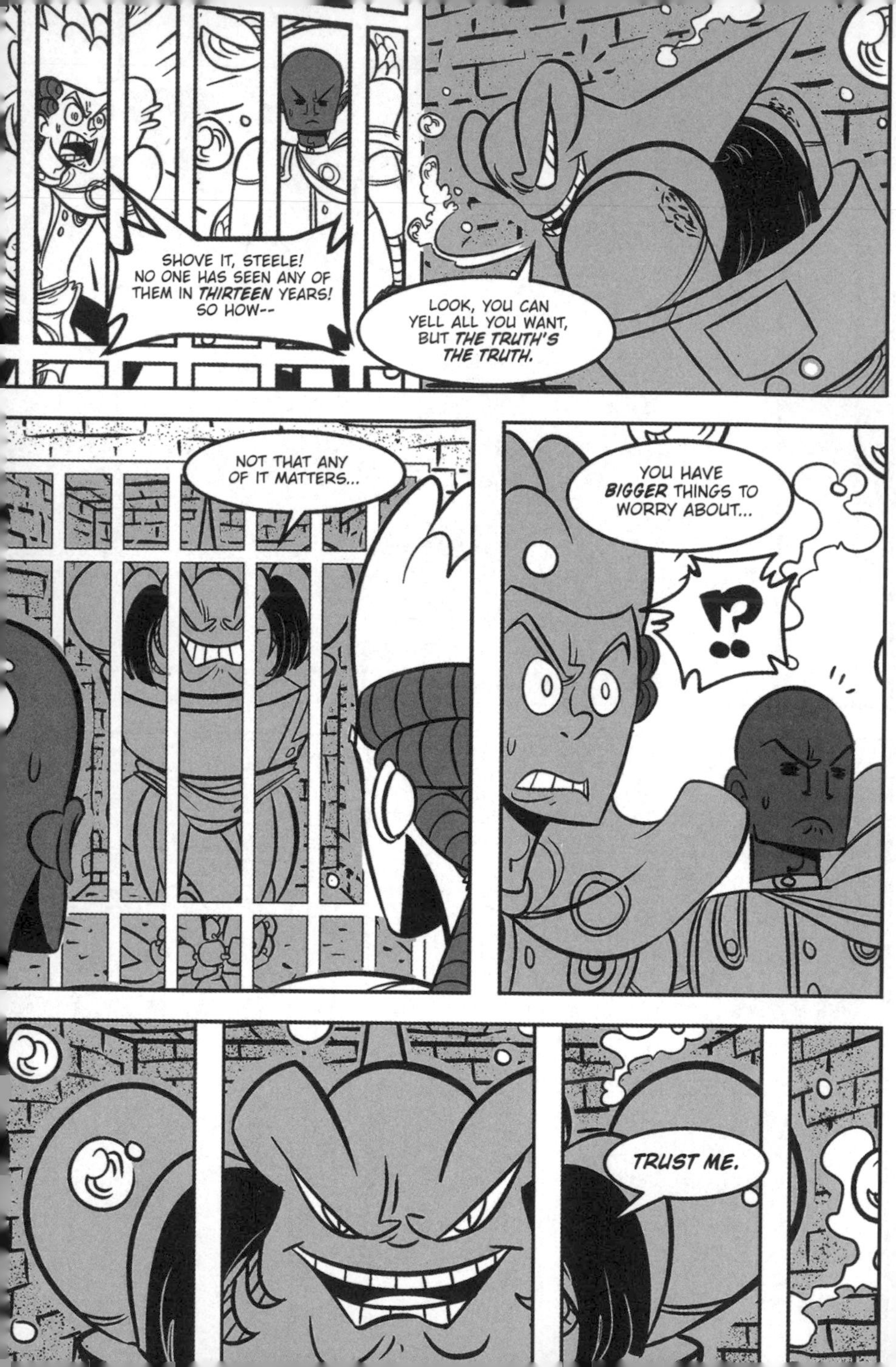
SHOVE IT, STEELE! NO ONE HAS SEEN ANY OF THEM IN *THIRTEEN* YEARS! SO HOW--
LOOK, YOU CAN YELL ALL YOU WANT, BUT *THE TRUTH'S THE TRUTH.*
NOT THAT ANY OF IT MATTERS...
YOU HAVE *BIGGER* THINGS TO WORRY ABOUT...
!?!!
TRUST ME.

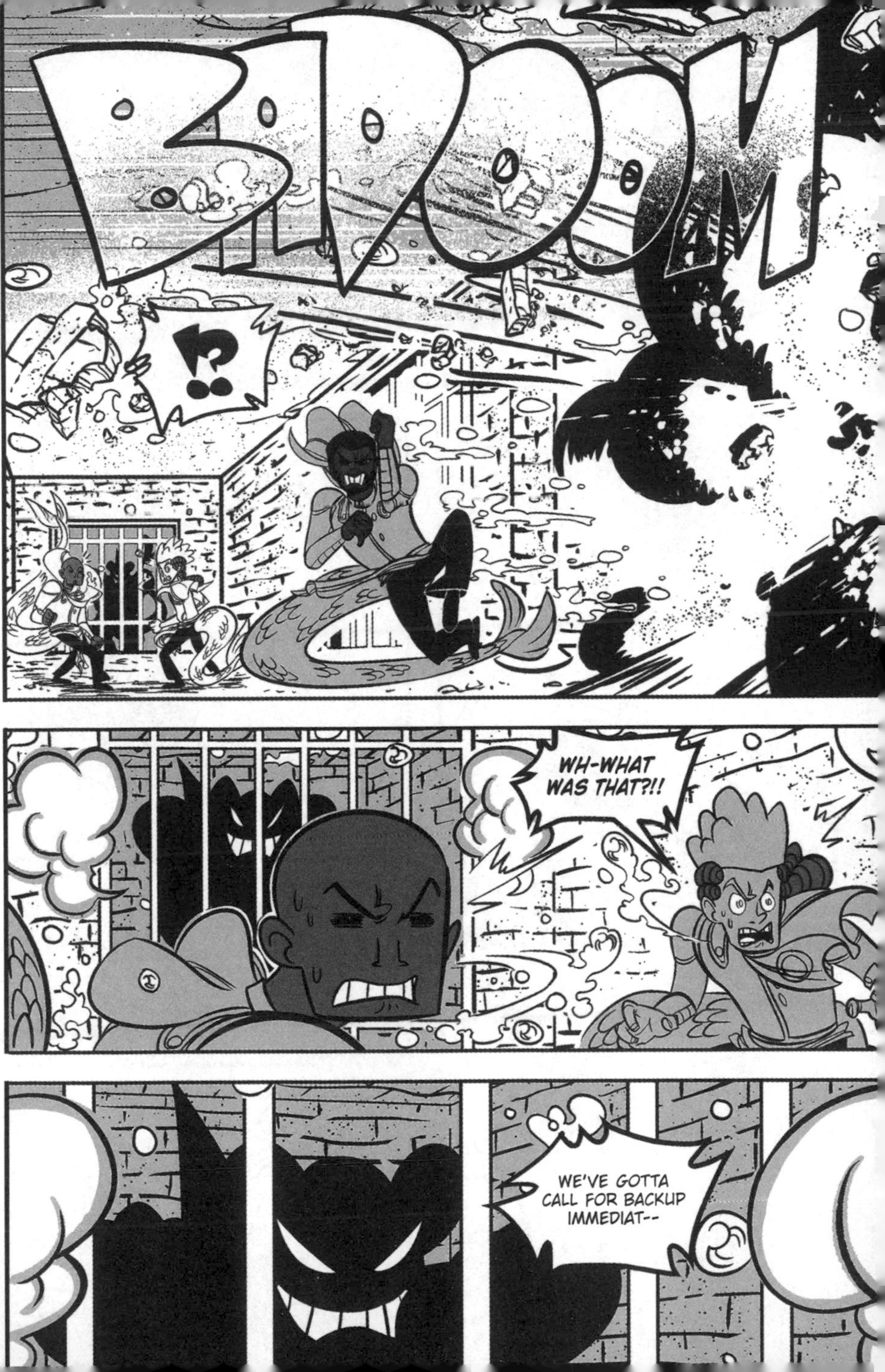
BADOOM
!?
WH-WHAT WAS THAT?!!
WE'VE GOTTA CALL FOR BACKUP IMMEDIAT--

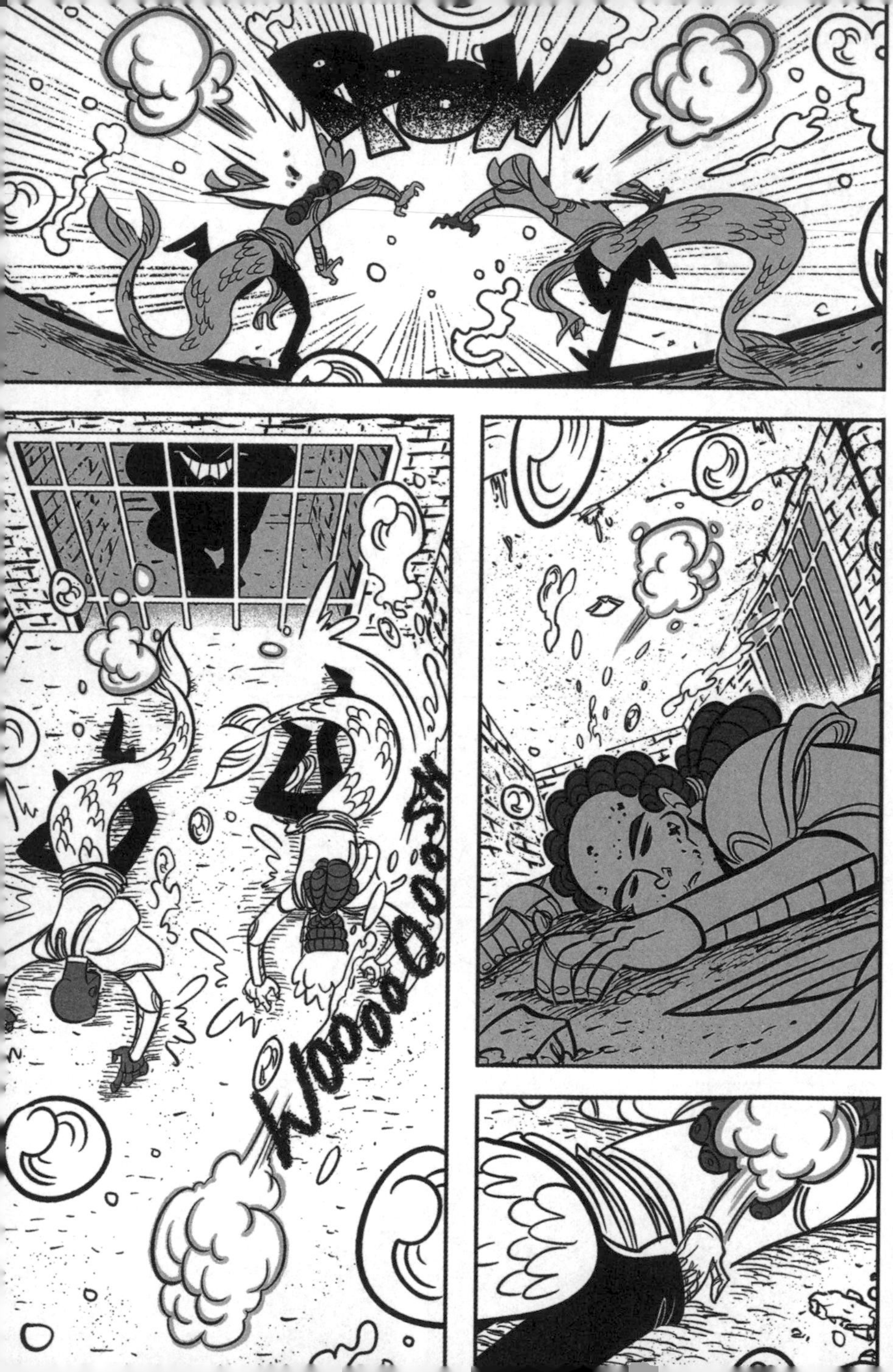
PROW
WOOOOOOOSH

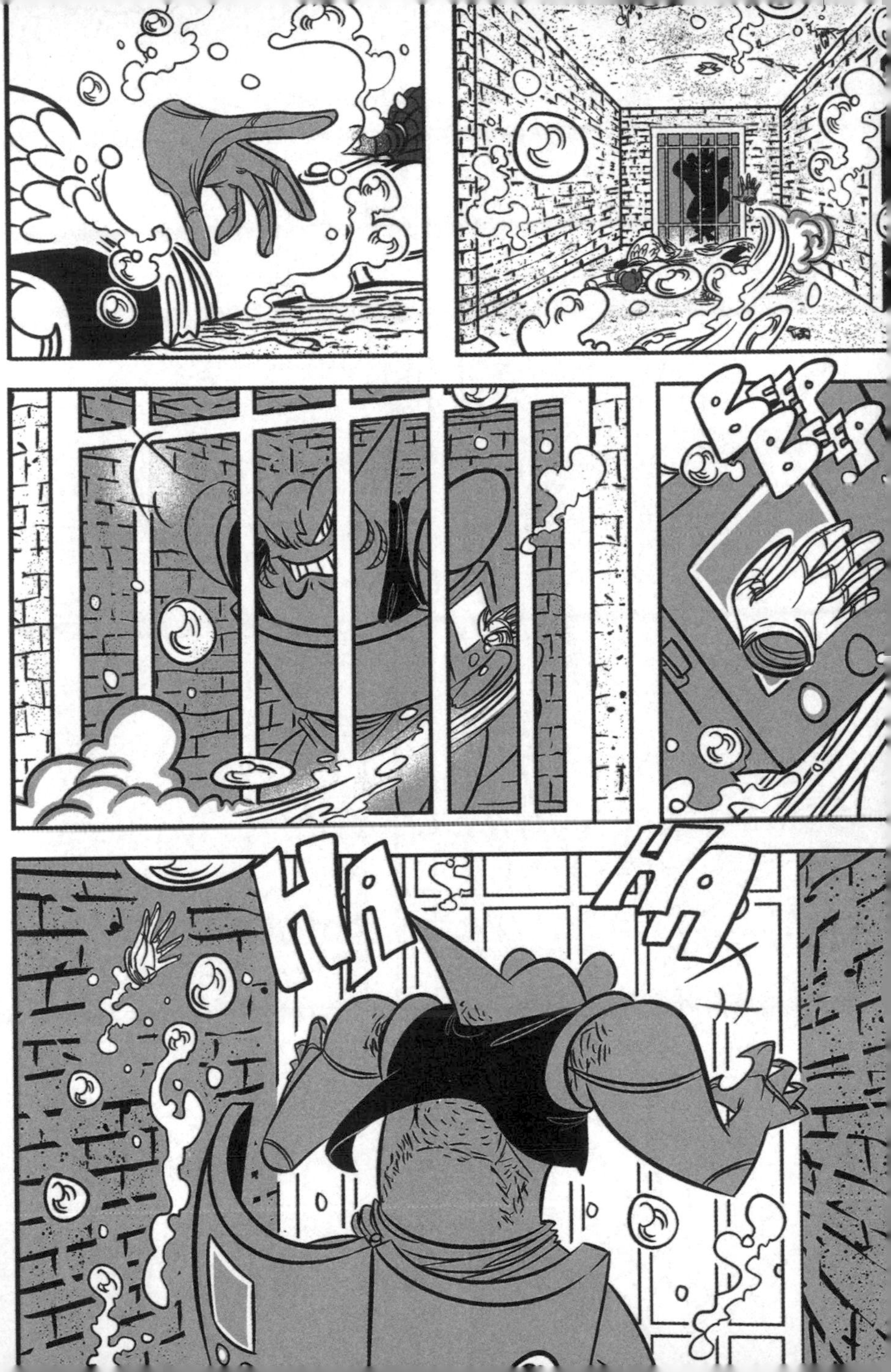
BEEP BEEP
HA HA

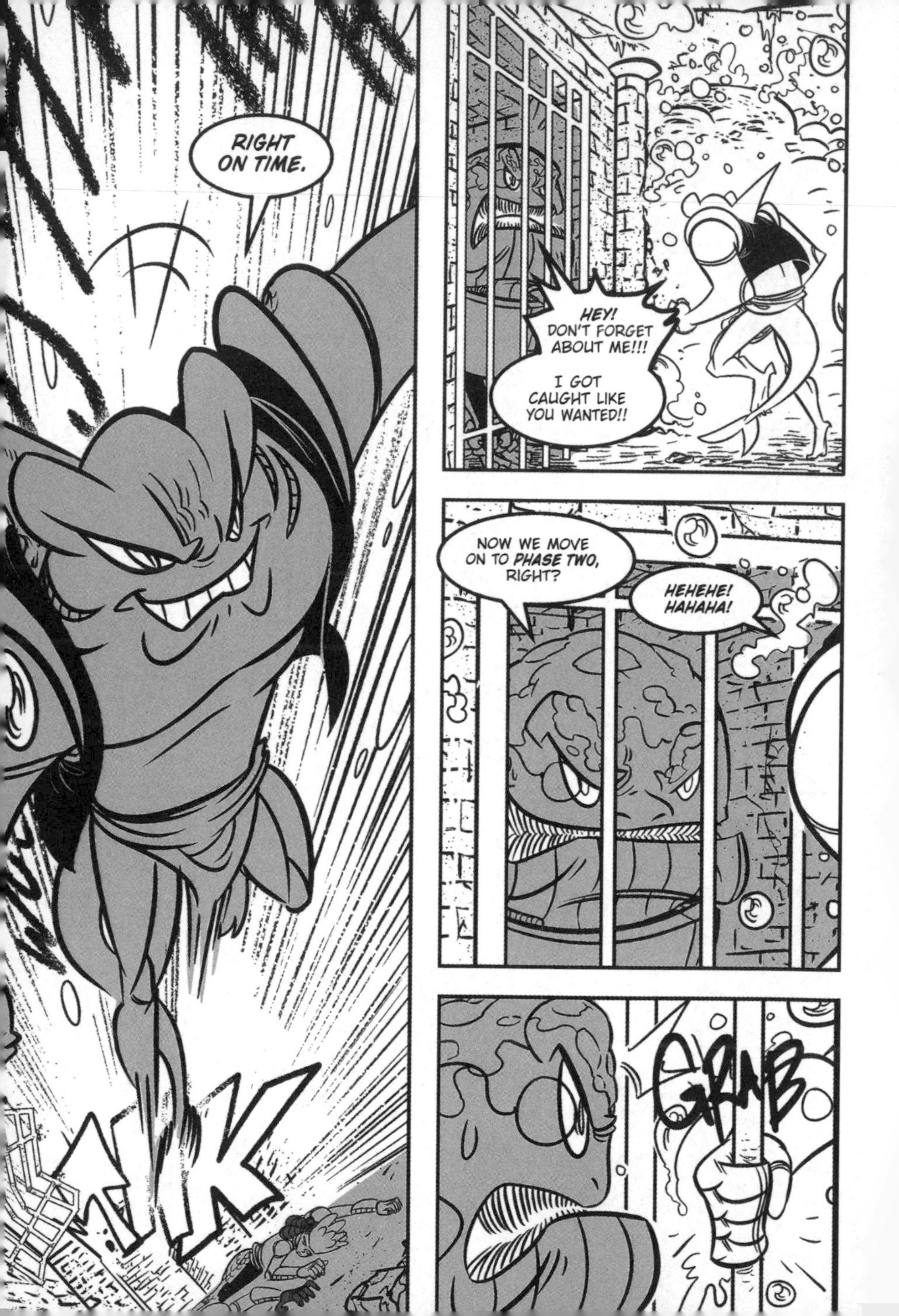
RIGHT ON TIME.
HEY! DON'T FORGET ABOUT ME!!!
I GOT CAUGHT LIKE YOU WANTED!!
NOW WE MOVE ON TO PHASE TWO, RIGHT?
HEHEHE! HAHAHA!

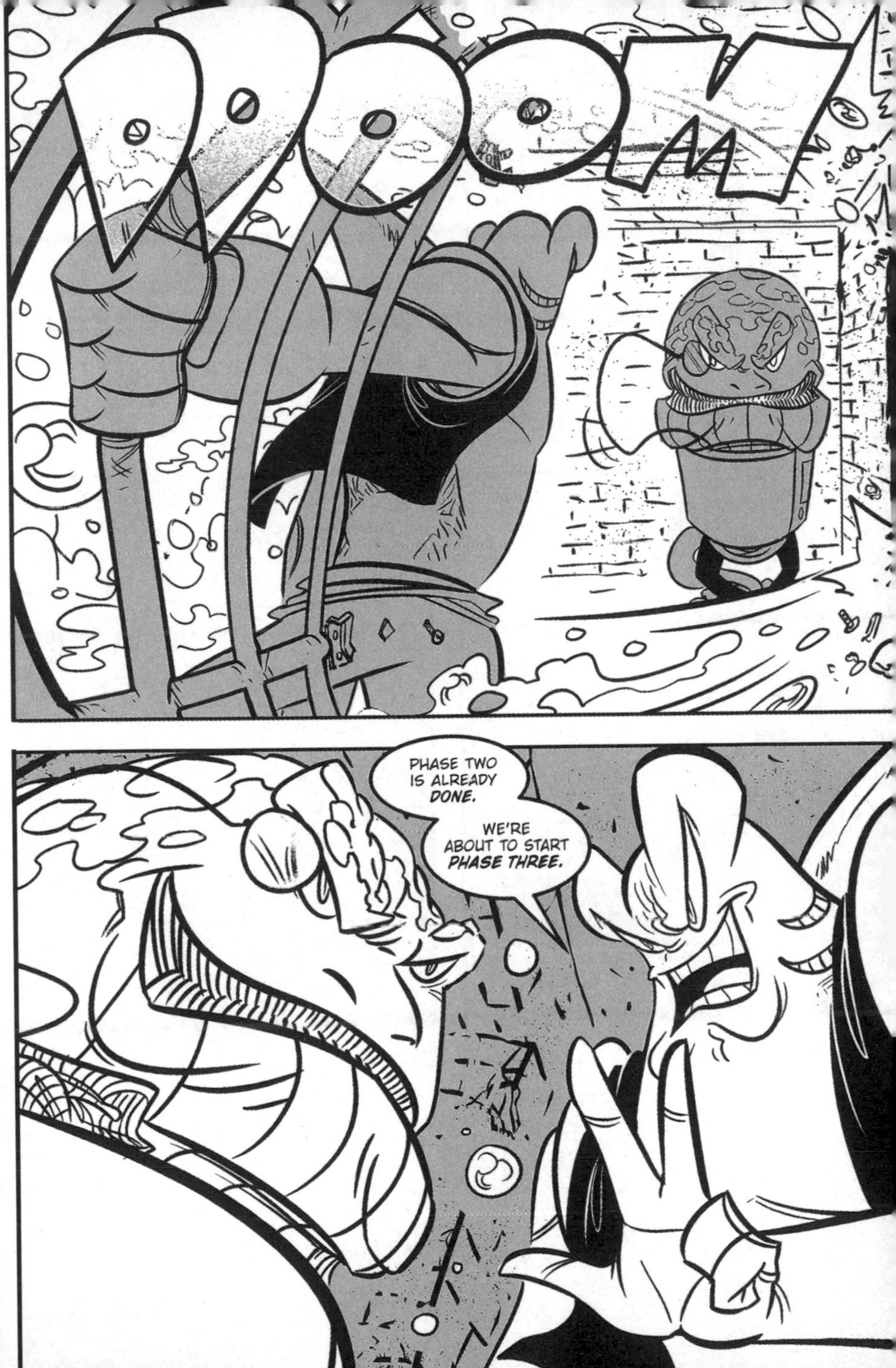
PHASE TWO IS ALREADY *DONE.*
WE'RE ABOUT TO START ***PHASE THREE.***

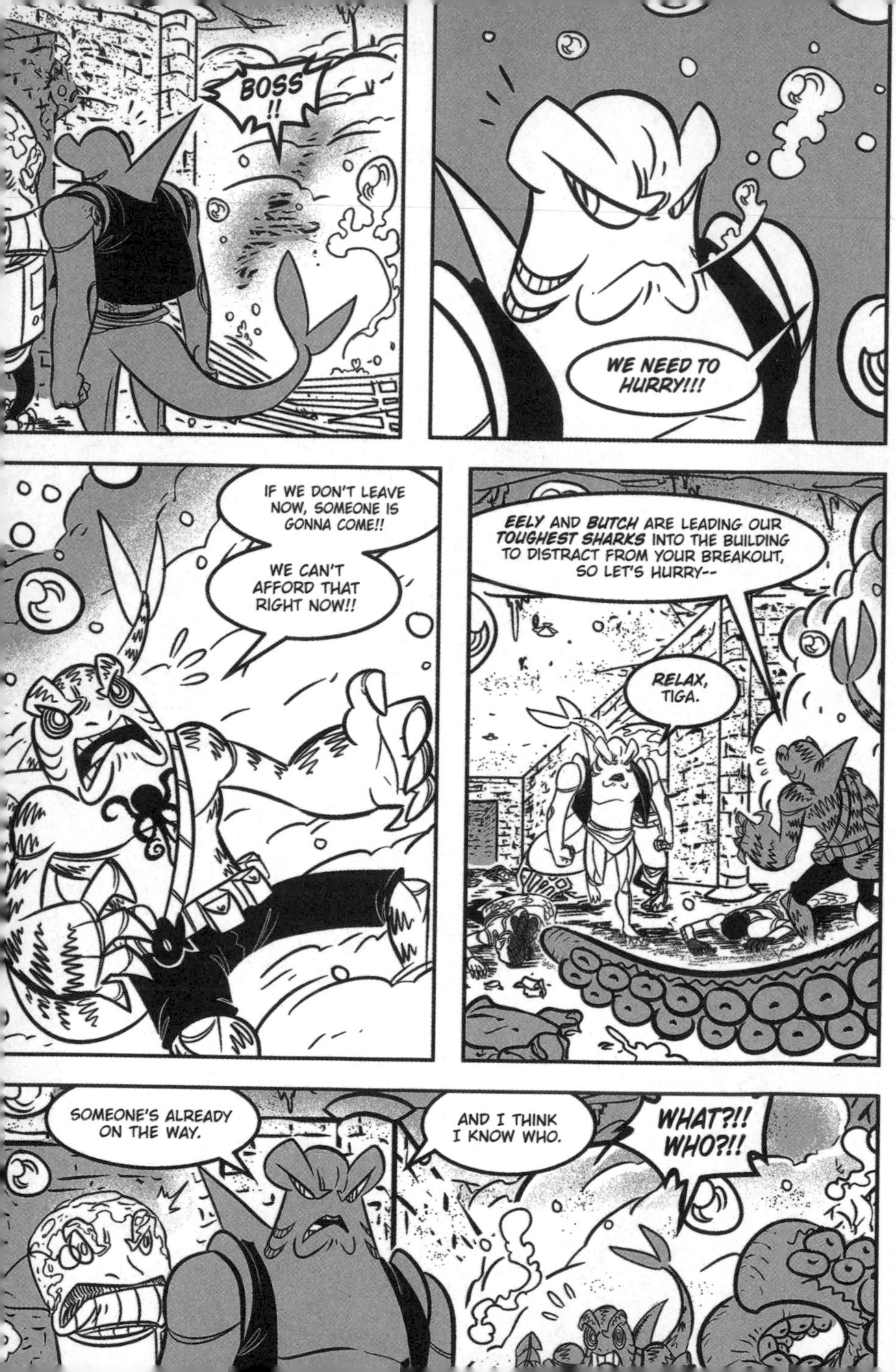
BOSS !!
WE NEED TO HURRY!!!
IF WE DON'T LEAVE NOW, SOMEONE IS GONNA COME!!
WE CAN'T AFFORD THAT RIGHT NOW!!
EELY AND BUTCH ARE LEADING OUR TOUGHEST SHARKS INTO THE BUILDING TO DISTRACT FROM YOUR BREAKOUT, SO LET'S HURRY--
RELAX, TIGA.
SOMEONE'S ALREADY ON THE WAY.
AND I THINK I KNOW WHO.
WHAT?!! WHO?!!

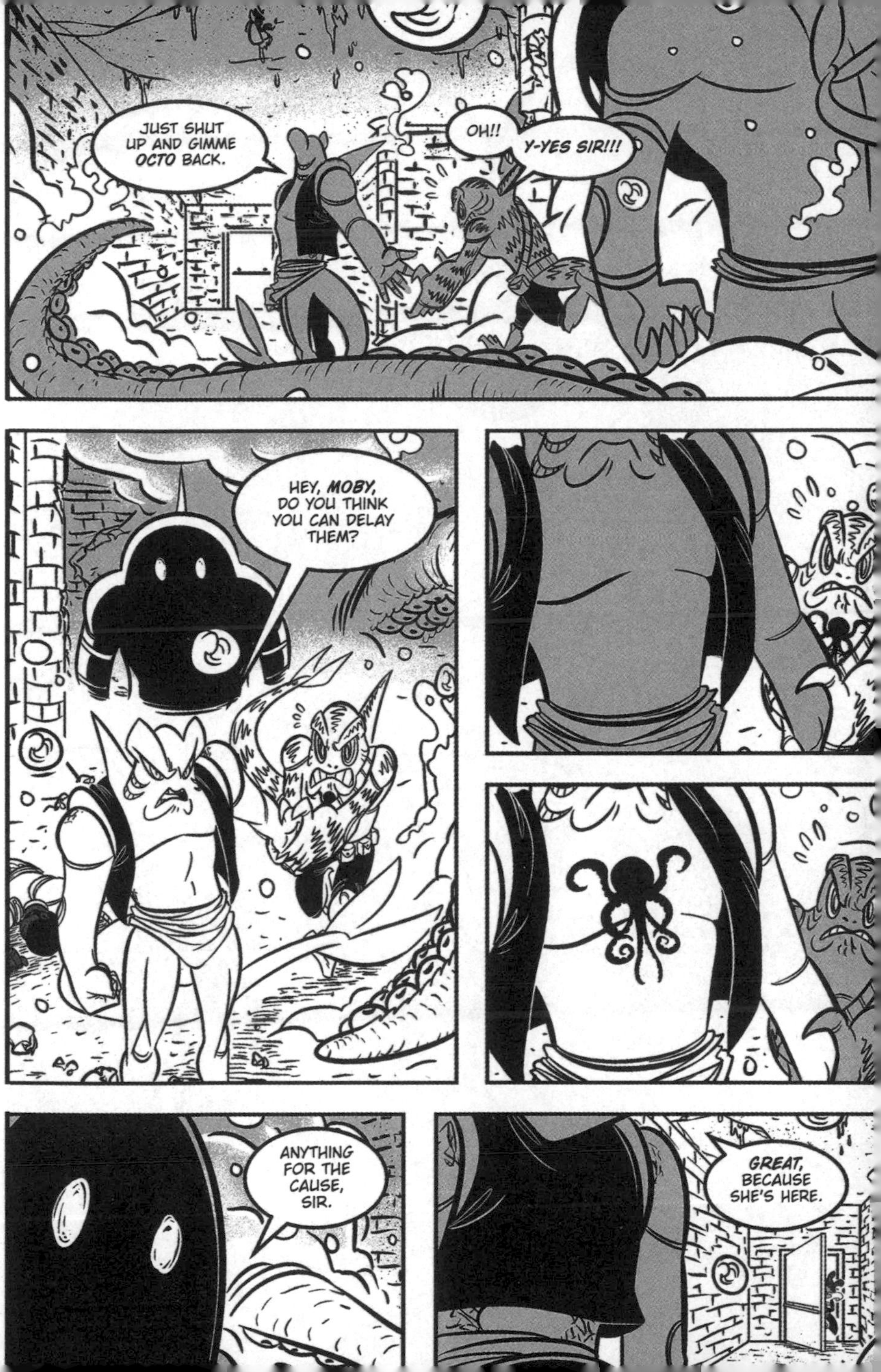
JUST SHUT UP AND GIMME OCTO BACK.
OH!!
Y-YES SIR!!!
HEY, MOBY, DO YOU THINK YOU CAN DELAY THEM?
ANYTHING FOR THE CAUSE, SIR.
GREAT, BECAUSE SHE'S HERE.

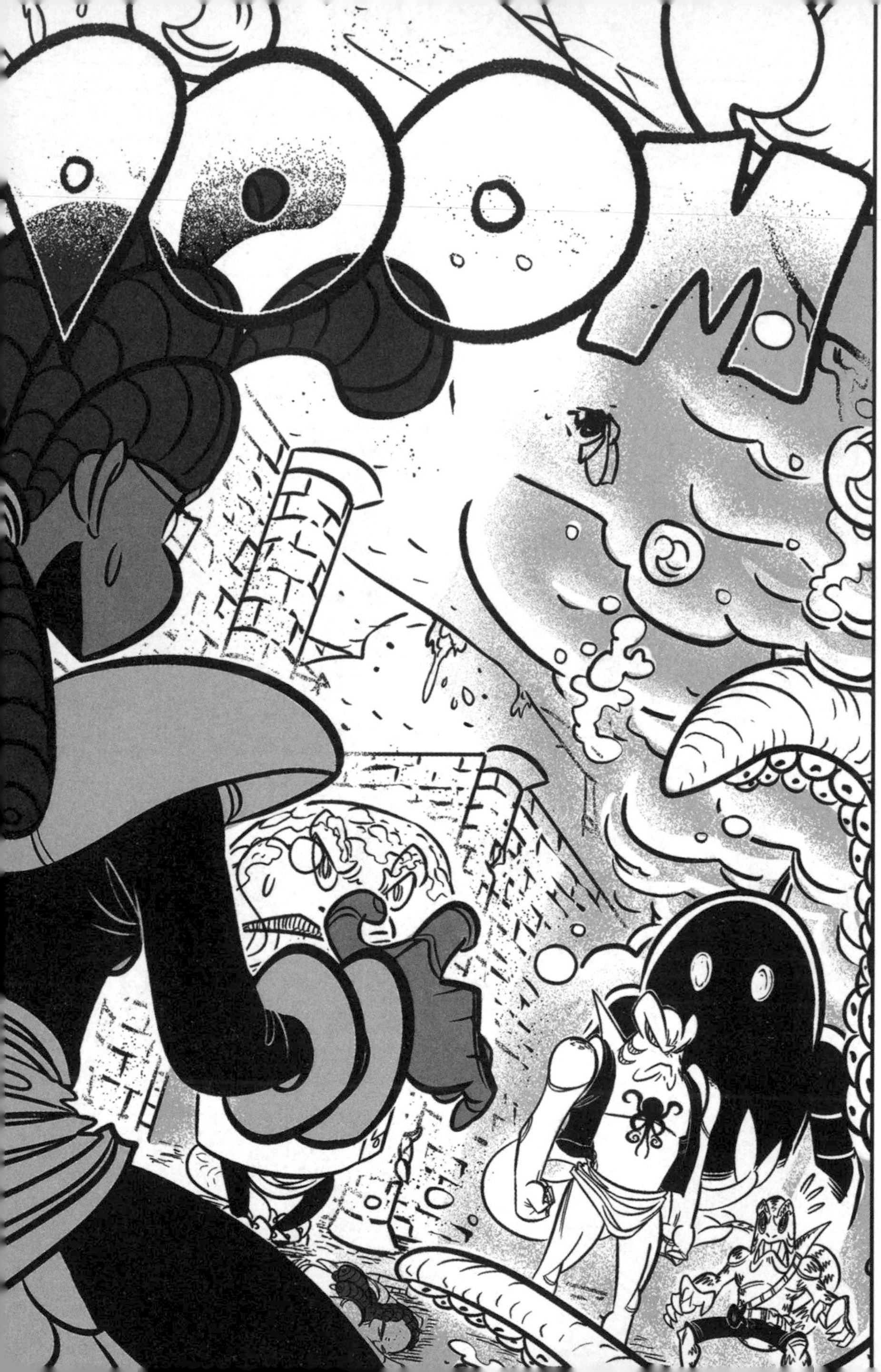
WOOM

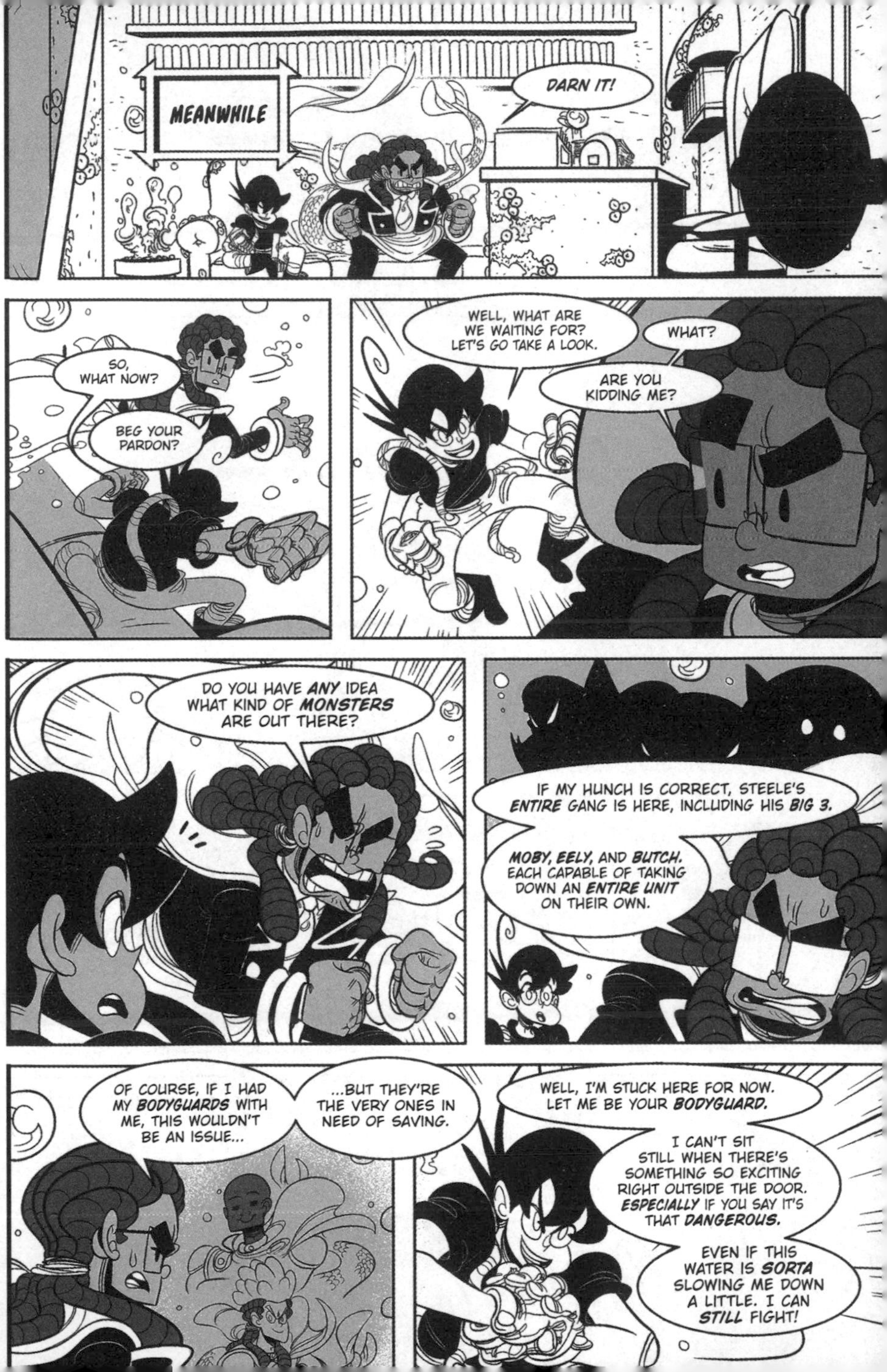
MEANWHILE
DARN IT!
SO, WHAT NOW?
BEG YOUR PARDON?
WELL, WHAT ARE WE WAITING FOR? LET'S GO TAKE A LOOK.
WHAT?
ARE YOU KIDDING ME?
DO YOU HAVE ANY IDEA WHAT KIND OF MONSTERS ARE OUT THERE?
IF MY HUNCH IS CORRECT, STEELE'S ENTIRE GANG IS HERE, INCLUDING HIS BIG 3.
MOBY, EELY, AND BUTCH. EACH CAPABLE OF TAKING DOWN AN ENTIRE UNIT ON THEIR OWN.
OF COURSE, IF I HAD MY BODYGUARDS WITH ME, THIS WOULDN'T BE AN ISSUE...
...BUT THEY'RE THE VERY ONES IN NEED OF SAVING.
WELL, I'M STUCK HERE FOR NOW. LET ME BE YOUR BODYGUARD.
I CAN'T SIT STILL WHEN THERE'S SOMETHING SO EXCITING RIGHT OUTSIDE THE DOOR. ESPECIALLY IF YOU SAY IT'S THAT DANGEROUS.
EVEN IF THIS WATER IS SORTA SLOWING ME DOWN A LITTLE. I CAN STILL FIGHT!

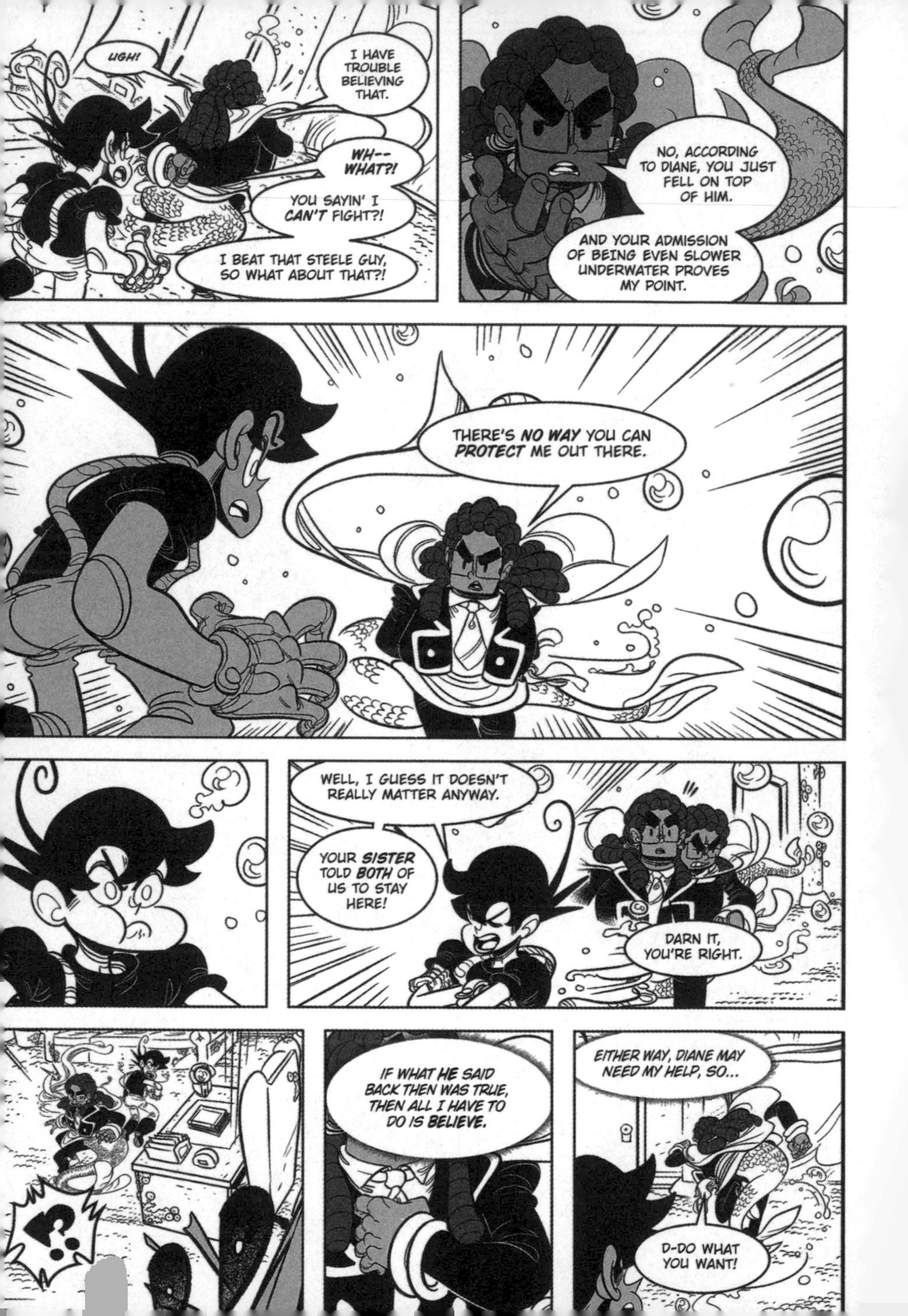
UGH!
I HAVE TROUBLE BELIEVING THAT.
WH-- WHAT?!
YOU SAYIN' I CAN'T FIGHT?!
I BEAT THAT STEELE GUY, SO WHAT ABOUT THAT?!
NO, ACCORDING TO DIANE, YOU JUST FELL ON TOP OF HIM.
AND YOUR ADMISSION OF BEING EVEN SLOWER UNDERWATER PROVES MY POINT.
THERE'S NO WAY YOU CAN PROTECT ME OUT THERE.
WELL, I GUESS IT DOESN'T REALLY MATTER ANYWAY.
YOUR SISTER TOLD BOTH OF US TO STAY HERE!
DARN IT, YOU'RE RIGHT.
IF WHAT HE SAID BACK THEN WAS TRUE, THEN ALL I HAVE TO DO IS BELIEVE.
EITHER WAY, DIANE MAY NEED MY HELP, SO...
D-DO WHAT YOU WANT!

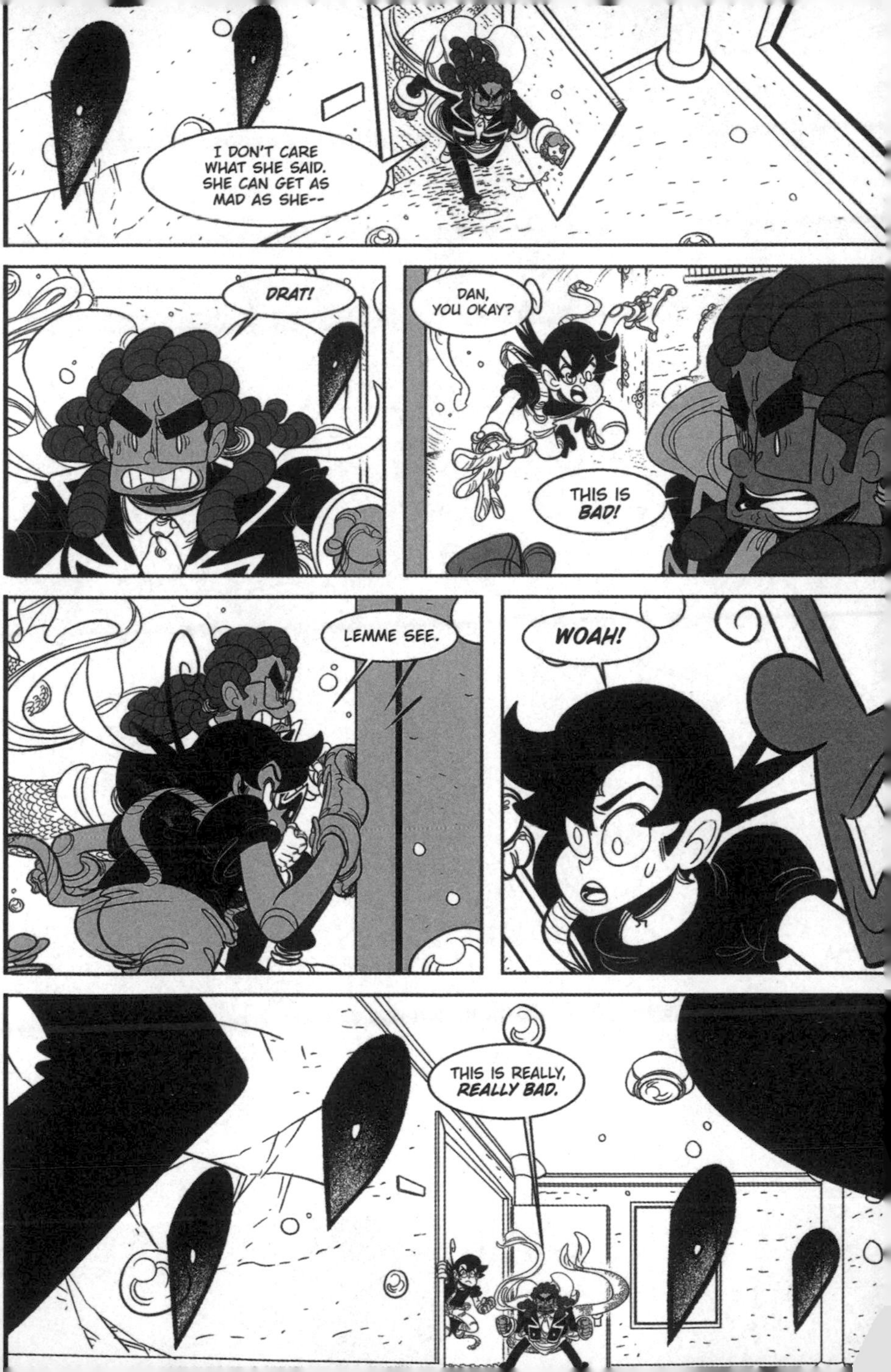
I DON'T CARE WHAT SHE SAID. SHE CAN GET AS MAD AS SHE--
DRAT!
DAN, YOU OKAY?
THIS IS BAD!
LEMME SEE.
WOAH!
THIS IS REALLY, REALLY BAD.

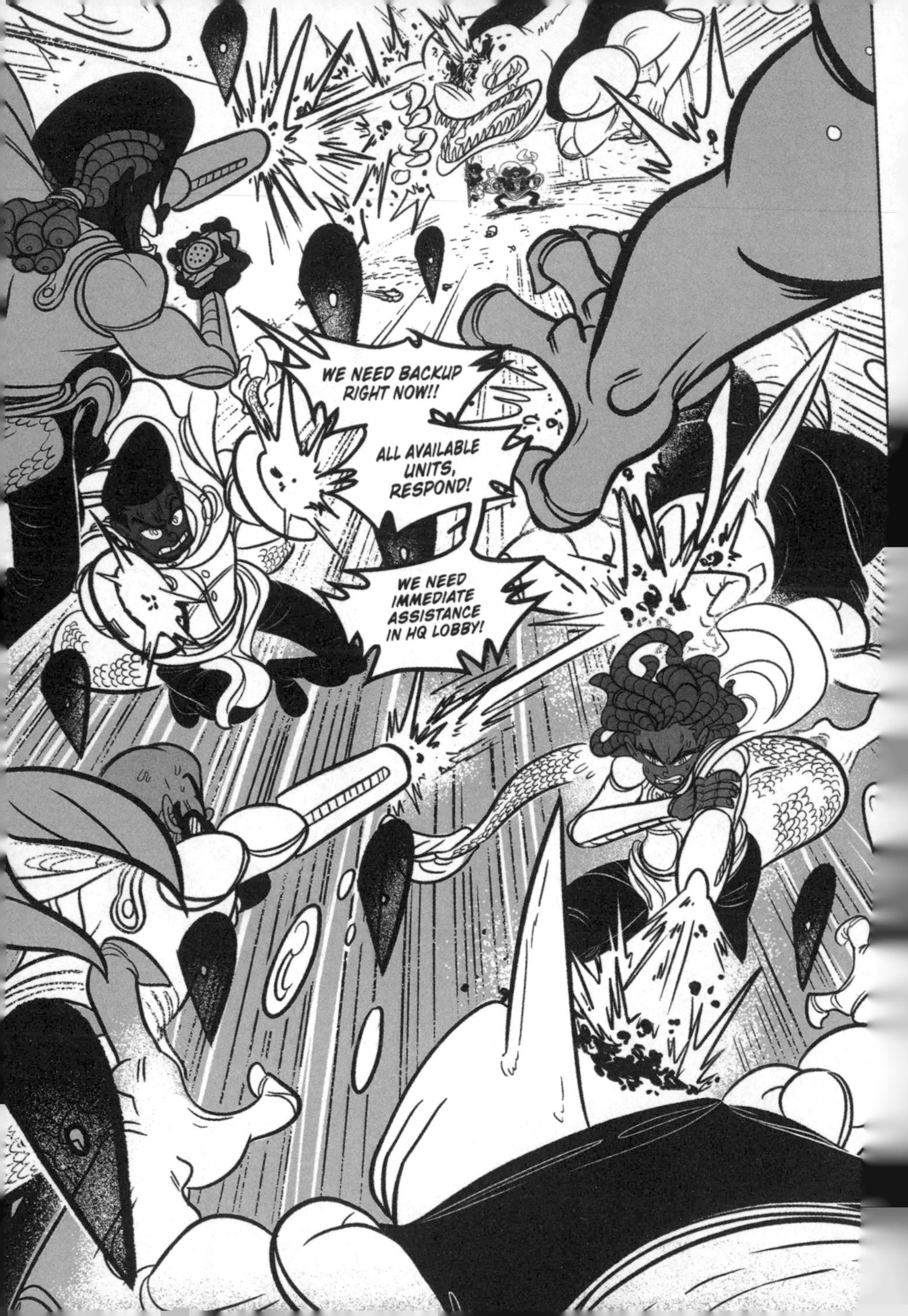
WE NEED BACKUP RIGHT NOW!!
ALL AVAILABLE UNITS, RESPOND!
WE NEED IMMEDIATE ASSISTANCE IN HQ LOBBY!

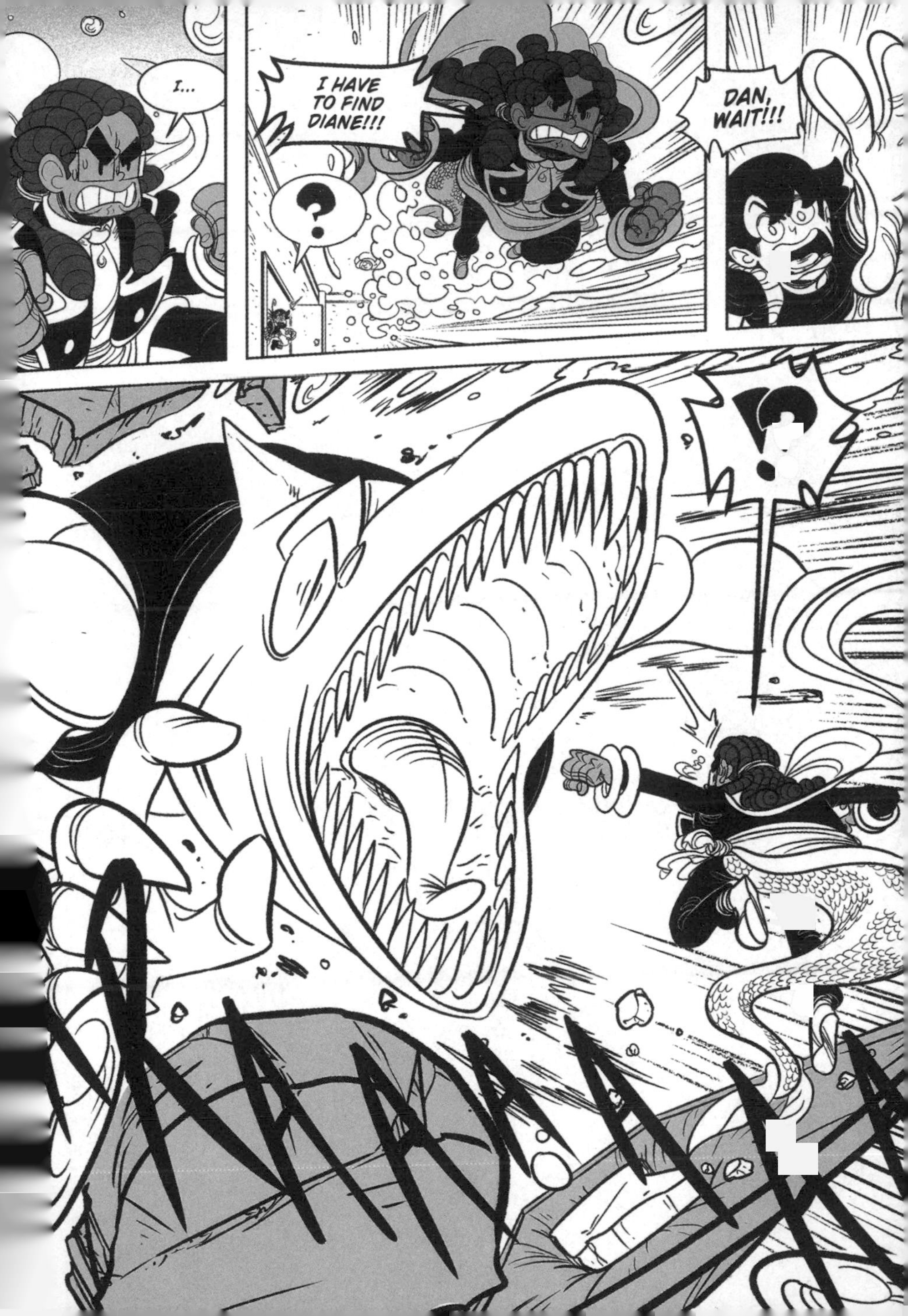
I...
I HAVE TO FIND DIANE!!!
?
DAN, WAIT!!!
?!

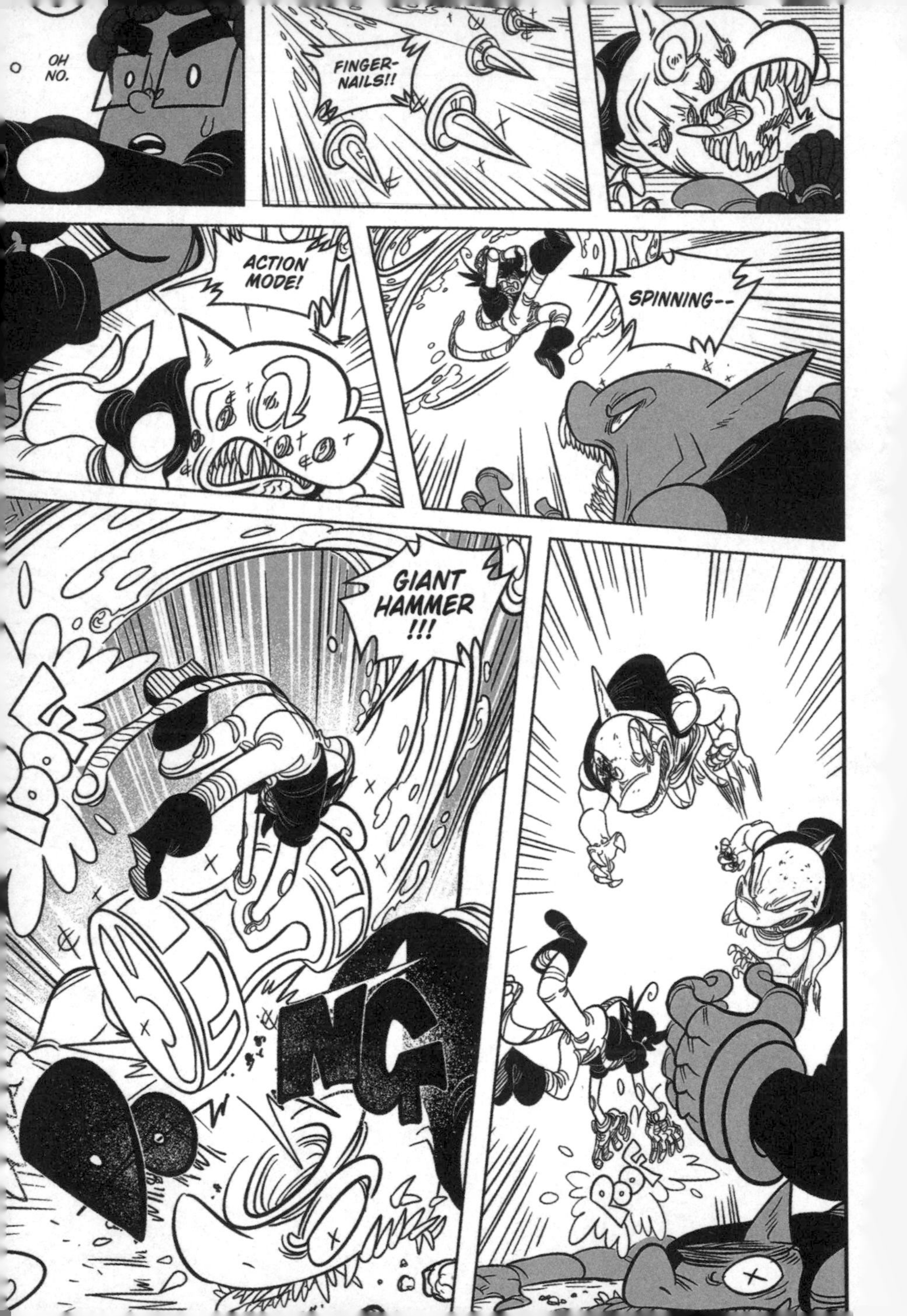
OH NO.
FINGER-NAILS!!
ACTION MODE!
SPINNING--
GIANT HAMMER !!!
POOF
NG
POOF

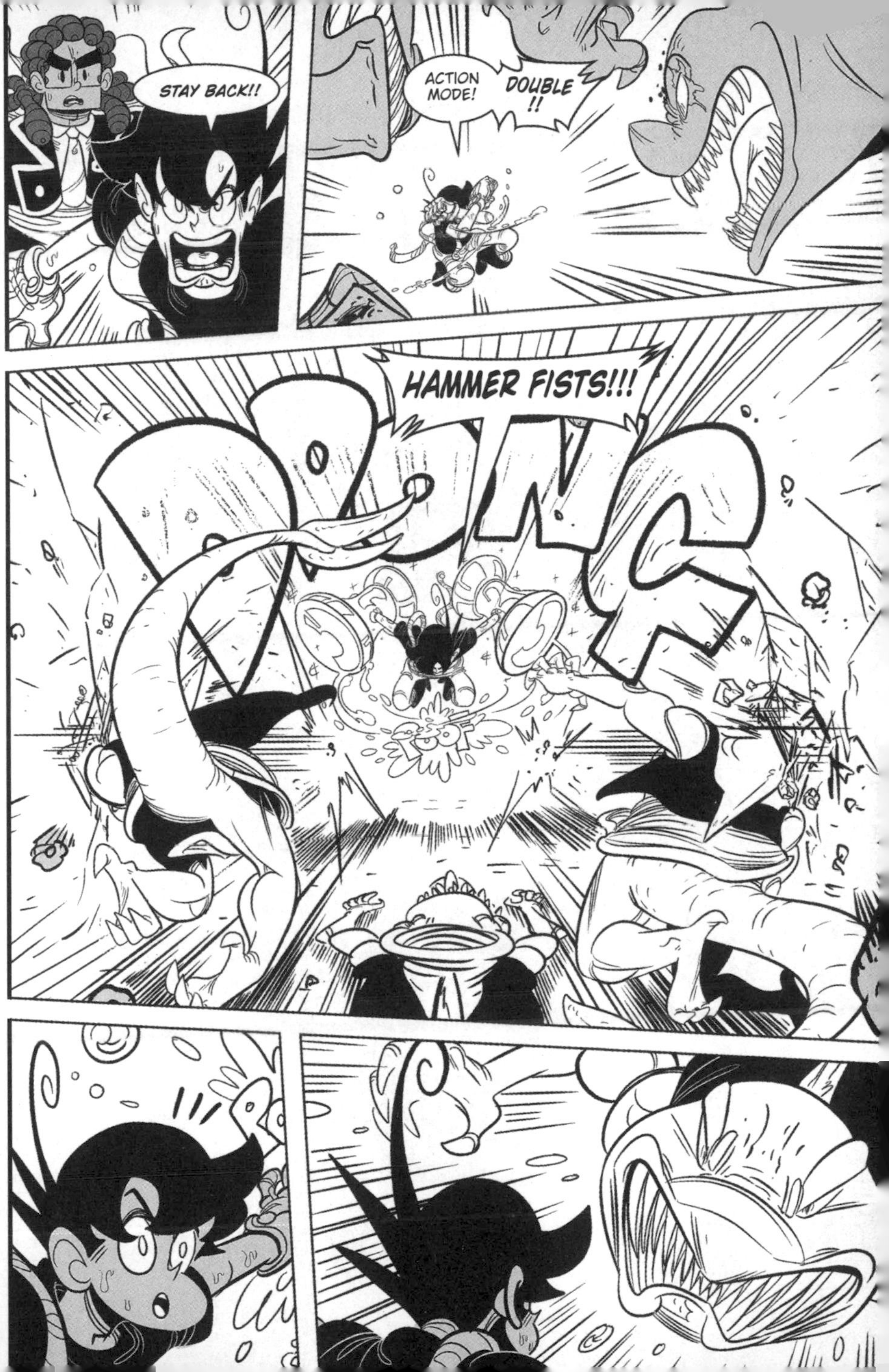
STAY BACK!!
ACTION MODE!
DOUBLE !!
HAMMER FISTS!!!
DONG

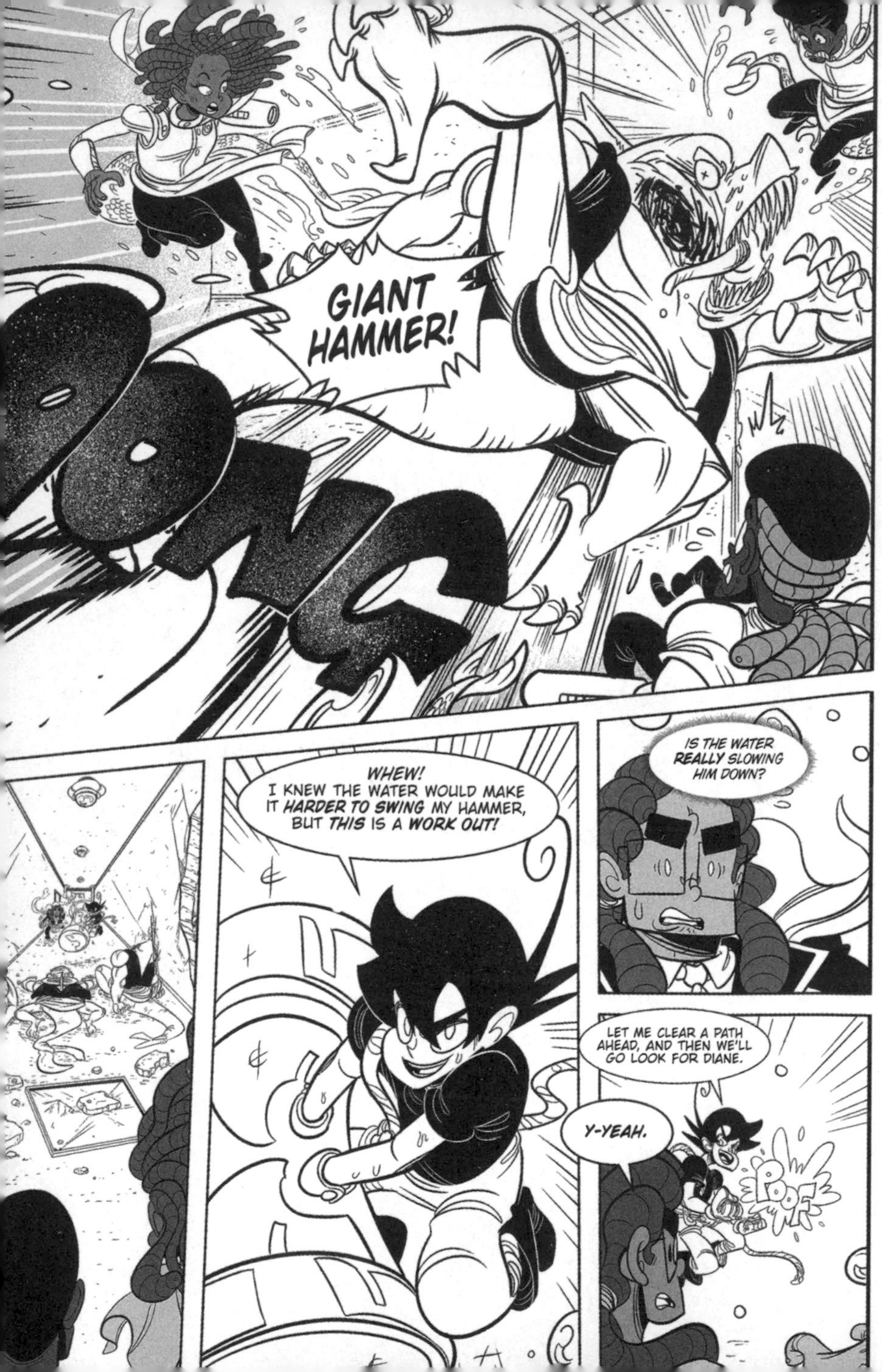
GIANT HAMMER!
WHEW! I KNEW THE WATER WOULD MAKE IT HARDER TO SWING MY HAMMER, BUT THIS IS A WORK OUT!
IS THE WATER REALLY SLOWING HIM DOWN?
LET ME CLEAR A PATH AHEAD, AND THEN WE'LL GO LOOK FOR DIANE.
Y-YEAH.
POOF

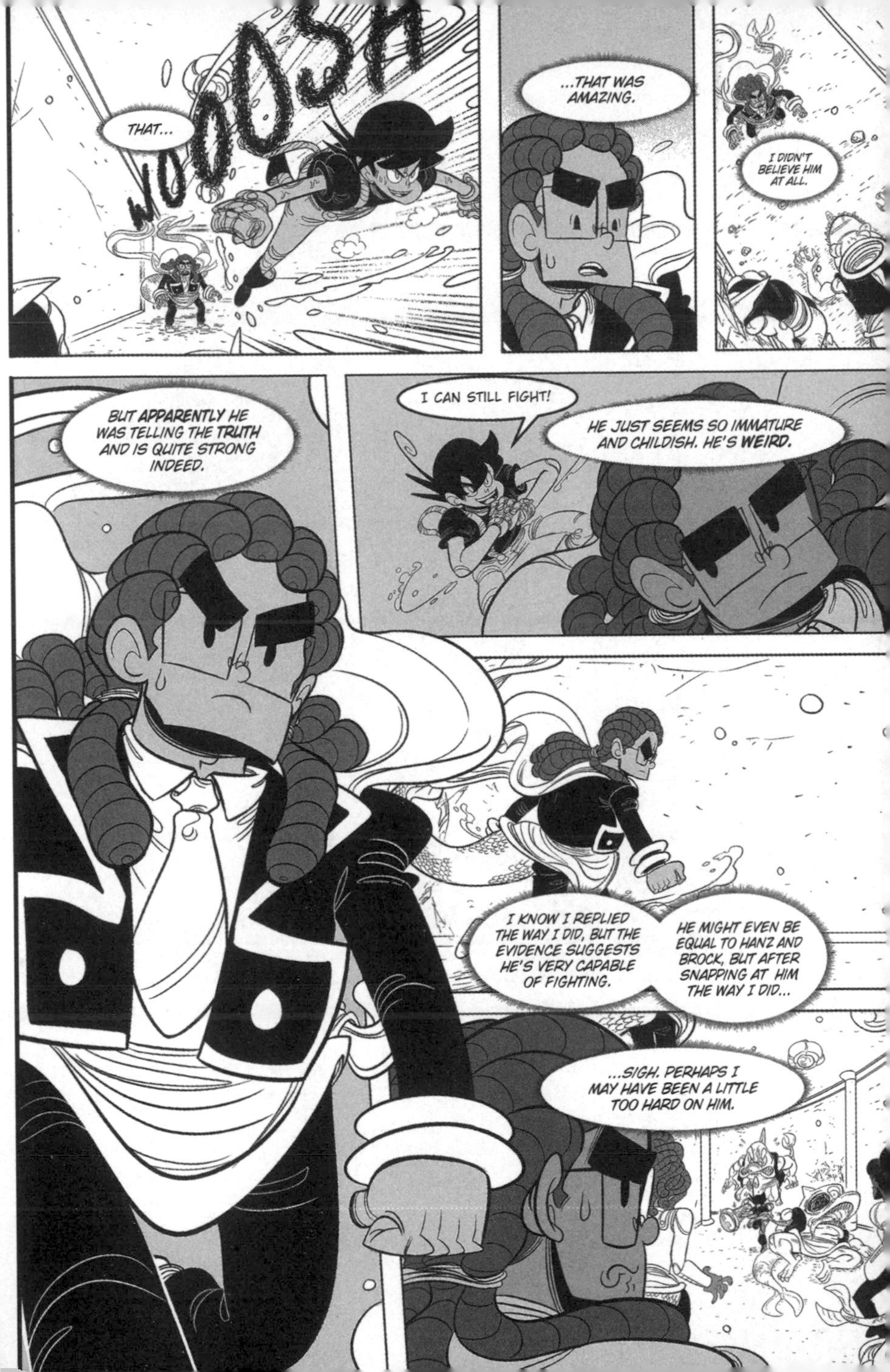
THAT...
WOOOSH
...THAT WAS AMAZING.
I DIDN'T BELIEVE HIM AT ALL.
BUT APPARENTLY HE WAS TELLING THE TRUTH AND IS QUITE STRONG INDEED.
I CAN STILL FIGHT!
HE JUST SEEMS SO IMMATURE AND CHILDISH. HE'S WEIRD.
I KNOW I REPLIED THE WAY I DID, BUT THE EVIDENCE SUGGESTS HE'S VERY CAPABLE OF FIGHTING.
HE MIGHT EVEN BE EQUAL TO HANZ AND BROCK, BUT AFTER SNAPPING AT HIM THE WAY I DID...
...SIGH. PERHAPS I MAY HAVE BEEN A LITTLE TOO HARD ON HIM.

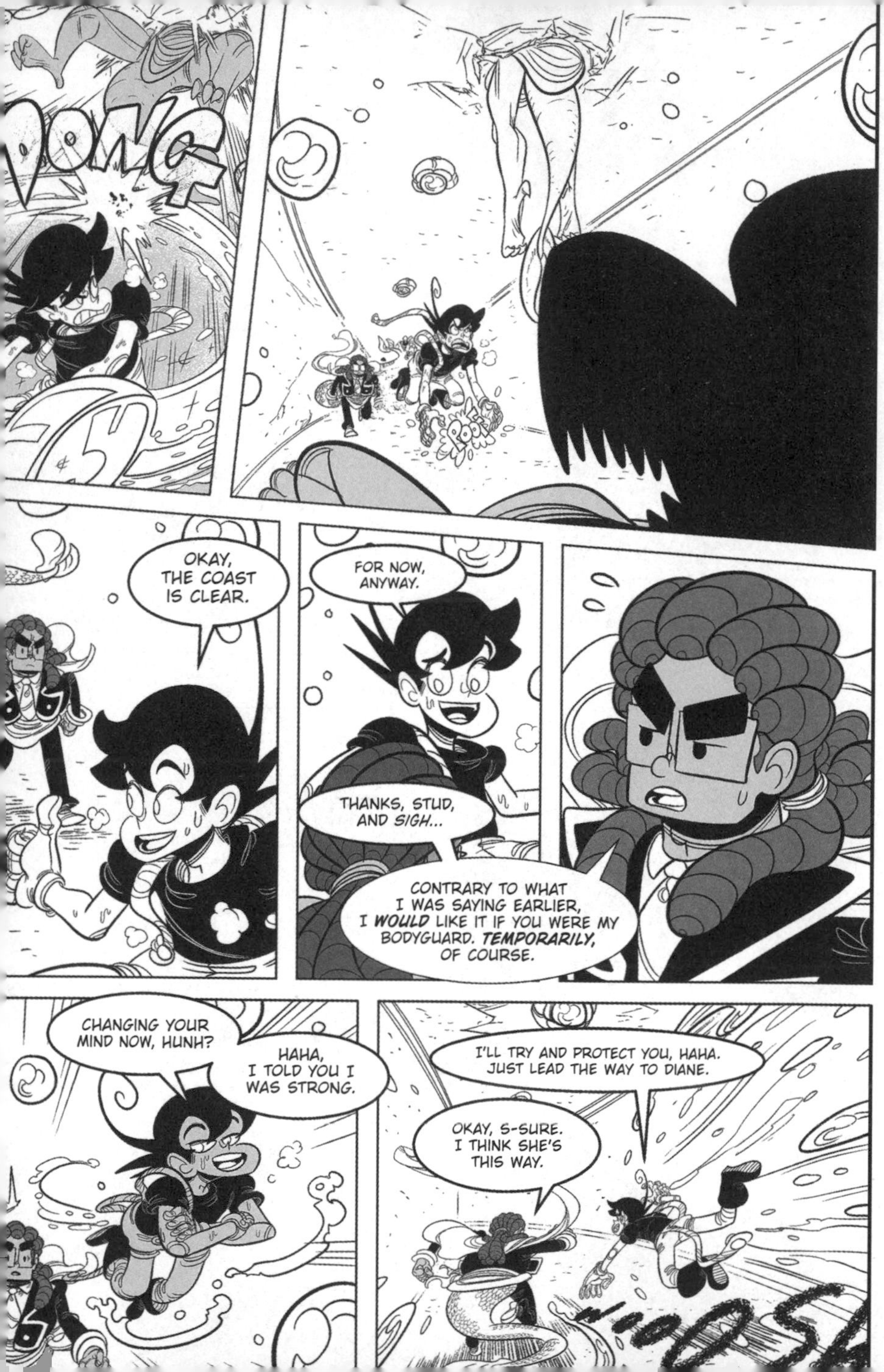
DONG
POP
OKAY, THE COAST IS CLEAR.
FOR NOW, ANYWAY.
THANKS, STUD, AND *SIGH*...
CONTRARY TO WHAT I WAS SAYING EARLIER, I ***WOULD*** LIKE IT IF YOU WERE MY BODYGUARD. ***TEMPORARILY,*** OF COURSE.
CHANGING YOUR MIND NOW, HUNH?
HAHA, I TOLD YOU I WAS STRONG.
I'LL TRY AND PROTECT YOU, HAHA. JUST LEAD THE WAY TO DIANE.
OKAY, S-SURE. I THINK SHE'S THIS WAY.

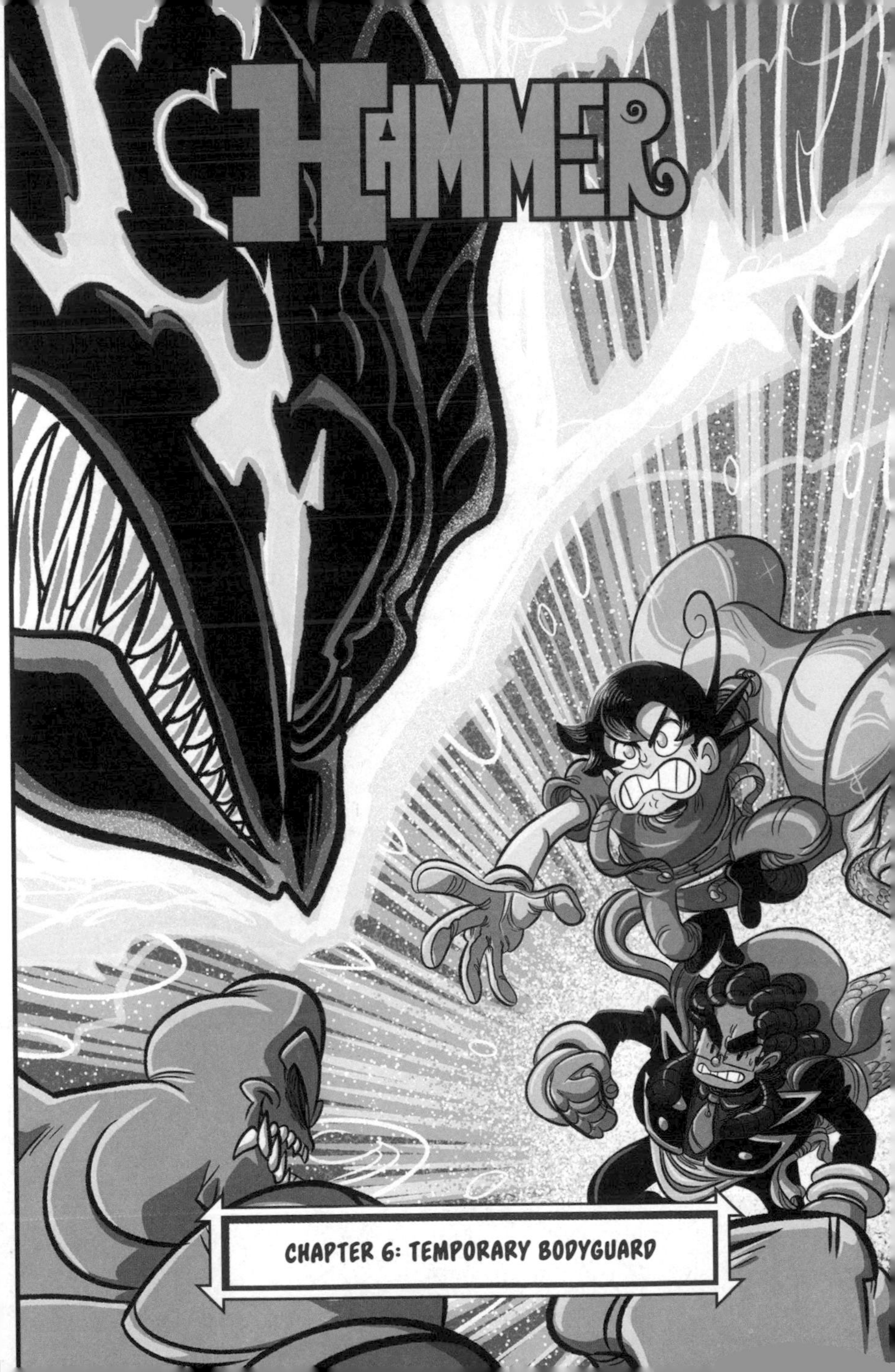
HAMMER
CHAPTER 6: TEMPORARY BODYGUARD

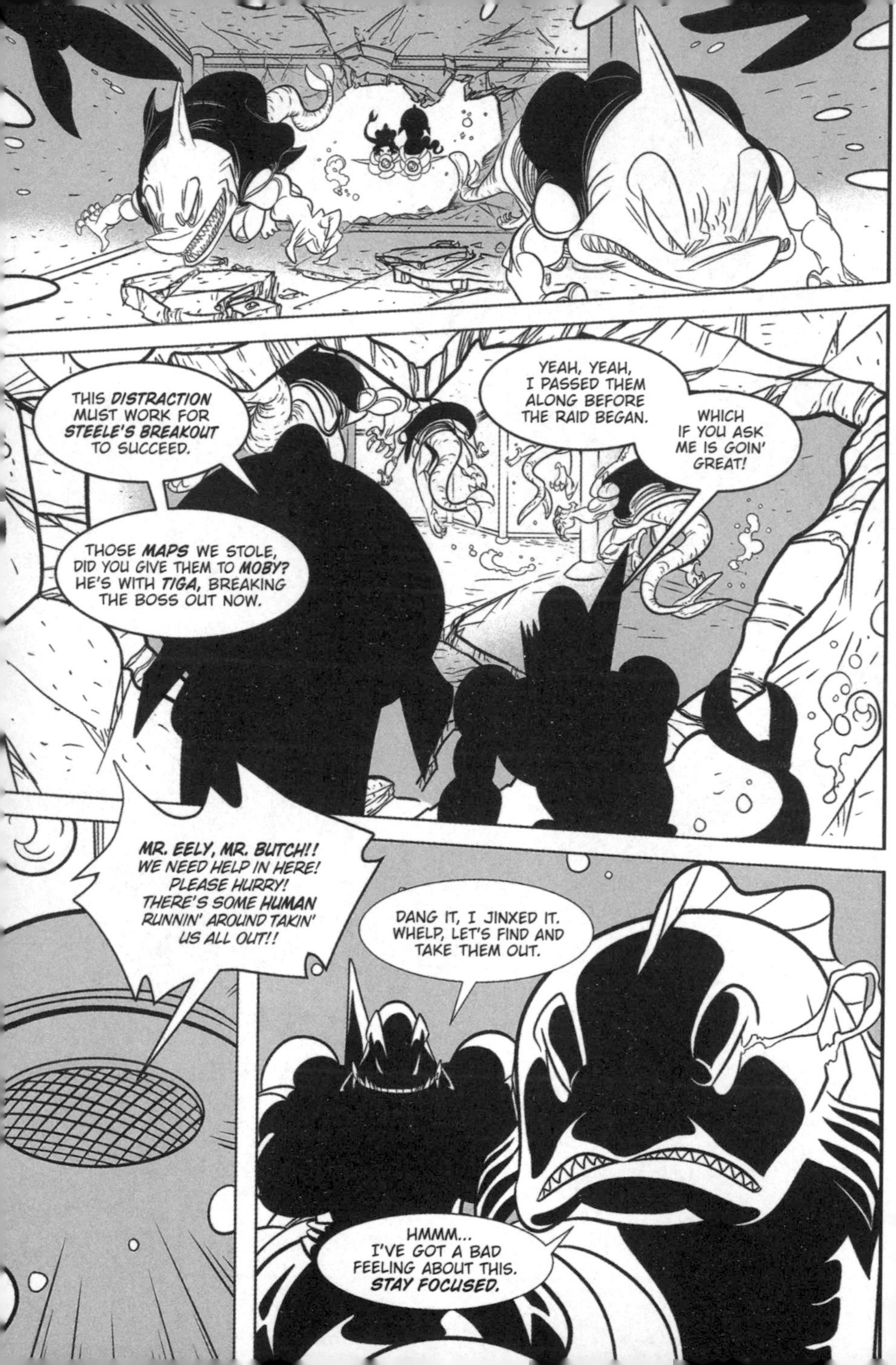
THIS DISTRACTION MUST WORK FOR STEELE'S BREAKOUT TO SUCCEED.
THOSE MAPS WE STOLE, DID YOU GIVE THEM TO MOBY? HE'S WITH TIGA, BREAKING THE BOSS OUT NOW.
YEAH, YEAH, I PASSED THEM ALONG BEFORE THE RAID BEGAN.
WHICH IF YOU ASK ME IS GOIN' GREAT!
MR. EELY, MR. BUTCH!! WE NEED HELP IN HERE! PLEASE HURRY! THERE'S SOME HUMAN RUNNIN' AROUND TAKIN' US ALL OUT!!
DANG IT, I JINXED IT. WHELP, LET'S FIND AND TAKE THEM OUT.
HMMM... I'VE GOT A BAD FEELING ABOUT THIS. STAY FOCUSED.

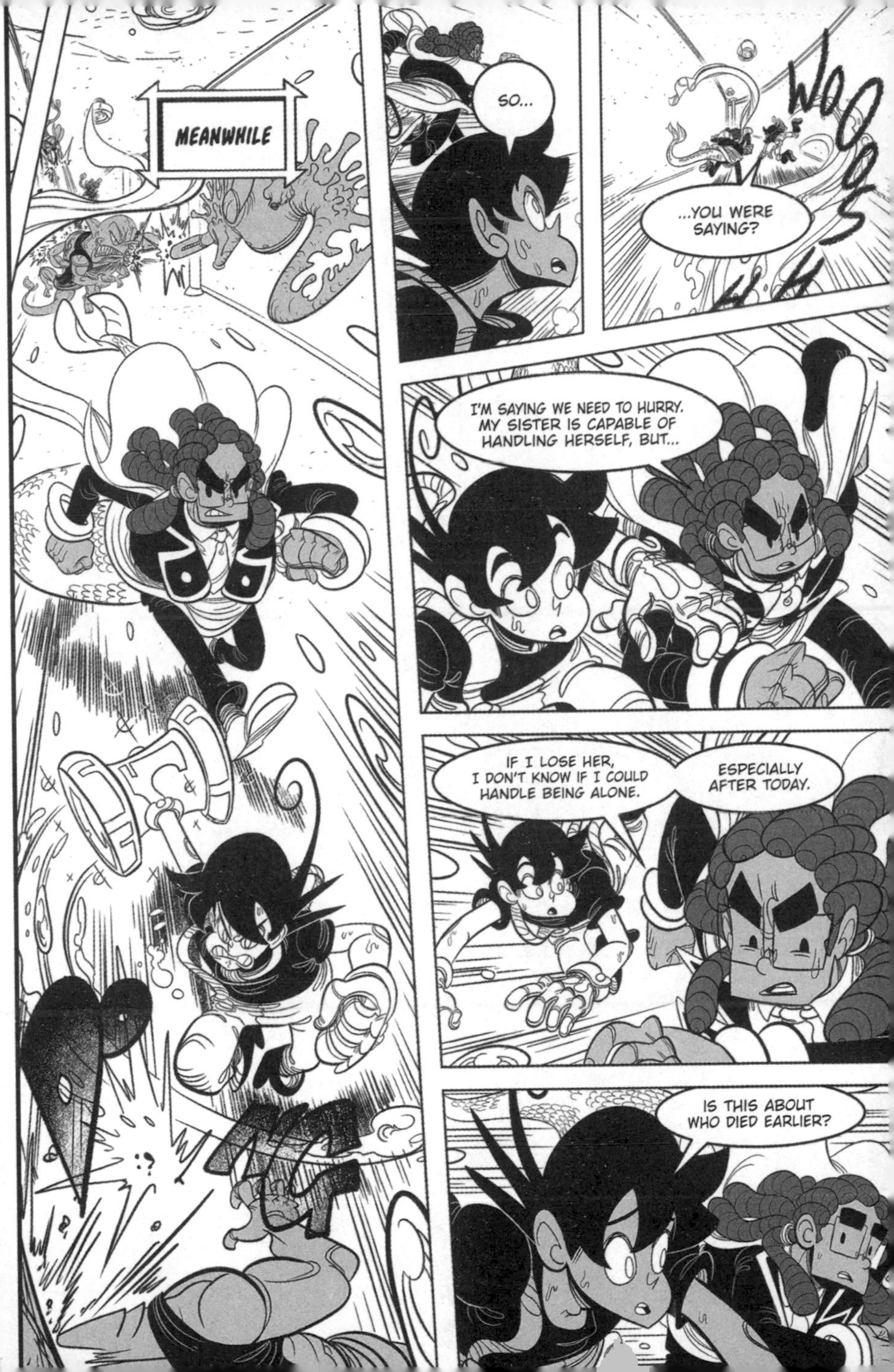
MEANWHILE
SO...
...YOU WERE SAYING?
WOOOSHH
I'M SAYING WE NEED TO HURRY. MY SISTER IS CAPABLE OF HANDLING HERSELF, BUT...
IF I LOSE HER, I DON'T KNOW IF I COULD HANDLE BEING ALONE.
ESPECIALLY AFTER TODAY.
IS THIS ABOUT WHO DIED EARLIER?

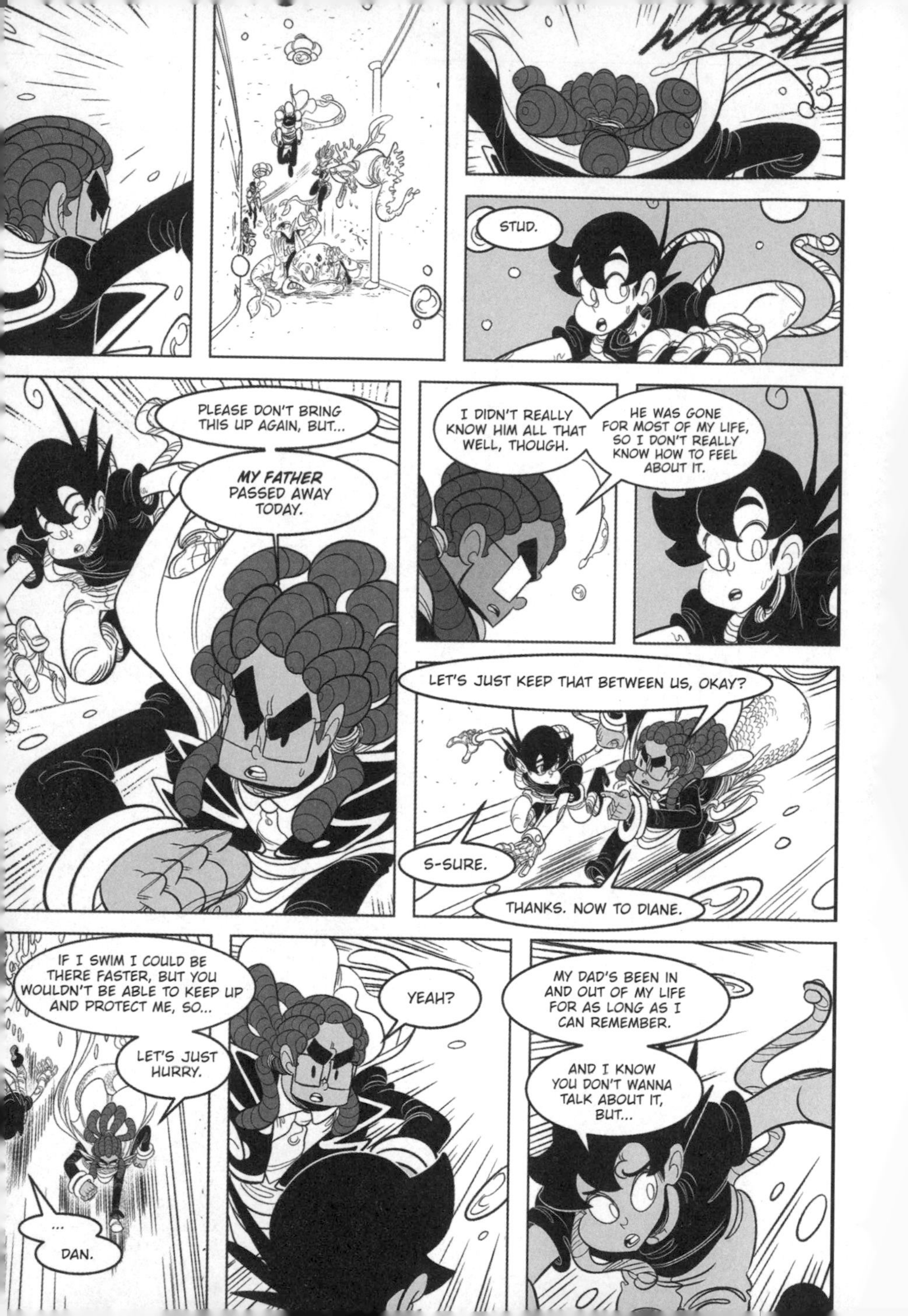
WOOSH
STUD.
PLEASE DON'T BRING THIS UP AGAIN, BUT...
MY FATHER PASSED AWAY TODAY.
I DIDN'T REALLY KNOW HIM ALL THAT WELL, THOUGH.
HE WAS GONE FOR MOST OF MY LIFE, SO I DON'T REALLY KNOW HOW TO FEEL ABOUT IT.
LET'S JUST KEEP THAT BETWEEN US, OKAY?
S-SURE.
THANKS. NOW TO DIANE.
IF I SWIM I COULD BE THERE FASTER, BUT YOU WOULDN'T BE ABLE TO KEEP UP AND PROTECT ME, SO...
LET'S JUST HURRY.
... DAN.
YEAH?
MY DAD'S BEEN IN AND OUT OF MY LIFE FOR AS LONG AS I CAN REMEMBER.
AND I KNOW YOU DON'T WANNA TALK ABOUT IT, BUT...

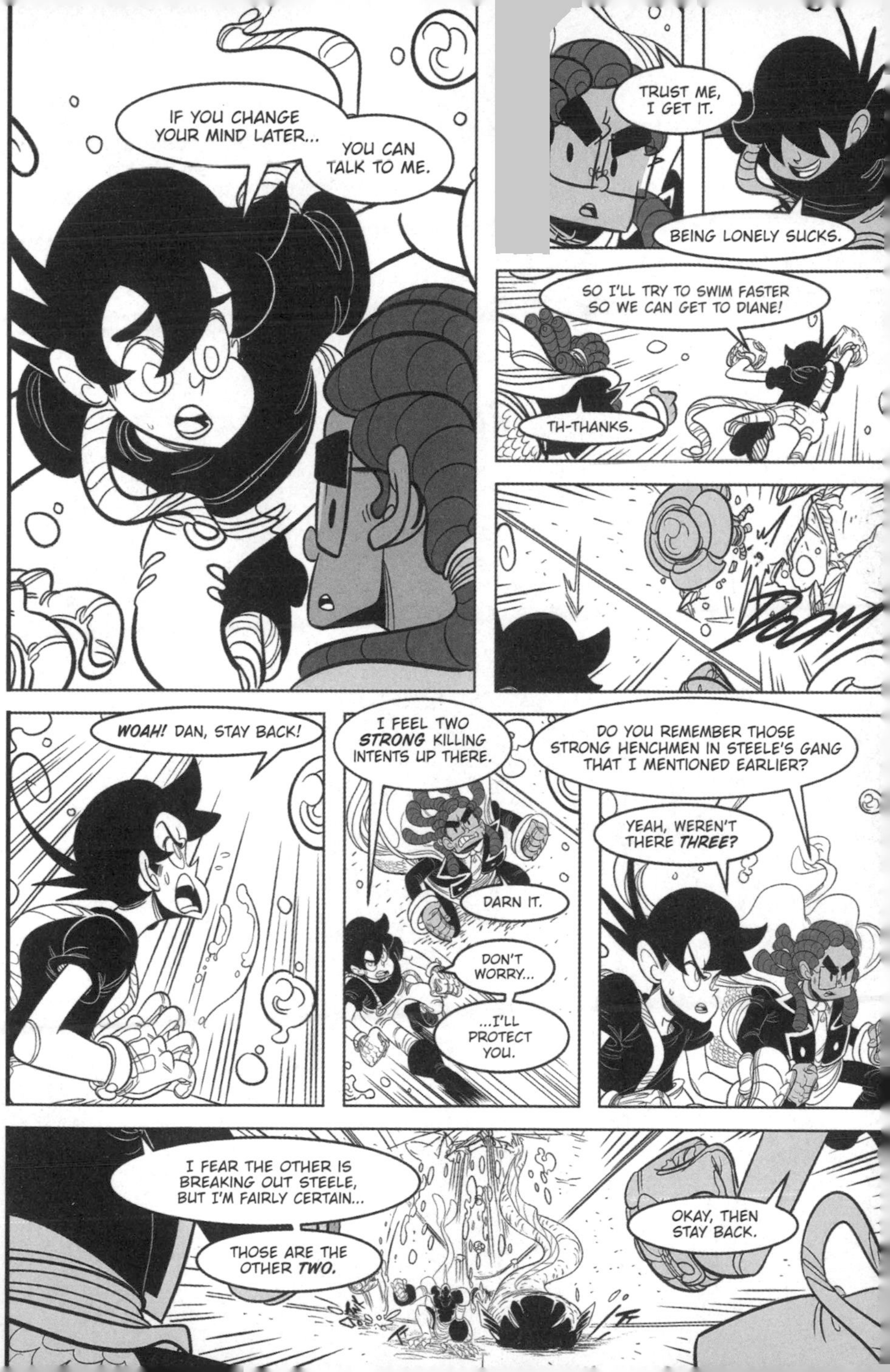
IF YOU CHANGE YOUR MIND LATER...
YOU CAN TALK TO ME.
TRUST ME, I GET IT.
BEING LONELY SUCKS.
SO I'LL TRY TO SWIM FASTER SO WE CAN GET TO DIANE!
TH-THANKS.
DOOM
WOAH! DAN, STAY BACK!
I FEEL TWO STRONG KILLING INTENTS UP THERE.
DARN IT.
DON'T WORRY...
...I'LL PROTECT YOU.
DO YOU REMEMBER THOSE STRONG HENCHMEN IN STEELE'S GANG THAT I MENTIONED EARLIER?
YEAH, WEREN'T THERE THREE?
I FEAR THE OTHER IS BREAKING OUT STEELE, BUT I'M FAIRLY CERTAIN...
THOSE ARE THE OTHER TWO.
OKAY, THEN STAY BACK.

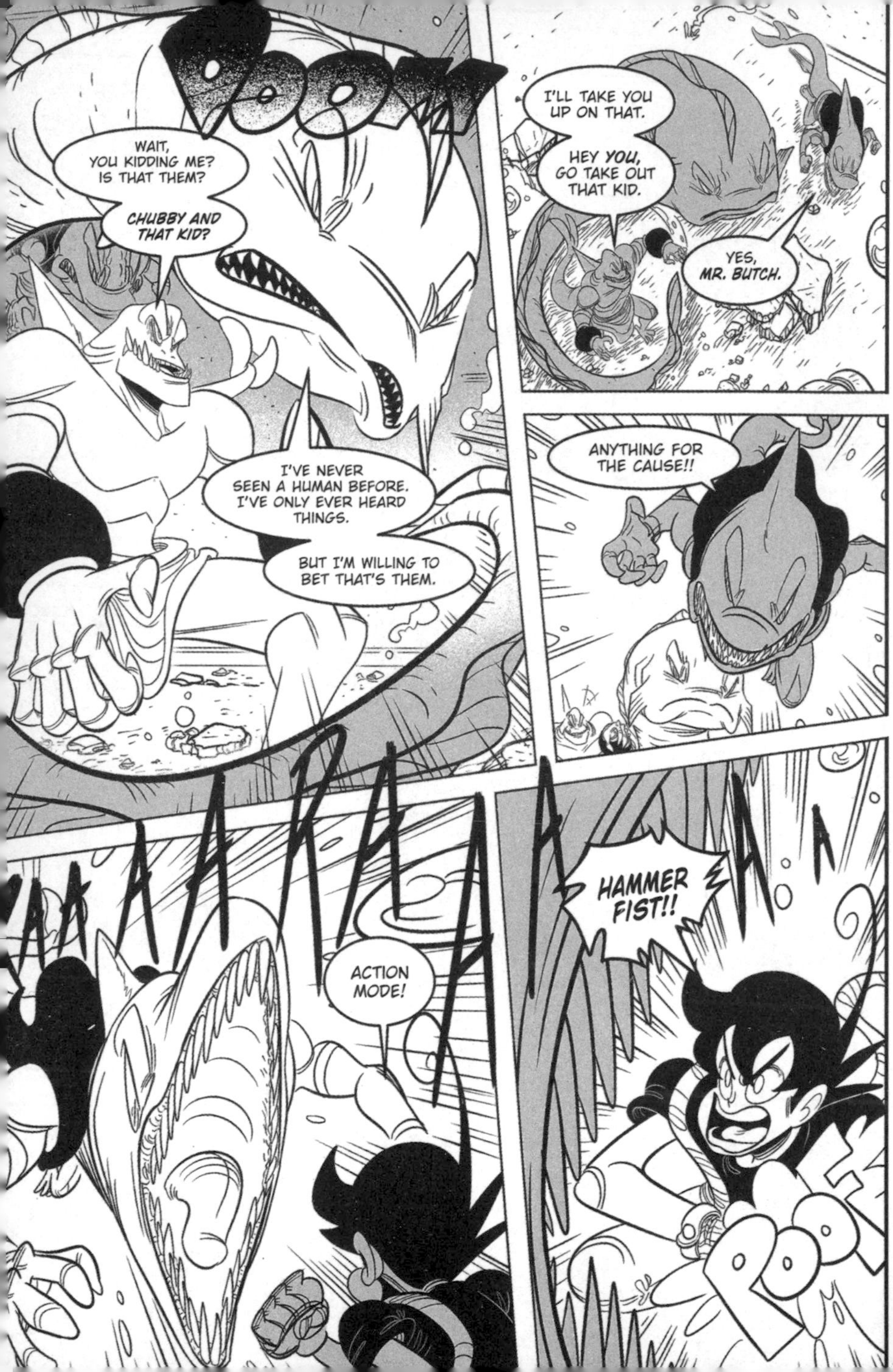
WAIT, YOU KIDDING ME? IS THAT THEM?
CHUBBY AND THAT KID?
I'VE NEVER SEEN A HUMAN BEFORE. I'VE ONLY EVER HEARD THINGS.
BUT I'M WILLING TO BET THAT'S THEM.
I'LL TAKE YOU UP ON THAT.
HEY YOU, GO TAKE OUT THAT KID.
YES, MR. BUTCH.
ANYTHING FOR THE CAUSE!!
ACTION MODE!
HAMMER FIST!!

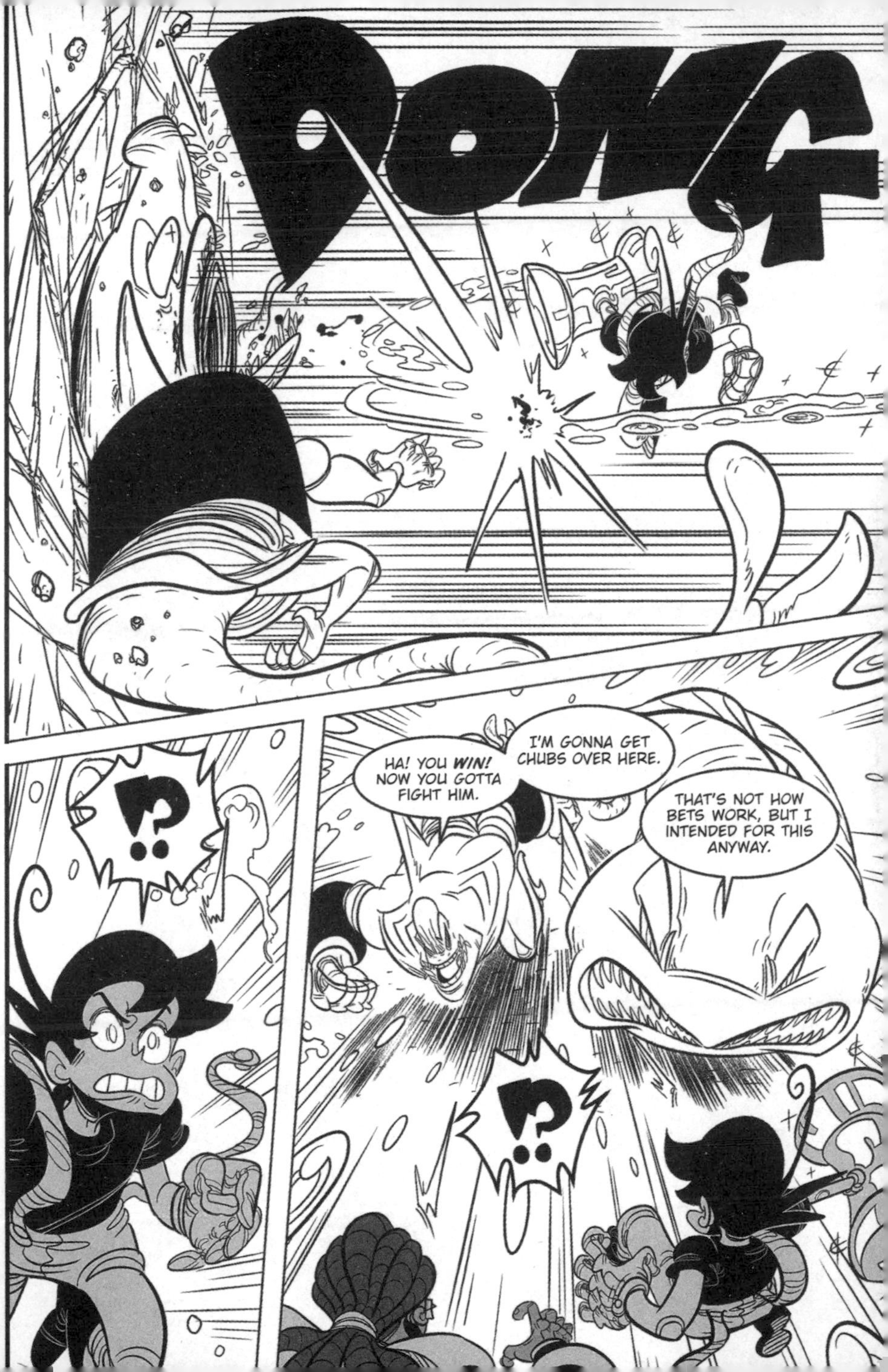
DONG
!?
HA! YOU WIN! NOW YOU GOTTA FIGHT HIM.
I'M GONNA GET CHUBS OVER HERE.
THAT'S NOT HOW BETS WORK, BUT I INTENDED FOR THIS ANYWAY.
!?

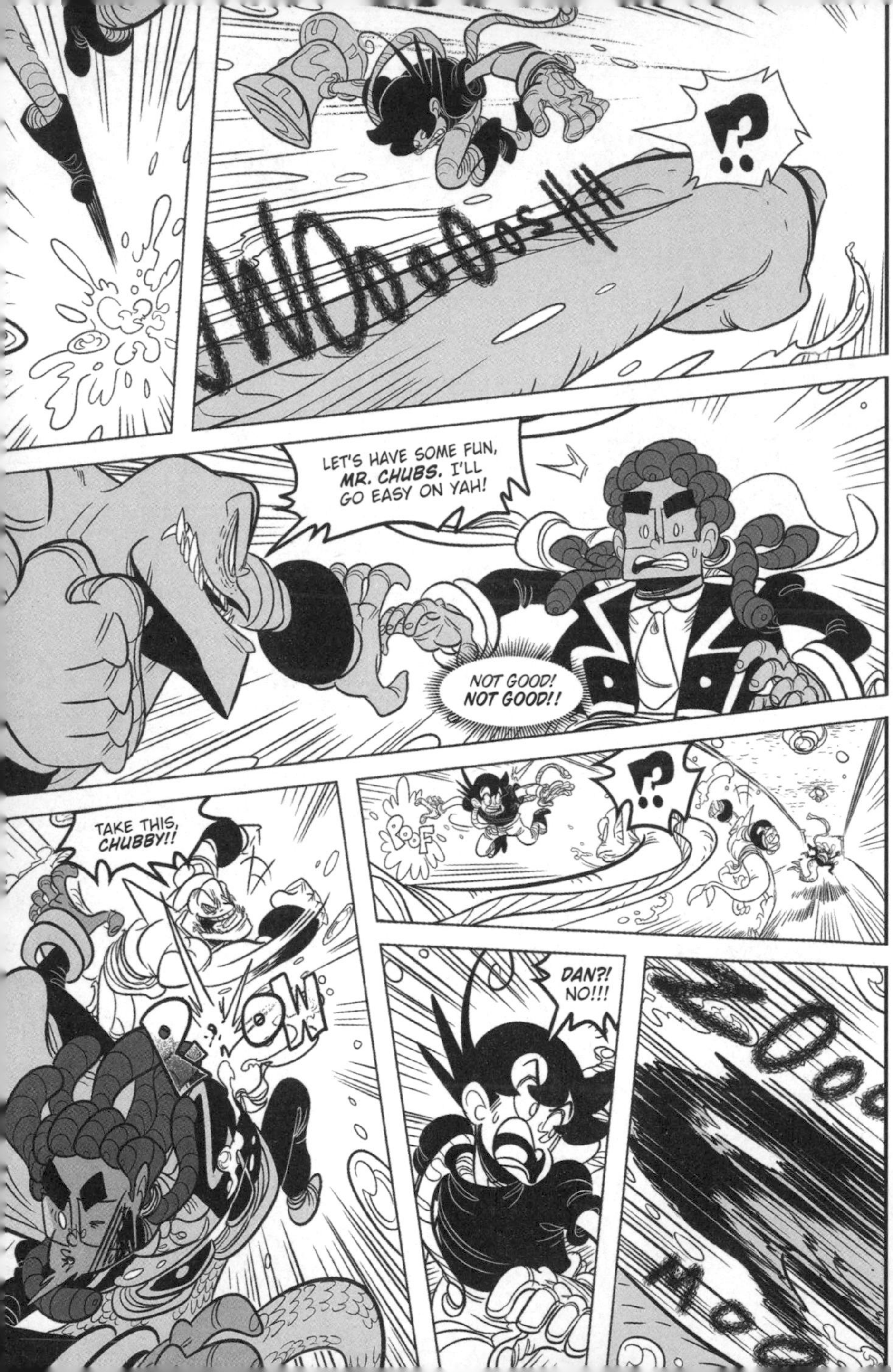
?!!
WHOOoOoOS!!!
LET'S HAVE SOME FUN, **MR. CHUBS.** I'LL GO EASY ON YAH!
NOT GOOD! ***NOT GOOD!!***
POOF
?!!
TAKE THIS, **CHUBBY!!**
POW
DAN?! NO!!!

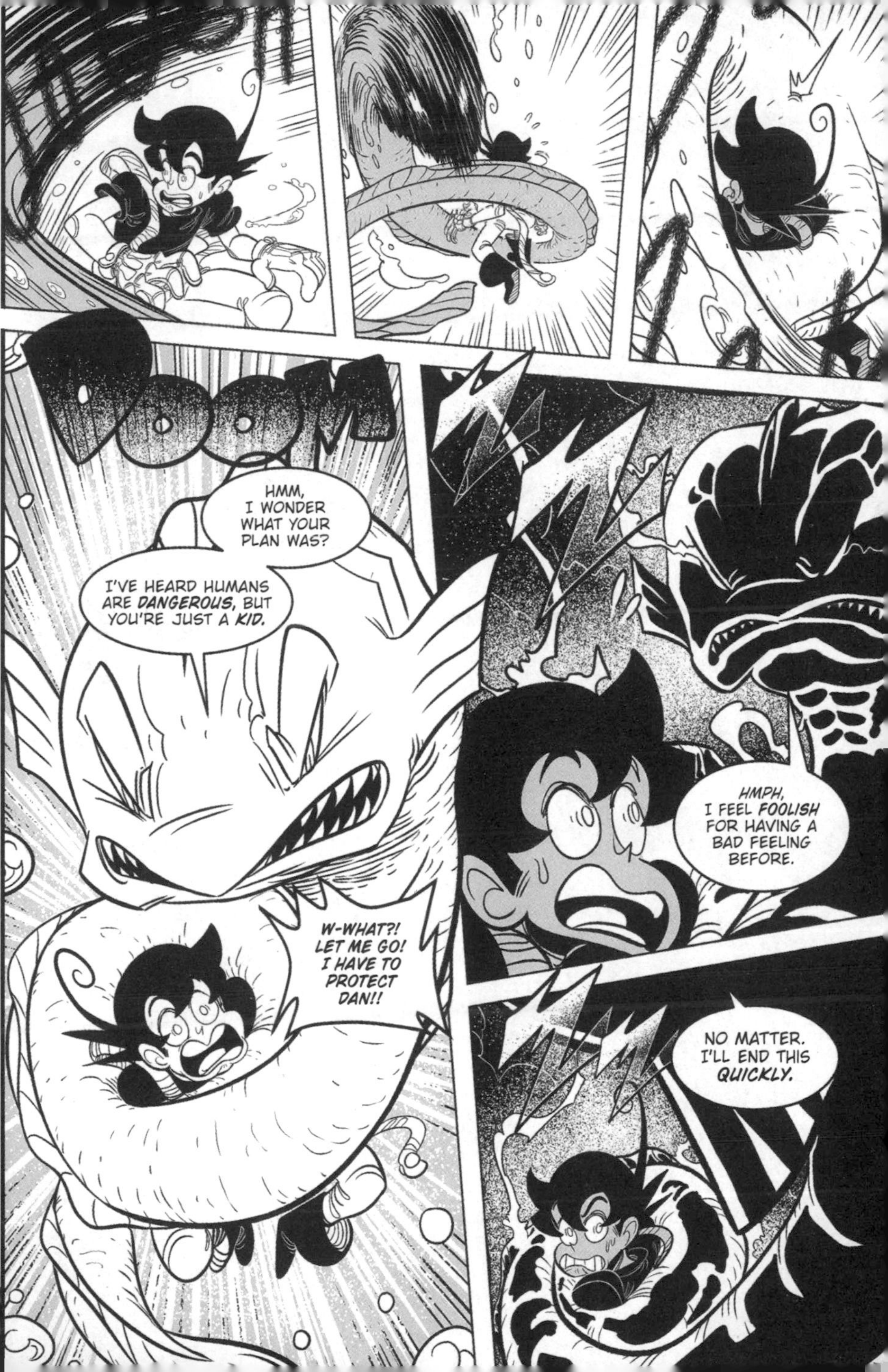
DOOOM
HMM, I WONDER WHAT YOUR PLAN WAS?
I'VE HEARD HUMANS ARE *DANGEROUS*, BUT YOU'RE JUST A *KID*.
W-WHAT?! LET ME GO! I HAVE TO PROTECT DAN!!
HMPH, I FEEL *FOOLISH* FOR HAVING A BAD FEELING BEFORE.
NO MATTER. I'LL END THIS *QUICKLY.*

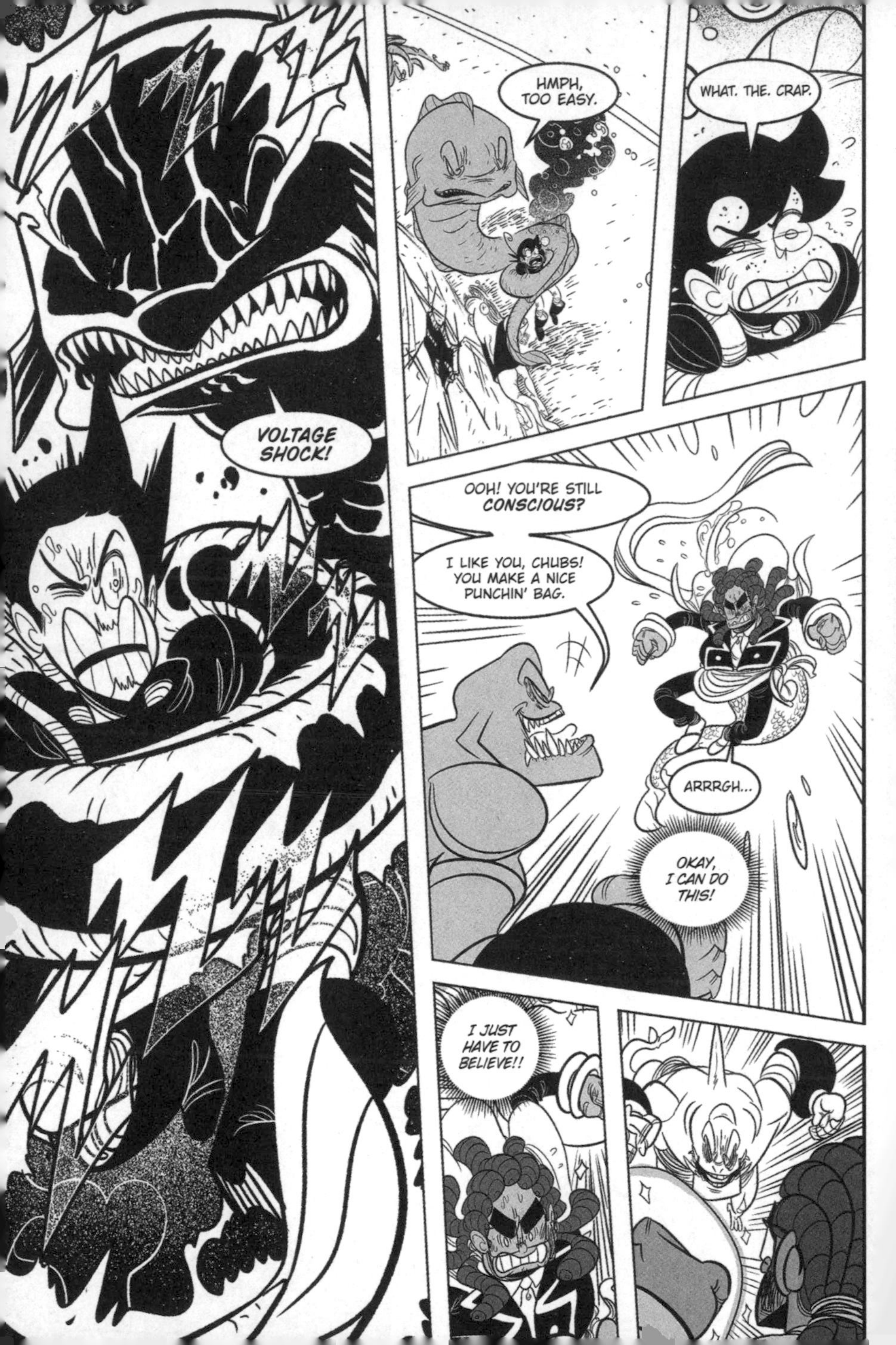
VOLTAGE SHOCK!
HMPH, TOO EASY.
WHAT. THE. CRAP.
OOH! YOU'RE STILL CONSCIOUS?
I LIKE YOU, CHUBS! YOU MAKE A NICE PUNCHIN' BAG.
ARRRGH...
OKAY, I CAN DO THIS!
I JUST HAVE TO BELIEVE!!

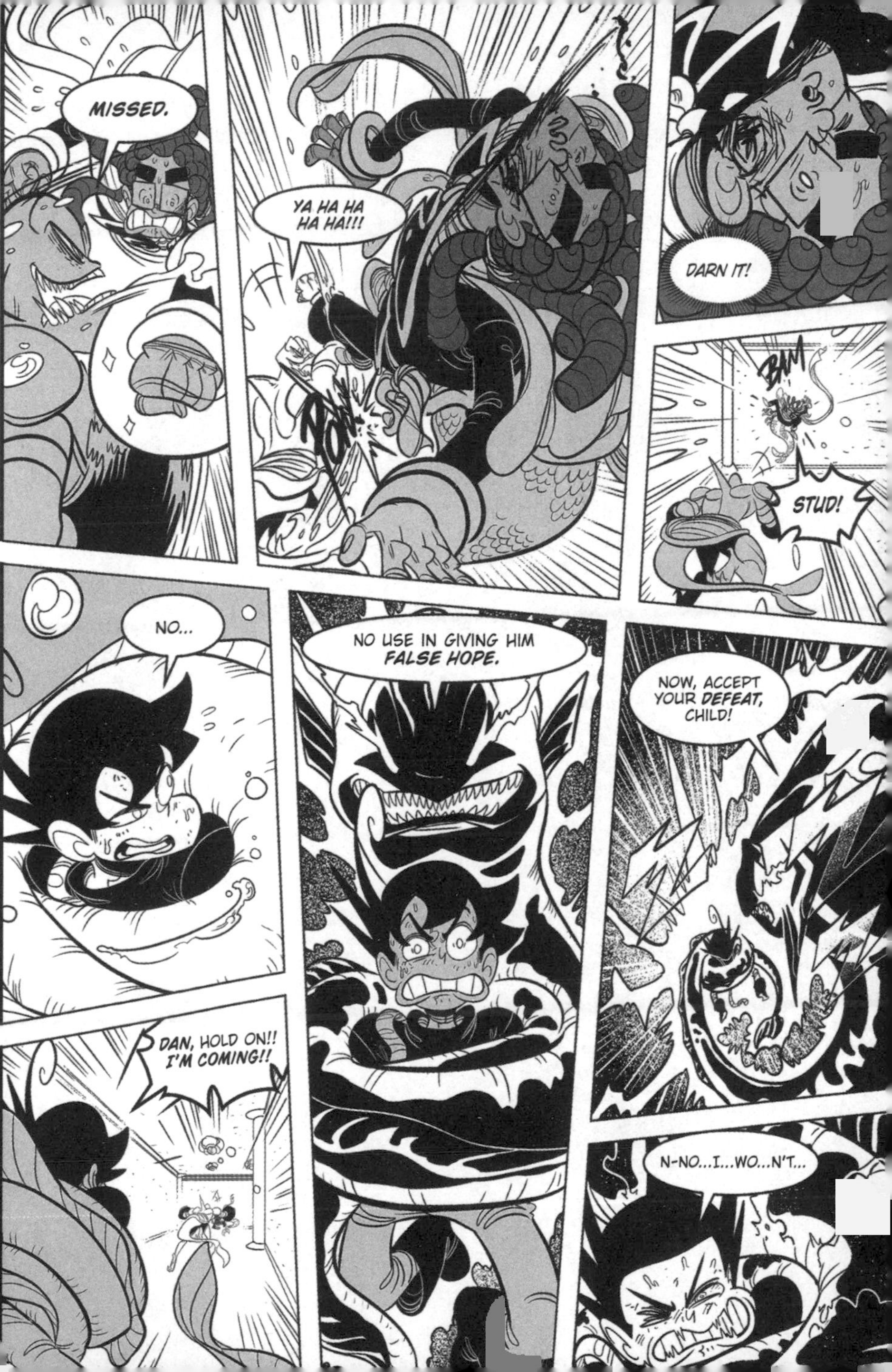
MISSED.
YA HA HA HA HA!!!
DARN IT!
BAM
STUD!
NO...
DAN, HOLD ON!! I'M COMING!!
NO USE IN GIVING HIM FALSE HOPE.
NOW, ACCEPT YOUR DEFEAT, CHILD!
N-NO...I...WO...N'T...

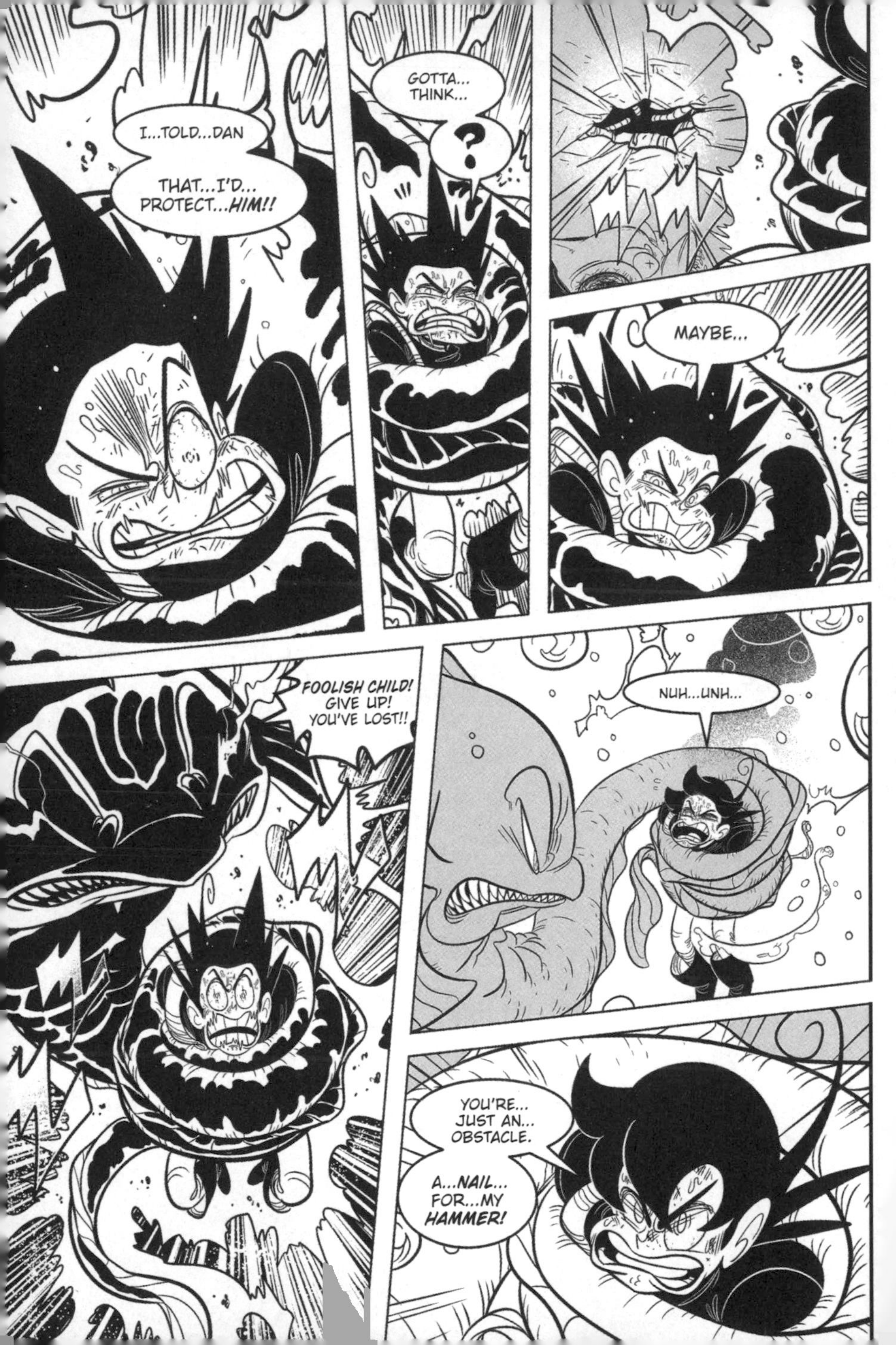
I...TOLD...DAN
THAT...I'D... PROTECT...HIM!!
GOTTA... THINK...
?
MAYBE...
FOOLISH CHILD! GIVE UP! YOU'VE LOST!!
NUH...UNH...
YOU'RE... JUST AN... OBSTACLE.
A...NAIL... FOR...MY HAMMER!

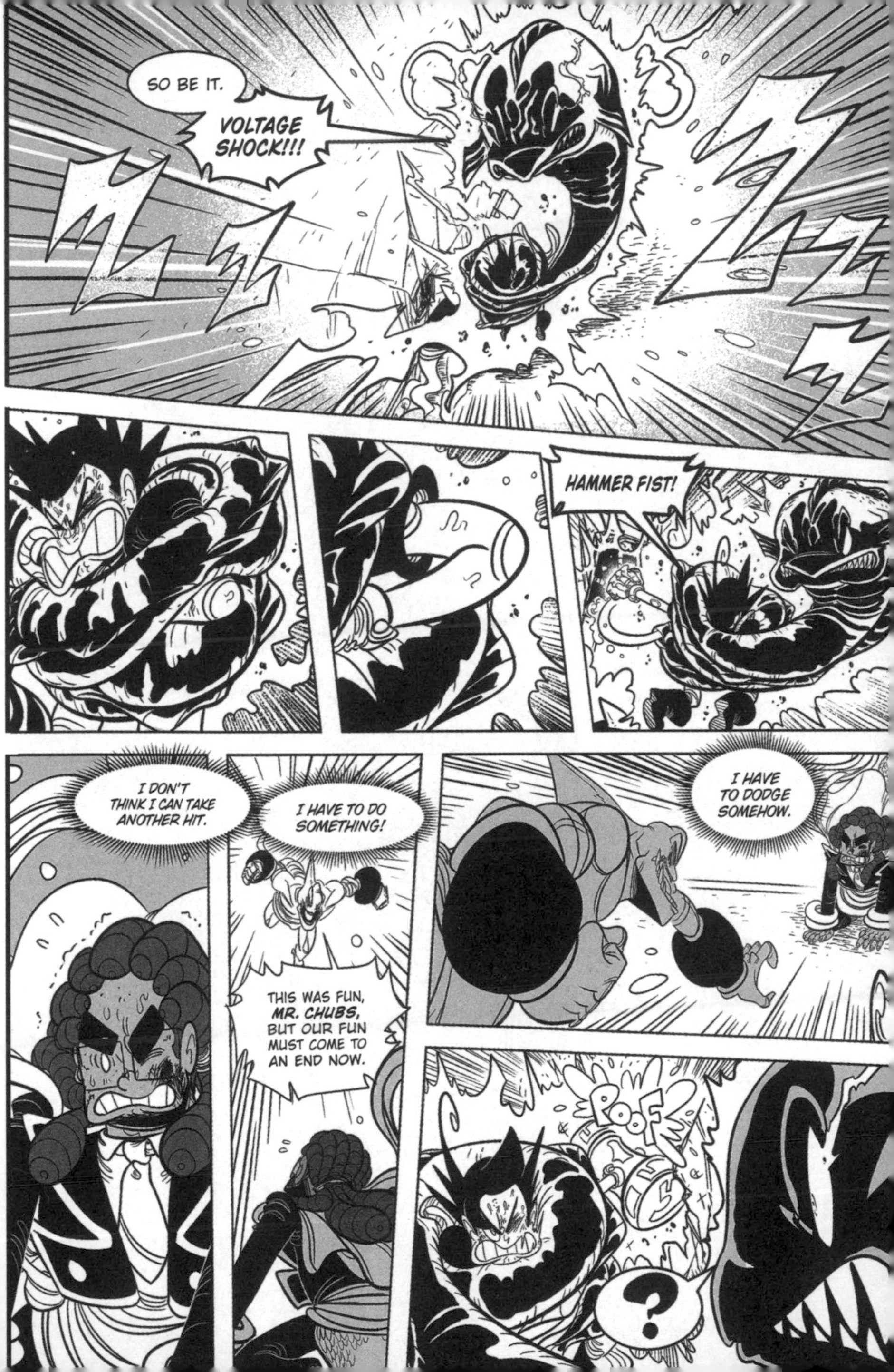
SO BE IT.
VOLTAGE SHOCK!!!
HAMMER FIST!
I DON'T THINK I CAN TAKE ANOTHER HIT.
I HAVE TO DO SOMETHING!
THIS WAS FUN, MR. CHUBS, BUT OUR FUN MUST COME TO AN END NOW.
I HAVE TO DODGE SOMEHOW.
POOF
?

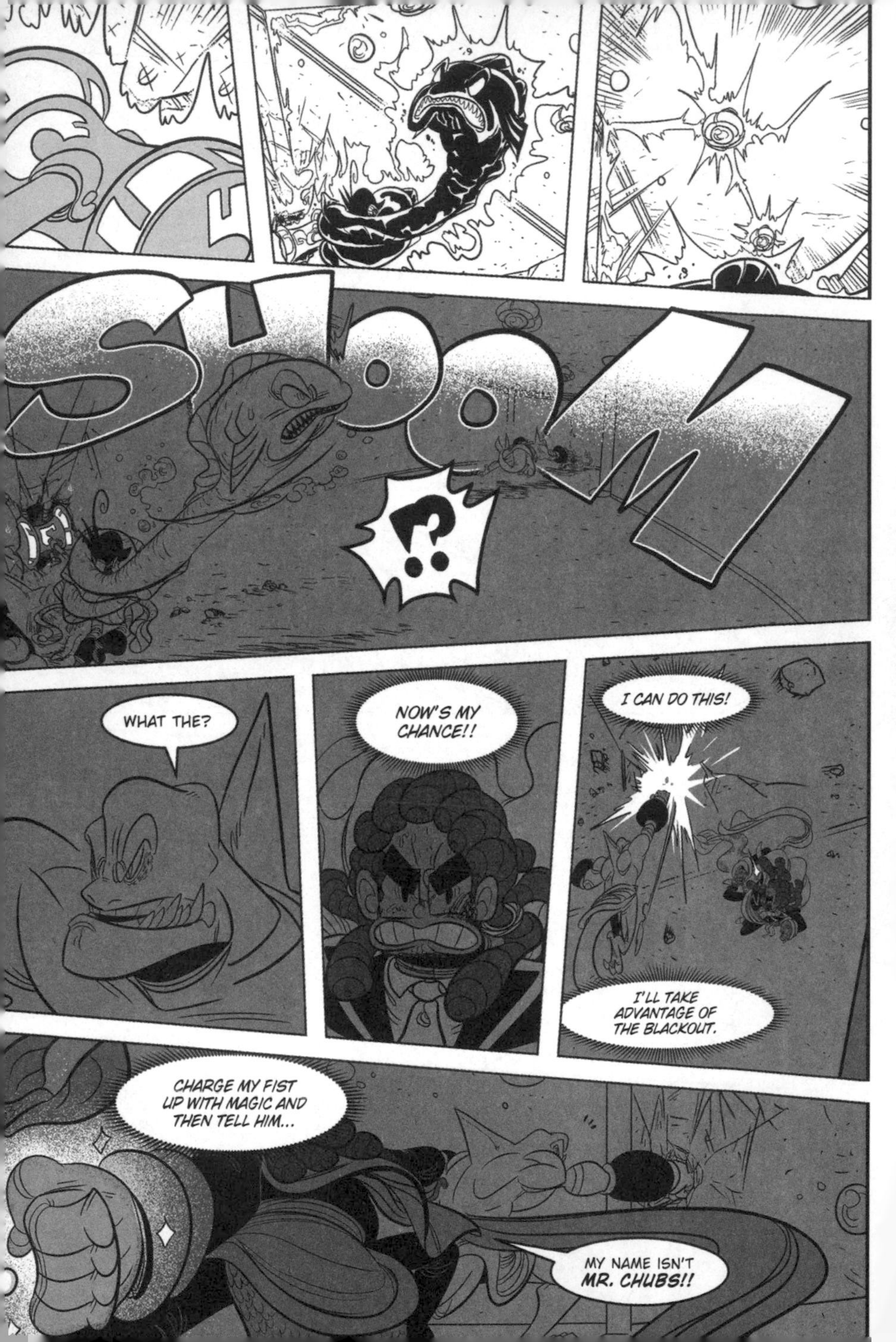
SHOOM
!?
WHAT THE?
NOW'S MY CHANCE!!
I CAN DO THIS!
I'LL TAKE ADVANTAGE OF THE BLACKOUT.
CHARGE MY FIST UP WITH MAGIC AND THEN TELL HIM...
MY NAME ISN'T **MR. CHUBS!!**

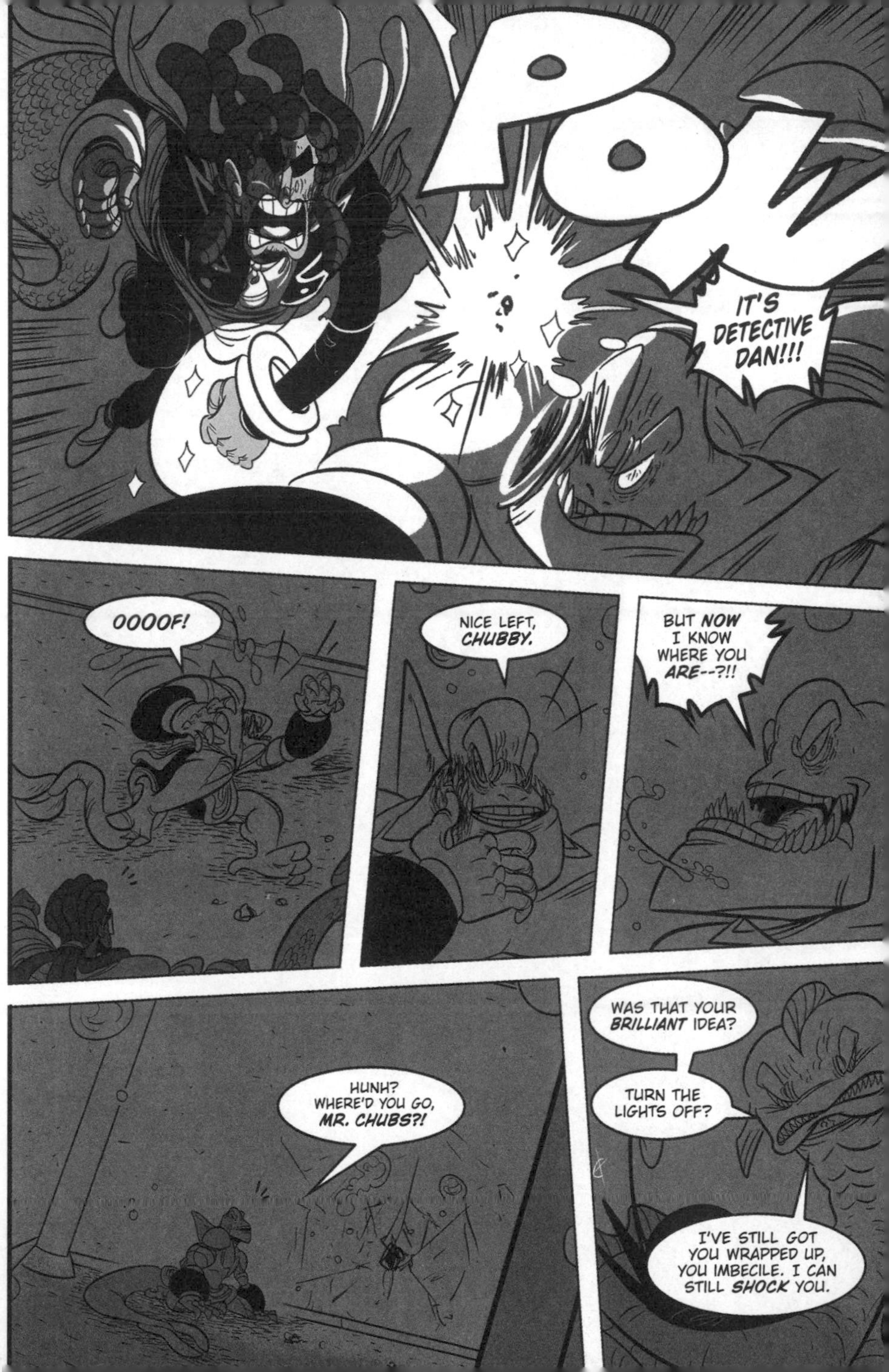
POW
IT'S DETECTIVE DAN!!!
OOOOF!
NICE LEFT, CHUBBY.
BUT NOW I KNOW WHERE YOU ARE--?!!
HUNH? WHERE'D YOU GO, MR. CHUBS?!
WAS THAT YOUR BRILLIANT IDEA?
TURN THE LIGHTS OFF?
I'VE STILL GOT YOU WRAPPED UP, YOU IMBECILE. I CAN STILL SHOCK YOU.

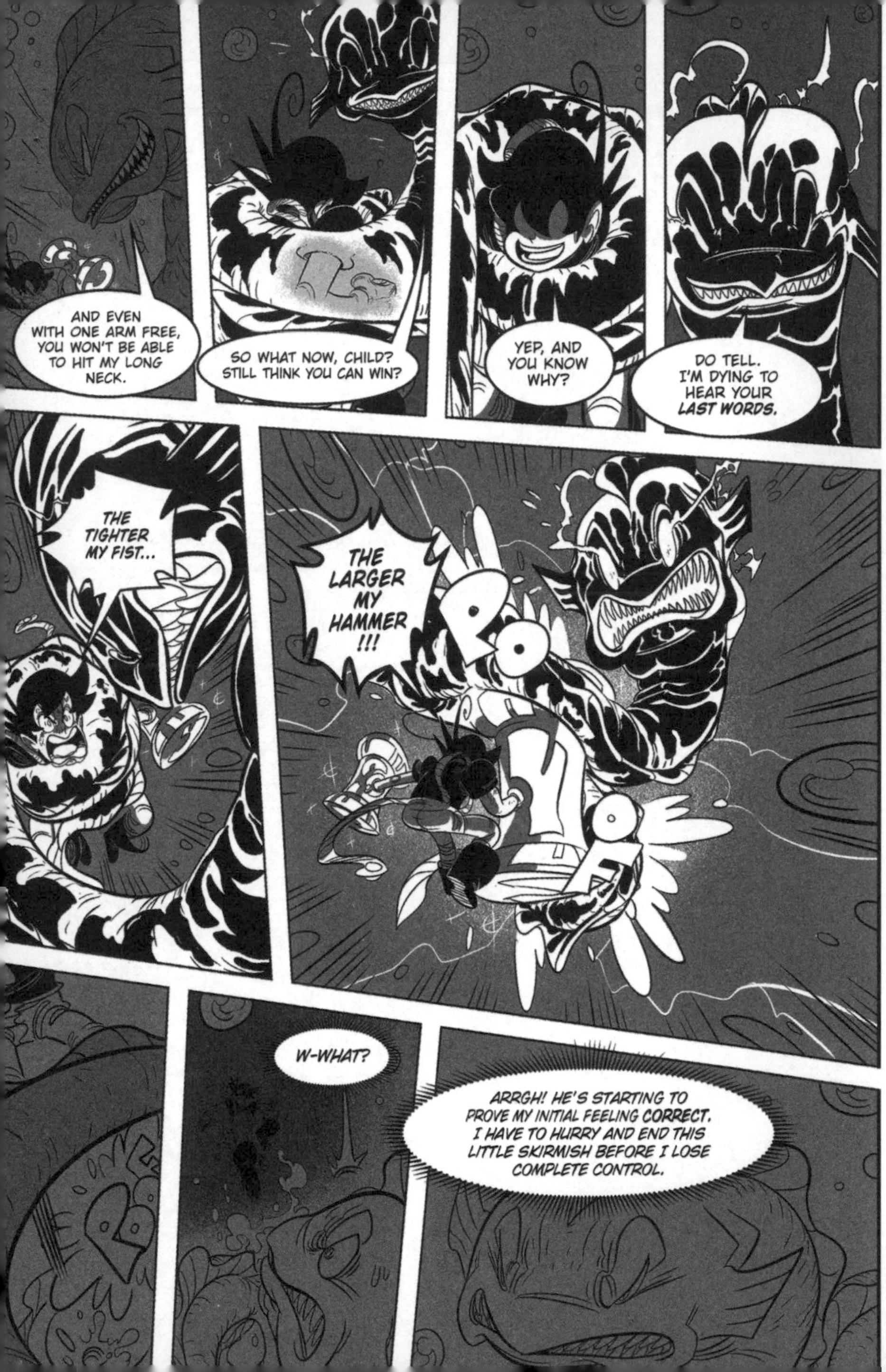
AND EVEN WITH ONE ARM FREE, YOU WON'T BE ABLE TO HIT MY LONG NECK.
SO WHAT NOW, CHILD? STILL THINK YOU CAN WIN?
YEP, AND YOU KNOW WHY?
DO TELL. I'M DYING TO HEAR YOUR LAST WORDS.
THE TIGHTER MY FIST...
THE LARGER MY HAMMER !!!
W-WHAT?
ARRGH! HE'S STARTING TO PROVE MY INITIAL FEELING CORRECT. I HAVE TO HURRY AND END THIS LITTLE SKIRMISH BEFORE I LOSE COMPLETE CONTROL.

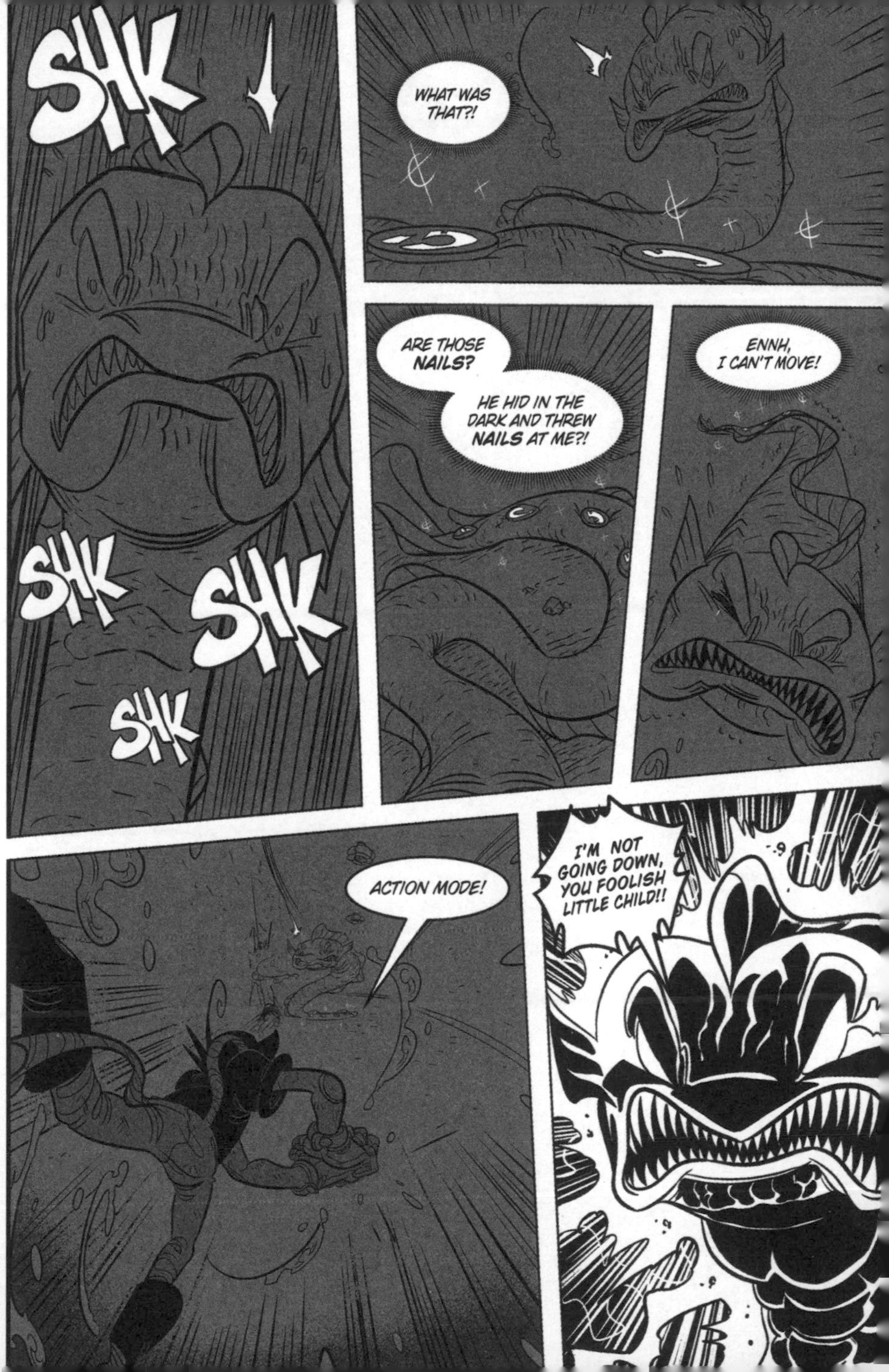
SHK
WHAT WAS THAT?!
SHK
SHK
SHK
ARE THOSE NAILS?
HE HID IN THE DARK AND THREW NAILS AT ME?!
ENNH, I CAN'T MOVE!
ACTION MODE!
I'M NOT GOING DOWN, YOU FOOLISH LITTLE CHILD!!

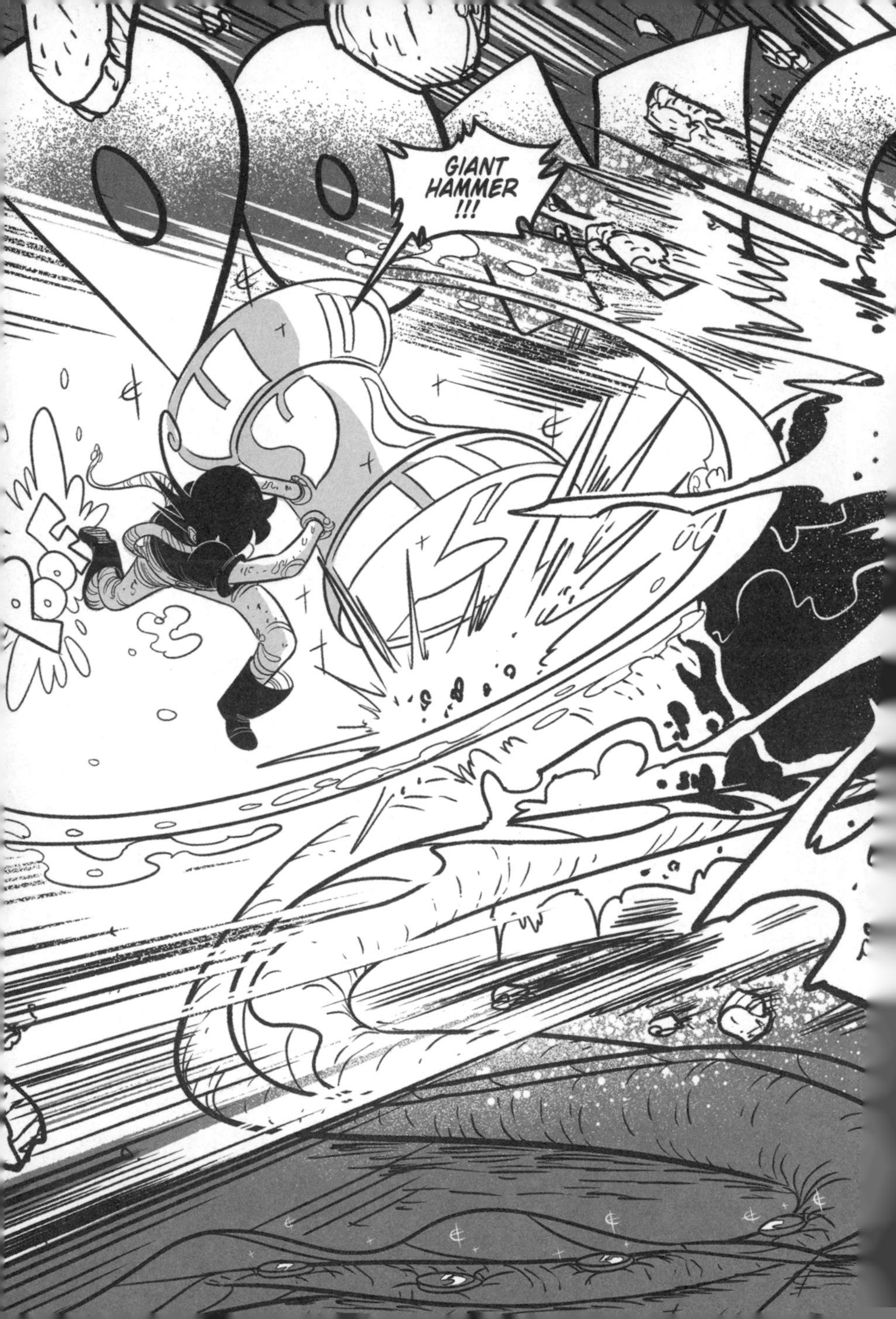
GIANT HAMMER !!!
LOOF

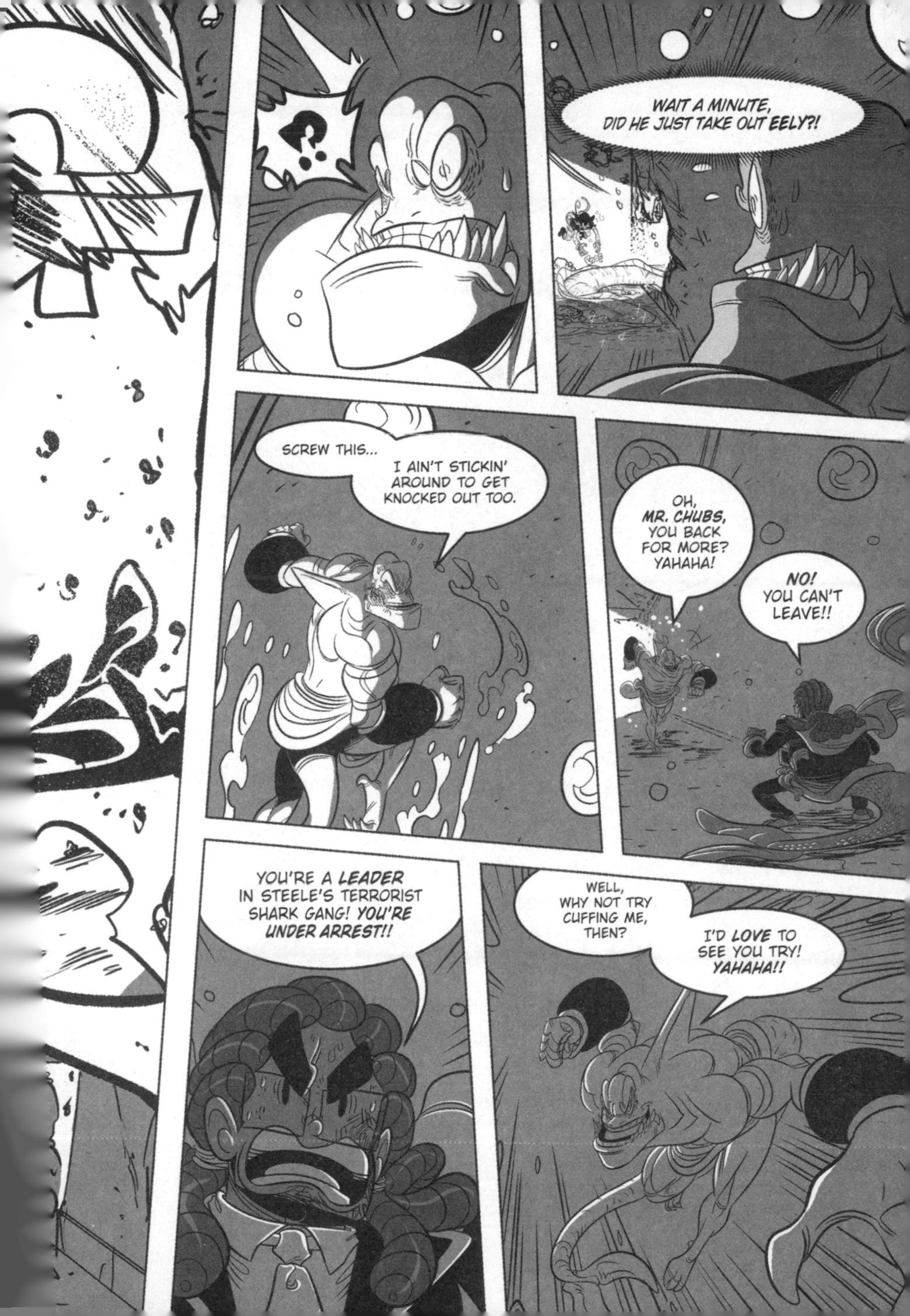
WAIT A MINUTE, DID HE JUST TAKE OUT EELY?!
SCREW THIS...
I AIN'T STICKIN' AROUND TO GET KNOCKED OUT TOO.
OH, MR. CHUBS, YOU BACK FOR MORE? YAHAHA!
NO! YOU CAN'T LEAVE!!
YOU'RE A LEADER IN STEELE'S TERRORIST SHARK GANG! YOU'RE UNDER ARREST!!
WELL, WHY NOT TRY CUFFING ME, THEN?
I'D LOVE TO SEE YOU TRY! YAHAHA!!

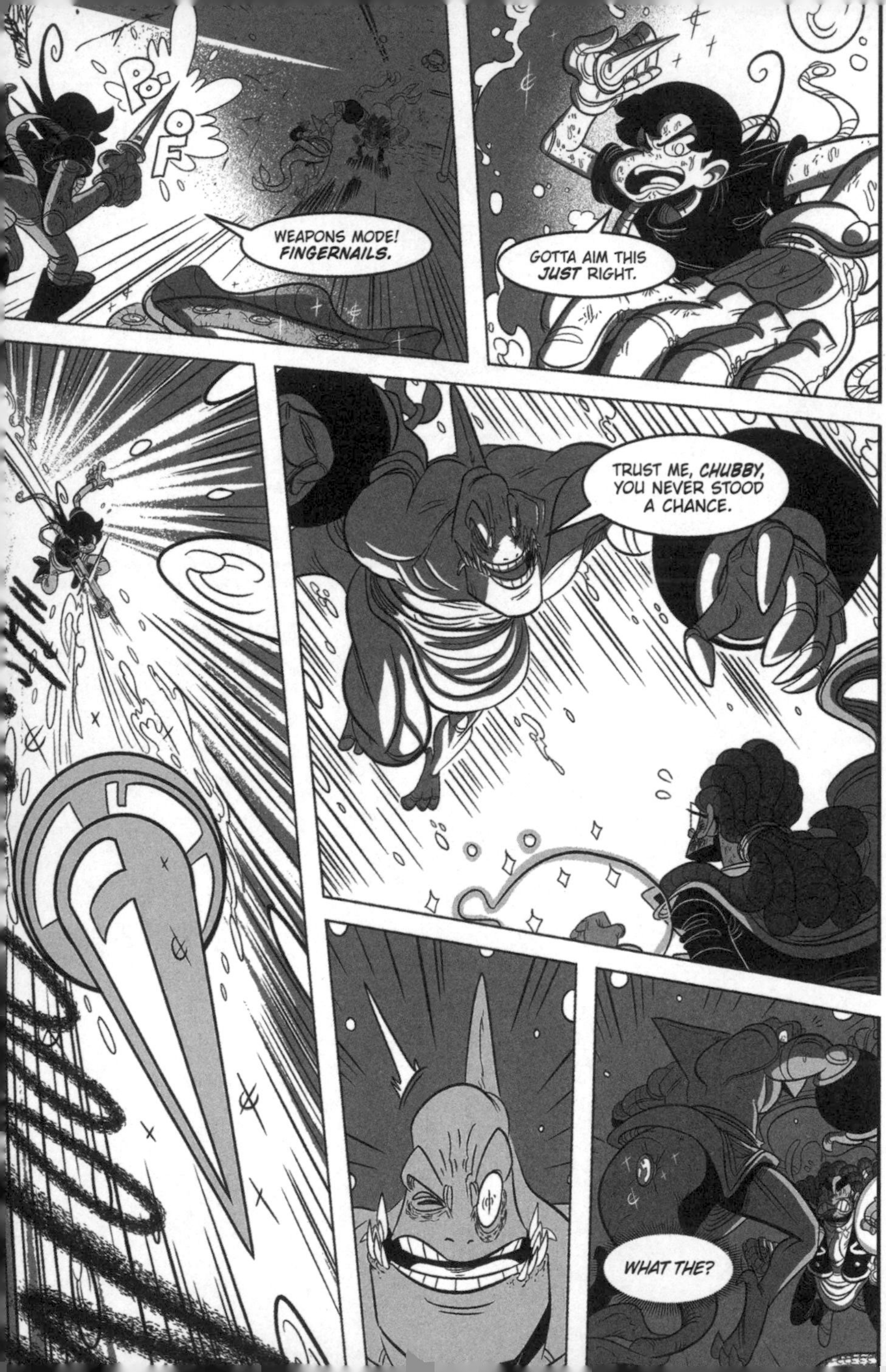
POOF
WEAPONS MODE! FINGERNAILS.
GOTTA AIM THIS JUST RIGHT.
TRUST ME, CHUBBY, YOU NEVER STOOD A CHANCE.
WHAT THE?

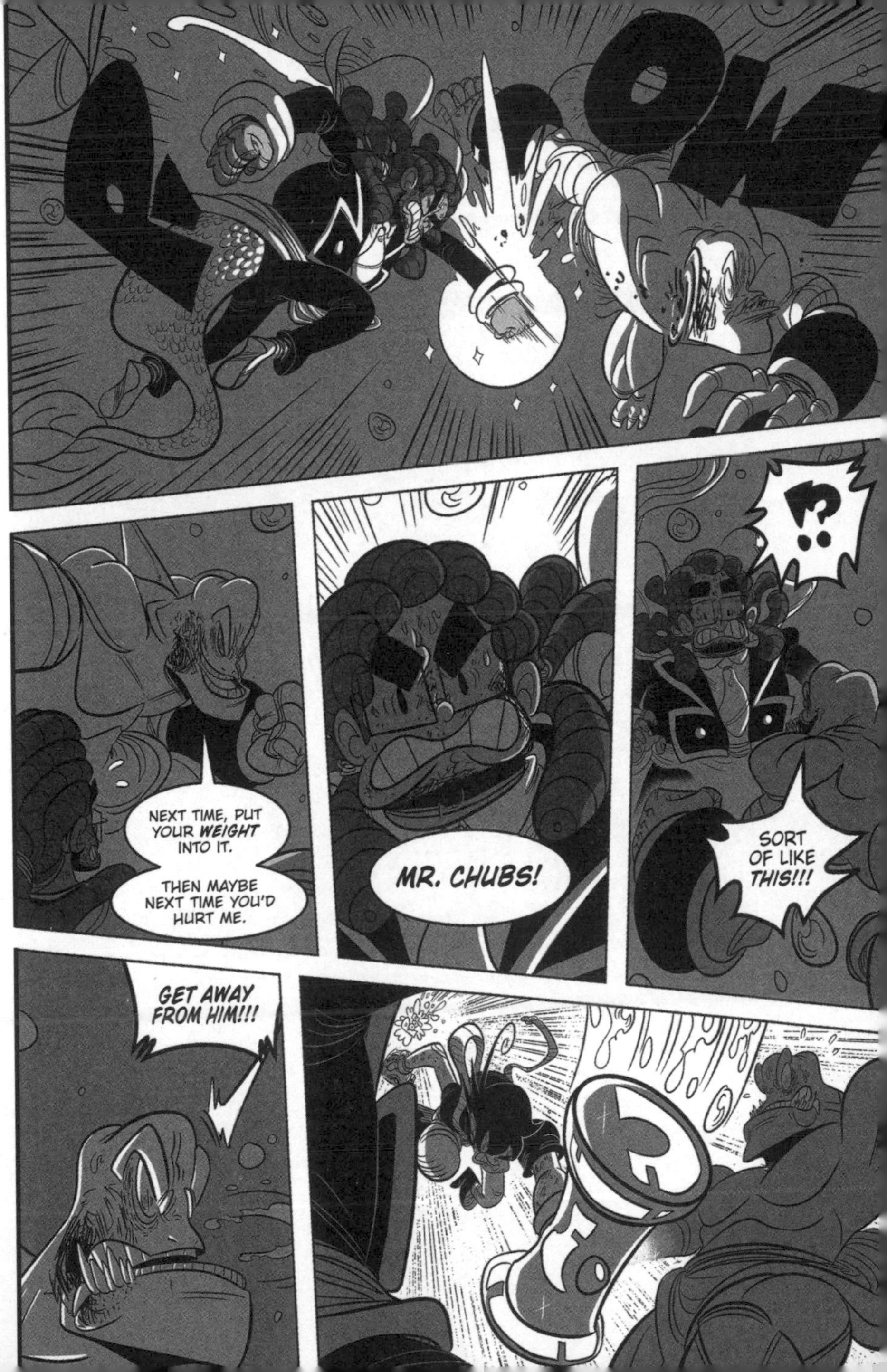
POW
NEXT TIME, PUT YOUR WEIGHT INTO IT.
THEN MAYBE NEXT TIME YOU'D HURT ME.
MR. CHUBS!
!?
SORT OF LIKE THIS!!!
GET AWAY FROM HIM!!!

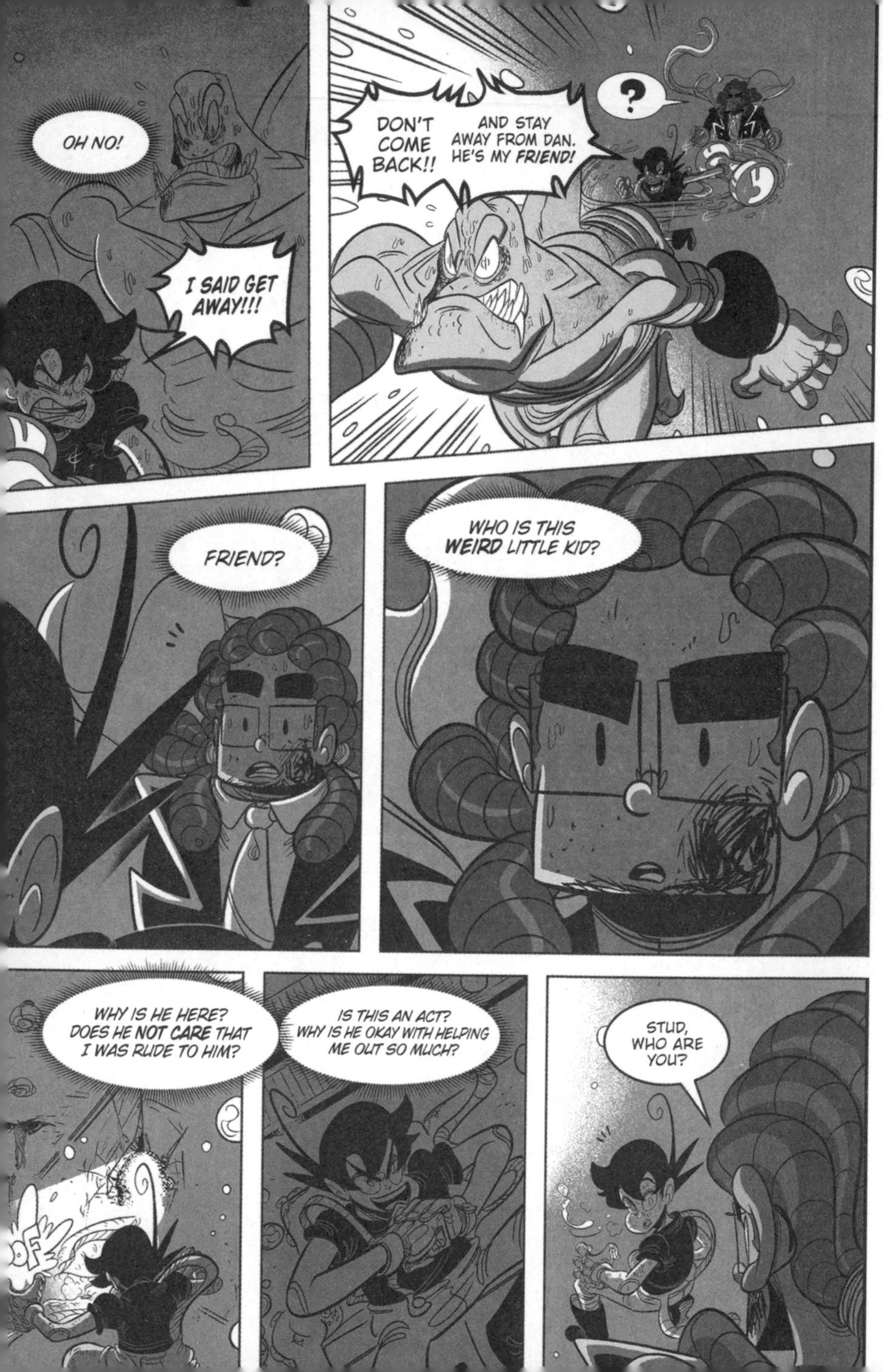
OH NO!
I SAID GET AWAY!!!
DON'T COME BACK!!
AND STAY AWAY FROM DAN. HE'S MY FRIEND!
?
FRIEND?
WHO IS THIS WEIRD LITTLE KID?
WHY IS HE HERE? DOES HE NOT CARE THAT I WAS RUDE TO HIM?
IS THIS AN ACT? WHY IS HE OKAY WITH HELPING ME OUT SO MUCH?
STUD, WHO ARE YOU?

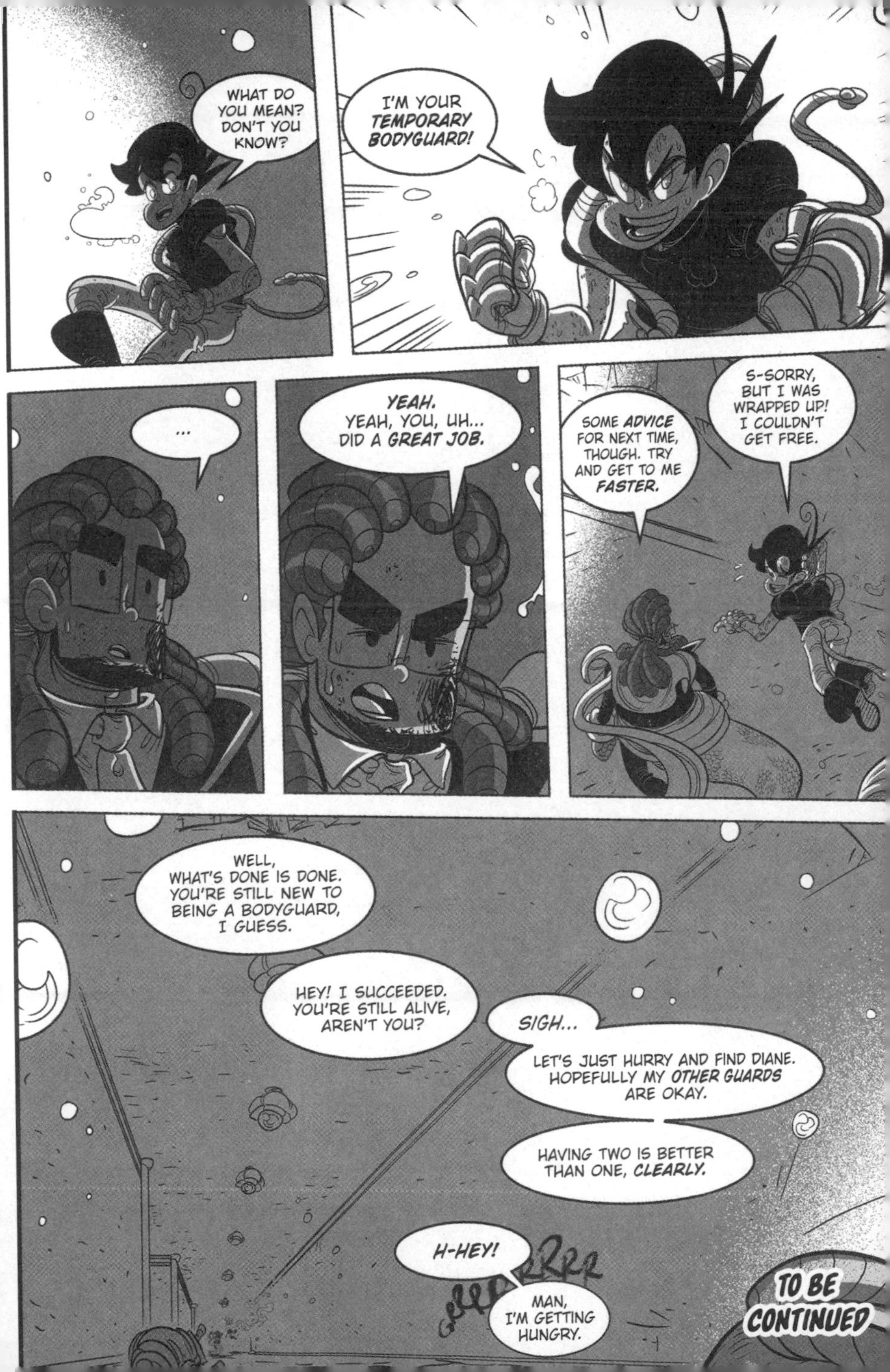
WHAT DO YOU MEAN? DON'T YOU KNOW?
I'M YOUR *TEMPORARY* *BODYGUARD!*
...
YEAH. YEAH, YOU, UH... DID A *GREAT JOB.*
SOME *ADVICE* FOR NEXT TIME, THOUGH. TRY AND GET TO ME *FASTER.*
S-SORRY, BUT I WAS WRAPPED UP! I COULDN'T GET FREE.
WELL, WHAT'S DONE IS DONE. YOU'RE STILL NEW TO BEING A BODYGUARD, I GUESS.
HEY! I SUCCEEDED. YOU'RE STILL ALIVE, AREN'T YOU?
SIGH...
LET'S JUST HURRY AND FIND DIANE. HOPEFULLY MY *OTHER GUARDS* ARE OKAY.
HAVING TWO IS BETTER THAN ONE, *CLEARLY.*
H-HEY!
GRRRRRRRR
MAN, I'M GETTING HUNGRY.
TO BE CONTINUED

HAMMER

END OF VOLUME 1

ABOUT THE AUTHOR

JEYODIN

Born in New Orleans, Louisiana, manga artist
JeyOdin attended Savannah College of Art and
Design in 2010, where he majored in sequential art.
In addition to Saturday AM, many top publishers
have published this prolific artist, including
Antarctic Press, *USA Today*, and Oni Press.

ACKNOWLEDGMENTS

DID YOU KNOW YOU CAN DO ANYTHING?

ALL IT TAKES IS HARD WORK, DEDICATION, PATIENCE, AND TIME. IT ALSO TAKES LUCK AND SOME MONEY, BUT IF YOU FOCUS ON THOSE FIRST FOUR THINGS, YOU'LL BE GOLDEN. MY DREAM COMING TRUE WITH THIS BOOK IN YOUR HANDS IS PROOF OF THAT. THANK YOU FOR ALL OF YOUR CONTINUING SUPPORT. I HOPE YOU HAVE FUN READING VOLUME 1 OF HAMMER.

-JeyOdin

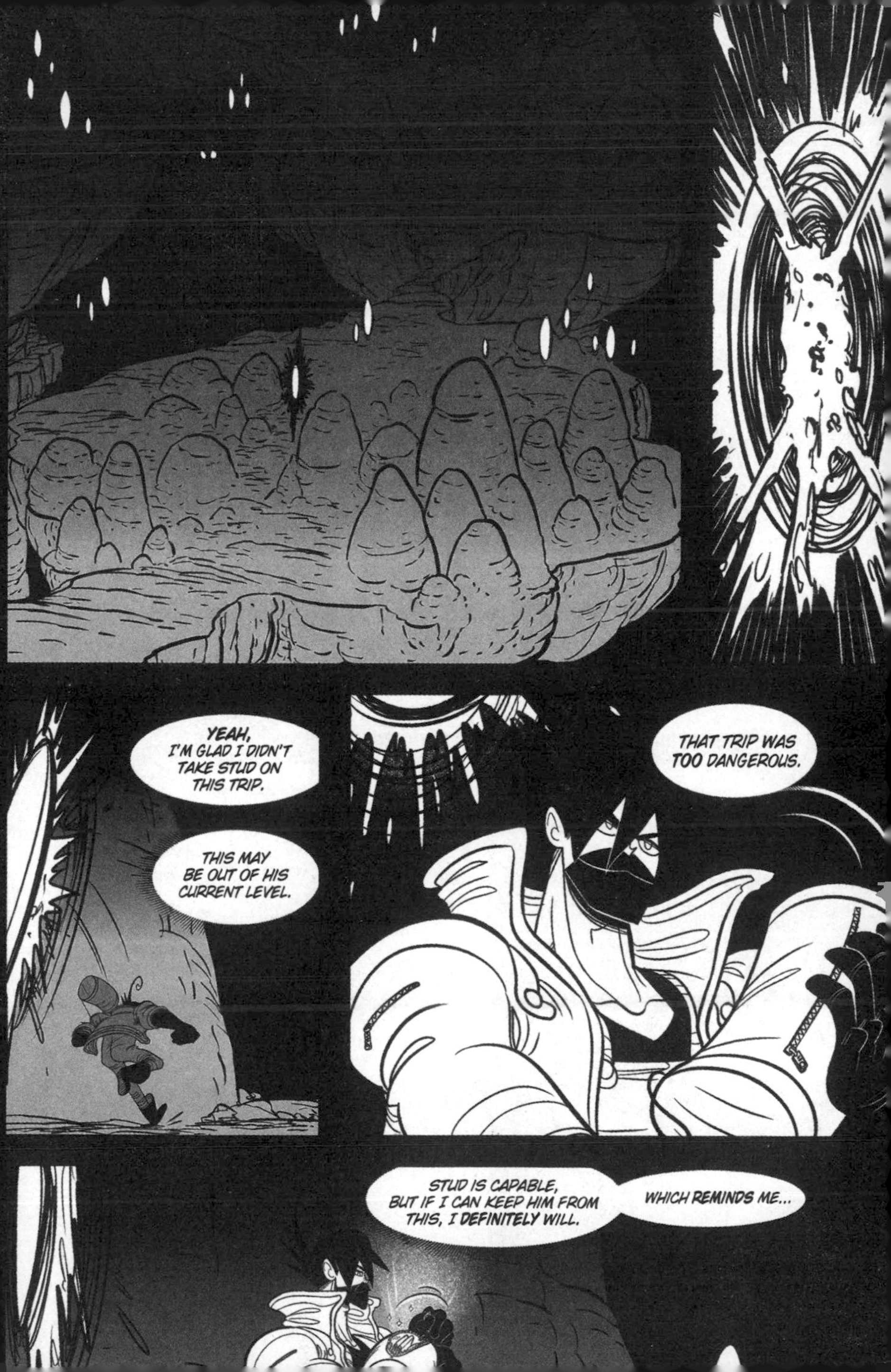
YEAH, I'M GLAD I DIDN'T TAKE STUD ON THIS TRIP.
THIS MAY BE OUT OF HIS CURRENT LEVEL.
THAT TRIP WAS TOO DANGEROUS.
STUD IS CAPABLE, BUT IF I CAN KEEP HIM FROM THIS, I DEFINITELY WILL.
WHICH REMINDS ME...

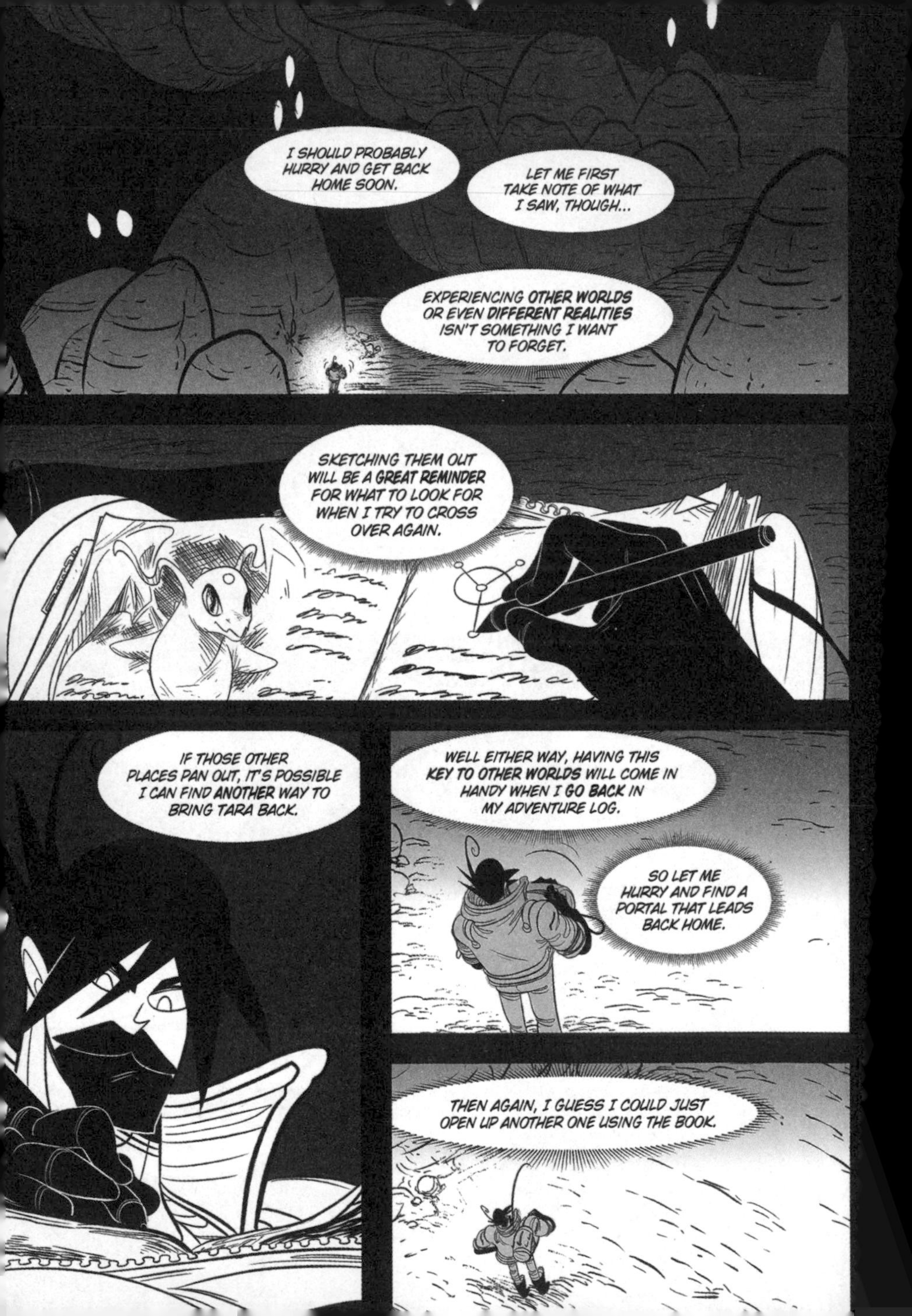
I SHOULD PROBABLY HURRY AND GET BACK HOME SOON.
LET ME FIRST TAKE NOTE OF WHAT I SAW, THOUGH...
EXPERIENCING OTHER WORLDS OR EVEN DIFFERENT REALITIES ISN'T SOMETHING I WANT TO FORGET.
SKETCHING THEM OUT WILL BE A GREAT REMINDER FOR WHAT TO LOOK FOR WHEN I TRY TO CROSS OVER AGAIN.
IF THOSE OTHER PLACES PAN OUT, IT'S POSSIBLE I CAN FIND ANOTHER WAY TO BRING TARA BACK.
WELL EITHER WAY, HAVING THIS KEY TO OTHER WORLDS WILL COME IN HANDY WHEN I GO BACK IN MY ADVENTURE LOG.
SO LET ME HURRY AND FIND A PORTAL THAT LEADS BACK HOME.
THEN AGAIN, I GUESS I COULD JUST OPEN UP ANOTHER ONE USING THE BOOK.

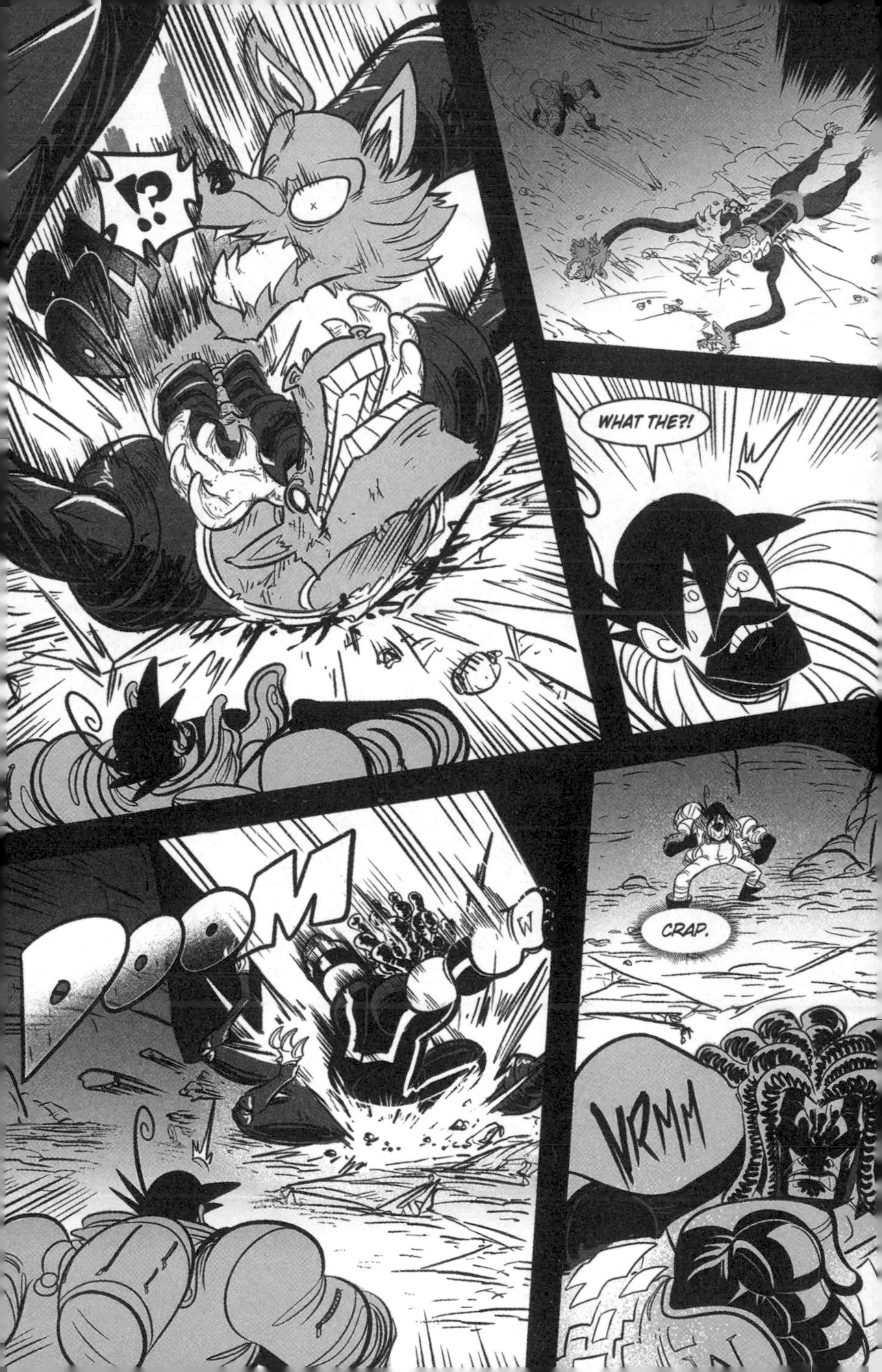
!?
WHAT THE?!
DOOOM
CRAP.
VRMM

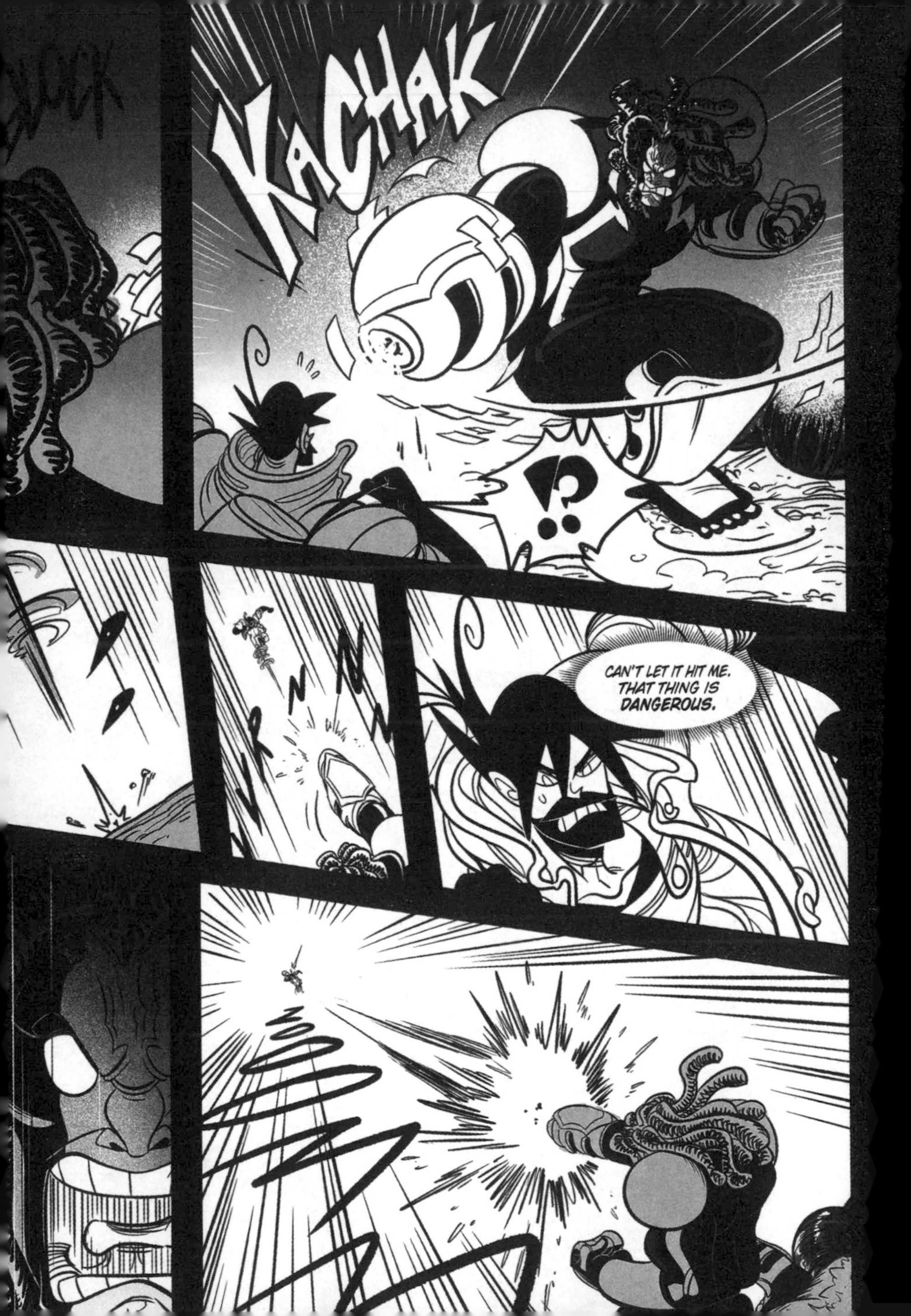
KACHAK
!?
CAN'T LET IT HIT ME. THAT THING IS DANGEROUS.

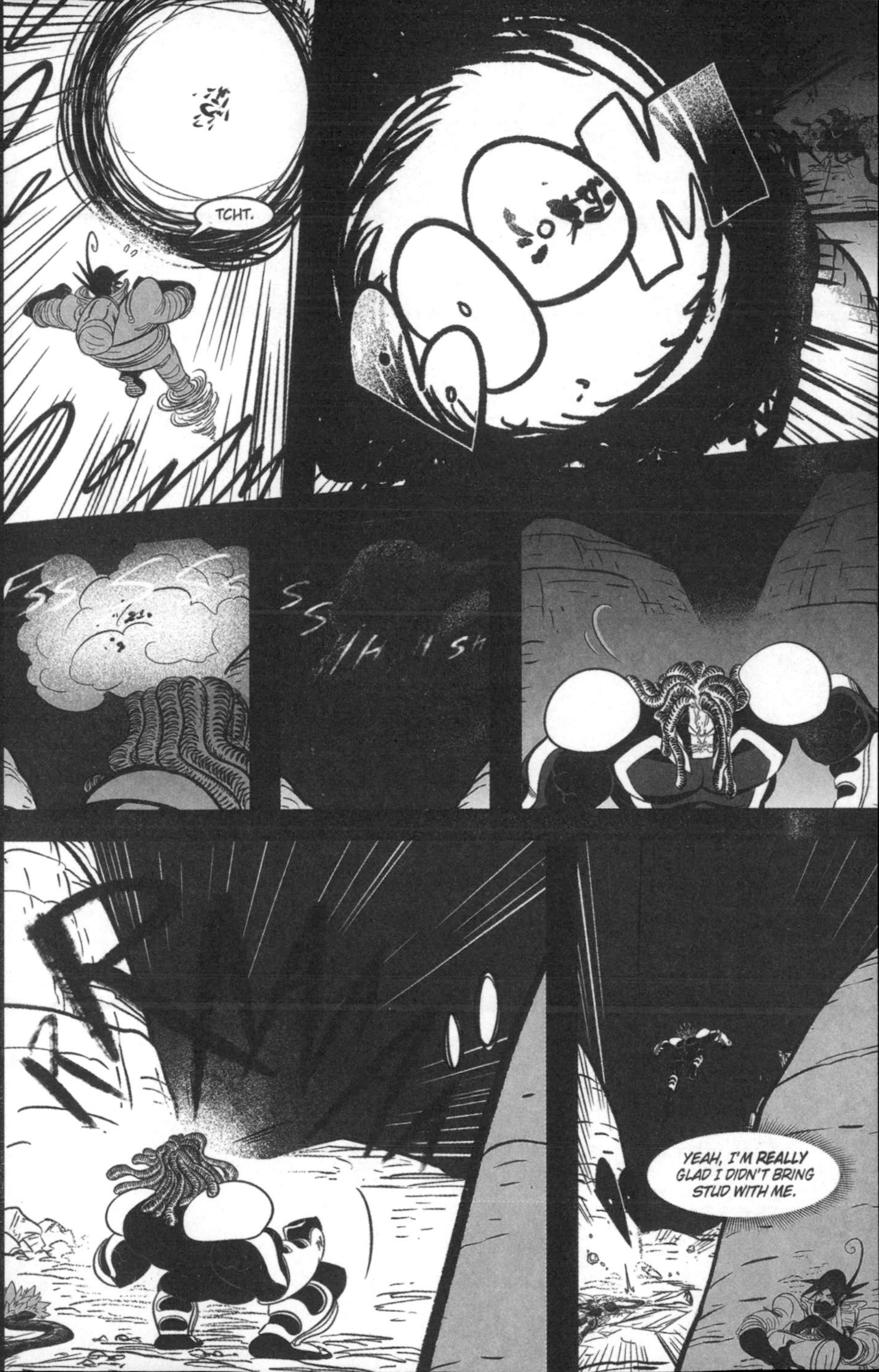
TCHT.
YEAH, I'M REALLY GLAD I DIDN'T BRING STUD WITH ME.

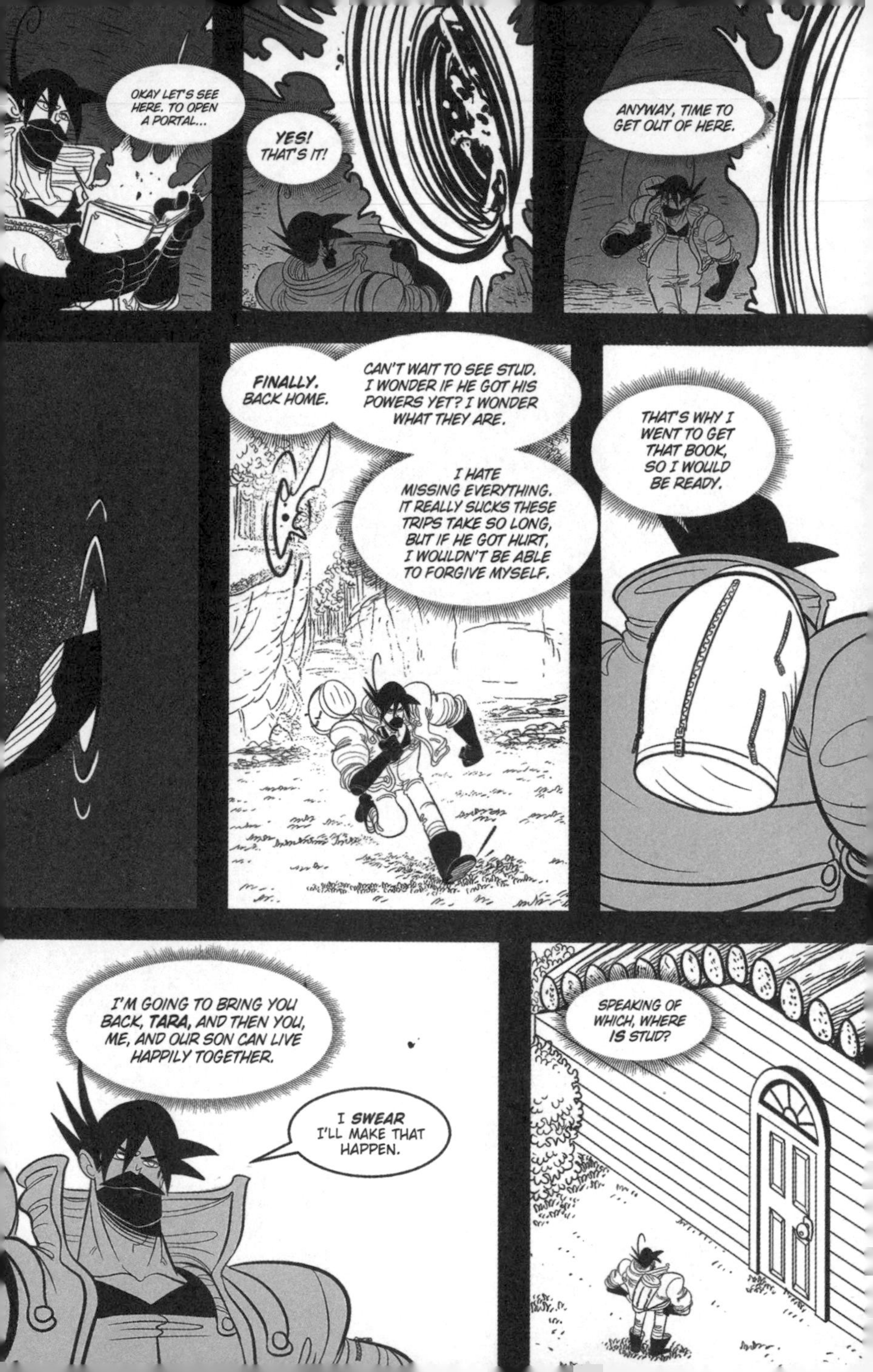
OKAY LET'S SEE HERE. TO OPEN A PORTAL...
YES! THAT'S IT!
ANYWAY, TIME TO GET OUT OF HERE.
FINALLY. BACK HOME.
CAN'T WAIT TO SEE STUD. I WONDER IF HE GOT HIS POWERS YET? I WONDER WHAT THEY ARE.
I HATE MISSING EVERYTHING. IT REALLY SUCKS THESE TRIPS TAKE SO LONG, BUT IF HE GOT HURT, I WOULDN'T BE ABLE TO FORGIVE MYSELF.
THAT'S WHY I WENT TO GET THAT BOOK, SO I WOULD BE READY.
I'M GOING TO BRING YOU BACK, TARA, AND THEN YOU, ME, AND OUR SON CAN LIVE HAPPILY TOGETHER.
I SWEAR I'LL MAKE THAT HAPPEN.
SPEAKING OF WHICH, WHERE IS STUD?

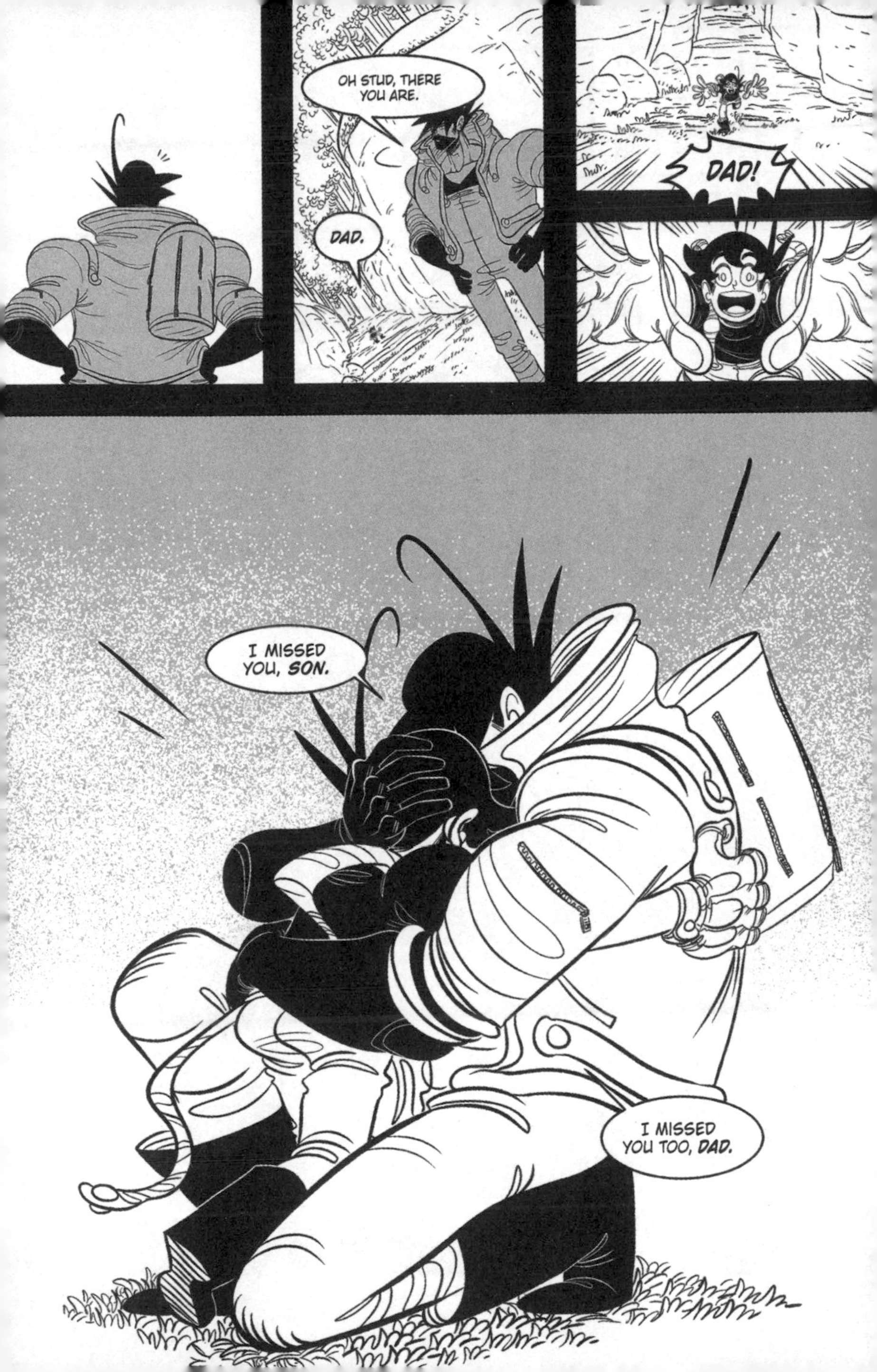
OH STUD, THERE YOU ARE.
DAD.
DAD!
I MISSED YOU, SON.
I MISSED YOU TOO, DAD.

HAMMER ART GALLERY

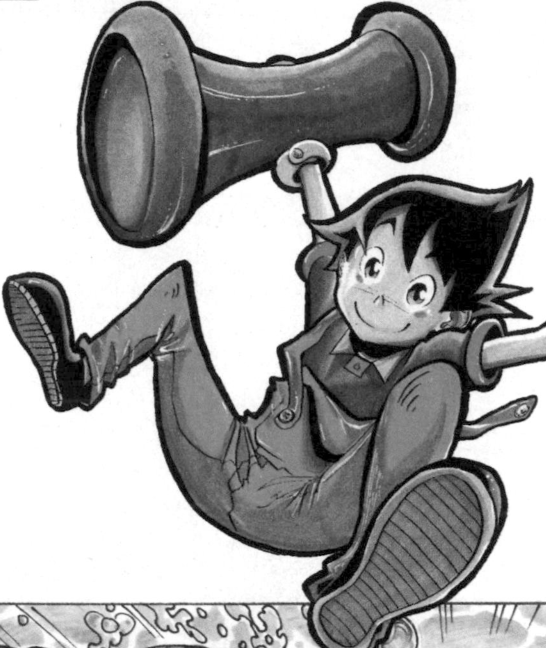

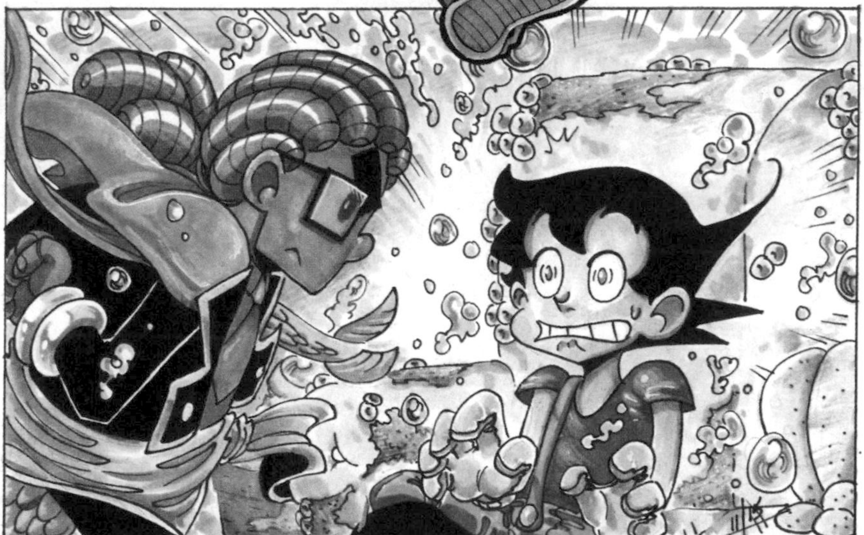

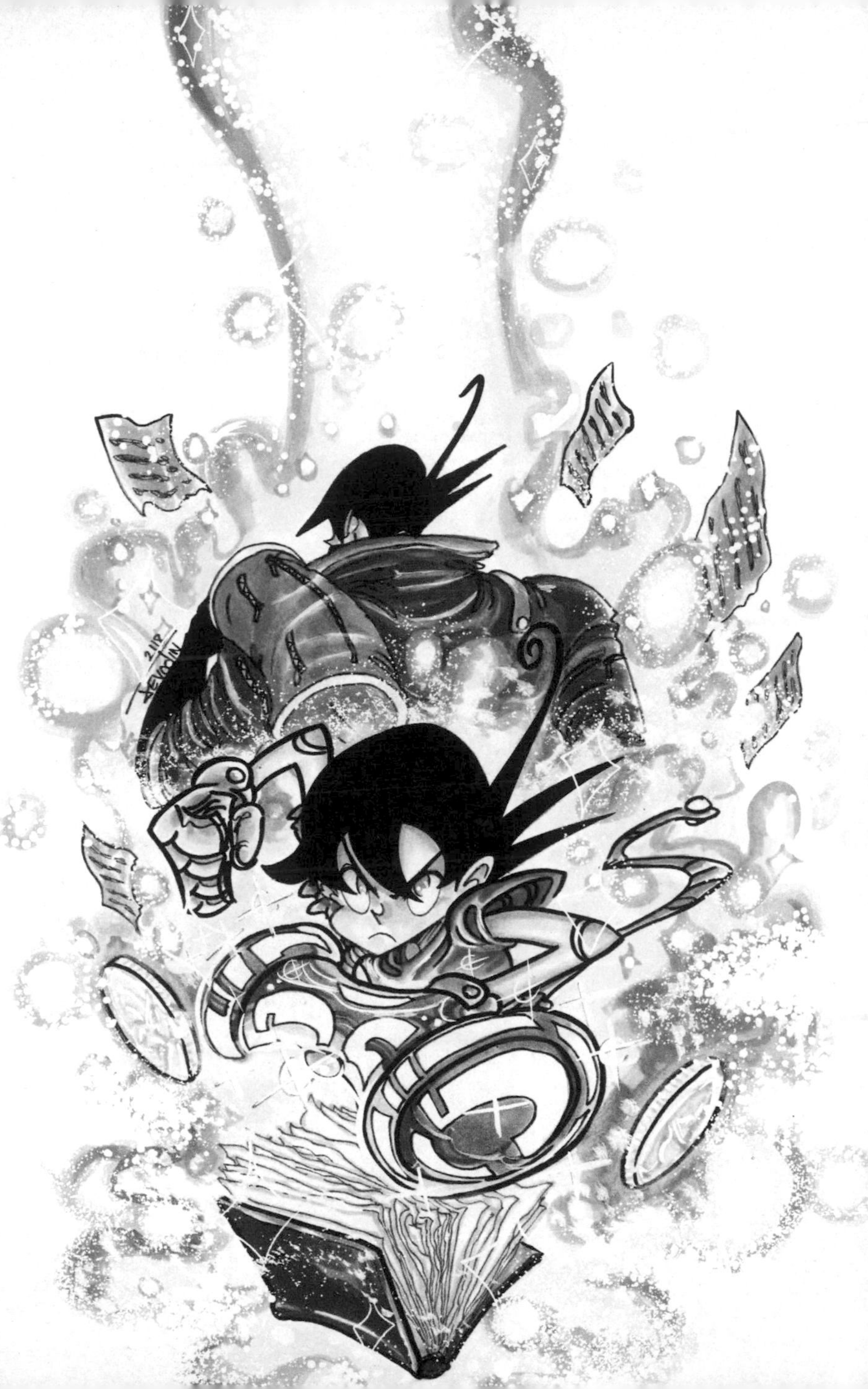

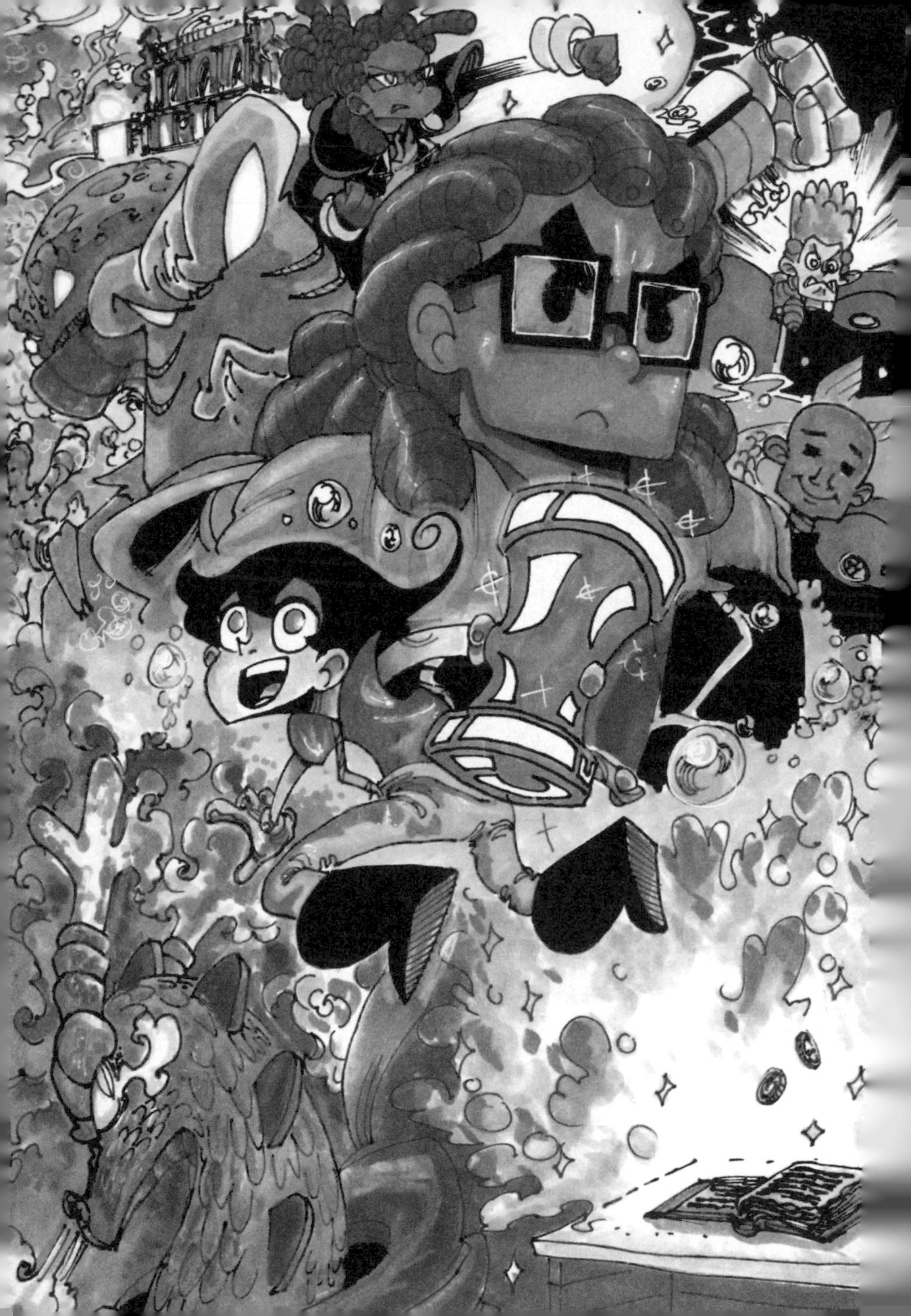

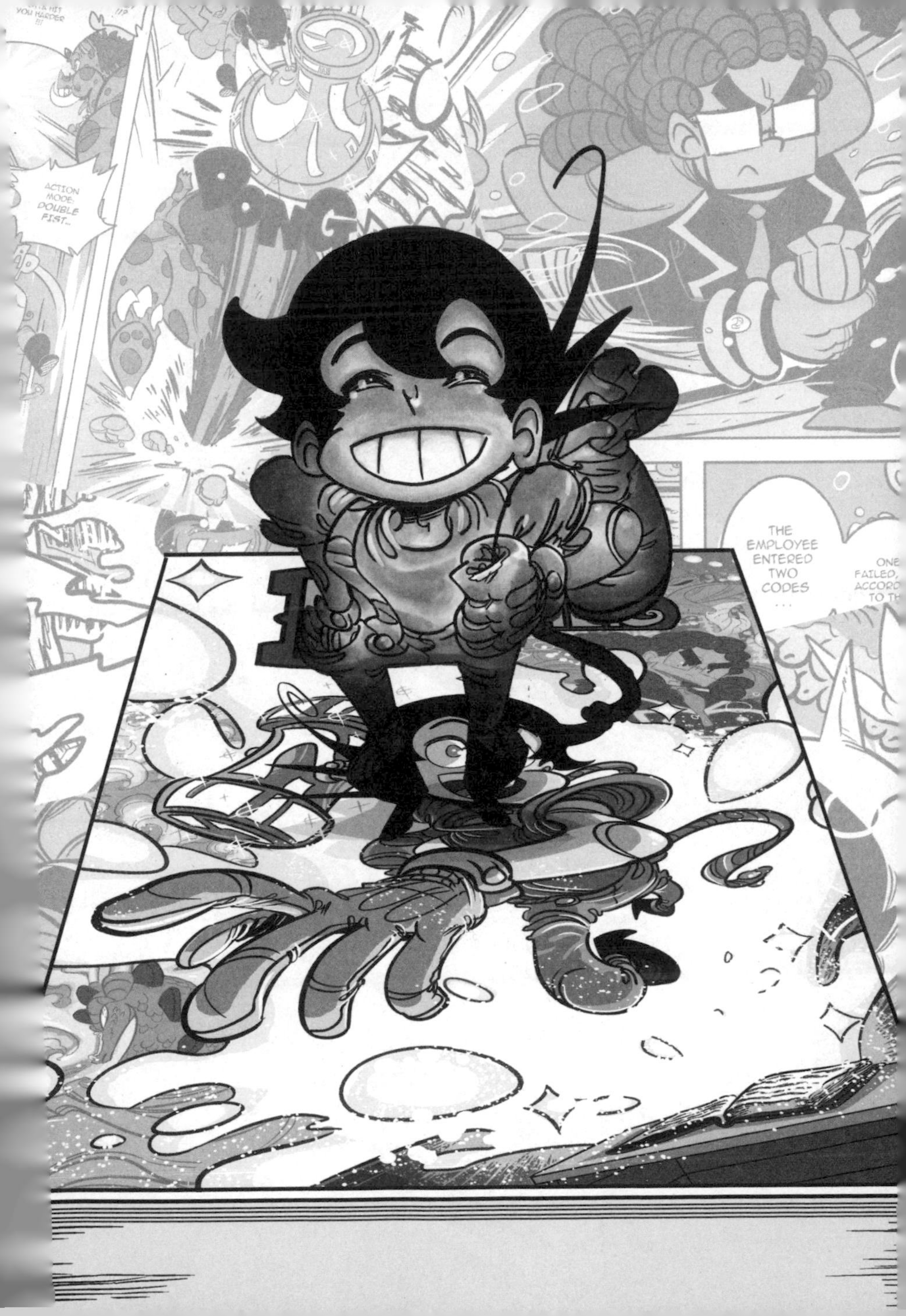

YOU HARDER !!!
ACTION MODE: DOUBLE FIST...
THE EMPLOYEE ENTERED TWO CODES ...

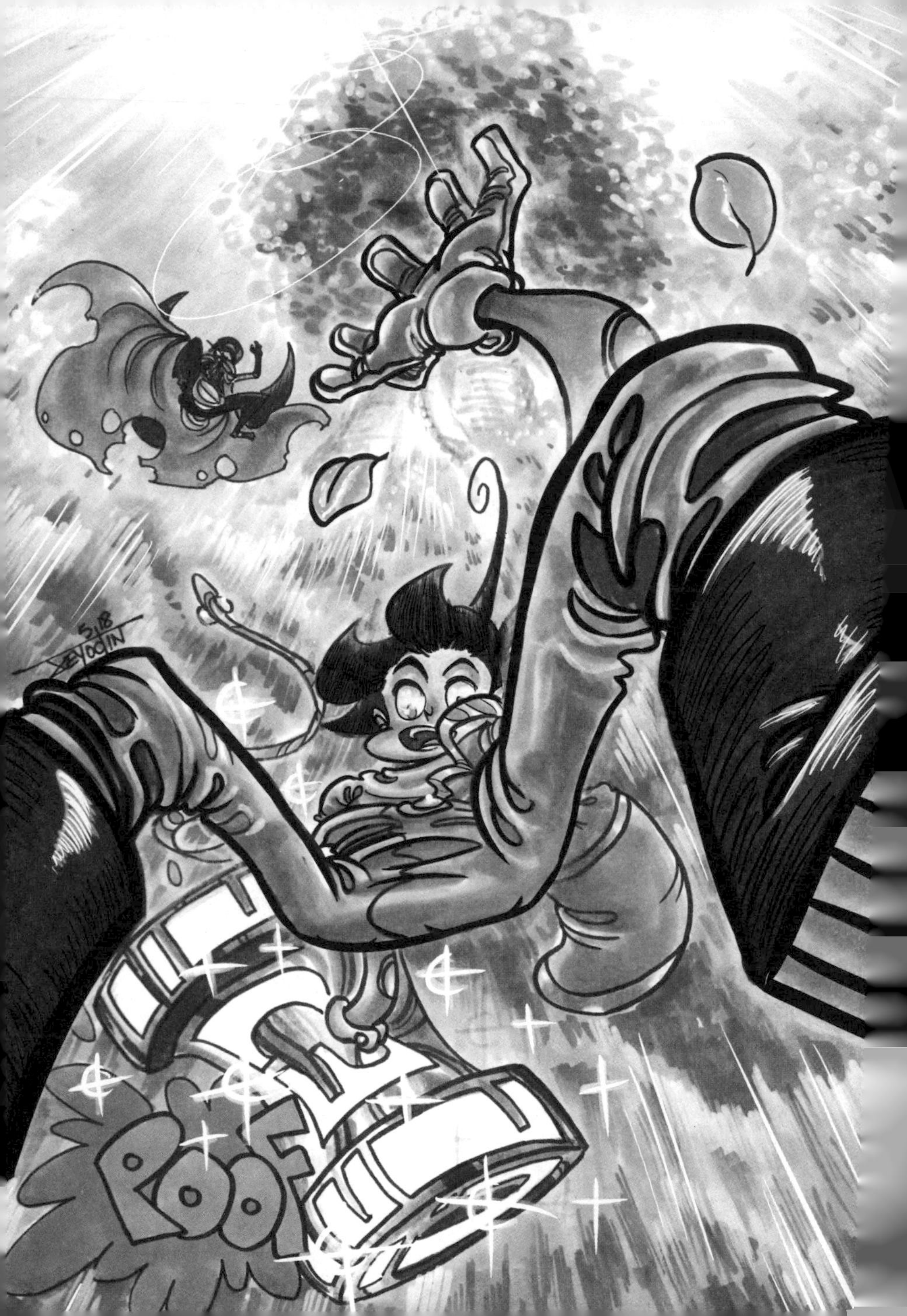
POOF